ICON OF THE KINGDOM OF GOD

STUDIES IN EASTERN CHRISTIANITY

SERIES EDITORS

Stefanos Alexopoulos
The Catholic University of America

Robin Darling Young
The Catholic University of America

ICON
of the
KINGDOM
of GOD

An Orthodox Ecclesiology

RADU BORDEIANU

The Catholic University of America Press

Washington, D.C.

Text and cover design by Reflective Book Design

Cataloging-in-Publication Data is available upon request
from the Library of Congress
ISBN: 978-0-8132-3689-6
eISBN: 978-0-8132-3690-2

To Frs. Paul and John and our parishioners

Contents

Introduction

Those who serve the Lord sincerely and truly ought to have
this one ambition—to bring back to unity the churches
which have been severed from each other

ST. BASIL THE GREAT[1]

What is the Church? Some would answer this question by studying the Scriptures, the history of the Church, and contemporary theologians, thus addressing the theological nature of the Church. Others would answer based on statistics, interviews, and personal observation, thus focusing on the experience of
the Church. These theological and experiential perspectives are in tension, or
at times even opposed. Whereas the first might speak about the local church
as the diocese gathered in the Liturgy presided over by its bishop, the latter
would describe the local church as the parish community celebrating the Liturgy together with the parish priest, never experiencing a sole liturgy that gathers
an entire diocese around its bishop. Whereas a theologian might abstractly
describe the Church as a reflection of the Trinity, a regular church-member
might concretely experience the Church as a community that manifests the
Kingdom of God in its outreach ministries. The present book attempts to
bring these two perspectives together, starting from the concrete experience
of the Church, engaging this experience with the theological tradition of the
Church, extracting ecclesiological principles from this combined approach, and
then highlighting concrete situations that reflect those standards or proposing
correctives, when necessary.

---

1. Saint Basil the Great, "Letter 114. To Cyriacus and His Followers at Tarsus," in *Saint Basil. Letters.
Volume I (1–185), Fathers of the Church* (Washington DC: The Catholic University of America Press,
1951), 241.

Yves Congar gradually became convinced that a complete treatise on the Church will never be written.[2] So this book presents an Orthodox ecclesiology that has no pretentions of being complete.[3] It is a scholarly endeavor, but a passioned one, written from a heart that beats for the Church—a living Church that breathes the Spirit. It attempts to bring together the past theological heritage and the present experience of the Church, being written for the Church and not simply as an academic exercise. When the members of the Church read this book, hopefully they will recognize their own experience of the Church in it and will be inspired to more richly embrace their ecclesial life.

The present book will have three methodological characteristics: experiential, Kingdom-centered, and ecumenical. While the third characteristic requires more attention in the second chapter, the description of these approaches will be kept here at a minimum. After all, considerations about method should be nothing more than "throat-clearing."[4]

EXPERIENTIAL APPROACH

Most of my publications to date have focused on various aspects of ecclesiology, and they will prove useful in this book. Like most other ecclesiologists, however, I have focused too much on theoretical issues and too little on the experience of the Church. Sometimes academic theology can be its own worst enemy, contributing to its own isolation from the life of the Church. An experiential approach to ecclesiology is sorely needed. Rather than limiting ourselves to abstract theological discussions, we need to encounter the Church, which exists and functions prior to our conceptualizing it, prior to our doing it violence by re-creating it in the image of our presuppositions. This phenomenological-like approach[5] emphasizes the importance of a non-objectifying or non-instrumental attitude towards the other, and of being "in relationship *with* others as the space where discernment takes place *between* people rather than exercising leadership *on*

---

2. Yves Congar, "My Path-Findings in the Theology of Laity and Ministries," *The Jurist* 32, no. 2 (1972): 169.

3. "Ecclesiology" comes from the Greek term for Church, namely *ekklesia*, which in turn derives from *ek-kaleo*, meaning "to be called out."

4. Jeffrey Stout, *Ethics after Babel: The Languages of Morals and their Discontents* (Boston: Beacon, 1988), 163.

5. Without claiming to do phenomenology proper, this book simply fits in a phenomenological vein that studies experience (in this case, of the Church), including perception, memory, imagination, desire, and embodied action.

people."[6] Thus, the present book can be first characterized as an experiential ecclesiology.

Purely theoretical, abstract ecclesiologies pose three great dangers. The first one has to do with power. As the late Catholic theologian, Gerard Mannion cautioned, "blueprint ecclesiologies" are models of the Church that are being imposed from the center (in his case, Rome) upon other localities, without concern for differing pastoral and theological contexts. If "blueprint ecclesiology" presupposes someone who has the power to impose it on others,[7] the antidote is an emphasis on locality and polycentrism, which fit quite well in the Orthodox context. That is not to say that Orthodoxy does not have its own version of "blueprint ecclesiology." On the contrary, that is particularly the case when one draws only one ecclesiological model from subjective readings of history, and this subjective idealization of history represents the second danger of abstract ecclesiologies.

As Rowan Williams points out, when looking at the Christian past, we cannot allow our contemporary theological interests "to settle historical questions," nor can we pretend that our Christian past has not been conditioned by "human motives and social or political" circumstances. He concludes that "good theology does not come from bad history."[8] Even correct readings of history that are idealized and regarded as normative do not provide a true foundation of ecclesiology insofar as they no longer correspond to the contemporary experience of the Church. If the best aspects of our church are all buried in a distant past and in very distant places, then we are unfaithful servants. But that is not the experience of the faithful: the glory of the Church is not only a thing of the past, rightly belonging in a museum, but is clearly—and primarily—discernable in the present. A theology that only lives in the past represents an unattainable, utopic model that cannot be applied in the present and is thus less relevant. The Holy Spirit has not deserted the Church after a supposed golden age of the first centuries, but guides the Church from its beginnings to this day, and until the end of time. That is why this book will include numerous historical considerations read in their proper context and nuance; many

6. Elizabeth Petersen and Jannie Swart, "Via the Broken Ones: Towards a Phenomenological Theology of Ecclesial Leadership in Post-Apartheid South Africa," *Journal of Religious Leadership* 8, no. 2 (2009): 28–29.

7. Gerard Mannion, *Ecclesiology and Postmodernity: Questions for the Church in Our Time* (Collegeville, MN: Liturgical Press, 2007), 63–70; 160–70.

8. Rowan Williams, *Why Study the Past? The Quest for the Historical Church* (Grand Rapids, MI: Eerdmans, 2015), 2.

of them will be regarded as in continuation with the present experience of the Church and as the foundation of our dreams for a better Church.

Karl Rahner identifies the third great danger of purely theoretical ecclesiologies: "It is the constant temptation of the church to conceive of herself *merely* in terms of her own nature ... and to conceal from herself her real concrete reality by hiding behind this portrayal of her nature, in other words behind that which she should be."[9] Instead of hiding behind an idealized, ontological description of the Church, theology needs to pay attention to the concrete experience of the Church both in the past and especially today, in all our varied contexts. That is why the present book contains numerous analyses of statistics about Church life, concrete observations, and ethnographic evaluations.[10]

A purely experiential approach is not desirable, either. While it is important to understand how the people of God understand and experience the Church, it is equally important to consider the reality of generalized misperceptions, faulty understandings, and sinful practices in the Church. As Nicholas Lossky warns, the state of mind of the people does not always coincide with the theology of the Church,[11] and as Georges Florovsky shows, the truth is not expressed in plebiscites, but sometimes it is proclaimed by a small minority exiled in the desert, as was the case during the Nicene controversy, when most of the East embraced Arianism or Semi-Arianism.[12] Hence the need to consider the experience of the Church in its totality of space and time and to balance the experiential with the theoretical–theological approaches to ecclesiology.

9. Karl Rahner, "Of the Structure of the People in the Church Today," in *Theological Investigations* 12: *Confrontations* 2 (New York: Seabury, 1974), 218.

10. Edward Hahnenberg proposes the method of ethnographic evaluation based on observation and lived experience, as opposed to a deductive theological method that starts from theological principles. Edward P. Hahnenberg, "Learning from Experience: Attention to Anomalies in a Theology of Ministry," in *A Church with Open Doors: Catholic Ecclesiology for the Third Millenium*, ed. Richard R. Gaillardetz and Edward P. Hahnenberg (Collegeville, MN: Liturgical Press, 2015), 159–80.

11. Nicholas Lossky, "Conciliarity-Primacy in a Russian Orthodox Perspective," in *Petrine Ministry and the Unity of the Church: "Toward a Patient and Fraternal Dialogue": A Symposium Celebrating the 100th Anniversary of the Foundation of the Society of the Atonement, Rome, December 4–6, 1997*, ed. James F. Puglisi (Collegeville, MN: Liturgical Press, 1999), 130.

12. Georges Florovsky, "The Historical Problem of a Definition of the Church," in *Ecumenism II: A Historical Approach*, Collected Works of Georges Florovsky, Emeritus Professor of Eastern Church History, Harvard University; vol. 14 (Belmont, MA: Nordland, 1989), 33.

KINGDOM-CENTERED APPROACH

A second overarching characteristic of the book is its Kingdom-centeredness. The Kingdom of God was the center of Jesus' preaching, so this theme will be addressed properly in its own chapter, in an attempt to correct both its marginal place in Orthodox theology and its conflation with the Church. The former has resulted in an impoverishment of preaching and the Church's social action, while the latter has had disastrous consequences for the relationship between Church and state. The Church is not the Kingdom, but neither are the two separate; the Church is both a sign and an instrument of the Kingdom by proclaiming the good news and by being a healing presence in the world through its work of charity, justice, reconciliation, and confrontation of sin—both individual and structural. The Church is the community of disciples that enacts the values of the Kingdom of God, while striving to be closer and closer to the eschatological Kingdom. In the words of Nicholas Afanasiev, "the Church is the beginning of the 'last days.'"[13] As the Kingdom is already here ... but not yet (to use a common phrase in biblical scholarship), the present book centers around the experience and expectation of the Kingdom in the Church, arguing that the Church is an icon of the Kingdom of God.

Since much more will be said in the next chapter about the relationship between the Church and the Kingdom, some remarks about the Church as icon are necessary here. According to Robin Jensen, the "icon is a kind of symbol—a thing that points to a reality that surpasses or transcends itself by far, but in which it participates. It is not the reality itself, but relates to it in such a way as to make it genuinely known or understood."[14] The icon is both a presence of grace and an instrument of grace, thus becoming a fitting image for the relationship between God and the Church: God is present in the Church and works through the Church. Eastern theologians have consistently affirmed this relationship, from Origen who wrote that "the Church is filled with the Trinity,"[15] to contemporary theologians such as Dumitru Staniloae who referred to the Trinity as "the structure of supreme love."[16] It is thus not surprising that

13. Nicolas Afanassieff, *The Church of the Holy Spirit*, trans. Vitaly Permiakov (Notre Dame, IN: Notre Dame University Press, 2007), 3.

14. Robin M. Jensen, "Icons and Iconography," in *The Cambridge Dictionary of Christian Theology*, ed. I. A. et al. McFarland (New York: Cambridge University Press, 2011), 232.

15. Origen. *Selecta in Psalmos* 23, 1 PG 12,1265B.

16. Dumitru Staniloae, *The Experience of God: Revelation and Knowledge of the Triune God*, trans. Ioan Ionita and Robert Barringer, 2nd ed., vol. 1 (Brookline, MA: Holy Cross Orthodox Press, 1998; repr., 1994), 67. Similarly, Georges Florovsky defined "the Church [as] the living image of eternity in

St. Maximus the Confessor used the image of the Church as an "icon and figure of God," adding that the Church "has towards us the same energy as God
does, as icon of the same energy as its archetype."[17] The Church is an icon of
God because it does what God does, conforming itself to its archetype, and
because, as God unites the faithful who are varied in their characteristics, so
does the Church.[18]

The title of this book does not refer to the Church as "icon of God," but
"icon of the Kingdom of God," in order to emphasize not only the divine aspect
of the Church (since the Kingdom is of God), but also the Church's human
aspect, especially its communitarian character. The Kingdom is present in the
world, although it remains distinct from both the world and the Church. The
Kingdom becomes visible in the Church to the extent that the Church enacts
the values of the Kingdom, and thus becomes an icon. Bridging the images of
the Church as icon of God and icon of the Kingdom, the *Trinity* icon of Andrei
Rublev portrays the three persons of the Trinity sitting at a table whose fourth
side remains open. The worshipper is invited to sit at the table—a reference
to the Kingdom as heavenly banquet—to participate in the communion of the
Trinity. That is precisely the role of the Church: to bring in its members and
the world in communion with the Trinity, to be a presence of the Kingdom of
God in the world.

ECUMENICAL APPROACH

Thirdly, this book is intrinsically ecumenical, in dialogue primarily with the
Catholic Church. I have long been involved in ecumenism, practically and theoretically, locally and internationally. I am a member of the North American
Orthodox-Catholic Theological Consultation—a body of theologians officially
delegated by our respective churches, with the task of contributing theologically to the union between the Orthodox and Catholic churches. On a local level,

---

time." Georges Florovsky, "The Catholicity of the Church," in *Bible, Church, Tradition*, Collected Works of
Georges Florovsky, Emeritus Professor of Eastern Church History, Harvard University; vol.1 (Belmont,
MA: Nordland, 1972), 45.

17. Translated in Alain Riou, *Le monde et l'église selon Maxime le Confesseur*, Théologie Historique 22,
(Paris: Beauchesne, 1973), 140–41. English translations tend to use the term "image" instead of "icon" for
the passages in which Maximus refers to the Church as *tupon kai eikona Theou*, e.g. PG 91, 663D.

18. Saint Maximus the Confessor, "The Church's Mystagogy in Which Are Explained the Symbolism
of Certain Rites Performed in the Divine Synaxis," in *Maximus Confessor: Selected Writings*, ed. and trans.
George C. Berthold, Classics of Western Spirituality (New York: Paulist Press, 1985), 187–88.

I am a member of Christian Associates of Southwest Pennsylvania (CASP), which gathers judicatories such as Orthodox, Roman Catholic, Byzantine Catholic, Lutheran, Presbyterian, United Church of Christ, etc. I have also studied Jewish rabbinical traditions at Shalom Hartman Institute in Jerusalem, I am a co-convener of the Christian-Jewish dialogue in Pittsburgh, and a member of a local priests-rabbis study group.

Theological studies, pastoral experience as an ordained priest, and ecumenical dialogues, have all converged in the conviction that Christian churches should share each other's gifts and be willing to adopt what is valuable in the faith of the other as an instance of God's revelation outside their canonical boundaries. In the twenty-first century, after significant ecumenical progress, it is time to allow our ecumenical encounters to shape our identities. Hence, to the question, "Can this book still be an Orthodox ecclesiology if it quotes Jewish, Catholic, and Protestant sources?" the answer is a resounding yes. Orthodoxy does not define its identity in isolation, but in dialogue with the other. Its roots spread wide, and they include (in a re-read form) the history of Israel and Orthodoxy's interactions with the West. Hence, throughout the book, I will attempt to address questions such as the following: What are the principles of Orthodox ecclesiology and how are they related to the reality of Church life in a pluralistic world? How does Orthodox ecclesiology express its principles with a special sensitivity to the rest of the Christian world and how can we translate previous Orthodox ecclesiologies into an ecumenical language? How has Catholic ecclesiology informed the life of the Orthodox Church and how could both Orthodox and Catholic churches grow together in their respective understandings of the Church? And how do inter-church relations and ecumenical discussions affect the lives of our faithful as they experience the Church as icon of the Kingdom?

ONE

The Kingdom of God

—

Jesus proclaimed the Kingdom, and
what came was the Church.

ALFRED LOISY[1]

It is improper to speak of the Church during Jesus' ministry on earth. Out of all the four gospels, the word "church" (*ecclesia*) appears only three times. In Matthew 16:18 Jesus tells Peter, "you are Peter [the rock] and on this rock I will build my church."[2] In Matthew 18:17, a person who cannot make peace with another member of the community in private or in the presence of two or three witnesses should "tell it to the church; and if the offender refuses to listen even to the church, let such a one be to you as a Gentile and a tax collector." Matthew is the only evangelist who puts the word "church" on Jesus' lips and, as most biblical scholars concur, these three occurrences of *ecclesia* reflect the post-Paschal context of early Christian communities that Matthew projects back into the life of Jesus, rather than Jesus's actual words.[3] Instead of the Church, most of Jesus' preaching centers around the Kingdom. Compared to the three (disputable) instances in which "church" is mentioned in the gospels, the expression "kingdom of heaven" or "kingdom of God" appears 99 times, 90 of which are Jesus' own words. Clearly, the central message of Jesus' preaching was not the Church, but the Kingdom.

What on earth does the Kingdom of heaven have to do with the Church?

---

1. Alfred Loisy, *L'évangile et l'église*, 2nd ed. (Bellevue: Picard, 1903), 155.
2. Throughout the book, unless otherwise stated, I use the NRSV translation.
3. John Meier, *Companions and Competitors*, vol. 3 of *A Marginal Jew: Rethinking the Historical Jesus* (New York: Doubleday, 2001), 228–35.

Should one take Loisy's affirmation in the epigraph of this chapter negatively, as if he ironically states that Christ's proclamation of the Kingdom of God was later distorted to result in the Church? Or should one take his affirmation positively, meaning that the Church represents the natural consequence of Christ's proclamation of the Kingdom, even though Jesus has not technically founded the Church? Loisy intended the latter. Sadly, the Kingdom is not always at the center of the life of the Church, but rather the reverse is true: the Church has become the center of Christians' religious life and even a reality that points to itself. But when the Church exists for itself instead of manifesting and expanding the Kingdom of God to the entire world, Loisy's epigraph morphs into an ironic statement.

In this chapter, I argue that the Church exists as a partial manifestation of the Kingdom between the two full manifestations of the Kingdom, first in the person of Jesus and, at the end of time, in the eschatological Kingdom of God. In the meantime, the Church is an icon of the Kingdom, functioning as a foretaste of the reality that is to come, while simultaneously bringing the eschatological Kingdom closer and closer.

THE KINGDOM OF GOD IN THE BIBLE

God is the King of Israel, and God will be the King of Israel. That is not to say that God is male (a king, rather than a queen), or that monarchy is God's preferred political system (as opposed to democracy, for example). Consequently, many theologians today refer to "the rule of God" or "the reign of God" instead of "Kingdom of God" to translate the biblical expression *basileia tou Theou* (e.g., Mk 1:15) or its circumlocution in Matthew who, as all pious Jews, prefers to not use the name of God, but a synonym, "the Kingdom of heavens" *basileia ton ouranon* (e.g., Mt 4:17).[4] William Thompson-Uberuaga supports another interesting possibility, namely the replacement of "kingdom" with "kin-dom," which

> avoids the unfortunate associations of dominating power expressive of many, most, or even all (?) kingdoms/reigns, at least the ones we know in human history. And "kin-dom" or "kindom" seems wide enough to embrace

---

4. Dale Allison affirms that the two expressions usually denote the same reality, although "Kingdom of heavens" has a more pronounced spatial connotation than "Kingdom of God." Moreover, he argues that "heavens" is not primarily a circumlocution that piously avoids the name of God, as most biblical scholars agree. Dale C. Allison, *Constructing Jesus: Memory, Imagination, and History* (Grand Rapids, MI: Baker Academic, 2010), 182.

our entire family, human and all animates. Praying for kindom's coming seems to express a yearning to refind in a new way our union with our earth, our cosmos, but also with those who are our kin, and yet we do not know them or even see them, persons certainly, but entire groups.[5]

Throughout the book I have a preference for inclusive language. And yet, most Christians are unfamiliar with the inclusivist expressions mentioned above, and these expressions do not include a territorial connotation. Hence, I continue to use the classical translation, "the Kingdom of God," with the understanding that I do not assume its gender and political implications.

These terminological remarks notwithstanding, the Scriptures, both old and new, proclaim that *God is the King of Israel*, an affirmation that has significant political and religious implications: Israel recognizes God alone, and no human king, as its absolute ruler, so no human force will be able to stand against God's will for Israel, either politically or religiously.

Israel as a nation and Judaism as a religion long preceded any form of monarchy in Israel. Judaism can exist fully without any reference to monarchy, and yet Judaism and various forms of worldly powers have crossed paths from the time of its first king, Saul, through the rejection of the Roman Emperor during Jesus' time, to today's Jewish expectation of a Messianic ruler. All along, the belief that God is the absolute ruler, the King of all, has always been at the center of the Jewish tradition.

A very small nation, ancient Israel was surrounded by larger nations that attributed their power to the gods they worshipped. But the Israel of the Bible endured because their ruler—God—was more powerful than the idols of the nations, so "dominion belongs to the Lord, and he rules over the nations" (Ps 22:28). God empowered his people to withstand foreign attacks, as long as Israel stayed true to the covenant that it made with God: if they respect God's will, God will be their God and provide them with land, prosperity, and descendants. As far as God was concerned, this covenant was going to be everlasting (Gn 17:1–9). According to the prophets, Israel broke this covenant and the people were taken into captivity in Babylon not because God was unfaithful, but because they broke the covenant that stated that they would remain in the land if they followed God's will. And yet, God's dwelling place among his people (the Shekinah[6]) accompanied them in exile, later returning with them

<hr/>

5. William Thompson-Uberuaga, *Your Kin-dom Come: The Lord's Prayer in a Global Age* (Eugene, OR: Cascade Books, 2018), 32.

6. While the Jewish tradition regarded God as omnipresent, the Scriptures also describe God as dwelling in certain locations, such as the temple in Jerusalem. The rabbis explained this paradox by

from captivity to the Promised Land. All along, God remained their ruler. After the return from the Babylonian captivity, messianic expectations became
more prominent than ever: God will again send a new Moses to establish a
new covenant:

> I have loved you with an everlasting love; therefore I have continued my
> faithfulness to you. Again I will build you, and you shall be built, O virgin
> Israel!... The days are surely coming, says the LORD, when I will make a new
> covenant with the house of Israel and the house of Judah. It will not be like
> the covenant that I made with their ancestors when I took them by the hand
> to bring them out of the land of Egypt—a covenant that they broke, though
> I was their husband, says the LORD. But this is the covenant that I will make
> with the house of Israel after those days, says the LORD: I will put my law
> within them, and I will write it on their hearts; and I will be their God, and
> they shall be my people. (Jer 31:3–4, 31–33)

By the time of Jesus' coming, in the consciousness of the people, God promised a Messiah who would establish a kingdom in which all would see that,
indeed, God is king. As God is just, there will be justice in his Kingdom; as
God gives abundantly, all will have food in abundance; as God is perfect and
immortal, all will be healed from sickness and even death so that our relationship of love with God would last forever; as God is love, there will be love; as
God is truth, his words will be made known; as God is King, no foreign king
can rule over an independent nation of Israel. Being under Roman occupation
and in a dire economic situation, Jesus' contemporaries expected a Messiah
who would liberate them from the Romans, possibly a zealot who would lead
a revolution, as many Jewish zealots tried. Moreover, a Messiah would provide
plenty of food for his people and heal their diseases, so the hope in the Messiah
became intrinsically intertwined with the expectation of the Kingdom of God.
At his trial, Jesus did not deny being an other-worldly "King" who came into
this world (Jn 18:36–37), so Pontius Pilate inscribed his accusation as "Jesus of
Nazareth, the King of the Jews." Little did he know how true this statement
would soon become for Jesus' followers, and how unfounded it would ring to
those who did not accept Jesus as the Messiah.

Jesus—the new Moses, the King, the Christ, or the Messiah—ended up
crucified at the hand of the Romans, disappointing his followers who harbored
worldly hopes, as the two disciples lament on their way to Emmaus: "but we

---

affirming that the Shekinah is God's presence on earth, where, through his own accord, God dwells in a
special way.

had hoped that he was the one to redeem Israel ..." (Lk 24:21). This attitude is representative of most of Jesus' co-nationals who did not accept the statement that Jesus was the Messiah who brought about the Kingdom of God, since politically they had not seen the demise of the Roman Empire and Israel's independence and prosperity. To this day Jews throughout the world are praying for the fulfillment of these Messianic hopes. But after the Resurrection and even more so after Pentecost, Jesus' followers made this statement a central part of their confession of faith: Jesus *is* the Messiah, the King of Israel.[7] They looked back at the promises of God in the Scriptures and at the life and sayings of Jesus and understood what they had previously missed: Jesus was the King of Israel and, in his person, the Kingdom of God was fully present. That is because Jesus' passion has a redemptive significance beyond his own individual experience. Rather, Jesus carries in his person the suffering, exile, and martyrdom of the entire Israel, as the suffering servant through whom God redeems Israel, followed by Israel's victory in Jesus' rising from the dead. As N. T. Wright explains, "the resurrection of Jesus demonstrated that he was indeed the Messiah, that Jesus had indeed borne the destiny of Israel on his shoulders in carrying the Roman cross outside the city walls, that he had gone through the climax of Israel's exile and had returned from that exile three days later according to and in fulfillment of the entire biblical narrative."[8]

Thus, if Jesus is the King who embodies the entire nation of Israel, then Israel was, indeed, defeated on the Cross, but only to resurrect on the third day. The Romans were ultimately unable to defeat Jesus and thus Israel. In light of the Resurrection, the one who bore the sufferings of many on the Cross is also the King of the Jews who brought glory to the nation of Israel, who ensured their victory over sin, suffering, hunger, injustice, and death, which is what the Messiah was supposed to do. The resurrected Jesus is the first fruits of the victory of God through Israel, who is collectively embodied in Jesus, the fulfillment of the Messianic promises made to the nation of Israel.[9] But early Christians did not stop at the affirmation that the Kingdom of God was

7. Believing in Jesus's messiahship does not require belief in his divinity. The gospels focus mainly on Jesus as Messiah, not as God. Though Jesus implies numerous times that he is divine, he is only once explicitly referred to as "God" in the four gospels, when Thomas calls the resurrected Jesus, "My Lord and My God" (Jn 20:28). Later Christianity has taken some other messianic titles (especially "Son of God") to refer to Jesus' divinity.

8. N. T. Wright, *The Challenge of Jesus: Rediscovering Who Jesus Was and Is* (Downers Grove, IL: InterVarsity Press, 1999), 148..

9. The Songs of the Suffering Servant (Is 42–53) could refer to a single individual (possibly a king), or to the entire nation of Israel, or—most probably—to a king who embodies the entire nation of Israel, as any good king would. In the eyes of Orthodox Christians, this collective person was Jesus. During

fully present in the person of Jesus, true though it may have been. They went further: "Jesus is the Kingdom in person," (*autobasileia*) wrote Origen,[10] which is certainly a valid way of interpreting Jesus' affirmation that "the kingdom of God is among you" (Lk 17:21).

The above considerations have explained how the Kingdom represents God's reign or rule over all things. But is it also a physical place? Some might think of the Kingdom of heavens as a purely spiritual reality, separate from the messiness of this material world. This gnostic temptation of regarding eschatology as an escape from history has endured throughout the centuries. But the end of times will not be a disappearance of the material world into heavens; it will be the descent of the heavens upon the earth. The prayer "Our Father" invokes the image of the descent of heaven upon the earth. In reference to both the Kingdom and the will of God, the order in the Greek original is different than in English. The English reads, "on earth as it is in heaven," mentioning earth first. But in Greek the order is reverse: *os en ouranon kai epi tis gis*, which could be translated: "as in heaven, so on earth." Starting with heaven and then mentioning earth creates the impression that heaven descends upon earth, where the Kingdom will be, as opposed to suggesting, as the common English translation does, that earth ascends into heaven, where the Kingdom will be. The first might suggest a heavenly earth, while the second might suggest a heavenly reality with the memory of the earth. In this sense, N. T. Wright defines the Kingdom of God or the Kingdom of heaven not as "... a place, called 'heaven,' where God's people will go after death," but rather as "the rule of heaven, that is, of God, being brought to bear in the present world. Thy kingdom come, said Jesus, thy will be done, *on earth as in heaven*. Jesus' contemporaries knew that the creator God intended to bring justice and peace to his world here and now. The question was, how, when, and through whom."[11] There was one answer to all these questions: Jesus. Hence, the Kingdom is the rule of God over all spiritual and material creation in Jesus.[12]

Proskomide, the priest recites verses from these Songs while preparing the bread that will become "the Lamb of God who takes away the sin of the world" (Jn 1:29–36).

10. Origen, *The Commentary of Origen on the Gospel of St Matthew, Volume II*, trans. Ronald E. Heine, Oxford Early Christian Texts, (New York: Oxford University Press, 2018), XIV: 7, 432. Translation modified compared to "he himself is the kingdom."

11. Wright, *The Challenge of Jesus*, 37–38.

12. Dale Allison analyzes the range of meanings of the expression "Kingdom of God," including God's dynamic activity as a ruler, the state of affairs when God rules over the world, places sometimes related to Jewish territorial expectations (including the Promised Land of a new exodus), an established realm under God's rule, a house or a city, territorial eschatology, eternal life, the age to come, and God's people. Allison, *Constructing Jesus*, 164–204.

Another interesting indication of spiritualized materiality both in this present new age and in the eschaton is the consistency with which the Scriptures refer to the Kingdom as a meal. Many of Jesus' Kingdom parables refer to a banquet. The same goes for his actions. To illustrate the Kingdom, Jesus has table fellowship with the sinners and the outcasts, showing that all will be invited to partake of this meal in the Kingdom. His multiplications of the loaves and fishes in the wilderness also signify that all will have abundant food in the Kingdom. Hence, it is not surprising that the center of the Church's life, the Eucharist, is a meal. Jesus instituted the Eucharist during a meal—the Last Supper. Early Christians first gathered to eat together. During this meal they would break the bread (i.e. have the Eucharist—1 Cor 10–11), deacons would help with the distribution of the food (Acts 6:1), and the poor were fed with the gifts that everybody brought to church. To this day, the Liturgy ends not with the reception of the Eucharist, but with the sending forth in order to minister to the world—"Let us go forth in peace." The ministry to the poor—the Liturgy after the Liturgy, or the Liturgy at the altar of the poor—is as important as the eucharistic Liturgy because both manifest the Kingdom of God, when all will have plenty, when the heavens will descend upon earth. Thus, a Kingdom-centered ecclesiology will consider that God is the King of all things, both spiritual and material, and that the eschatological rule of God over all is already visibly present in the person of Jesus, the community of disciples, and in the Church's liturgy and care for the poor. What are *the main values of this Kingdom-centered ecclesiology?*

Like the Forerunner John the Baptist, Jesus began his preaching with the words, "Repent, for the Kingdom of God is at hand" (Mt 4:17, Mk 1:15). This coming of the Kingdom fully in the person of Jesus was the good news, the *euangelion*. Jesus manifested the Kingdom by proclaiming the good news (the gospel) and by healing the world of injustice, suffering, disease, hunger, death, and sin. When John the Baptist sent his disciples to ask Jesus whether he was the Messiah, Jesus answered positively, albeit indirectly: "Go and tell John what you hear and see: the blind receive their sight, the lame walk, the lepers are cleansed, the deaf hear, the dead are raised, and the poor have the good news brought to them" (Mt 11:4–5). Moreover, "Jesus went throughout Galilee, teaching in their synagogues and proclaiming the good news of the kingdom and curing every disease and every sickness among the people" (Mt 4:23, 9:35). Throughout the book, we shall consider these two elements—*healing and proclamation*—as the fundamental values of a Kingdom-centered ecclesiology.

The first of these values is *healing*. Jesus heals because God is perfect, he created human beings perfect. The world upon which he rules is to be free of suffering and disease, as opposed to the part of the world that is still under the dominion of evil, which needs to be conquered. If the Essenes of his time envisaged a messianic kingdom that excluded those with physical ailments, Jesus' proclamation of God's kingdom also heals the world of its elitist exclusivism that rejects the sick and the suffering, embracing them and reconstituting Israel.[13] Jesus conquers death when he resurrects people from the dead and, most importantly, when he himself is risen. Jesus shows that God's Kingdom provides in abundance when, like Moses before him, he twice feeds the multitudes in the wilderness (Mt 14:19–21; 15:36–38); the first time the disciples gather twelve baskets of crumbs, reminiscent of the twelve tribes of Israel and symbolizing the fullness of Israel, and the second time they gather seven baskets, evocative of the creation of the world in seven days and thus signifying that the entire world will be part of the Kingdom. Jesus forgives the sins of many, manifesting the absolute holiness of the King. Jesus defends the woman caught in sin, revealing the Kingdom of the absolutely just God, in contrast to what humans consider justice but is actually a system corrupted by sin; as St. Gregory of Nazianzus points out, only the woman was going to be stoned, and not the man with whom she sinned, because the rules are written by men and thus unjustly favor males.[14] Since God's perfect love extends to both the righteous and sinners, Jesus commands his followers to love their enemies (Mt 5:44–48). Amy-Jill Levine explains that Second Temple Judaism did not allow one to "mistreat the enemy, but love was not mandated.... [Jesus] may be the only person in antiquity to have given us this instruction [to love the enemy]."[15] Thus, healing extends from physical ailments and death to sin and broken human relationships.

The other aspect of the Kingdom is the *proclamation of the good news*, namely that the Kingdom is at hand. The Kingdom is good news for an oppressed people, a nation that suffered great injustice. But while at that time Israel associated their identity of covenantal people with political independence,

13. N. T. Wright contrasts Jesus' inclusivist healings that express the reconstitution of Israel with the "messianic rule" from Qumran (1QSa) that excluded the blind, the lame, the deaf and the dumb from membership in the community of God's restored people. Wright, *The Challenge of Jesus*, 68–69.

14. Saint Gregory of Nazianzus, "Oration 37 on Matthew 19:1," in *Cyril of Jerusalem, Gregory Nazianzen*, transl. Charles G. Browne, NPNF II, vol. 7 (Grand Rapids, MI: Eerdmans, 1893), #6, 679. In the same passage, St. Gregory of Nazianzus contrasts the Law of Moses that treated men and women equally with the customs introduced by men that are "unequal and irregular." The saint clearly states that he does not approve this custom that is "hard on women."

15. Amy-Jill Levine, *Short Stories by Jesus: The Enigmatic Parables of a Controversial Rabbi* (New York: HarperCollins 2014), 93–94.

God reigns in all contexts, including under Roman occupation. And so, Jesus is already able to renew the covenant at the Last Supper, sealing it not with the blood of animal sacrifices, as did the old Moses (Ex 24:1–8), but with his own blood: "Drink of this all of you, this is the blood of the new covenant, which is shed for you and for many for the forgiveness of sins."[16] The Kingdom of God is here; this is the center of Jesus' proclamation.

Jesus shared his mission with *the community of disciples*. As if re-creating the nation, Jesus chooses twelve men to represent the twelve tribes of Israel. The disciples are told that they will sit on twelve thrones, judging the twelve tribes of Israel (Mt 19:28), meaning that they symbolize the renewed Israel.[17] Of course, the community of disciples extended well beyond "the twelve." Luke mentions seventy disciples (Lk 10:1, 17), alluding to the coming of the LORD in the form of a cloud upon the seventy elders who were faithful in the time of Moses, who gathered around the tabernacle and the Spirit of the Lord rested upon them, enabling them to speak like prophets (Nm 11:24–25).[18] Again, the community of disciples is meant to represent the renewed Israel, of which Jesus is the Messiah and God is King.

Even though initially the twelve were sent "only to the lost sheep of Israel" (Mt 10:5–6), after the resurrection he sent them to "make disciples of all nations, baptizing them in the name of the Father and of the Son and of the Holy Spirit, teaching them to observe all that I have commanded you. And behold, I am with you always, to the end of the age" (Mt 28:19–20). The Kingdom of God, fully manifested in the person of Jesus, was to be expanded to include the community of disciples, which in turn was to become larger and larger, to include all the nations. Because Jesus promised to be with his disciples "always, to the end of the age," his followers began referring to their community as "the Body of Christ." They became the extended Jesus, the Body of Christ that includes all the nations. Thus, the renewed Israel was not oriented only towards itself, to strengthen its own members, but also towards the outside, to bring new members from among the nations.

16. These words from the Divine Liturgy are a combination of several biblical passages: Mt 26:26, Mk 14:24, Lk 22:20, 1 Cor 11:25.

17. The Essene community of Qumran anticipated the coming of the Priest Messiah who would lead a Messianic feast at which "the chiefs of the [clans of Israel] shall sit before him." *Rule of Congregation* 1QSa 2.20, quoted in Bryan D. Spinks, *Do This in Remembrance of Me: The Eucharist from the Early Church to the Present Day* (London: SCM Press, 2013), 10.

18. Oftentimes the numbers seven and seventy represent fullness, as when Ex 1:5 mentions the seventy children of Jacob who went into Egypt as a way of saying that all of Israel was present in Egypt. In this light, Luke might be implying that all of Israel is called to be a disciple of Jesus.

The orientation outside of Israel was in line with the destiny of Israel, as intended by God from the beginning. As Israel wandered through the desert, it was called to be a "priestly kingdom and a holy nation" (Ex 19:5–6); it was chosen out of all the nations in order to minister to the others. The community of disciples is commissioned by Jesus to do just that. So, we come full circle: the Chosen People that was called to be "a priestly kingdom and a holy nation" (Ex 19:5–6) and whose destiny is lived out in the Messiah, now ministers to the nations. Later on, the Church will take on the same mission, of being "a chosen race, a royal priesthood, a holy nation, God's own people, in order that you may proclaim the mighty acts of him who called you out of darkness into his marvelous light" (1 Pt 2:9).

A further distinction is necessary here. The references from Ex 19:5–6 and 1 Pt 2:9 emphasize the role of the Chosen People to minister *to* the nations, while the expansion of the Chosen People to include all the baptized (Mt 28:19–20) emphasizes the inclusion of the nations *in* the renewed Israel. Ministering to the nations and including them in the Chosen People are not necessarily separate emphases, as they could be congruent. But ministering to the nations can also mean the preservation of the nations' identity while the Chosen People brings them healing. Christ's messianic work embraces both emphases.[19]

The community of disciples remained within Judaism for much of the first century; they were Jews who believed in Jesus, who went to the Temple, but also broke bread (that is, had the Eucharist) at home (Acts 2:46). Because of the commemoration of Jesus' death and resurrection in the Eucharist, and because of their expansion towards the Gentiles, soon the Church had no choice but to part ways with institutional Israel. These considerations lead to the question: *what is the Church in relation to Israel?*

When describing the relationship between Israel and the Church, one needs to avoid two extremes: at one end of the spectrum, supersessionism contends that the Jewish tradition of scriptural interpretation has completely lost its value without reference to the New Testament, not to be confused with the genuine Christian position that the New Testament provides a new lens of reading the Old Testament, which does not cancel the Jewish tradition

---

19. The healing of the Centurion's servant (Mt 8:5–13) is a relevant passage in this regard: on the one hand, Jesus marvels at the faith of the Centurion and heals his servant without requiring conversion to Judaism. On the other hand, as a result of this encounter, Jesus says that "many will come from east and west and will eat with Abraham and Isaac and Jacob in the kingdom of heaven," suggesting their inclusion in the kingdom.

of interpretation. Supersessionism also considers that Christianity has replaced Judaism, the Church has replaced the Temple, and Christians are now God's people, while Israel is no longer the chosen one. At the other end of the spectrum, extreme forms of pluralism contend that all religions are—at their core—the same, we all worship the same God and there are no substantial differences between the Church and Israel; they are both similar paths leading to the same mountaintop. While the first extreme does not take into account the eternal character of God's covenant with Israel and the Jewish character of the early Jesus movement[20] (after all, Jesus, Virgin Mary, and the Apostles lived and died as Jews), the latter extreme fails to account for both the lack of recognition of Jesus as the Messiah in Judaism and the centrality of Christ in Christianity.

But it is much easier to say which extremes we should avoid than to describe positively the relationship between Israel and the Church. This difficulty is augmented today as we, Christians, confess in repentance and carry with remorse the heavy burden of our history of systematic persecutions of Jews, physical violence, murders, unjust legislation, and forced conversions. All attempts to relate the Church and Israel will be imperfect. Vatican II speaks of the "new Israel"—an expression that risks supersessionist connotations. Another possibility might be "remnant Israel" based on Rom 9:27–11:5 and numerous prophetic utterances, but the same risk of supersessionist connotations remains. A happier possibility might be "inclusive" Israel.

The best I can suggest is that the Church is the "expanded Israel" and the "renewed Israel." As the renewed Israel, Jesus also expanded it to include Gentiles. Paul makes the argument that a Jew is defined inwardly by the circumcision of the heart, and not by outward circumcision (Rom 2:28–29). His next step is to write that, in Christ, Gentiles have been grafted into the olive tree that is Israel (Rom 9–11, especially 11:16–24). Those who are baptized into Christ and who receive the Eucharist become one with Christ. Since Christ was a Jew, Gentiles who are united with Christ become incorporated into Israel. Today it is important to acknowledge that this argument worked for Paul and his followers, many of whom were Jews. But from a contemporary Jewish perspective, that is not the case, primarily because Jewish identity is understood in a very complex way that involves ethnicity, including being the inheritor of a history

---

20. Biblical scholars describe Jesus's public ministry, with its dynamism and constantly moving character, as "the Jesus Movement," avoiding the potentially static and institutional connotations of the term, "Church." Daniel J. Harrington, *The Church According to the New Testament: What the Wisdom and Witness of Early Christinity Teach Us Today* (Franklin, WI: Sheed & Ward, 2001), 1.

marked by persecution, often at Christian hands. From a religious perspective, Jewish identity is related to observance of rituals and teachings, which Gentiles would need to embrace through conversion to Judaism. Needless to say, all my attempts to explain to my Jewish friends the Christian sense in which I regarded myself as a Jew inwardly have failed.

And yet, the New Testament—again, at a time when most followers of Jesus were Jews—boldly affirms that the Church is "the Israel of God" (Gal 6:16). In this regard, Alexander Golitzin's definition of the Church deserves to be quoted at length:

> For the Orthodox tradition, the church is nothing more nor less than Israel in the altered circumstances of the Messiah's death, resurrection, and the eschatological outpouring of the Spirit. This "inaugurated eschaton", to borrow a phrase from the late Fr Georges Florovsky, is at the same time a "new creation" (Gal 6:15). In Jesus of Nazareth, Mary's son and eternal Son and Word of the Father, Israel has in a sense itself been crucified, raised, and changed, such as to become the "first-fruits" of the new creation (1 Cor 15:20), the "new" or "heavenly Adam" (cf. 1 Cor 15:45ff.; Rom 5:12ff.), the beginning of the world to come (Col 1:18). Yet, at least in Orthodox tradition, it would be most wrong to emphasize this change, these altered circumstances, as denoting rupture pure and simple with the Israel of the patriarchs, kings and prophets. True, far and away the majority of Israel did not accept the change, and they carry on to the present apart from the church, but I would maintain that the separation was and is not so much between church and Israel as between two separate and discrete entities, as it is a schism within Israel, a schism which, if we are to believe the apostle, God—and only God!—will heal at the end of days (see Rom 9–11). Christian and Jewish polemics, both in the early centuries of the church and in more recent times, may have often obscured this fundamental linkage and kinship, but they could not erase it. It is built into the earliest documents of Christianity and reflected continuously thereafter in Orthodox literature and liturgy. Thus for St. Paul, as I read him, the discussion at issue in epistles such as Galatians and, especially, Romans centres not on the rejection of Israel, but rather, through the Messiah, on the expansion of Israel's boundaries so as to include the nations.[21]

21. Alexander Golitzin, "Scriptural Images of the Church: An Eastern Orthodox Reflection," in One, Holy, Catholic and Apostolic: Ecumenical Reflections on the Church, ed. Tamara Grdzelidze (Geneva: WCC Publications, 2005), 255–56.

To recap the two main points thus far, the central message of Jesus' preaching was the Kingdom of God, with its two components: healing and proclamation. The Kingdom was to expand to include the community of disciples as the renewed Israel and all the Gentile nations. So, did Jesus found a Church understood as a separate religion from Judaism? No. Did he proclaim the Kingdom of God that was fully manifested in his person, which then extended to include the community of disciples and gentiles—what we call today, Church? Yes. This is the meaning of Loisy's words in the epigraph of this chapter: "Jesus proclaimed the Kingdom, and what came was the Church."

THE KINGDOM IS ALREADY HERE ...
BUT NOT YET

On the one hand, the Kingdom of God is already here fully in the person of Jesus as well as in instances when the community of disciples (and later the Church) acts according to the values of the Kingdom, namely healing and proclamation. On the other hand, the Kingdom of God is waiting for its fulfillment, when God will be the King of all and his power will be manifested in all places, for which reason Christians still pray, "Thy Kingdom come." In other words, the Kingdom of God is already here ... but not yet.

Perhaps no moment in Jesus' earthly ministry signifies the "already but not yet" aspect of the Kingdom as much as the Transfiguration on Mt. Tabor. For St. Maximus the Confessor, the Transfiguration is the promised anticipatory vision of the eschatological Second Coming of Christ, as a reference to the glory the Son possesses eternally by which "he glorified the assumed humanity because just as he was seen transfigured on the mountain in the body that is subject to suffering, so also we shall be in the resurrection when we receive an incorruptible body."[22] Similarly, St. Gregory Palamas understands the Transfiguration as the manifestation of the Kingdom of God in Jesus as already here, but not yet: "The King of all is everywhere, and so is His kingdom, so the coming of his kingdom does not mean it arrives here from somewhere else, but that it is revealed through the power of the Divine Spirit."[23] While the Kingdom was partially revealed to Peter, James, and John, the disciples who stood

---

22. "Question 190," Saint Maximus the Confessor, *Questions and Doubts*, trans. Despina D. Prassas (DeKalb, IL: Northern Illinois University Press, 2010), 137.

23. Saint Gregory Palamas, *The Homilies*, trans. Christopher Veniamin (Waymart, PA: Mt. Tabor Publishing, 2009), 34.7.

with the Lord, it will be fully revealed in the eschaton—the "manifestation to come."[24]

Just as on Mt. Tabor, the eschaton also pierces through time in the Church. Paul writes that all things are under Christ's authority who has been raised above all things in this world and in the world to come. Christ is the head of the Church, his Body, which is then defined as "the fullness of him who fills all in all" (Eph 1:23), meaning that Christ's dominion over all, which will be fully revealed in the eschaton, is already partially manifested in the Church. While the world is still waiting for its transformation into the Kingdom, the Church is meant to be a prefiguration (icon) of the eschaton, when God will visibly rule over all things and be "all in all." There is thus a continuum between Jesus (full manifestation of the Kingdom), the Body of Christ (reign within the Church, but incompletely in the world), and the eschaton (full manifestation of the Kingdom).

The relationship between the Kingdom and the Church took on different meanings in subsequent centuries. Karl L. Schmidt writes that, on the one hand, post-apostolic fathers distinguish between the Kingdom and the Church (Epistle of Barnabas 8:5), especially when considering the eschatological aspect of the Kingdom, which obviously is not yet present. Similarly, the eucharistic prayer of the Didache distinguishes between the Kingdom and the Church that Christ gathers into his Kingdom. On the other hand, however, 2 Clement 14:3 and Hermas reduce the distance between the Kingdom and the Church since the Church must be received like the Kingdom of God. From there on, the East has emphasized Kingdom as future-oriented and other-worldly (eschatological), while the West has emphasized its active realization on earth, culminating with Augustine's identification of the Kingdom with the Church.[25] Schmidt's remark about the difference of emphasis between East and West, while revealing a general trend, is not a hard-and-fast rule, given for example the Orthodox emphasis on the Liturgy as realized eschaton and the West's concept of beatific vision, so the difference of emphasis should not be taken to an extreme.

Augustine himself was more nuanced than Schmidt gives him credit for. Augustine points out that, on the one hand, the New Testament presents the community of disciples as already reigning with Jesus in his Kingdom on this side of the eschaton (e.g. "remember, I am with you always, to the end of the age" (Mt 28:20); or the parable of the tares (Mt 13:39–41) in which the

24. Gregory Palamas, The Homilies, 34.12.

25. Karl Ludwig Schmidt, "Basileus, Basileia," in Theological Dictionary of the New Testament, ed. Gerhard Kittel (Grand Rapids, MI: Eerdmans, 1964/1993), 592–93.

righteous, though intermingled with the unrighteous, are already part of the Kingdom). On the other hand, he notes that the New Testament speaks also of times when only those who are pure will be in the Kingdom (e.g. Mt 5:19–20). The first set of sayings refers to how the Church is now, while the second set refers to how the Church will be at the end of times. Thus, Augustine concludes, "the Church, even in this world, here and now, is the kingdom of Christ and the kingdom of heaven. Here and now Christ's saints reign with Him, although not in the way they are destined to reign hereafter; but the "weeds" do not reign with Him, even now, though they grow along with the "wheat" in the Church.... Those alone reign with Christ whose presence in His kingdom is such that they themselves *are* His kingdom."[26] Thus, Augustine identified the Church with the Kingdom of God both in this present age and in the age to come, but made the distinction that the members of the Church will reign differently in the eschaton, since then they will have conquered evil, while in the present age they are still fighting it.

Inspired by Augustine, John Calvin distinguishes between the Kingdom and the (visible) Church when he writes about the (visible) Church being a mix of righteous and unrighteous, of good seeds and tares, and the Church not being free from all wrinkles and spots until the Day of Judgment. When he writes especially of the positive aspects of the Church, however, Calvin identifies it with the Kingdom. In his commentary on the parable of the sower (Mt 13:24–30, 36–43), he even goes so far as to limit the Kingdom to the Church. Though Christ identifies "the field" in that parable with "the world," Calvin considers that Jesus was in fact talking about the Church and that "the field" actually refers to "the Church."[27]

These remarks connecting the Kingdom of God and the Church show how gradually the Church became identified with the Kingdom even while some pre-eschatological differentiation remained. The Church became the Kingdom "already here" and hoped for a full identification after the "not yet." But the "not yet" remained an important corrective to the full identification between the Church and the Kingdom. It is important to maintain the differentiation between the Church and the Kingdom in order to maintain the consciousness that the Church is not the end-point of creation; rather, the Kingdom is. In its relationship with the world, the Church ministers to the Kingdom, not to

26. Augustine, *The City of God, Books XVII–XXII*, trans. Gerald G. Walsh and Daniel J. Honan, The Fathers of the Church, (Washington, DC: The Catholic University of America Press, 2008), XX:9, 276.

27. John Calvin, *A Harmony of the Gospels Matthew, Mark and Luke*, trans. T. H. L. Parker, vol. 2 (Grand Rapids, MI: Eerdmans, 1995), 73–84, esp. 75, 84.

itself. In other words, the Church's mission is not to expand its own structures, but to be an icon of the Kingdom to the world—a presence of grace of the Kingdom in the world.

THE CHURCH: ICON OF THE KINGDOM OF GOD

Existing between the full manifestation of the Kingdom in the person of Jesus and the full manifestation of the Kingdom in the world at the end of time, the Church is called to be, as John Zizioulas proposes, "an *eikon* of the Kingdom to come."[28] As an icon, presence, sign, or foretaste of the Kingdom, the Church makes visible and present the values of the Kingdom, namely healing and proclamation. Until the Church arrives at the end of its pilgrimage to the eschaton, the Church reflects the Kingdom only imperfectly. These considerations are not intended critically, as if the Church is not already related to the Kingdom or as if it has strayed away from its calling. Rather, one should think of the days of creation, when God created the world gradually; at the end of each day, his partially finished creation was "good," and, at the end of the sixth day, it was "very good" (Gn 1:31). Being created in stages does not mean that the world (or the Church) is bad. It is simply incomplete, on the way toward fulfillment. It is as when an iconographer looks with content at some basic colors on a piece of wood because she can see the elements that will contribute to a beautiful icon when it is finished. So the Church now contains the elements that will be put together and manifested fully at the end of time. The Church is already a partial presence of the Kingdom and an instrument actively bringing about the fullness of the Kingdom of God, or better put, providing the space for God to bring his Kingdom, gradually, in stages, until the end of time.

Jesus is the inauguration of the eschaton, and the Church lives "within this eschatological framework, between, so to speak, the beginning of the End and the end of the End."[29] The eschatological state of the Church is not simply the endpoint of its pilgrimage; it is also what informs the Church's current state. According to Zizioulas, "the Church does not draw her identity from what she is but from what she will be."[30] Eschatology is no longer the last chapter of Christian Dogmatics, but the first; hence the abundant references to

28. John D. Zizioulas, "The Mystery of the Church in Orthodox Tradition," *One in Christ* 24, no. 4 (1988): 300.
29. Wright, *The Challenge of Jesus*, 181.
30. Zizioulas, "The Mystery of the Church in Orthodox Tradition," 296.

eschatology in the first chapter of the present book, which will in turn inform the subsequent chapters. Indeed, we shall later see that eschatology is crucial to ecclesiology. The Church receives its identity from what it is going to be. For example, the Liturgy is an experience of the eschaton. The end of time, when all creation will be transfigured, is already happening in the Eucharist. Moreover, as the Kingdom is not purely spiritual, but encompasses the visible world, the Church does not resign itself in the expectation of justice only in a fleshless afterlife. As the world suffers greatly, most of those who hurt from illness, persecution, or discrimination, do not have a voice. They silently carry the burden of their pain, with no one to help, with no one to hear their cry, with no one to speak for them. The Church is called to hear their suffering, bring healing, and give a voice to the voiceless. Already here, enlivened by the Spirit, the Church manifests the Kingdom in the transfigured inter-human relationships that its members experience in the community, in their advocacy for the world, and these relationships will be perfected in the eschaton. As Staniloae writes, at the end of times, Jesus

> will then perfect the communion among all the people from all times and he will change the image of the present world according to this perfect communion. The entire Church will resurrect in the new world together with the Lord. Then Jesus will subdue for the Father the world that would be saved and transfigured, and he will also subdue himself together with [the world], so that God would be all in all. Then will begin the day of perfect brotherhood among people and perfect sonship in relationship to the Father.[31]

That is the sense in which eschatology is not the last, but the first chapter of theology, representing not simply the endpoint of history, but also its source of inspiration, the beginning that nurtures it throughout the way. In the Church, we strive to live now as we will live at the end.

At that point, the Church will cease to exist as the gathering of the elect, the chosen ones, the ones that are holy (or separated) from the rest in order to be a holy priesthood to the world; there will be no more holiness in the sense of separation, since God will be "all in all" and the world will all be holy. Perhaps a better way to express this eschatological hope is to affirm that—instead of the disappearance of the Church—the Church will encompass all reality and praise God with one voice.

By way of conclusion, let us return to our original questions. What on earth

---

31. Dumitru Staniloae, *Iisus Hristos sau restaurarea omului* [*Jesus Christ or the Restoration of Humankind*], 2nd ed. (Craiova: Editura Omniscop, 1993), 427.

does the Church have to do with the Kingdom of Heavens? How should we take Loisy's affirmation that "Jesus proclaimed the Kingdom, and what came was the Church"? The center of Jesus' preaching was not the Church, but the Kingdom of God understood as the rule of heaven upon the earth. The Kingdom was fully present in Jesus, and then expanded to the community of disciples, the Church that includes the nations, and to the entire world in the eschaton. The task of the Church is to be an icon, sign, foretaste, and instrument of the Kingdom of God, where the good news is being proclaimed, where the world is being healed of sin and suffering and death. Throughout the centuries, the Church enacted the values of the Kingdom of God, while praying for the Kingdom to come. The Kingdom is already here, but not yet. The Church is not the entire Kingdom, but neither are the Church and the Kingdom separate. The Church brings together both the experience and the expectation of the Kingdom in the Church. In the eschaton, when God will be "all in all," the entire world will be a Church, filled with God's presence, and we already experience that eschatological reality in the Church.

TWO

Baptism

———

For in one Spirit we were all baptized into one body

I COR 12:13

The Church is the community of the baptized. Baptism is not merely a brief liturgical rite, but a long process that culminates in entry into the Church. For adults, this process begins with the moment of their conversion, followed by a period of catechesis, Baptism proper, Chrismation (what Western Christians call Confirmation), and receiving the Eucharist. Hence, the epigraph of this chapter captures several elements of the rite of initiation: the receiving of the Spirit through Chrismation, Baptism proper, and entry into the Church, which is the Body of Christ—the same designation also referring to the Eucharist. And since Orthodox liturgical books include under the rite of Baptism all these three sacraments, most of the references to Baptism in this chapter refer to the entire rite of Christian initiation. This theme could very well be treated from a liturgical-historical perspective. Instead, this chapter focuses on the ecclesiology that emerges from the experience of Baptism, in line with the general approach of this book.

Most commonly today, Orthodox faithful are baptized as infants and thus become members of the Church unawares. It may seem unusual to begin an experiential discussion of the Church with the rite of initiation that most Orthodox faithful do not remember experiencing. And yet, there is not a profound difference between infant and adult baptisms in this regard, since entry into the Church remains—with the exception of adult catechesis—an unexplainable phenomenon. Baptism is a *mysterion*, as the Greek word for "sacrament" emphasizes the inexplicable character of the ritual. Similar to infants, adults who are aware of going through the rite of initiation still cannot explain it. All faithful experience their entry into the Church in a way that is even more real than other realities that they can explain rationally. The first members of the Church experienced the same type of individual transformation, when they "were cut to the heart" and received baptism at Pentecost. When Peter preached the risen Jesus as Lord and Messiah, so the people who heard him

> ... were cut to the heart and said to Peter and to the other apostles, "Brothers, what should we do?" Peter said to them, "Repent, and be baptized every one of you in the name of Jesus Christ so that your sins may be forgiven; and you will receive the gift of the Holy Spirit." ... They devoted themselves to the apostles' teaching and fellowship, to the breaking of bread and the prayers. Awe came upon everyone, because many wonders and signs were being done by the apostles. All who believed were together and had all things in common; they would sell their possessions and goods and distribute the proceeds to all, as any had need. Day by day, as they spent much time together in the temple, they broke bread at home and ate their food with glad and generous hearts, praising God and having the goodwill of all the people. And day by day the Lord added to their number those who were being saved. (Acts 2:37–38, 42–47)

Several themes stand out in this quotation, providing an outline to the present chapter. The call to repentance (v. 38) hearkens back to the beginning of John the Baptist and Jesus' ministries and their centeredness on the Kingdom of God, also alluded to in the references to "many wonders and signs," (v. 43) which refer primarily to healings—a significant component of the Kingdom. Forgiveness of sins, the reception of the Spirit (v. 38) and the breaking of the bread (v. 42) point to Baptism, Chrismation, and the Eucharist, or to the rite of Christian initiation. Peter's teaching before anyone is baptized (v. 37) is indicative of a community that, while technically not yet baptized, is related to the Church in a very real sense, which will lead to a detailed discussion of the different types of Baptism and their consequences for how Orthodoxy delineates the limits of the Church. Verses 44–47 reflect the new nature of the ecclesial persons making up the community, especially with its social justice overtones. In addition to these elements stemming from Acts 2, this chapter will address Baptism as consecration into royal (universal or baptismal) priesthood and the permanence of Baptism, even when a person leaves the faith.

BAPTISM AND THE KINGDOM OF GOD

In the New Testament, the Kingdom of God is closely associated with Baptism. John the Baptist began his ministry with the call to "Repent, for the kingdom of heaven has come near" (Mt 3:2), baptizing the people who confessed their sins. In other words, because the Kingdom of God is here, people should repent and be baptized. Then Jesus himself was baptized and, after coming from the desert (a clear reference to the people of God sojourning through the desert before coming into the Promised Land), he preached the same words: "Repent, for the kingdom of heaven has come near" (Mt 4:17), after which he called the first disciples who were to represent the renewed Israel. Beginning with Pentecost (Acts 2:38), the community of disciples began baptizing as a result of their preaching of Jesus as Messiah—a title interrelated with the Kingdom. These brief mentions suffice to say that Baptism, repentance, the renewed Israel, the Church, and the Kingdom of God are closely connected in the Bible.

Since the New Testament first relates baptism to John, it is important to see what this ritual meant at the time. There are several precedents in Second Temple Judaism that might shed some light on this matter. First, John's baptism (from the Greek term, *baptizo* meaning "to immerse") could be similar to the rituals of purification of priests and purification of vessels, which were referred to as dipping into the water,[1] so the meaning of John's baptism could be the purification of a new priestly kingdom. Others have speculated that it could be similar to the Essene rites of purification, but there is a major difference between them; whereas John's baptism was a once in a lifetime occurrence, Essene rites were repeatable.[2]

While the above possibilities have their ecclesiological merit, they do not go to the heart of the matter. The main way to interpret John's action is to regard it as proselyte baptism, or the ritual of conversion into Judaism. There is, of course, a significant difficulty with looking at John's baptism as a conversion ritual, namely that most of the people who were coming to the river Jordan to be baptized were already Jews.[3] John's baptism and call to repentance imply that

---

1. For more on the Old Testament practice of priests going through a rite of water purification before carrying out their duties (Ex 40:12, 30–32), the high priest bathing on the Day of Atonement (Leviticus 16), ritual washings to end uncleanness (Leviticus 11–15), the insistence of the Pharisees to extend these priestly practices to the entire Israel and ritual purifications in the Essene community at Qumran, see Harrington, *The Church*, 43–44.

2. Albrecht Oepke, "Bapto, Baptizo, Baptismos," in *Theological Dictionary of the New Testament*, ed. Gerhard Kittel (Grand Rapids, MI: Eerdmans, 1964/1993), 530–35.

3. Lk 3:14 mentions soldiers who could be Jewish, as for example the Temple guard, in which case the

those who are already ethnically Jews need to re-orient their mind (the meaning of repentance derived from the Greek, *metanoite*) and convert to the renewed Israel, as the Kingdom of God is about to be inaugurated in this messianic age. Thus, as Oepke affirms, "The baptism of John is an initiatory rite for the gathering Messianic community."[4]

Israel's integration into the Kingdom also constitutes the reason for Jesus' baptism. Clearly, in Jesus' case, none of the purification symbolism and forgiveness of sins apply personally. But the communitarian explanation of baptism is in full force here: Jesus is the corporate personality that embodies the entire Israel, a nation that is now being converted into the renewed Israel as Jesus enters the waters of Jordan.

The community of disciples will later continue Jesus' work.[5] In this regard, Sandra Schneiders establishes a parallel between Jesus' baptism as described in the gospel of John and the commissioning of the apostles:

> [John the Baptist testified that he was] sent to bear witness to someone coming after him whose status far surpassed his own.
>
> The next day [John] saw Jesus coming toward him and declared, "Behold, the *Lamb of God* who *takes away the sin of the world!*.... [T]he one who sent me to baptize with water said to me, 'He on whom you see the *Spirit descend and remain* is the one who *baptizes with the Holy Spirit.*' And I myself have seen and have testified that this is the Son of God" (Jn 1:29–34).

John's witness to Jesus at this inaugural moment, seen in light of the commissioning of his disciples in John 20:19–23, shows the continuity between his vocation and theirs: here the Spirit descends and remains on Jesus empowering him for his mission to "take away the sin (singular) of the world." When he has accomplished this great work through his life, death, and resurrection Jesus will "baptize," that is, empower his followers with the Holy Spirit for their mission to "forgive sins (plural)."[6]

---

above argument stands. But these soldiers might have also been Gentiles, especially since John baptizes in the wilderness closer to Gentile territories, in which case John's baptism signifies the inclusion of Gentiles into the new Israel.

4. Oepke, "Bapto," 537.

5. Although several biblical passages refer to Jesus as baptizing with the Spirit, Jesus himself did not baptize: "Now when Jesus learned that the Pharisees had heard, 'Jesus is making and baptizing more disciples than John'—although it was not Jesus himself but his disciples who baptized—he left Judea and started back to Galilee" (Jn 4:1–3).

6. Sandra M. Schneiders, "Whose Sins You Shall Forgive ... The Holy Spirit and the Forgiveness of Sin(s) in the Fourth Gospel," in *It Is the Spirit Who Gives Life: New Directions in Pneumatology*, ed. Radu Bordeianu (Washington, DC: The Catholic University of America Press, 2022), 73.

The purpose of these brief biblical considerations is to relate Baptism to the Kingdom. The experience of later Christians will continue in the same tradition, as they will experience Baptism, Chrismation, and the Eucharist as entry into the Church—icon of the Kingdom.

THE RITE OF CHRISTIAN INITIATION AND ITS ECCLESIOLOGICAL CONNOTATIONS[7]

Orthodox liturgical books include under the heading, "Baptism" three components: Baptism, Chrismation, and the Eucharist, all of which aggregately represent the rite of Christian initiation. This was the means by which adults were received into the Church in the first Christian centuries, and, later on, this practice remained in the Orthodox Church even when infant baptism became the norm. To this day, after the making of the catechumen, the rite begins with the words, "Blessed is the kingdom of the Father and the Son and the Holy Spirit," which are not repeated before Chrismation and the reception of Communion, thus making Baptism a unified rite of entry into the Church. This section will address two main questions: first, is Baptism a sacrament of forgiveness of original sin, or is it entry into the Church? Second, what ecclesiology emerges from the rite of Baptism?

The question whether Baptism is the sacrament through which a person receives forgiveness of original sin would be more or less an irrelevant theoretical speculation—and thus out of place in an experiential ecclesiology as this book intends—had it not been for infant baptisms. Does the Orthodox Church baptize babies to offer them *forgiveness of original sin?*

The practice of infant baptism has existed since the beginning of the Church's history. While it cannot be proven beyond any doubt on biblical grounds, the New Testament offers some important indications that the early Church practiced infant baptism.[8] For example, Acts 16:25–33 presents the liberation of Paul and Silas from jail after an earthquake. When the jailer asked,

> "Sirs, what must I do to be saved?" They answered, "Believe in the Lord Jesus, and you will be saved, you and your household." They spoke the word

---

7. I have explored some of these considerations in Radu Bordeianu, "Baptism as Entry into the Church, The Boundaries of the Church, and Mutual Recognition among Churches," in *Tendances et directions dans les recherches actuelles des théologiens orthodoxes roumains de la diaspora*, ed. Ciprian C. Apintiliesei and Constantin Pogor (Paris: Editions du Cerf, 2022), 101–20.

8. Harrington, *The Church*, 45.

of the Lord to him and to all who were in his house. At the same hour of the night he took them and washed their wounds; then he and his entire family were baptized without delay.

Similarly, Lydia "and her household were baptized" (Acts 16:14–15) and Paul baptized the household of Stephanas (1 Cor 1:16). Noteworthy in all these instances is that baptisms were not limited to adults (which was clearly the norm in those times), but comprised the entire household, which included the family as well as its servants. A household most likely included children and infants, and their baptism is a logical deduction stemming from these passages, which should not be surprising, given both the Jewish and Greco-Roman understandings of the family as one unit, with children following the religious practices of their parents.

In contrast with the implied character of infant baptism in apostolic times and the normative practice of adult baptisms, nowadays the majority of Orthodox baptisms are of infants. And yet, the rite of Baptism is replete with prayers that ask for forgiveness of sins and renunciation of old ways, reminiscent of adult baptisms; also prominent are the exorcisms that address the devil and its evil spirits in very strong language. Experientially speaking, the strong language of these exorcisms contrasts with the innocence of the infant to be baptized. Given the over-emphasis on casting out demons and sin at the expense of explicit references to baptism as entry into the Church, perhaps a revision of the service for infant baptism is long overdue. To be clear, I do not advocate a complete elimination of all references to sin and exorcisms; for example, the paragraphs below will emphasize the need to exorcise the entire cosmos of the demonic powers that have hijacked it. My suggestion is to add more explicit references to Baptism as entry into the Church and to avoid the application of texts that initially referred to the (adult) neophyte's personal sin to innocent infants. Such a multitude of references to sin that were initially intended in reference to adults, when applied to infants, risks further propagating the rather recent Orthodox insistence on Baptism as forgiveness of original sin, based on an unhealthy Western influence.[9]

9. One can recommend the updating of a liturgical service only after a long process of discernment and with trepidation. A later chapter will address Prosper of Aquitaine's principle that the rule of prayer should lay down the rule of faith—*lex orandi lex credendi*. According to this venerable principle, there should be complete agreement between the faith of the Church and its liturgical life. When a disagreement arises, one has to establish whether the faith or the liturgy needs readjustment—a process that is most difficult when, by keeping the same liturgical forms, we risk their misunderstandings in a new theological context. Presently, the references to sin generally refer to the infant to be baptized and thus there is a high risk of equating these mentions of "sin" with "original sin," which was not their initial intent. So, in

It is not necessary here to enter into a long discussion of what constitutes original sin. Manual Orthodox theology[10] up to the twentieth century was influenced by the medieval controversies between the Reformation and post-Tridentine Catholic thought, letting itself be drawn into discussions of whether original sin resulted in the loss of super-abundant grace or in the destruction of the image of God in human beings. Both of these extremes (and everything "Orthodox" in between) were actually very similar in a crucial regard: original sin was considered an actual sin, in the sense of a diminished relationship with God that requires personal forgiveness. In other words, this type of scholastic theology concluded that all human beings are born guilty of original sin, which is an actual sin that necessitates forgiveness, despite not being the result of deliberate behavior. This actual sin is inherited from Adam and Eve and justly imputed on all human beings who are born with a corrupted nature. In this line of thought, all babies who die unbaptized die guilty of original sin without having received forgiveness. The practical consequence of such beliefs varied greatly, from the belief that babies who die unbaptized go to hell, to the Catholic tradition of limbo as the place reserved to unbaptized babies that is in between heaven (where nothing unclean enters) and hell (where those who sin intentionally suffer), to the current Catholic understanding that unbaptized babies go to heaven.[11] We shall return to this theme shortly, but in the meantime, it is important to point to the inconsistency of affirming that nothing unclean enters heaven, original sin is an actual sin, and that unbaptized babies go to heaven, as contemporary Catholics believe.

---

order to stay true to the original intent, the service should be revised in a way that avoids this confusion and adds more explicit references to Baptism as entry into the Church. Throughout this book, there will be numerous cases where the reverse is true, namely the liturgical text in its ancient form is a corrective to our contemporary theology, hence the need for discernment and trepidation before recommending the revision of a liturgical text.

10. The fall of Constantinople in 1453 marked the beginning of a period of crisis for Orthodox theology, known as "the Western captivity" of Orthodox theology, during which the East uncritically adopted Western arguments, generating a neo-scholastic theology or "manual theology." Its overly rationalistic approach is highly speculative, to the detriment of apophatic theology, spirituality, and the Liturgy. Its ecclesiology in particular is juridical, organizational, and hierarchical, as opposed to being sacramental and communal. For more, see Radu Bordeianu, *Dumitru Staniloae: An Ecumenical Ecclesiology* (New York, London: T&T Clark/Continuum, 2011),13–18.

11. A 2007 statement of the International Theological Commission grapples with the universality of sin, Pelagius' position that infants could be saved without Baptism, Augustine's response that infants who die unbaptized are consigned to hell, the development of the teaching about limbo (which never became a dogmatic definition of the Magisterium), and the hope that God will save unbaptized infants. International Theological Commission, *The Hope of Salvation for Infants Who Die Without Being Baptized* (2007). http://www.vatican.va/roman_curia/congregations/cfaith/cti_documents/rc_con_cfaith_doc_20070419_un-baptised-infants_en.html.

While manual Orthodox theology thought about original sin along the same lines, contemporary Orthodox theologians are reluctant to speak about original sin, and when they do, they regard it not as an actual sin that is punishable, but rather as an inclination to sin, or a predisposition. As Kallistos Ware explains, we are born into a world in which it is easier to do evil than to do good, and all human beings, interconnected as we are, participate in this sin.[12] But having an inclination in our hearts to sin does not mean that we are going to act on it. And since this is a predisposition and not an actual sin, therefore, we are not born guilty, and later in life we can learn to resist this sinful inclination.

To consider original sin not an actual punishable sin, but an inclination, challenges the understanding of baptism as forgiveness of the original sin. It is impossible to confirm with certitude that a baptized child has less of a tendency to sin than an unbaptized one, or that the baptized experience a world in which it is easier to do good than to do evil. On the contrary, as the ascetical tradition consistently warns, the closer we are to God, the more we fight against the temptations that come upon us with even greater strength. That is why earlier Church Fathers dealing with baptism, such as Tertullian and Cyril of Jerusalem, did not address an original sin of which they did not even know, but Baptism as entry into the Church, renunciation of old sinful ways in the case of adult catechumens, and a life of virtue after Baptism, as we shall see shortly.

Today's practice of *infant baptism should not be regarded as forgiveness of original sin, but as entry into the Church—a return to the lost communion with God.* John the Baptist's call to repentance did not refer to original sin; Judaism in fact does not have anything similar to the Catholic belief in original sin. Rather, Judaism acknowledges that we are born outside of the Garden of Eden and that sin stands between God and us. One should not project the doctrine of original sin back into biblical texts such as, "I was born guilty, a sinner when my mother conceived me" (Ps 51:5), but should look at John's call to repentance and baptism within the context of the Judaism of its day, which has been faithfully transmitted in the Orthodox Church: we are born outside of the Garden of Eden, not in communion with God, and we need to re-enter the Garden, as God's people, in communion with him. As we shall see momentarily, the liturgical celebration of Baptism illustrates this perspective. That is not to say that there is an abundance of explicit references to Baptism as entry into the Church. In fact, the only audible prayer that contains an explicit reference to Baptism as entry into

---

12. Kallistos Ware, *The Orthodox Way*, rev. ed. (Crestwood, NY: St. Vladimir's Seminary Press, 1995), 62.

the Church is intercalated between the third exorcism and the renunciations and reads:

> Make him (her) a reason-endowed sheep of the holy Flock of Your Christ, an honorable member of Your Church, a hallowed vessel, a child of Light, and heir of Your Kingdom. So that, having ordered his (her) life according to Your commandments, and having guarded the Seal and kept it unbroken, and having preserved his (her) garment undefiled, he (she) may attain unto the blessedness of the Saints of Your Kingdom.

Additionally, a prayer that the priest recites inaudibly (because it is about asking God's help for himself) contains the second explicit reference to Baptism as entry into the Church, but this prayer is not heard by the faithful: "Form the image of Your Christ in him (her) who is about to be born again through my humility. Build him (her) on the foundation of Your Apostles and Prophets. Cast him (her) not down, but plant him (her) as a plant of truth in Your Holy, Catholic, and Apostolic Church." Hence, Schmemann contrasts the definitions of Baptism found in manual theology and in the liturgical rite:

> In these manuals Baptism is defined almost exclusively as being the "removal" of original sin and as the conferring of grace, both acts being "necessary," in a juridical sense of this word, for salvation. But Baptism [is] the sacrament of regeneration, as re-creation, as the personal Pascha and the personal Pentecost of man, as the integration into the *laos*, the people of God, as the "passage" from an old into a new life and finally as epiphany of the Kingdom of God.[13]

Thus far, an experiential approach to ecclesiology grappled with the reality that infant baptism is no longer the exception, but the norm, which challenges the understanding of baptism primarily as forgiveness of sin. Instead, baptism is first and foremost entry into the Church. Two explicit references (of which one is inaudible) do not suffice to make this claim. So, *without attempting a comprehensive liturgical-historical analysis*, the following paragraphs will outline *the ecclesiology that emerges from the liturgical celebration of Baptism*.

Given that Christian Baptism is a reimagination of the *Jewish proselyte (or conversion) baptism*, it is not surprising that both share several elements in common. Both require a time for catechesis spanning various amounts of time, followed by the ritual proper, which involves questioning the candidate,

13. Alexander Schmemann, *Of Water and the Spirit: A Liturgical Study of Baptism* (Crestwood, NY: St. Vladimir's Seminary Press, 1974), 118.

the guarantee of the godparents,[14] a profession of faith, and immersion into water.[15]

The period of instruction before Baptism, or the catechumenate, is particularly relevant for adult baptisms or, as we shall see later, for conversions into Orthodoxy. In the early Church, it spanned over at least one year, time in which the catechumen learned foundational Christian teachings from the catechist who was not necessarily a clergy person. The teachings disclosed to the catechumens did not include all aspects of the faith, some of which (particularly in regard to the Eucharist) being reserved for those already initiated through Baptism. Adding some interesting details to this description of the catechumenate, including the practice of communal fasting, Justin Martyr writes:

> Those who are convinced and believe what we say and teach is the truth, and pledge themselves to be able to live accordingly, are taught in prayer and fasting to ask God to forgive their past sins, while we pray and fast with them. Then we lead them to a place where there is water, and they are regenerated in the same manner in which we ourselves were regenerated.[16]

This practice is similar to the Jewish tradition in which the catechumen is instructed in some of the major commandments and some of the minor ones, with the understanding that most of the learning will happen after conversion, throughout one's life. Pastoral experience shows that throughout a person's life, the major teachings of the faith are not questioned; rarely—if ever—does a priest have to correct a parishioner who has embraced a heresy. It is usually the less central aspects of the faith that need to be addressed prior to conversion. It is not surprising that both Baptism and conversion through Chrismation contain only a basic profession of the faith, namely the Nicene-Constantinopolitan Creed. True, the Creed includes in a concise form the entire major elements of our faith, and the need for brief confessions existed for a long time. Rabbi Hillel—Jesus's contemporary—is said to have been asked by a would-be convert to explain the entire Law while standing on one foot; Hillel's answer was, "What is hateful to you, do not do to your fellow. That is the whole Torah. The rest is

---

14. For the role of godparents as guarantors of the neophyte's faith, see Tertullian, *On Baptism*, #18, 38–39. Nowadays, the role of godparents is to profess the faith on behalf of the infant being baptized, to guarantee the Christian upbringing of the child, and, in the tragic case of the death of the parents, to be prepared to assume the parenting duties for their godchild.

15. See *Babylonian Talmud* tractate "Yevamot" 47a-b.

16. Justin Martyr, "First Apology," in *Saint Justin Martyr: The First Apology, the Second Apology, Dialogue with Trypho, Exhortation to the Greeks, Discourse to the Greeks, the Monarchy or the Rule of God*, Fathers of the Church (Washington, DC: The Catholic University of America Press, 1965), #61, 99.

commentary."[17] Jesus, too, when asked to summarize the Law, did so either by mentioning only some of the commandments (e.g. Mt 19:18–19) or by summarizing the entire Law and the prophets thusly: "'You shall love the Lord your God with all your heart, and with all your soul, and with all your mind.' This is the greatest and first commandment. And a second is like it: 'You shall love your neighbor as yourself.' On these two commandments hang all the law and the prophets" (Mt 22:37–40; see also Dt 6:5). Such concentrated summaries of the faith are an invitation to continuous education in the Church. They represent an entry way into the mysteries of the faith that are inexhaustible, no matter how much one studies throughout their lives. Such wealth of knowledge and of wisdom should be the focus of sermons, Bible studies, catecheses, which are now open to all who are already baptized and those who are not, since the Church does not face the same danger of being misunderstood by its persecutors as it did in the first Christian centuries. In those early centuries, some aspects of the faith that could have been misunderstood had to be protected, so catechumens and visitors were dismissed before the Creed, which is still introduced in the Liturgy with the words, "the doors, the doors"—reminiscent of closing the doors to protect the mystery. It is ecclesiologically relevant, however, that in the early Church catechumens were allowed to attend the Divine Liturgy of the word; it means that not-yet-baptized catechumens were considered, in a certain partial sense, members of the Church.

Technically speaking, the catechumenate also pertains to infant baptisms, since the first part of the Baptism service is entitled "The Making of a Catechumen." It includes three exorcisms that are perhaps too adversarial in tone, given that the one to be baptized is an innocent infant, and maybe some liturgical differentiation between the baptism of adults and of infants is necessary in this regard. These exorcisms are followed by the questioning of the candidate (through godparents) in the form of renunciation of evil and the expressed desire to be united with Christ.

To this professed desire to be united with Christ, the liturgical celebration responds with entry into the Church in the form of a *procession*. When baptisms were performed outside of the church building proper, that meant entry into the building. When baptisms happen within the building (as is mostly the case today), that procession moves from the back of the church to inside the sanctuary, near the baptismal font. Either way, this procession symbolizes that

---

17. Babylonian Talmudic Tractate *Shabbat* 31a, quoted in Michael Fagenblat, "The Concept of Neighbor in Jewish and Christian Ethics," in *The Jewish Annotated New Testament*, ed. Amy-Jill Levine and Marc Zvi Brettler (New York: Oxford University Press, 2011), 543.

union with Christ happens in Baptism understood as entry into the Church. As the epigraph of this chapter reminds us, "we were all baptized into one body" (1 Cor 12:13). If, as stated above, we are born outside of the Garden of Eden, as catechumens we renounce our life of sin and become ready to return to Eden. Outside of the Garden we are separated from God; inside we are in communion with God by being members of the renewed Israel—the Church.

Schmemann aptly emphasized this communitarian aspect of Baptism, in contrast with today's understandings of Baptism that stem from its association with the forgiveness of original sin: either it is a private affair relevant only to the one being baptized and family, or it is a sacrament that does not result in consecration, which happens only through the sacrament of Ordination. Therefore, the focus of this overly scholastic approach of manual theology became the validity of Baptism, as opposed to its ecclesiological ramifications. In the same vein, Lent became a time of repentance and chest-beating, as opposed to the ecclesiological act of preparation for the consecration taking place at Easter. In other words, the entire Church community is fasting in preparation for the Paschal consecration into baptismal priesthood—an act done by the entire community, with ecclesiological significance, and not simply a private affair as it is seen today.[18]

This ecclesiological approach to Baptism is much more relevant than regarding the sacrament as forgiveness of original sin, as manual theology contends. If forgiveness of original sin is something that happens once and then has few repercussions, entrance into the Church as consecrated implies a ministry that will follow; the life of each and every baptized Christian is a holy life, a priestly ministry for the others, a renewal of life after the model of the new Adam—the crucified Messiah. That is why this procession symbolizing entry into the Church and consecration into the priestly new Israel is only the beginning. Another procession will take place at the end of the service, namely from the baptismal font to the altar, when the newly baptized receives Communion. That is when the return to Eden is complete, when we receive the fruit of the Tree of Life—the Body and Blood of the crucified Christ.

Returning to the order of the liturgical act of Baptism, the service continues with *the exorcising prayers over water and its blessing.* Orthodox faithful pray such lengthy exorcisms both at the blessing of the waters at Epiphany and—with almost identical prayers—at baptisms, but the idea of waters needing to be exorcised is rather foreign to the modern mind. Of course, as with many

18. Schmemann, *Of Water and the Spirit*, 118.

things in Orthodoxy, there is a historical explanation that is rich in ecclesiological meaning and could make this experience more meaningful.

Most icons of the Baptism of the Lord depict evil creatures living in the
water, later subdued by Jesus' entry into the river Jordan. Such depictions are
reminiscent of ancient cosmological myths that regarded the waters as inhabited by dragons that hold captive the souls of the dead.[19] But it would be a cynical mistake to think that Orthodox services are simply syncretistic rituals that
carry, under Christian guise, the pagan religions so embedded in the minds of
those newly converted to Christianity. Despite their similarities with Egyptian
cults and Greco-Roman religions,[20] these beliefs were mainly based on biblical
accounts and were far superior in the minds of early Christians such as Tertullian and Cyril of Jerusalem.[21]

As Christopher Lockwood shows, from the opening verses of the Bible
to Jesus' Baptism, water is associated with the dwelling place of evil forces,
the destruction of sin, and with sanctification. Thus, water was created good,
and initially the Spirit of God "was hovering over the waters" (Gen 1:2). But
soon after the Fall, the same waters had to drown the sin of humankind, all
but Noah and his family. It is not surprising that Ps 74:13–14 refers to dragons that are lurking in the waters. This, however, is only the first part of the
story. The same Spirit of God that hovered over the waters of creation is again
symbolized by the dove bearing an olive branch which signals to Noah that
God has again recreated the world by water (Gen 8:8–12). And just like Noah
emerged victorious from his battle with the sin that was drowned in the waters
and became the father of a renewed humanity, so did Moses conquer sin when
the armies of the Egyptians were drowned in the Red Sea, as Israel sojourned
towards the Promised Land where they were renewed as a nation. Even more
so, Jesus the Messiah emerged victorious from his battle with the evil forces
dwelling in the waters of the river Jordan[22] and again renewed Israel and restored the entire humankind as Noah and Moses did. That is why the Orthodox liturgical tradition is so adamant in its affirmation that Jesus' immersion

19. Christopher Lockwood, "Hagismos: Water Symbolism in Orthodox Christianity," St. Vladimir's
Theological Quarterly 61, no. 1 (2017): 21.

20. Oepke, "Bapto," 532–35.

21. Tertullian, Homily on Baptism, trans. Ernest Evans (London: SPCK, 1964), #5,13–14. Cyril compares the purification of waters of evil spirits with the liberation of Israel from Egypt by drowning pharaoh's
armies into the Red Sea. See Saint Cyril of Jerusalem, "Mystagogical Lectures," in The Works of Saint Cyril
of Jerusalem Volume 2, Fathers of the Church (Washington DC: The Catholic University of America Press,
2000), I:3, 154.

22. Lockwood, "Hagismos," 21.

into the river Jordan sanctified all waters and all creation, and we partake of that sanctification by blessing the waters of Epiphany and of the baptismal font with the following prayer: "You hallowed the streams of the Jordan, sending down from the Heavens your Holy Spirit, and [you] crushed the heads of the dragons that lurked therein."[23]

So significant is this tradition that the liturgical prayers also affirm that, recognizing its Master, the river Jordan turned back in fear. Naturally, this is a portrayal of Jesus as the new Moses, who delivers his people through parting the waters (then at the Red Sea, now at Jordan) to take them to the Promised Land. But what is often overlooked is that Moses did not in fact enter the Promised Land; instead, Joshua, his successor, did. When Joshua led the people of Israel to the river Jordan, the waters of the river turned back,[24] and the people crossed into the Promised Land as on dry land. Joshua then elected twelve representatives from each tribe of Israel to commemorate the crossing of the Jordan by picking up stones from the river (Joshua 3:15–4:5) and finally, in victory over their adversaries, Israel settled into their land. Now, the new Joshua (for this is a better English translation for Christ's name, rather than Jesus) enters the river Jordan, which turns back, then chooses the Twelve who represent the renewed Israel, and brings them into the Kingdom of God victorious over their adversaries. His disciples will continue this same tradition of baptizing so that a renewed nation—and, indeed, humankind—emerges victorious. As Lockwood continues, "the creative aspect of baptism is subtly expressed through the supernatural combat and victory of God over the demonic demigods dwelling within the waters, and the divine triumph over them effectively ushers in a new creation wrought by the power of the Holy Spirit in the likeness of a dove."[25] Those who are baptized into the Church, therefore, partake of that new humanity in Christ, and the entire world is sanctified in the victory of Christ.

The sanctification of the world through the waters of baptism and at Epiphany point to another ecclesiological significance of Baptism: in it we are consecrated into priesthood or, more specifically, natural priesthood that is directed towards creation. Because of our baptismal consecration, we are called to exorcise creation of the evil that exists in the world, offer it to God, invoke the Holy Spirit upon creation, and thus sanctify it. Such a rich view stands in stark contrast with the manual theology that regards Baptism primarily as forgiveness

23. Quoted in Lockwood, "Hagismos," 20.
24. The tradition of Jordan turning back is later mentioned in Ps. 114:3–5.
25. Lockwood, "Hagismos," 21.

of sin and consecration as something that happens at Ordination. As Schmemann points out, the baptismal references to exorcisms and the power of the devil have a cosmic relevance because the entire world has been hijacked by evil forces that need to be exorcized; in our exercise of priestly cosmic priesthood, or natural priesthood, we need to offer creation back to God.[26] This is the cosmic relevance to repentance and forgiveness. Again, because our modern world does not share in the presuppositions of our ancestors about water, the prayers might seem outdated, but historical explanations and the call to eco-activism as briefly outlined above should bring history back to life and hopefully make the experience of Baptism richer.

Equally outdated might seem the next major point in the ritual, namely *the anointing with the oil of gladness.* The person about to be baptized is anointed with oil over their entire body. This oil—not to be confused with Chrismation—is reminiscent of ancient sporting events when wrestlers anointed themselves so that their adversaries would not be able to take hold of them and thus be defeated. The same custom applied to soldiers. Corresponding to this athletic and military imagery, the person to be baptized is anointed so that they may complete "the race" or to be a soldier in the army of Christ, respectively.[27] Schmemann goes as far as to say that the soldiers of Christ form into a militia.[28] This pre-baptismal anointing is subversive; it shows that we are going to fight.

Joining this militia, of course, comes with its training regimen and ethical norms, but these are not preconditions to Baptism. Being baptized is primarily about belonging to the Church and only secondarily about ethical requirements. Naturally, Christians are going to have to change—a soldier will train and act differently—so Baptism has ethical implications. But just as with the discussion in the previous chapter about the Kingdom not having ethical prerequisites, so here the main concern is to establish that the neophyte belongs to a new kingdom, with a new King, serving in the new militia of the anointed ones.

The next major liturgical step is *immersion in the baptismal font.* This act represents first of all sharing in the Baptism of the Lord in the river Jordan, and

26. Schmemann, *Of Water and the Spirit*, 41–43.
27. "I have fought the good fight, I have finished the race, I have kept the faith" (2 Tm 4:7). Moreover, the first exorcism refers to the one to be baptized as "newly-enlisted soldier of Christ."
28. Alexander Schmemann, *For the Life of the World: Sacraments and Orthodoxy*, 2nd ed. (Crestwood, NY: St. Vladimir's Seminary Press, 1973), 71. Schmemann, *Of Water and the Spirit*, 125–26. Schmemann also writes about the medicinal role of oil, its use as a source of light and a symbol of peace, signifying the healing power of Baptism, our reconciliation with God and the world, and the call of the neophyte to become "light to the world" (cf. Mt 5:14–16). Schmemann, *Of Water and the Spirit*, 51–53.

second, partaking of Jesus' death and resurrection. The above comments about the blessings of the waters at Baptism and Epiphany should suffice to show that the neophyte shares in the Baptism of the Lord when being immersed in the baptismal font. To give just one more biblical example, Paul writes, "as many of you as were baptized into Christ, have clothed yourselves with Christ" (Gal 3:27). This baptismal hymn is embedded in Orthodox consciousness, as these words are sung both in the procession around the baptismal font and in the Divine Liturgy on special feast days, such as Epiphany, Pascha, and Pentecost. Though these festal Liturgies no longer include baptisms, the *typikon* retained the singing of the baptismal hymn in remembrance of the times when early Christians were baptized. Unfortunately, the ecclesiological significance of this liturgical variation is less obvious today, since most baptisms are a private matter, taking place outside of the Liturgy, and the neophyte receives communion from the reserved sacrament. In the early Church, as well as in the rare instances today when Baptisms take place within the Liturgy, the singing of the Galatians 3:27 baptismal hymn has obvious ecclesiological significance: by sharing in the Baptism of the Lord, the newly baptized has become one with Christ, a member of the Body of Christ, and thus has entered the Church—a public act in which the entire congregation participates, not just the immediate family and friends.

Regarding the second meaning of the immersion, namely partaking of the death and resurrection of the Lord, one of the petitions of Baptism reads: "That he (she) may grow in, and become a partaker of the Death and Resurrection of Christ our God; let us pray to the Lord." Water is both a symbol of death (as in the flood or the drowning of the Egyptian armies), and of life (as when the Spirit who gives life hovered over the waters of creation).[29] Lockwood correlates the waters of baptism with the Old Testament ritual of circumcision[30] based on Colossians 2:11–12: "In [Christ] also you were circumcised with a circumcision made without hands, by putting off the body of flesh in the circumcision of Christ; and you were buried with him in baptism, in which you were also raised with him through faith in the working of God, who raised him from the dead." These insights are highly significant for our theme because they show that Baptism is entry into the renewed Israel, and that the

29. For St. Gregory of Nyssa, the pursuant Egyptians represent temptation and the sinful passions, which one is to drown in the Red Sea and it is lamentable when "many of those who receive the mystical baptism,... even after crossing the water they bring along the Egyptian army, which still lives with them in their doings." Saint Gregory of Nyssa, *The Life of Moses*, trans. Abraham J. Malherbe and Everett Ferguson, The Classics of Western Spirituality, (New York: Paulist Press, 1978), 83–84.
30. Lockwood, "Hagismos," 20–21.

sign of this entry is no longer physical circumcision but baptism, which in turn is connected with re-creation. In physical circumcision, a part of the flesh dies in order to symbolize the entry of that person into Israel and the belonging of that entire person to God. Immersed entirely under water, the "circumcision made without hands" at baptism symbolizes the death of the old self that walked according to the flesh in order to resurface as an entirely new person who has died to the flesh, walks according to the Spirit, lives wholly for God, and is part of the renewed Israel.

The Orthodox Church today uses exclusively the Matthean baptismal formula; after his resurrection, Jesus told the eleven disciples to "make disciples of all nations, baptizing them in the name of the Father and of the Son and of the Holy Spirit" (Mt 28:19). The early Church, however, used multiple formulas for baptisms that were considered equally valid. Before the "trinitarian" baptismal formula became the norm beyond Matthew's community, Baptisms were initially done "in Christ," "in the name of Christ," and "in the name of Jesus,"[31] always in conjunction with the reception of the Holy Spirit. As Sarah Coakley explains,

> What, first, lay behind the initial construction of the triadic baptismal formula (Matthew 28.19)?... The obvious answer is the example of Jesus's own baptism (Mark 1.9–11 and parallels), with its conjunction of the Father's voice, the Son's baptismal calling, and the Spirit's descent. But this is perhaps not the whole story. It is worth also recalling the testimony of Acts, which refers in its early chapters to a baptism simply "in the name of Jesus Christ," but promises as a specific mark of that baptism the 'gift of the Holy Spirit' (Acts 2.38).... Rivalry with John's baptism (mentioned already in Acts 1.5) may have caused the early community to draw attention to the *special* gifts of the "holy Spirit" (tongues and prophecy) which marked out baptism in Jesus's name as superior (Acts 19.1–6).... it was dramatic charismatic gifts—involving the ecstatic capacity—which were the hallmark of some of the earliest Christian baptisms. Acts associates the Spirit with manifest "signs and wonders" (Acts 2.43), whereas Paul's association of the Spirit with baptism is, as we have seen, more concerned with the incorporation into the effects of Christ's death and resurrection (Rom 6.3–11, 8.9–11).[32]

Thus, Baptism—whether in the name of the Father and the Son and the Holy Spirit, or in the name of Jesus, or Lord Jesus, or Christ—is always asso-

---

31. Oepke, "Bapto," 539.
32. Sarah Coakley, *God, Sexuality, and the Self: An Essay 'On the Trinity'* (Cambridge: Cambridge University Press, 2013), 118–19.

ciated with receiving the Holy Spirit. To give just one example from the Acts of the Apostles:

> While Apollos was in Corinth, Paul passed through the interior regions and came to Ephesus, where he found some disciples. 2 He said to them, "Did you receive the Holy Spirit when you became believers?" They replied, "No, we have not even heard that there is a Holy Spirit." 3 Then he said, "Into what then were you baptized?" They answered, "Into John's baptism." 4 Paul said, "John baptized with the baptism of repentance, telling the people to believe in the one who was to come after him, that is, in Jesus." 5 On hearing this, they were baptized in the name of the Lord Jesus. 6 When Paul had laid his hands on them, the Holy Spirit came upon them, and they spoke in tongues and prophesied— 7 altogether there were about twelve of them (Acts 19:1–7).

Noteworthy here are several elements already explained above: baptism "in the name of the Lord Jesus" and not in the name of the Trinity (v. 5), the laying on of hands (v. 6), and the number twelve (v.7), which is an allusion to Israel. This instance is by no means singular (e.g. Acts 8:14–16, 10:44–48), but it suffices to prove that, from the beginning of the Church, Baptism was accompanied by the reception of the Holy Spirit. In the Orthodox Church, that association persisted continuously until today, since all persons who are being baptized, including infants, also *receive the Holy Spirit in Chrismation* (or what the West calls Confirmation). Again, liturgically speaking, Chrismation is not a separate service, but it is intercalated seamlessly between the trifold immersion in the water, tonsure, vesting into a garment of light, the singing of the baptismal hymn "As many of you as were baptized into Christ, have clothed yourselves with Christ" (Gal 3:27), the biblical readings referring to Baptism, and the reception of the Eucharist.

In the first Christian centuries, each community was headed by what we call today a bishop. At that time, Christians were initiated into the Church at special feast days that gathered the entire diocese, and the celebrant of Chrismation was the bishop, through the imposition of hands and anointing with oil. With the emergence of the parish and the diminishing number of bishops as leaders of the local assemblies, the priest became the regular celebrant of the rite of Chrismation and thus the one who anoints with Holy Chrism, without however being allowed to bless the oil of the Chrism. The Chrism today is blessed on Holy Thursday by the bishops of each autocephalous Church and then distributed throughout their jurisdiction.[33] Thus, in a rather indirect

---

33. For more on the evolution of the rite, see Nicholas E. Denysenko, *Chrismation: A Primer for Catholics* (Collegeville, MN: Liturgical Press, 2014), 1–39.

sense, the bishop remains the celebrant of Chrismation. Experientially speaking, however, Chrismation is mostly separated from the ministry of the bishop since the priest administers it on a regular basis and the majority of the faithful do not participate in the blessing of the Chrism on Holy Thursday. Moreover, it is not the local bishop who blesses the Chrism, but bishops from throughout the autocephalous church; this reality is both positive, in the sense that Chrismation transcends the limits of the local church and marks more acutely one's entry into the universal Church, and negative, since it consolidates sacramentally the superiority of the regional church over the local diocese, since Chrismation cannot be consecrated locally. This impression of the priority of the regional church over the local diocese is then corrected experientially, since Baptism only happens in a local community, albeit in the parish and not the diocese.

If the emergence of the parish headed by a priest forced the Orthodox East to separate the bishop from the administration of Chrismation, the same phenomenon of the emergence of the parish forced the Catholic West to separate Baptism from Chrismation (Confirmation) and the Eucharist. In the Catholic Church, infants are first baptized, then later receive the first Eucharist, and even later Confirmation. This order is not supported by the Tradition (which placed Confirmation before the Eucharist)[34] and diminishes the importance of the reception of the Holy Spirit. As established above, the Bible associates entry into the Church with both immersion into water and reception of the Holy Spirit, sometimes in the opposite order. It would follow that in order to be a *full* member of the Church, a person would have to receive both Baptism and Confirmation. Since only members of the Church were allowed to receive Communion, the practice of allowing first the Eucharist and then Confirmation is out of balance. Again, the Catholic Church did not choose this course of action freely; it was forced by the emergence of the parish headed by a priest, the need to perform Baptisms in a timely fashion, and the desire to not separate the faithful from the Eucharist unnecessarily long. But the bishop remained unable to visit all his parishes at short intervals of time, so, in its desire to preserve the early practice of the bishop administering the sacrament of Confirmation, the reception of the Holy Spirit is delayed until an episcopal

---

34. George Tavard writes: "The widespread delay of confirmation until after first communion, which is often favored for pastoral or educational reasons, is opposed to the tradition, and it is abnormal from the point of view of the proper ordering of spiritual life." George H. Tavard, "The Ecclesial Dimension of Spirituality," in *The Gift of the Church: A Textbook on Ecclesiology in Honor of Patrick Granfield, O.S.B.*, ed. Peter C. Phan (Collegeville, MN: Liturgical Press, 2000), 225.

visit is feasible. There are more and more voices among Catholic theologians who call for a revision of this practice to be closer aligned to the tradition of the early Church of having a unified rite of initiation, as it is already the practice of adult baptisms, when a person receives the full rite of initiation at the Easter vigil and receives the full rite of initiation celebrated by the priest.

The departure of both the Orthodox and Catholic churches from the practice of the early Church raises two more ecclesiological considerations. First, if Baptism takes place in infancy, marking one's entry into the Church, is it necessary to have a rite of passage later in life so that each Christian would also express their own will to be a member of the Church, based on a solid understanding of what that entails? While the answer is clearly yes, the nature and appropriate time for such a rite of passage is less clear. In the Catholic Church, first Communion and Confirmation, with the education that precedes them, function as rites of passage. The Orthodox Church does not have a similar rite, although more and more parishes have designated Sundays to renew our baptismal vows and confess our faith. Both churches, however, have to recognize that the time when a baptized Christian chooses freely to be a member of the Church varies from person to person and is even akin to a conversion moment—certainly impossible to associate with a specific ritual. Pastorally speaking, most young people do not consciously choose their faith when they live with their parents or when they first leave to live on their own. In fact, this rarely occurs even upon marriage. Confirmation truly takes place when a couple has their first child and they decide to raise their child in a specific Church. In North America, being most probably a mixed couple, one of the spouses is likely to convert to the faith of the other spouse and, statistically, most conversions take place before the first child is ten years old,[35] showing that the spouses fully embrace their faith when they choose to pass it down to their child. That moment, of course, will not be the last time that a person chooses their faith—it is a life-long struggle. Thus, while the Orthodox Church should emphasize more the need to accept freely one's membership into the Church, the Catholic Church does not gain much from postponing the first Communion and Confirmation until the age of reason when a person can make a free and informed choice. Moreover, one should not presume that there is an age when we can fully understand the mystery of Baptism, so it is better to baptize infants with the full rite of initiation, recognizing that choice and

---

35. Dean R. Hoge, "Sociological Research on Interfaith Marriage in America," in *InterMarriage: Orthodox Perspectives*, ed. Anton C. Vrame (Brookline, MA: Holy Cross Orthodox Press, 1997), 91.

understanding—with major qualification as shown above—come later in life.

Second, while the priest certainly consecrates objects and blesses people's undertakings, in Orthodox consciousness it is the bishop who consecrates into priesthood. The presence of the bishop at every Chrismation, with his imposition of the hands upon the head of every person being baptized, would certainly create the image of Baptism as consecration into the universal priesthood of the Church. But since the presence of the bishop at every Baptism is practically impossible, perhaps the imposition of the hands by the priest could be more emphasized. As it stands, the rite of baptism stipulates that the priest put his hand upon the head of the person who is approaching to be made a catechumen right at the beginning of the service. The second time that the priest puts his right hand upon the head of the newly baptized and Chrismated person is at the prayer of tonsure, which has pneumatological overtones by referencing the anointing of King David through Prophet Samuel and invokes the visitation of the Holy Spirit upon the neophyte. The image of Baptism as consecration into universal priesthood would be strengthened if the priest could lay both hands upon the head of the person to be baptized, and especially if this same gesture could take place at Chrismation, when a person receives the Holy Spirit—a moment associated with the imposition of the hands in the biblical texts mentioned above.

These brief and certainly incomplete references to the rite of Christian initiation present Baptism as much more than an abstract forgiveness of the original sin. Baptism is communitarian, it marks one's entry into the Church as the renewed Israel partaking in the death and resurrection of Christ, consecration into the universal priesthood, membership in the Body of Christ, and the beginning of a journey into the Kingdom of God. At the same time, regarding the Church as the community of the baptized according to these parameters raises questions about the different types of Baptism and their ecclesiological consequences.

TYPES OF BAPTISM

In the early Church, when adult Baptism was more prevalent, candidates would be catechumens for long intervals of time in order to learn the faith and be tested in their determination to join the Church. But under exceptional circumstances, a person would be considered a member of the Church through two alternatives to baptism by water, namely baptism by blood and baptism of desire, both of which are still relevant today.

Jesus refers to his own martyred death as baptism (Mk 10:38, Lk 12:30), and the ritual of Baptism represents voluntarily dying with Christ (Rom 6:3ff.). From its inception in the New Testament, the history of the early Church is replete with accounts of martyrdom. Sometimes those who died for their faith in Christ were not yet baptized, but were catechumens or even persecutors who, inspired by the witness of the martyrs, instantly decided to embrace the Christian faith and they too were martyred.[36] As Tertullian wrote, the blood of the martyrs became the seed of Christianity.[37] If a martyr was unable to go through the regular journey from catechumenate to Baptism before their death, their witness was considered as *baptism by blood*.[38] Despite their lack of baptism by water, martyrs are not only members of the Church through baptism by blood, they are also venerated as saints and commemorated on feast days; the faithful take their names and consider them saint protectors, are inspired by their lives, and raise churches dedicated to them.

Because the New Testament offers an ideal of Christian life centered around witness and martyrdom, it is not surprising that even in countries that enjoy religious liberty some Christians regard themselves as being persecuted

36. Venerable Bede describes the martyrdom of St. Alban in fourth century Roman Britain. As he was being taken to the place of his execution, St. Alban dried up a river and one of the Roman soldiers converted instantly and refused to execute the saint. Moments later, that Roman solider was martyred together with St. Alban. Then Bede describes the Roman soldier as follows: "though he was not regenerated by baptism, yet he was cleansed by the washing of his own blood, and rendered worthy to enter the kingdom of heaven." Bede, *Ecclesiastical History of the English People*, ed. Bertram Colgrave and R. A. B. Mynors (Oxford: Clarendon Press, 1969), I:7. It is important to note that the Orthodox Church commemorates St. Alban together with the Roman soldier who is thus not only a regular member of the Church, but also a venerated saint.

37. Tertullian writes: "We become more numerous every time we are hewn down by you: the blood of Christians is seed [*semen est sanguis Christianorum*]." Tertullian, "Apology," in *Tertullian, Apologetical Works and Minucius Felix, Octavius*, The Fathers of the Church (Washington, DC: The Catholic University of America Press, 1950), 50:13, 125.

38. Hyppolytus of Rome writes: "If violence is brought against [the catechumen] and he is killed before receiving baptism for the remission of sins, he will be justified, for he has received baptism in his own blood." Hippolytus, *On the Apostolic Tradition*, second ed., ed. Alistair C. Stewart (Crestwood, NY: St. Vladimir's Seminary Press, 2015), par. 19. Similarly, St. Cyril of Jerusalem writes: "If a man does not receive baptism he does not attain salvation, excepting only the martyrs, who, even without the water, receive the kingdom. For the Savior who redeemed the world by the Cross, when His side was pierced, poured forth blood and water, that in time of peace men might be baptized in water, but in time of persecution in their own blood. For the Savior could call martyrdom a baptism, saying: "Can you drink the cup of which I drink or be baptized with the baptism with which I am baptized? [Mk 10:38]" Saint Cyril of Jerusalem, "Lenten Lectures (Catecheses) I–XII," in *The Works of Saint Cyril of Jerusalem Volume 1*, Fathers of the Church (Washington DC: The Catholic University of America Press, 1969), III:10, 114.

for their faith and needing to offer witness to their beliefs.[39] And yet, a proper appreciation of the suffering of early Christians should reserve the concepts of martyrdom and persecution for instances of true martyrdom and genuine persecution, and not disrespect the sacrifice of the millions of martyrs who died for their faith in Christ. Unfortunately, in this true sense of martyrdom, baptism by blood continued to be relevant well past the early history of the Church, and remains so today. Christianity continued to find its seed in the martyrs of the Ottoman Empire, of the communist regime, or of the terrorist groups that commit violence in the name of religion today. Indeed, even in the twenty-first century, there are martyrs who suffer displacement, destruction of churches, confiscation of property, kidnappings, severe punishments under the false accusations of blasphemy, incarceration, and pay the ultimate price for their Christian faith.[40]

Just as in the early Church, the blood of the martyrs is the seed of Christianity, as was evident in post-communist Romania, to give just one example. Shortly after the December 1989 Revolution and the subsequent liberation of religion, a 1992 census revealed that 86.8% of the population identified as Orthodox and only 0.2% as atheists or not part of an organized religion. When the next census took place in 2002, 86.7% were Orthodox and 0.1% atheists or not religious. In both cases, the rest of the population belonged to various religious groups, with Roman Catholics as the next largest category, around 5%.[41] Despite systematic communist persecutions, faith in general, and Orthodoxy in particular, not only survived, but got even stronger and sustained similar levels ten years later, while the percentage of atheists remained miraculously small. Clearly, Tertullian's words resonate throughout Orthodox history: the blood of the martyrs is the seed of Christianity.

Another alternative to baptism by water has been *baptism of desire.* In antiquity, the catechumens who suffered sudden (not martyred) death before having a chance to be baptized, were considered part of the Church by virtue

---

39. In the United States, especially among white evangelical churches, the political subject that is most talked-about from the pulpit is that of religious liberty. Almost half of respondents (49%) reported hearing sermons about religious liberty, and only 1% of those respondents heard messages stating that religious liberty is *not* under attack. Pew Research Center, *Many Americans Hear Politics from the Pulpit* (2016), 2–3, 7. www.pewresearch.org. Without denying individual experiences, this attitude seems inappropriate in a country in which religion has a major influence upon the public sphere, churches sue the government, enjoy tax-exempt status, and clergy have special tax benefits.

40. See for example the April 2020 "Annual Report of the U.S. Commission on International Religious Freedom" https://www.uscirf.gov/sites/default/files/USCIRF%202020%20Annual%20Report_Final_42920.pdf.

41. http://www.infotravelromania.ro/recensamant.html

of their desire to join the Church. The necessity to speak about baptism of desire was inevitable, given that the catechumenate spanned over long periods of time; but this situation was exacerbated by the custom to postpone baptism until one's deathbed. The main reason to postpone baptism so late was the early Church's belief that the last opportunity for forgiveness of sin is baptism. After that, a Christian was supposed to live a life worthy of Christ, and there was no sacrament of confession as we know it today.[42] In the second and third centuries in Northern Africa, Tertullian testified that, except in martyrdom, one cannot receive forgiveness of sins after baptism: "we enter into the bath once only, once only are our sins washed away, because these ought not to be committed a second time."[43] At the end of the fourth century in Antioch, St. John Chrysostom did not know the sacrament of Confession as it exists today, in which a person who has been baptized can confess to a priest and receive forgiveness of sins.[44] In the early Church, one could be forgiven either at Baptism or in martyrdom (the latter also giving birth to the belief that tonsure into monasticism, as a new form of martyrdom, offered forgiveness of sins). Thus, for a brief period of time, some Christians postponed baptism until their deathbed, the most notable example being Emperor Constantine the Great. The practice of baptism on one's deathbed clearly indicates the emphasis on the forgiveness of sins over entry into the Church; Constantine considered himself a "bishop in the externals," preached sermons, convened and participated at the first ecumenical council of Nicaea (325), indicating that he was not regarded as an outsider. Even after he received baptism from a Semi-Arian bishop on his deathbed, Constantine still came to be considered a saint and equal to the Apostles in the Orthodox Church, so clearly baptism became more centered around forgiveness of sins than entry into the Church. The gradual emergence of Confession in its present form is a welcome development that re-emphasizes the communitarian ramifications of Baptism and of the Church as the icon of the Kingdom of God where healing from sin takes place.

Similar to baptism by blood, baptism of desire is still relevant today.

42. The Church of the first nine centuries did not know the sacrament of Confession as we know it today. While some provisions for Confession are mentioned in the writings of Hermas in the second century, and afterward various local churches (though not all) accepted Confession for the sins of adultery, apostasy, and murder that were causing public scandal, Confession as a form of devotion did not exist. In fact, most Christians in that period spent their entire lives without ever having Confession. Kenan B. Osborne, *Reconciliation and Justification: The Sacrament and Its Theology* (Eugene, OR: Wipf and Stock, 2001), 82.

43. Tertullian, *On Baptism*, #15, 34–35.

44. Saint John Chrysostom, *On Wealth and Poverty*, trans. Catharine P. Roth (Crestwood, NY: St. Vladimir's Seminary Press, 1984), 89–96.

Acknowledging that Orthodox theology does not approach ecclesiologically the subject of *unborn babies* either through miscarriage or through abortion, I contend that baptism of desire applies to babies who pass away in the womb, and thus before being baptized. In other words, I propose combining the belief that life begins at conception with the ancient tradition of baptism of desire and applying them to the membership in the Church of babies who died unbaptized and whose parents desired to baptize them had their child survived.

Sometimes, friends of good faith try to console parents who grieve after a miscarriage by telling them that they did not lose a child; that "it" was not yet a human being. Well intended though these friends may be, parents who believe that life begins at conception know differently; and this pro-life stance is a difficult cross to bear. It would be much easier to believe that life does not begin at conception. Those parents have lost their child; they did not merely experience a fleeting physiological anomaly. And their numbers are great, since an estimated 20% of pregnancies end in miscarriage.

Grieving parents need a church community for support and consolation that convey the love of the Church for them and for their departed baby. Unfortunately, in some jurisdictions, the designated prayers for miscarriage ascribe blame to the sins of the mother (but not of the father) for the loss of pregnancy that is equated with murder. Moreover, these lives are never commemorated in the public prayer of the Church, at Proskomide, in memorial services, or not even as a general category of children who died before being baptized.[45] For an Orthodox Church that is committedly pro-life in the sense of affirming the sanctity of life in the womb, for a Church that prays for all kinds of general categories of people in its public worship (including many who are not members of the Church, such as the military or the civil authorities), this is a stark omission.[46]

The lack of recognition of the existence and even less so of the ecclesial status of babies who died prematurely does not reflect the experience of the family that grieves and our desire for communion in the Church with all those departed before us. Consequently, in some countries such as Romania, there is the unsanctioned practice of naming miscarried babies "John," for St. John the Baptist, and commemorating them during the Liturgy or memorial services,

45. See more in Carrie Frederick Frost, *Maternal Body: A Theology of Incarnation from the Christian East* (Mahwah, NJ: Paulist Press, 2019), 16–19.
46. The use of the expression "pro-life" in this context transcends the unduly limited understanding of this expression in U.S. political and religious discourse, where it refers almost exclusively to protecting life in the womb. A more encompassing understanding of "pro-life" includes expanding access to affordable health care, passing legislation that reduces gun violence, and abolishing the death penalty.

even though officially this practice is forbidden. Without contradicting the official position of the Church, it is important to recognize that, experientially speaking, the faithful long for communion with their loved ones who died unbaptized. Relevant in this regard is Paul's ironical reference to "people who receive baptism on behalf of the dead" (1 Cor 15:29); while the Apostle made this reference to prove the reality of the resurrection, he also documented the care that people had for their loved ones who died without baptism. The same remains true today when, especially on the Feast of the Baptism of the Lord, some Romanian priests go against the discipline of their church and immerse a candle into the baptismal font, in the hope that this ritual substitutes the baptism of children who have been aborted or miscarried. Such unofficial rituals would not be necessary if we stated boldly that these babies are members of the Church by virtue of baptism of desire.

Again, this is my personal contribution to this ecclesiological problem: had those babies been born, their parents would have desired to baptize them; but since the babies went into the heavenly kingdom prematurely, just as early Church catechumens who died before baptism were considered members of the Church—and even saints!—so nowadays we should apply the same baptism of desire and consider these babies as members of the Church. Obviously, in today's context, desire refers to the intent of the parents to baptize their child, and not to the desire of the unbaptized baby, the latter being an impossibility. Consequently, parents do not need to focus on original sin and fear that their children might be in hell; their children are members of a Church whose communion encompasses the living and the dead.

In light of the above considerations about original sin that was sometimes misunderstood to mean that unbaptized babies go to hell, the Church cannot repent enough for the unnecessary suffering that it has brought upon the parents who, instead of receiving consolation in their grief, were left feeling guilty and doubting the salvation of their children. Not merely as individuals regretting their sins, but after an honest ecclesial repentance, the Church as a community needs to be there for the parents and reassure them that, just as in the early Church, baptism of desire is no less valid, effective, and a source of hope as baptism by blood or water. The Church also needs to console the families who lost their children before they were born and, if Orthodoxy is indeed pro-life in the sense of affirming the sanctity of life in the womb, it must treat these events just as it treats the untimely death of a baptized child, namely with sympathy, hope that life conquers, and trust in the unity of the Church in heaven and on earth, where parents pray for their children and children pray for parents as one Body of Christ. Applying baptism of desire in these situations results in the need for a different prayer at miscarriage, one that encompasses the entire family and not just the mother, a prayer that is not penitential in character, but offers consolation and hope, as some jurisdictions have already done. For the same reason, commemorations in the public worship of the Church should also be encouraged, including Proskomide, petitions, and memorial services.

In this section we have seen how the boundaries of the Church—the community of the baptized—expand considerably through baptisms by blood and of desire as alternative types to baptism with water. Next, we will see how there are also cases in which the boundaries of the Orthodox Church expand, but the boundaries of the *Una Sancta* remain the same, namely when a Christian validly baptized in another Church joins Orthodoxy without repeating Baptism.

CONVERSION INTO ORTHODOXY

Cyprian of Carthage uttered the (in)famous words, *extra ecclesiam nulla salus*— "there is no salvation [outside] the Church."[47] In this section, the question of salvation outside the Church will be divided into two parts: first, what are the best ecclesiological and pastoral practices for receiving converts into Orthodoxy? Second, what is the relationship between the community of the baptized and the community of the saved and its relevance to the limits of the Church.

In traditionally Orthodox countries, converts form a relatively small percentage of the Orthodox parishes. In the United States, those who convert to Orthodoxy from other churches represent a significant number.[48] For example, 51% of the faithful in the Orthodox Church in America (OCA) and 29% of the Greek Archdiocese of America (GOA) faithful are converts; in the OCA, the percentage of clergy who are converts is even higher—59%.[49] In cases where

---

47. "Letter 73 to Jubaian," in Saint Cyprian of Carthage, *Letters (1–81)*, trans. Sister Rose B. Donna, Fathers of the Church, (Washington, DC: The Catholic University of America Press, 1964), #21, 282. Cyprian reacted against the Novatians who rebaptized those who had already been baptized in Cyprian's Church. His words are a strong condemnation of rebaptism and yet, ironically, in some contemporary circles, they represent the basis for rebaptism.

48. Despite a large influx of converts, the growth of American Orthodoxy was slightly outpaced by the growth of the U.S. general population between 1936 and 2010. If the Orthodox population increased by 138%, the general American population saw an 141% increase. Alexei Krindatch, *Fast Questions and Fast Answers about the Geography of Orthodoxy in America* (2018), 24. http://assemblyofbishops.org/news/research.

49. Alexei Krindatch, *Orthodox Church Today* (Berkeley, CA: Patriarch Athenagoras Orthodox Institute, 2008), 13.

a person who desires to join the Orthodox Church but has not been previously baptized with water and in the name of the Father and the Son and the Holy Spirit, entrance into Orthodoxy happens through Baptism. The typical convert to Orthodoxy, however, has already been baptized with water in the name of the Father and the Son and the Holy Spirit in another church. Most of the Orthodox world recognizes the baptisms of other churches and receives their faithful into Orthodoxy most commonly through Confirmation and, in some cases, through Confession.

There are significant differences within Orthodoxy in regard to *the reception of baptized non-Orthodox Christians into the Orthodox Church.*[50] In the Russian Orthodox Church, Catholics, Oriental Orthodox, and Old Believers are received through the sacrament of Confession; in the case of a clergyman, the Orthodox bishop's absolution also brings the ability to serve as a clergy in good standing.[51] The Synodal Theological Commission of the Russian Orthodox Church recently reaffirmed this longstanding practice:

> Vatican II called the Orthodox Church a Sister Church, thus recognizing the blessed nature of the Orthodox Church and the salvific nature of her sacraments. The Orthodox Church, in her turn, always recognized the validity of the sacraments of the Catholic Church.[52] The evidence to that is the fact that the Catholic Christians are accepted into the Orthodox Church by the so-called *Third Order* for joining the Orthodox membership—not through Baptism, as non-Christians or sectarians, nor through Chrismation, like the Protestants, but through repentance, like schismatics. Roman Catholic clergymen are accepted in their existing orders to which they had been ordained by the Roman Catholic Church. It is no coincidence that Old Believers, who are also in schism from the Orthodox Church are accepted back in the same manner as the Roman Catholic Christians. This

50. For the variety of practices in various Orthodox jurisdictions and even within a single jurisdiction, regarding the reception of baptized Catholics in the Orthodox Church by re-baptism, Chrismation (in various ways), confession of faith, or simply by aggregation, see John H. Erickson, "Reception into the Orthodox Church: Contemporary Practice," *The Ecumenical Review* 54, no. 1 (2002): 66–75.

51. Georges Florovsky, "The Boundaries of the Church," in *Ecumenism I: A Doctrinal Approach, Collected Works of Georges Florovsky, Emeritus Professor of Eastern Church History, Harvard University; vol. 13* (Belmont, MA: Nordland, 1989), 40.

52. The affirmation that the Russian Orthodox Church has always recognized the validity of Catholic sacraments is somewhat exaggerated. While this is indeed the norm, as George D. Dragas shows, there is also historical evidence of reception of Latins into the Russian Orthodox Church by rebaptism between the thirteenth and seventeenth centuries, although this practice is in minority. George D. Dragas, "The Manner of Reception of Roman Catholic Converts into the Orthodox Church with Special Reference to the Decisions of the Synods of 1484 (Constantinople), 1755 (Constantinople) and 1667 (Moscow)," *Greek Orthodox Theological Review* 44, no. 1–4 (1999): 250–51.

fact shows that despite serious fundamental differences on a number of doctrinal and spiritual issues between the two Churches, Roman Catholicism in the Orthodox mind and Tradition is viewed as a Christian community in schism with the Orthodox Church which nevertheless has preserved apostolic succession.[53]

In other traditions—such as the Ecumenical Patriarchate—converts already baptized with water in the name of the Father, Son, and Holy Spirit in other churches enter the Orthodox Church through Chrismation. In this practice, Confession precedes Chrismation, but is not considered sufficient, as in the Russian tradition. A generous ecclesiology emerges from these practices related to conversion. First, it is significant that in both practices mentioned above, a person who is not yet Orthodox receives the sacrament of Confession; thus, the boundaries of the Orthodox Church do not align strictly with its canonical limits, since the grace of an Orthodox sacrament such as Confession is bestowed upon a faithful who, technically speaking, is not yet Orthodox. Second, both these practices accept the validity of baptisms outside the canonical boundaries of the Orthodox Church and thus take Paul's words that "there is one Lord, one faith, one baptism ..." (Eph 4:5) to mean that Baptism is unrepeatable. While this practice is almost generalized, there are few modern ecumenical statements in this regard, such as Moscow's statement above, or the North American Orthodox-Catholic Theological Consultation's declaration that

> The formal expression of the recognition of Orthodox baptism has been constant in the teaching of the popes since the beginning of the sixteenth century, and was emphasized again at the Second Vatican Council. The Synods of Constantinople in 1484 and Moscow in 1667 testify to the implicit recognition of Catholic baptism by the Orthodox churches, and do so in a way fully in accord with the earlier teaching and practice of antiquity and the byzantine era.... The Orthodox and Catholic members of our Consultation acknowledge, in both of our traditions, a common teaching and a common faith in one baptism.... We are therefore moved to declare that we also recognize each other's baptism as one and the same. This recognition has obvious ecclesiological consequences.[54]

53. April 18, 1997. https://mospat.ru/archive/en/1997/07/ve110771/. The 1988 Statement on "Ordination" of the Joint Committee of Orthodox and Catholic Bishops in North America affirms the same prohibition of "reordination." John Borelli and John H. Erickson, eds., *The Quest for Unity: Orthodox and Catholics in Dialogue* (Crestwood, NY: St. Vladimir's Seminary Press, 1996), 151.
54. North American Orthodox-Catholic Theological Consultation, "Baptism and 'Sacramental

As this statement affirms, the recognition of Baptisms outside the Orthodox Church is not a recent innovation. Additionally, it is important to remember
that the first ecumenical council of Nicaea (325) has allowed for the reception of
Arians through Chrismation, thus recognizing their baptism. But the same first
ecumenical council also rejected Sabellian baptisms, for their lack of recognition
of the Trinity and thus the practice of not baptizing in the name of the Father
and the Son and the Holy Spirit.[55] Summarizing the early canonical tradition
within the framework of St. Basil the Great's distinction among various levels
of division, John Erickson writes:

> In one of the earliest authoritative statements on this subject, St. Basil the
> Great (canon 1) indicates with approval that "the ancients" distinguished
> between heresies, schisms, and illegal congregations: "heresies, those who
> are completely broken off and, as regards the faith itself, alienated; schisms,
> those at variance with one another for certain ecclesiastical reasons and
> questions that admit of a remedy; illegal congregations, assemblies brought
> into being by insubordinate presbyters or bishops, and by uninstructed
> laymen." As examples of heretics he gives Manichaeans, Montanists and
> various gnostic groups, whose understanding of God and of God's rela-
> tion to creation was altogether at variance with the Christian faith and
> who signaled this (in the case of the Montanists) by their use of a falsified
> baptismal formula ("In the name of the Father and of the Son and of the
> Lord Montanus"). Such baptisms, Basil states, the ancients quite properly
> rejected. On the other hand, he notes, they accepted the baptism not only
> of those coming from illegal congregations but also of schismatics—and
> in Basil's understanding this category included many groups, such as the
> Novatianists, who differed with the Church on some very serious doctrinal
> issues. By the late fourth century, the term "heretic" comes to be applied to
> many of these groups, in part so that civil legislation against heretics could
> be enforced against them. Yet the practice of the Church, as set forth in a
> number of liturgical and canonical texts (I Nicaea canons 8 and 19, "Laodi-
> cea" canons 7–8, "1 Constantinople canon 7," the presbyter Timothy's treatise
> "On the Reception of Heretics," the *Euchologion* of the Great Church of
> Constantinople, Trullo canon 95, etc.) continued to distinguish between
> heretics in the earlier sense of the word, who were to be received as hea-
> thens (i.e., baptized), and those who were to be received by anointing with

Economy' (1999)," in *The Journey Toward Unity: The Orthodox-Catholic Dialogue Statements*, ed. Ronald
Roberson, Thomas FitzGerald, and J. Figel (Fairfax, VA: Eastern Christian Publications, 2016), 132–33, 41.
55. Tertullian, too, intimated that the early Church did not recognize its own reality of baptism in the
baptisms of heretics in Tertullian, *On Baptism*, #15, 34–35.

chrism (e.g., Novatianists, mainstream Arians, *pneumatomachoi*) or simply by profession of faith (e.g., the non-Chalcedonians).[56]

A traditional Orthodox who respects the patristic tradition and the ecumenical councils needs recognize Catholic and Protestant baptisms as well, since the differences between East and West today pale in comparison with the Arian disputes over the divinity of the Son. And yet, emerging practices among some Protestant churches have unfortunately forced the Orthodox to insist on performing baptisms in the name of the Father and the Son and the Holy Spirit after the Matthean model. Some Pentecostal churches that are not clearly trinitarian have revived the biblical practices of baptism "in the name of Jesus" and insistence on baptism in the Spirit. Despite the biblical nature of their baptismal formulas, the Orthodox Church cannot recognize such baptisms because of their rejection of trinitarian theology. Another sensitive situation arises when Christians are baptized in the name of the Creator, Redeemer, and Sustainer. In the worthy effort to use inclusive language, some churches chose to completely abandon the male language inherent in the names of the Father and the Son. But the biblical character of the baptismal formula and the problematic nature of this solution are good reasons to maintain the Matthean language. It is a (perhaps unintended) modern form of Sabellianism to consider the Father as the Creator, when in fact the Word and the Spirit also participate in creation; the Son as the redeemer, when Jesus is the Christ by virtue of the dwelling of the Spirit upon him; the Spirit as Sustainer, when providence and sanctification are the attributes of the entire Trinity.

Clearly, the Orthodox Church does not indiscriminately accept all baptisms. But at the same time, there are some Orthodox who reject absolutely all baptisms outside the Orthodox Church, ignoring the longstanding practice to recognize the baptisms of those who are in schism. In these circles, baptisms outside the canonical boundaries of Orthodoxy (and sometimes even within Orthodoxy if there is a suspicion that certain minute technicalities have not been followed strictly) are considered invalid; hence, the convert is rebaptized, even though in their eyes baptism happens validly for the first time. There are even cases in which a person is received into Orthodoxy through Chrismation, lives an Orthodox life for a long time, and then joins a group in which they are rebaptized. This practice of rebaptizing other Christians, especially Catholics, does not stand on solid historical footing. The overwhelming majority of the

---

56. John H. Erickson, "On the Cusp of Modernity: The Canonical Hermeneutic of St. Nikodemos the Haghiorite" (1748–1809)," *St. Vladimir's Seminary Quarterly* 42, no. 1 (1988): 53–54.

history of the East does not support it, but, as always, there are late historical anomalies that could be forcefully seen as precedent.

The means of accepting Catholics into the Orthodox Church varied between the eleventh and nineteenth centuries, depending on the Latin practice of using a single or triple immersion, sprinkling, as well as the relationships between East and West, such as immediately following the 1204 Crusade when the crusaders sacked Constantinople or in times when Catholics rebaptized Orthodox who converted. Within these various Eastern practices, George Dragas identifies rebaptism, Chrismation and confession of faith, and confession of faith. The latter two options are the most common, while the first is the exception. Besides several earlier canonists and hierarchs who advocated rebaptism, the culmination of this first option was promulgated at the 1755 Synod of Constantinople. The synod was convened in a tense climate, marked by the return of Patriarch Cyril V of Constantinople to the throne after having been overthrown by Latin instigators, a schism that Latin missionaries caused in Syria, Latin attempts to convert the Orthodox in the East, and the fact that, in 1729, the Roman congregation for missionaries, *Propaganda fide*, prohibited eucharistic sharing with non-Catholics. Unsurprisingly, the official statement (or *Definition*) of the Council did not recognize the validity of Catholic baptisms, forbade eucharistic sharing with Catholics, and considered converts to Orthodoxy as unbaptized. While the main objection to Catholic baptism was the manner in which it was celebrated, the *Definition* also makes a significant ecclesiological statement: "we recognize only one Church, our holy catholic and apostolic Church. It is her sacraments, and consequently her Baptism, that we accept," and, therefore, Catholics are counted among the heretics. And yet, the decisions of the 1755 Council did not become a universal norm; they were vigorously challenged shortly thereafter, and their implementation varied greatly.[57] The polemical character of the Council's over-reaction and the astonishingly recent character of its faulty ecclesiological innovation stand out.[58]

---

57. Dragas, "Manner of Reception," 235–47. See also St. Irenaeus Joint Orthodox-Catholic Working Group, "Serving Communion: Re-thinking the Relationship between Primacy and Synodality," (2018): 9.11.

58. Erickson argues that the 1755 *Definition* should be read in conjunction with St. Nikodemos the Haghiorite's influential (and innovative) re-reading of the canonical tradition. If previously the Cyprianic position and other similar canons regarding rebaptism were regarded as marginal, Nikodemos considers them the true witness of the canonical tradition. He affirms that, whenever non-Orthodox baptisms were accepted, it was by *oikonomia* as a temporary measure in order to attract them to the truth, but *akrebeia* is required presently, thus setting the two readings of the canons in opposition—another novel approach, as opposed to a harmonious approach to the two readings of the canons in earlier forms of spirituality. According to Erickson, Nikodemos' innovation was both ecclesiological and canonical. Erickson, "Cusp of Modernity," 59–66.

These very strict (and innovative as opposed to truly traditional) anti-ecumenical groups within Orthodoxy consider that the limits of the Church confessed in the Creed coincide with the canonical limits of Orthodoxy, hence they regard as invalid all Baptisms administered outside the Orthodox Church. Such groups then choose to administer their own Baptisms to Christians who have been previously baptized in Western churches and even to converts received elsewhere in the Orthodox Church through Chrismation. Their practices should be condemned as rebaptisms and as actions that contradict the longstanding Orthodox tradition of recognizing many of the baptisms outside its canonical boundaries, which in turn has serious ecumenical consequences.

These consequences become clear when the same practice is applied to Orthodox faithful who convert to churches in the Anabaptist tradition, which recognizes only the validity of adult Baptisms and considers all infant baptisms as invalid. The person who has previously been baptized Orthodox as an infant is re-baptized when they convert into a Baptist church. While from an Orthodox perspective this practice is offensive, for Baptists it takes a different meaning. Some Baptist churches permit the repetition of the rite of Baptism if it is deemed that it was not preceded by a sincere acceptance of Christ, even when these rituals take place in the same parish. Such is the case when a person accepts Jesus Christ as their personal Lord and Savior and is baptized, but then falls into a grievous sin thus revealing that their initial acceptance of Jesus was not heartfelt, rendering their prior Baptism invalid. Consequently, such a person would again accept Jesus and be baptized, in practice showing Baptism as a repeatable ritual. The tension stems not only from differing views regarding infant Baptism, but also from differences regarding Baptism itself; if for the Orthodox Baptism represents entry into the Church and is thus unrepeatable, for Baptists it represents the rite that seals one's salvation understood as the acceptance of Jesus Christ as personal Lord and Savior.

Having said that already-baptized Christians who convert to Orthodoxy should be received by either Confession or Chrismation, it is also important to admit that there are cases when a person should not be received into the Orthodox Church. Some of them are systemic, while others are more personal or pastoral in nature. In the first systemic category fall those Orthodox dioceses that do not allow marriages between Orthodox and non-Orthodox Christians. For the marriage to go forward, sometimes the non-Orthodox spouse hurriedly converts to Orthodoxy—often as a formality, rather than the result of deep conviction. Such practices are in fact instances of proselytism, since they apply pressure on the non-Orthodox spouse to convert. Although some converts

might end up faithful Orthodox Christians, others might even resent Orthodoxy for cornering them into conversion. Orthodoxy does not need half-hearted
converts. It is better that all Orthodox abandon the requirement for conversion
into Orthodoxy prior to marriage, as in fact most Orthodox jurisdictions do.
Even if the non-Orthodox spouse is committed to embracing Orthodoxy, unless
they are entirely proven in their determination, conversion should wait until
after marriage, to ensure that there are no undue pressures. It is more likely
that during their own period of catechumenate, when they are instructed in the
faith and experience the life of the Orthodox Church for a meaningful period
of time, they become honestly interested in the faith and might even elevate the
commitment to the faith of their Orthodox spouse.

The priest and the community could also refuse conversion if they discern that a catechumen wants to embrace Orthodoxy for the wrong reasons.
Such reasons could include haste, lack of understanding of the teaching of the
Church, or family pressure. Especially in the US, Catholics and Protestants
who are disillusioned with their churches for being too liberal look at the Orthodox Church as the community that aligns more squarely with their political convictions. Such cases should be treated with great caution, as conversion
should be all encompassing, not motivated by ideological issues. At its best,
Orthodoxy does not fit in the artificial liberal-conservative divide of U.S. politics. Moreover, the Orthodox faithful in the U.S. are distributed equally across
the conservative–liberal divide, artificial as it is. A 2008 study of Orthodox
parishes in the U.S. affirms that

> the gaps between the "left" and the "right" wings in American Orthodoxy,
> and between "conservative-traditional" and "moderate-liberal" Church
> camps are very wide.... [On a spectrum of] "conservative," "traditional,"
> "moderate" and "liberal,"... the relative majority (41%) of church members
> prefer to be in the safe "middle" and describe their personal theological po-
> sition and general approach to church life as being "traditional." Yet, quite
> sizeable factions of Orthodox laity identify themselves with either "con-
> servative" (28%) or "moderate-liberal" (31%) Church camps.... the greatest
> differences in the approach of American Orthodox clergy and laity to the
> various aspects of Church life are based *not* on distinctions between various
> Orthodox jurisdictions (denominations), and not on variations between
> different age-groups, or between cradle-Orthodox Christians and converts
> to Orthodoxy, but on their individually chosen "micro-theological" stance.
> That is, the self-identification of the priests and parishioners as being ei-
> ther "liberal" or "moderate" or "traditional" or "conservative" serves as the

strongest predictor for their attitudes towards wide range of issues related to "Status of Priesthood," "Democracy and Pluralism in the Church," "Changes and Innovations in the Church," and "Religious 'Particularism' and Ecumenism."[59]

A person converting to Orthodoxy in search for an ideological haven created in the image and likeness of their political ideologies will be greatly disappointed.

THE BOUNDARIES OF THE CHURCH: IS THERE SALVATION OUTSIDE THE CHURCH?

These considerations about the various means through which converts are received into the Orthodox Church and the recognition (or lack thereof) of non-Orthodox baptisms raise a significant ecclesiological question: where are the boundaries of the Church?[60] The term "Church" here refers to the "one, holy, catholic, and apostolic Church" confessed in the Creed—sometimes referred to as "the Church," or "the Church of Christ," or "the *Una Sancta.*" For the minority who do not recognize non-Orthodox baptisms, the charismatic boundaries of the *Una Sancta* coincide with the canonical boundaries of the Orthodox Church. For the majority of the Orthodox, however, the Church of Christ surpasses the canonical boundaries of the Orthodox Church since non-Orthodox baptisms are accepted as valid.

Furthermore, the Church offers means of salvation, so it is no surprise that the relationship between the community of the Church (here on earth) and the community of the saved (in heaven) often surfaces in discussions about the Church so, before investigating the limits of the Church, a word of caution: *the Church is not the community of the saved.* Who is saved and who is not saved should be left to God alone; we mortal human beings were not given to judge our neighbor's state in the afterlife.[61] The community of the saved will be the

---

59. Krindatch, *Orthodox Church Today,* 179–80.

60. Cyril Hovorun prefers to write about frontiers that are constantly expanding, as opposed to borders that remain as fixed demarcations. Cyril Hovorun, *Scaffolds of the Church: Towards Poststructural Ecclesiology* (Cambridge: James Clarke & Co, 2017), 163–80.

61. Throughout history, theologians of good faith took very different attitudes towards eternal life and eternal damnation. Their views ranged from the late Augustine who considered that the majority of people are condemned (and deservedly so, since they are born with the original sin) to Origen who hoped in the restoration of all (*apokatastasis*), even the devil and his angels. Kallistos Ware considers that without contradicting the biblical and patristic testimony about the existence of hell, one could hope that hell will

eschatological Kingdom. Within this eschatological framework, one could look at all those saved at the end of the world, at the community that they form with God and among themselves, at their worship of God, and identify these elements as characteristic of the Church. But those saved are not necessarily baptized Christians, as for example in the case of Old Testament prophets. So, it would be improper to refer to those who are saved as the Church in the eschaton. That is why, on this side of the eschaton, where we cannot know who will be saved, the Church is not the community of the saved, but of those who are duly baptized. The Church is not only a community of holy people, but also a hospital for sinners in which the greatest sinner is equally a member of the Church as the greatest saint. In the eschaton, either the Church and the heavenly Kingdom will coincide, or—to be perhaps speculative—the Church will not exist, since it is a mediator, an icon of the Kingdom. The Kingdom will be fully manifested in the entire world, un-mediated through the sacraments or the community of the Church, and the entire cosmos will participate in the praise of God. Thus, the discussion of the limits of the Church and salvation are best treated separately, despite their inter-relatedness.

Contemporary theologians seem overly concerned with clearly defining *the limits of the Church in general and the Orthodox Church in particular*, often along canonical lines. For a small but quite vocal anti-ecumenical faction that does not recognize all baptisms described above, even the canonical limits of the Orthodox Church are too large; they prefer to see only their own followers as truly Orthodox, as if those who are open to dialogue are not true members of the Church.[62] They claim an epistemic certainty that excludes the other, in

---

be totally unpopulated. Timothy (Kallistos) Ware, *The Orthodox Church*, New ed. (London, New York: Penguin Books, 1997), 261–62. David B. Hart argues that the idea of an eternal hell has been adopted widely despite its lack of biblical support and its problematic relationship with truly free choice informed by the vision of God. David Bentley Hart, *That All Shall Be Saved: Heaven, Hell, and Universal Salvation* (New Haven, CT: Yale University Press, 2019). Given this very wide range of opinions, the difficulty in interpreting the various meanings of the biblical term "salvation," the parabolic character of New Testament references to damnation, the difficulty of interpreting texts about "eternal punishment" (Mt 25:46) and about afterlife—a concept that is marginal at best in the Jewish tradition—and most importantly because God alone is merciful and just in his judgment, it is preferable not to speculate about who might go to heaven and who might go to hell, no matter how tempting it might be for mere mortals to take the divine judgment seat.

62. While defining the Church as the place where the word of God is preached and the sacraments are duly performed (thus visibly), the Reformers added an emphasis on God's free gift of grace upon those who are saved, upon God's election of the true Church known only to him – the latter being a Calvinist emphasis. In response, the Catholic Counter-Reformation over-emphasized the visible character of the Church, defining it primarily as submission to the Roman Pontiff and stressing the role of the ordained priesthood and the sacraments. Some Orthodox factions today espouse this same, medieval Western approach that equates membership in the Church with salvation, and even say, along Calvinist lines, that

contradistinction to the apophatic approach that Orthodoxy has traditionally taken to ecclesiology, and which Paul Evdokimov summarized best: "We know where the Church is, but we cannot judge where the Church is not."[63]

Instead of applying select elements of canon law, history, and theology in a rigorous, unloving, and untrue way, traditions should be read in their original context and applied carefully today. Given how all Christians agree on the essential dogmas that have been challenged by heretics in the early Church, the canons that precede the East-West schism and the birth of Protestantism do not apply directly today. And even the later canons should be seen in their proper context, often marked by enmity motivated primarily by cultural and political concerns. That combative environment stands in stark contrast with the experience of the majority of the faithful today, who live irenically with their Western neighbors. A return to an irenic spirit would square contemporary theology with both the experience of the faithful and the Orthodox Tradition at its best.

Theologically speaking, the Eastern tradition has been concerned with expanding the limits of the Church, not with reducing them. This concern goes beyond the Great Commission, "go therefore to all nations, baptizing them ..." For example, Pseudo-Dionysius does not consider only the ecclesial hierarchy, but also the celestial hierarchy as components of the Church. Maximus the Confessor expands the Church to the entire universe, which celebrates a cosmic liturgy.[64] (Obviously, these elements of non-human creation are not members of the Church in the same sense in which baptized humans are, and yet, they worship God with the rest of the Church.) While such theological accounts remain quite intricate, they are not only intellectually fascinating, but also concretely reflected in the liturgical life of the Church. By way of example, one need only remember the above considerations about the blessing of the waters at Epiphany, when Christ entered the Jordan river and thus blessed the entire river, which in turn blesses all rivers that flow into the seas, which then become clouds, and come back to us—all sanctified. The grace of Jesus' Baptism extends to all creation and is renewed in the liturgical celebration of the Church at Epiphany and at all baptismal celebrations. This is one of the

---

not all who are part of the canonical (visible) Church are part of the true Church, the significant difference being that this true Church is not invisible, as in Calvinism, but visible, defined similarly to Catholic identity: belonging in communion with a certain group.

63. Paul Evdokimov, *L'Orthodoxie* (Paris: Desclée de Brouwer, 1979), 343. See the same idea adopted in Ware, *The Orthodox Church*, 308.

64. Radu Bordeianu, "Maximus and Ecology: The Relevance of Maximus the Confessor's Theology of Creation for the Present Ecological Crisis," *The Downside Review* 127, no. 447 (2009): 103–26.

senses in which Orthodox theology speaks of the sacramentality of all creation, in a sense baptizing all the universe that becomes a vehicle of God's grace— which is one of the essential functions of the Church. Hence, the concept of sacramentality is important in expanding the limits of the Church beyond the sacraments.

In this same generous patristic spirit that continuously expands the limits of the Church, it is now the time to ask: what does the Orthodox practice of receiving converts through Chrismation or Confession say about the limits of the Church and how is this question relevant for Orthodox involvement in the ecumenical movement? What does the practice of rebaptism say about the same ecclesiological themes? At stake is a different understanding of the boundaries of the Church: if the ecumenical group recognizes the reality of the Church in other Christians, the anti-ecumenical group denies it. For the latter, there is no church outside of Orthodoxy and thus there is little or no difference between non-Orthodox and non-Christians.[65]

Orthodox participants in ecumenical dialogues consistently affirm that the Church is already one, as the image of the Body of Christ suggests. There is only one head, Jesus Christ, and one Body, the Church *Una Sancta*. Consequently, ecumenism is concerned with re-establishing not the unity of the Church, which can never be lost, but rather that of Christians, who are visibly disunited. And yet, Orthodox representatives have also consistently referred to the *churches* (plural) that make up the Christian family. As early as 1902, the Ecumenical Patriarchate consulted all major Orthodox sees on the initiation of dialogue with the West, especially with Old Catholics and Anglicans, whose teachings were regarded as very close to Orthodox doctrine. In the 1904 letter of Patriarch Joachim III of Constantinople, which included the responses of the other Orthodox sees, he referred to Western churches as "holy local Churches of God."[66] Most notably, other Christian communities were called *churches* in the unprecedented 1920 initiative of the Ecumenical Patriarchate to

65. For examples of old and new anti-ecumenical attitudes that restrict the boundaries of the Church to Orthodoxy, see Dragas, "Manner of Reception," 246. Will Cohen, "Does the Long-Contested Question of Orthodox Ecumenism Remain Open after Crete?," *International Journal of Systematic Theology* 23, no. 1 (2021): 12–13. As previously stated, St. Nikodemos Haghiorites was highly influential for this type of reading of Eastern patristic and canonical tradition. In doing so, he did not hide his anti-Catholic sentiments (sentiments of explicit hatred, unfortunately); he wrote in his *Enchiridion on Baptism*: "The very fact that we have entertained so much hatred and aversion against them for so many centuries is a plain proof that we loathe them as heretics.... So the Latins cannot even perform a baptism because they are heretics and have lost the grace required to celebrate Christian rites." Quoted in Erickson, "Cusp of Modernity," 61–62.

66. Gennadios Gennadios Limouris, ed., *Orthodox Visions of Ecumenism: Statements, Messages and Reports of the Ecumenical Movement 1902–1992* (Geneva: WCC Publications, 1994), 3–8.

form a fellowship, in the programmatic encyclical entitled, "Unto the Church-es of Christ Everywhere," which is considered a foundational document of the ecumenical movement. This designation remained consistent throughout the process of preparation for the Holy and Great Council of the Orthodox Church held in Crete in 2016. Notwithstanding pressure from anti-ecumenical circles, after affirming that the unity of the Church cannot be perturbed and generally avoiding references to Catholics and Protestants as "churches," the Crete Council rather timidly states that "the Orthodox Church accepts the historical name of other non-Orthodox Christian Churches and Confessions that are not in communion with her," and describes the WCC as being made up of "non-Orthodox Christian Churches and Confessions," thereby continuing to recognize non-Orthodox *churches* as such.[67]

It is important to note that the terms "communion" and "confession," as distinct from "church," rarely appear in Orthodox statements, and only most recently. Such a distinction, however, has no grounding in the Eastern tradition. It is in fact a Catholic influence, surprisingly taken up in anti-ecumenical circles, most likely unknowingly. Vatican II designates the churches of the Reformation as "ecclesial communities," as opposed to "churches"—terminology reserved to Catholics and Orthodox in *Unitatis Redintegratio* 13–22. An in-depth discussion of this subject is impossible here, but it is noteworthy that Vatican II initially placed the emphasis on "ecclesial" in the expression, "ecclesial communities," meaning that the churches of the Reformation are, indeed, Churches (they have an ecclesial character) and took into consideration that some Christian families, such as the Anglicans, refer to themselves as "communion."[68]

Thus, the first theological question related to ecumenism is an ecclesiological one: how do Orthodox understand the relationship between the Orthodox Church and the church described in the Creed as the *Una Sancta*, and what does that understanding mean for the ecclesial status of other Christian churches? In other words, is the Body of Christ limited to Christians belonging

---

67. "Relations of the Orthodox Church with the Rest of the Christian World" par. 6, 16 in Council of Crete, *Official Documents* (2016). https://www.holycouncil.org/official-documents. Will Cohen offers an excellent analysis of Crete's references to non-Orthodox churches. He presents the maximalist and minimalist readings of these texts among various Orthodox theologians; the shift from pre-conciliar drafts that spoke about the "ontological existence" of non-Orthodox churches (1971), to their "real / actual existence" (1986), to "historical existence" (2015), to the final text that speaks about their "historical name" (Crete 2016), all of which went further than other previous councils; and about Crete's endorsement of ecumenism for the first time in the Orthodox conciliar tradition. Cohen, "Ecumenism after Crete," 21.

68. J.-M.-R. Tillard, *Church of Churches: The Ecclesiology of Communion*, trans. R. C. De Peaux (Collegeville, MN: Liturgical Press, 1992), 314–15. Francis A. Sullivan, *The Church We Believe In: One, Holy, Catholic and Apostolic* (New York: Paulist Press, 1988), 30–32.

to just one denomination—in this case, Orthodoxy—or can various denominations be considered as members of the same Body of Christ?

First and foremost, the official position of all autocephalous Orthodox churches and the view of most contemporary theologians is that Orthodoxy needs to engage in dialogue with other churches and that all those baptized with water in the name of the Trinity are validly baptized members of the *Una Sancta*. Undeniably, there is tension between Orthodoxy's claim to be the Church and the recognition of non-Orthodox as members of the Church, validly baptized. Orthodox theologians who hold together both these aspects do not deny the ecclesial status of non-Orthodox churches, but they cannot say positively what that ecclesial status is. Here is where I suggest that *the language of fullness of belonging to the Church* is helpful: the grace of God is at work fully in the Orthodox Church, which represents the fullness of the *Una Sancta*, but also in other churches, which share in that fullness to different degrees. "Fullness" language simultaneously speaks to the Orthodox self-identification with the Church and affirms the ecclesial character of other Christian churches.

The affirmation that Orthodoxy represents the fullness of the Church sounds arrogant to Protestant ears, but the Orthodox do not mean it in the sense that they live a sinless life or that their church, in its historical manifestations, has been perfect at all times. On the contrary, sin and human weakness are undeniable realities in the life of the church. But, with deep humility and seeing it as a calling, the Orthodox believe that the fullness of truth and church life has been preserved since the beginning of Christianity, without interruption, in Orthodoxy. It is a calling both in the sense of witness to other Christians and in the sense that the Church is still in need of perfection: the fullness of the Church in Orthodoxy is already here, but not yet; it is both indicative and imperative.

I propose a subjective recognition of the fullness of the Church in one's community, with the acceptance of the fact that other Christians will recognize that same fullness in their own community. This would be no different from a Catholic experiencing the Church of Christ "subsisting in" the Catholic Church,[69] while recognizing elements of the Church in others, or from a Methodist choosing to be a Methodist as opposed to a member of any other church based on where they experience the Church to the highest degree possible. Such an experiential approach to ecumenical ecclesiologies seems to point

69. Vatican Council II, *Lumen Gentium* (November 21, 1964), par. 8, in Austin Flannery, ed., *Vatican Council II: The Conciliar and Postconciliar Documents*, New Revised ed., vol. 1 (Northport, NY: Costello Publishing Company, 1998), 357.

to one's experience of the fullness of the Church in their own denomination. Hence the Orthodox claim to be the fullness of the Church is not meant to be exclusivist, arrogant, or derogatory, but rather is descriptive of their experience.

When the discussion shifts to *the views of major individual theologians*, one notes that most theologians agree that the boundaries of the *Una Sancta* extend beyond the Orthodox Church. And yet, there is great diversity among them. Georges Florovsky distinguished between the canonical and charismatic boundaries of the Church. He identified the former boundary with the unified early Church and its continuation today, namely the Orthodox Church, and the latter one with the entirety of Christianity. Florovsky pointed out that some heretics were received into the early Church without the administration of Baptism and their orders were recognized as valid. These sacraments are validly performed "by virtue of the Holy Spirit." Moreover, according to Florovsky, "the unity of the Church is based on a twofold bond—the 'unity of the Spirit' and the 'union of peace' (cf. Eph 4:3). In sects and divisions the 'union of peace' is broken and torn apart, but in the sacraments the 'unity of the Spirit' is not terminated. This is the unique paradox of sectarian existence." Thus, Florovsky considered that the canonical and charismatic boundaries of the Church do not coincide because of the extended presence of the Holy Spirit outside the canonical Orthodox Church, manifested in sacraments, particularly in Baptism.[70]

Florovsky's concerns were to say that the Church confessed in the Creed still exists today and to not exclude other Christians from the Church. Under his direct influence, the newly formed WCC declared in 1950 at Toronto that membership of the *Una Sancta* is more inclusive than the membership of individual churches, and that members of the WCC recognize in other churches "elements of the true Church,"[71] as in Florovsky's distinction between the canonical and charismatic limits of the Church. His theological insights have become, with a surprising consistency, the basis for most of the documents signed by Orthodox delegates at ecumenical gatherings.

Another great ecumenical theologian, Nicolas Afanasiev, was very much in favor of Christian unity but disagreed with the idea that non-Orthodox churches have only a diminished ecclesial existence or "vestiges" of the Church, affirming that "[t]he nature of the Church presupposes that either she exists

70. Florovsky, "The Boundaries of the Church," 37–42. Besides this sacramental approach, eschatology, too, weakens the importance of the boundaries between Christian churches. As Metropolitan Platon of Kiev famously said, "the boundaries of the churches do not reach up to heaven." Quoted in John A. Jillions, "Ecumenism and the Paris School of Orthodox Theology," *Theoforum* 39 (2008): 150.

71. Michael Kinnamon and Brian E. Cope, *The Ecumenical Movement: An Anthology of Key Texts and Voices* (Grand Rapids, MI: Eerdmans, 1997), 467.

in her fullness or she does not exist at all, but there can be no partial existence nor can there be vestiges existing here and there."[72] He believed that if other Christians have a valid Eucharist they are fully the church, and he therefore considered the Roman Catholic Church to be a local church of the *Una Sancta* as was the Orthodox Church. For Afanasiev, the division between the Orthodox and Catholic Churches has affected only the surface of their ecclesiastical lives and has merely a canonical character.[73]

A final remark regarding the limits of the Church has to do with secularization and the growing phenomenon of *"the nones" or "spiritual but not religious."* In our internal quarrel, our Christian families often forget the scandal that we cause with our disunity and the need to minister to those who are positively disposed towards believing but hesitate to join our churches—a challenge that all Christians face together. While we count those who are not active in their faith as members of our churches because they entered the Church through Baptism, they belong only in name. In this sense, WCC's 2005 document, *The Nature and Mission of the Church* states that

> Many of our communities face the challenge that some of their members seem to "belong without believing", while other individuals opt out of Church membership, claiming that they can, with greater authenticity, "believe without belonging". The challenge of living our faith as believing communities in such a way that all those who belong are seriously committed Christians, and all who sincerely believe want to belong, is a challenge that we share; it crosses the lines which divide us.[74]

Besides our canonical divisions, all churches experience the separation from those who "belong without believing" and those who "believe without belonging." Especially younger generations are highly suspicious of institutions in general and religious institutions in particular.[75] The number of those "spiritual but not religious," of whom the youth represent the majority, is growing exponentially.

In just seven years, from 2007 to 2014, the percentage of unaffiliated among U.S. adults rose from 16.1 to 22.8, making them the fastest growing religious

72. Nicolas Afanassieff, "Una Sancta," in *Tradition Alive: On the Church and the Christian Life in Our Time: Readings from the Eastern Church*, ed. and trans. Michael Plekon (Lanham, MD: Rowan & Littlefield, 2003), 8.

73. Afanassieff, "Una Sancta," 25.

74. WCC, *The Nature and Mission of the Church: A Stage on the Way to a Common Statement* (Geneva: WCC Publications, 2005), par. 51.

75. Both humorously and sadly, Orthodox Christians can respond to those who are against organized religion: "have I got a religion for you …"

group in America.[76] When asked, "with which religion do you identify?" they answer, "none," hence their designation as "the nones." They believe in God, they make significant life decisions based on their faith, they volunteer, and they do acts of kindness associated with the Kingdom of God, but outside the canonical boundaries of our churches.[77] Even among those affiliated with the Orthodox Church, not just among the nones, there is the conception that one does not need to participate in the life of the Church in order to be a good Christian; faith is in one's heart. When the nones say "I am spiritual, but not religious," they divorce personal spiritual growth from communal worship and reduce religion to ethical behavior, while the public worship of the Church seems less relevant to personal spiritual ascent.

Orthodox theology offers a compelling alternative to this individualistic and fragmented approach to religion in general and to spirituality in particular. The Church is a community in which the Lord acts and is not simply the sum of isolated individuals; the Church worships God communally and not only privately; the Church has a Creed shared throughout the centuries and throughout the world and not simply personal beliefs; and the Church brings healing to the world by serving those in need communally, as opposed to separate individual initiatives. Moreover, spirituality as a personal endeavor finds its fulfillment in the communitarian, liturgical aspect of the Church. At the same time, the reverse is true: the more each faithful grows in relationship with Christ, the more their spiritual progress creates communion. Thus, the mission of the Church addresses not only the individual, but also the community, not only the spirit, but also the body, not only one's immediate context, but the world.

The nones long for this sense of community, communal worship, as well as nourishment and confirmation from a community of faith. A sincere spirituality and study of the Bible that might start out individually, should lead to the community. Of course, one can be a good person without religion; but one cannot individually have the same level of liturgical life, creedal tradition, and charitable presence as when belonging in a community.

---

76. Pew Research Center, *America's Changing Religious Landscape: Christians Decline Sharply as Share of Population; Unaffiliated and Other Faiths Continue to Grow* (2015), 3. www.pewresearch.org.

77. The most important reason why the nones leave the Church is because they disagree with the Church's teachings. 49% of "nones" say that they do not believe, in the sense of being disenchanted with Church teaching, considering that their views have evolved, and because they went through a crisis of faith. The second most important reason for leaving the Church is that they dislike organized religion. Under this umbrella fall "anti-institutional religion; religion focuses on power/politics, and religion causes conflict." Pew Research Center, *Choosing a New Church or House of Worship* (2016), 29. www.pewresearch.org.

In response, the community of the Church needs to understand and rectify the reasons for the nones' departure. While this question will resurface repeatedly throughout this book, relevant to our theme here is to advocate an experiential approach to ecclesiology and ecumenism. From this perspective, the question of the limits of the Church, even canonical limits, becomes more complicated: those who "believe without belonging" belong in a real sense. Without resolving the paradox, it is helpful to remember Augustine's words: "how many sheep there are without, how many wolves there are within!"[78]

These considerations complement the assertion that Church is an icon and instrument of the Kingdom, but the reverse is also true: the Kingdom is an icon and instrument of the Church. The Kingdom of God is already present outside the visible boundaries of the Church and leads to the Church. God works in mysterious ways and those who do the work of the Kingdom even without God, might end up in the Church (the icon of the Kingdom), or directly into the heavenly Kingdom.

THE ECUMENICAL IMPERATIVE AND
ANTI-ECUMENICAL ATTITUDES

Based on the understanding that the Church is both one and divided, the Orthodox Church sees it as an imperative to participate in the ecumenical movement. Shortly before his Passion, Jesus prayed that all his disciples and the generations to come "may be one, as [Jesus and the Father] are one, I in them and you in me, that they may become completely one, so that the world may know that you have sent me and have loved them even as you have loved me" (Jn 17:22–23). When the Church fulfills its call to unity and love, the world will recognize the presence of the Father and of the Son in the disciples. In this sense, the prayer for the disciples is also a prayer for the world, that the world might know Christ. In the meantime, our disunity is a counter-testimony to Christ, affecting mixed families, international relations, and individual interactions. Moreover, there have been many mission-trips to places that never heard of Christ. Episcopalian, Methodist, and Baptist missionaries spoke in one voice about Christ. Then people wanted to be baptized into *the* Church. But that was impossible; they had to be baptized into *a* church, namely Episcopalian,

78. Augustine, "Tractate 45 on John 10.1–10," in Augustine, *Tractates on the Gospel of John 28–54*, trans. John W. Rettig, Fathers of the Church, (Washington, DC: The Catholic University of America Press, 1993), #12, 198.

Methodist, or Baptist. Seeing our disunity, some catechumens renounced the idea of becoming Christians. Others accepted to be baptized into the disunity that we brought to them. Disunity is not from God, and so Orthodox Christians pray at every service "for the unity of all."[79]

Ecumenism represents the movement that attempts to bring Christian churches into visible unity. The term comes from the Greek *oikos*, which means "house." To restore the unity of the house means to recognize the life of Christ in the other not simply as individuals, but as church. That is not to say that unity is an end in itself. Unity is, indeed, the goal of the ecumenical movement, but not the goal of the Church's existence. In fact, Christian unity is a means, a necessary condition for fulfilling the missionary calling of the Church: to live as a foretaste of the Kingdom by sharing life in Christ, as his Body, in the bond of the Spirit, as children of the Father.

In what concerns theological matters, the ecumenical *Grundaxiom* that unity does not mean uniformity holds true for Orthodoxy both internally and in its approach to ecumenism. There is a significant degree of diversity in the East, from the ways in which different national churches celebrate the Liturgy, to the calendar that they use, to various practices concerning divorce, the election of bishops, or the means by which converts are received into Orthodoxy. And yet, all autocephalous Orthodox churches affirm their unity in faith and dogma. The same model of theological unity in diversity applies to Orthodox participation in the ecumenical movement. Diversity, understood as constitutive of unity, is a blessing. But seen as an end in itself, diversity becomes division, schism, or "illegitimate diversity" that damages unity. Ecumenism is thus concerned with establishing the limits of acceptable diversity. That is not to say that ecumenism is concerned exclusively with removing obstacles, but also with sharing our gifts with one another. This type of "receptive ecumenism" seeks to learn from the other, rather than simply asking the other to learn from us, in the conviction that both can grow in faith, life and witness to Christ if they are open to being transformed by God's grace mediated through each other.

Ecumenical dialogue is neither the search for the lowest common denominator, nor a negotiation of the faith. On the contrary, it is here that churches are most creative, proclaiming their faith together. Simply repeating old positions when in fact they were often based on terminological misunderstandings and inimical attitudes is un-faithful to Tradition. One notices over the years a

79. It is appropriate to quote C. S. Lewis here: "If I have not directly helped the cause of reunion, I have perhaps made it clear why we ought to be reunited." C. S. Lewis, *Mere Christianity* (New York: HarperCollins, 2001), xi.

reassessment of past controversies. Such is the case with regard to Christology in relations between Eastern Orthodox and Oriental Orthodox (pre-Chalcedonian or non-Chalcedonian) Churches. Their Joint Theological Commission's most important statements of Anba Bishoi (1989) and Chambésy (1990) show that, despite centuries of alienation and terminological confusion, the two churches share the same Orthodox faith.[80] After more than fifteen centuries of separation, this is *perhaps the most important accomplishment of any bilateral dialogue* involving the Orthodox Church and it is already bearing fruit in pastoral life in some jurisdictions in Western Europe and North America, where members of the two churches share in the Eucharist.

Orthodox theologians have also retraced the lines between church-dividing and non-church-dividing issues. Noteworthy is the recommendation of the North American Orthodox-Catholic Theological Consultation that the Filioque "need no longer divide us," but that the different ways of understanding the procession of the Holy Spirit in the East and in the West should be placed in their proper theological, historical, and terminological context. The differences do not pertain to the essence of our faith regarding the divinity of the Spirit, but to diverse ways of theologizing about the manner of the Spirit's origin in various contexts.[81] Without an official recognition, it would be an exaggeration to state that this issue has been completely resolved, but the silence on this subject speaks loudly: this statement's (mostly tacit) reception put to rest the thorny issue of the Filioque.

Looking at previous agreed upon statements, a pessimist might say that everything has been said, but nothing has been done. It is true that sometimes theological agreements do not result in concrete action and are slowly forgotten. One of ecumenism's significant problems is the loss of memory.[82] For example, prior Orthodox-Catholic agreements on Marriage are still waiting their full implementation; this book will make an argument in this direction.

80. Kinnamon and Cope, *The Ecumenical Movement*, 147–49. Thomas FitzGerald and Peter Bouteneff, eds., *Turn to God, Rejoice in Hope: Orthodox Reflections on the Way to Harare: The Report of the WCC Orthodox Pre-Assembly Meeting and Selected Resource Materials* (Geneva: Orthodox Task Force, WCC, 1998), 145. The Eastern Orthodox churches of Alexandria, Antioch, and Romania and the Oriental Orthodox churches of Alexandria, Antioch, and Malankara-India have officially accepted the agreed statements and proposals of the Commission.

81. Consultation, "The Filioque: A Church-Dividing Issue? An Agreed Statement of the North American Orthodox-Catholic Theological Consultation. Saint Paul's College, Washington, D.C. October 25, 2003," 183.

82. Sometimes memory loss—or rather a healing of memory—is necessary for ecumenical progress. That is the case of wars with partial religious motivations, such as between Catholics and Protestants in Ireland or Orthodox and Catholics in ex-Yugoslavia.

Sometimes, however, the lack of ecumenical progress is also rooted in an unwillingness to change for the other or to acknowledge that the other has changed. Perfectionism is another excuse for lack of action: instead of taking small steps together based on what we have accomplished, we wait for full resolution of all dissentions before we make even the smallest step, and thus perfection becomes the enemy of the good. Lastly, after an initial ecumenical enthusiasm, we are now experiencing an "ecumenical winter." As Vladimir Latinovic has pointed out, it seems that Orthodox ecumenism works better backwards: Orthodox theology was much more open and progressive in the beginning of the twentieth century than it is today. Hence, to register progress in Orthodox ecumenical thought, one should begin nowadays and go backwards in time.[83]

An optimist, however, would look at the last ecumenical century and emphasize the major accomplishments highlighted above regarding Eastern-Oriental Orthodox relations and the Orthodox-Catholic dialogue. These have addressed centuries-long controversies in a very short term, since *the ecumenical movement has a rather brief history.*[84]

As stated above, in 1902, the Ecumenical Patriarchate consulted all major Orthodox sees on the initiation of dialogue with the West. In 1904, Patriarch Joachim III of Constantinople issued a letter that included the responses of the other Orthodox sees, calling for a dialogue with the Western churches, which he called "holy local Churches of God."[85] Most notable is the unprecedented 1920 invitation of the Ecumenical Patriarchate "unto the Churches of Christ everywhere" to form a fellowship (*koinonia*) of churches. It affirmed that Christians are not strangers, but all part of the household of Christ. This invitation, which became programmatic for the entire ecumenical movement, acknowledged that some degree of rapprochement need not await the resolution of dogmatic differences, but it was necessary as an initial stage before reaching theological agreement.[86] These initiatives were the result of intra-Orthodox consultations and all local Orthodox churches felt the urgency to act together towards Christian unity.

83. Vladimir Latinovic, "Konservativer als zuvor? Die orthodoxe Beteiligung am ökumenischen Dialog," in *Damit alle eins seien: Programmatik und Zukunft der Ökumene*, ed. Bernd Jochen Hilberath, Hans Küng, and Johanna Rahner (Ostfildern: Grünewald Verlag, 2015), 111.
84. I have explored the following considerations in Radu Bordeianu, "The Unity We Seek: Orthodox Perspectives," in *The [Oxford] Handbook of Ecumenical Studies*, ed. Geoffrey Wainwright and Paul McPartlan (New York: Oxford University Press, 2021), 577–93. Radu Bordeianu, "Getting from Conflict to Communion: Ecclesiology at the Center of Recent Lutheran-Orthodox Dialogues and the 2016 Orthodox Council of Crete," *Worship* 91, no. Nov. (2017): esp. 529–30.
85. Limouris, *Orthodox Visions of Ecumenism*, 9–11.
86. Kinnamon and Cope, *The Ecumenical Movement*, 12–13.

Having already mentioned the early twentieth century calls of the Ecumenical Patriarchate to dialogue with other churches, the next major development in Orthodoxy's relationship with the West was the founding of the
World Council of Churches (WCC). A number of Orthodox churches were
represented as founding members at the WCC's inaugural assembly in Am-
sterdam in 1948, namely the Ecumenical Patriarchate, the Churches of Cyprus
and Greece, as well as the Romanian Orthodox Episcopate of the USA. The
Orthodox churches behind the Iron Curtain all refused to join the WCC in
1948, and a synod that took place in the USSR in the same year invoked an ecclesiological reason, namely their refusal to recognize Protestants as churches.
(On a more practical level, it is important to acknowledge that all these churches emulated the isolationist attitude of the communist regimes in which they
existed.) Their concerns were answered shortly thereafter in 1950 at Toronto,
when the WCC stated that its members recognize in other churches elements
of the true Church, but are not obligated to recognize them as churches in
the full sense of the term. As stated above, Georges Florovsky was one of the
influential figures who tailored this statement.[87] Other Orthodox theologians
of the first rank from that period, such as Nicholas Afanasiev, Paul Evdokimov,
and Dumitru Staniloae, embraced this attitude of ecumenical openness.

The Orthodox churches from communist countries later joined the WCC
between 1961 and 1965. At that time, the Orthodox Church of Albania was
unable to exist officially within its territory, so it joined the WCC only in 1994.
All canonical Orthodox churches have therefore been involved in the WCC at
some stage.

Unfortunately, internal Orthodox struggles—rooted primarily in secular
politics, not theology—complicated the relationship with the WCC. First, there
was the suspicion that churches from the Eastern bloc became WCC members
to further the communist propaganda of their countries: they gave the impression of openness, peace, and understanding, while using the WCC meetings
as opportunities to gather information about the West. Second, the Russian
Orthodox Church justified its membership in the WCC not as a common initiative with the West (which would have been a political faux pas), but by its
decision to seek Christian unity virtually by canonical absorption within Orthodoxy. Third, the internal quarrels among Orthodox delegates increased because

87. Matthew Baker and Seraphim Danckaert, "Georges Florovsky," in *Orthodox Handbook on Ecumenism: Resources for Theological Education—"That They All May Be One" (John 17, 21)*, ed. Pantelis
Kalaitzidis and Thomas FitzGerald (Oxford/Volos: Regnum Books International / Volos Academy Publications, 2013), 214.

they rarely met outside the limited pre-Assembly meetings, due mainly to their inimical geopolitical situations. Fourth, the tension between Orthodox representatives and the WCC became more pronounced when Orthodox refused to sign common statements and the number of separate Orthodox statements increased, when the Orthodox did not share in eucharistic services with Protestant members, and when Orthodox delegates became increasingly dissatisfied with the nature of the unity that the WCC was seeking and with its voting procedures. The number of autocephalous Orthodox churches was unlikely to increase, but the WCC continued to admit a great number of Protestant churches as members, thus limiting the impact of the Orthodox delegations who were easily outvoted.

The main quarrel did not revolve so much around ecumenism as around ecumenical institutions, so in 1997 and 1998 respectively, the Georgian and Bulgarian Patriarchates withdrew from the WCC. In response, at its eighth assembly in Harare (1998), the WCC created a Special Commission on Orthodox Participation in the WCC. The 2006 Final Report of the Commission deals with common prayer at WCC gatherings, decision-making by consensus (a significant Orthodox contribution!), and theological criteria for churches applying for membership in the WCC. Although opinions could differ regarding the real changes that this Report has brought about, the willingness of the WCC to accommodate Orthodox concerns is exemplary. This good will proved enormously influential on the 2016 Council of Crete's positive attitude towards the WCC.[88]

The WCC, however, embodies but one model of institutional ecumenism. Bilateral dialogues have also proved immensely fruitful, especially between the Orthodox and Catholic churches. The Second Vatican Council (1962–1965) marked the change of an era in this regard. Orthodox observers contributed meaningfully to the documents and ecumenical atmosphere of the Council; among these, Nicholas Afanasiev, Nikos Nissiotis, and André Scrima, stand out.[89] Moreover, although Patriarch Athenagoras of Constantinople was un-

---

88. Crete's "Relations" par. 17 affirms: "The local Orthodox Churches that are members of the WCC participate fully and equally in the WCC.... The Orthodox Church readily accepted the WCC's decision to respond to her request concerning the establishment of the Special Commission on Orthodox Participation in the World Council of Churches, which was mandated by the Inter-Orthodox Conference held in Thessaloniki in 1998. The established criteria of the Special Commission, proposed by the Orthodox and accepted by the WCC, led to the formation of the Permanent Committee on Consensus and Collaboration."

89. See Radu Bordeianu, "Orthodox Observers at the Second Vatican Council and Intra-Orthodox Dynamics," *Theological Studies* 79, no. 1 (2018): 86–106.

able to visit Vatican II as he intended, he initiated the lifting of the mutual excommunications of 1054. A moment of grace occurred at the concluding vigil of the council, on December 7, 1965. After the reading of the decision to "lift the sentences of excommunication, remove them from the midst of the Church, and consign them to oblivion,"[90] Pope Paul VI and Metropolitan Meliton of Heliopolis embraced each other to the enthusiastic applause of the assembly.

As a result of this atmosphere of openness, Orthodox-Catholic theological dialogues proliferated. The oldest and most productive among regional dialogues is the North American Orthodox-Catholic Theological Consultation, whose first meeting took place on September 9, 1965. Other regional dialogues followed, culminating with the establishment of the Joint International Commission for Theological Dialogue between the Roman Catholic Church and the Orthodox Church in 1979. In its initial stage, the international dialogue focused on sacramental theology, especially the Eucharist and Holy Orders. In its second stage, it responded to the new context created out of the fall of communism but entered a period of crisis in the late 1990s, when the Orthodox protested the re-emergence of Byzantine Catholic Churches in Eastern Europe. After a six-year hiatus, the international dialogue resumed in 2006, and in this third stage it has focused on primacy and synodality.

One of the reasons why the ecumenical dialogue is progressing so slowly is that it tends to focus on issues of ecclesiology. The Bible and the ecumenical councils do not speak authoritatively about the nature of the Church, and so there is no official Orthodox ecclesiological dogma. The same holds true for the nature of the unity we seek: no commonly-agreed model exists, although many have been proposed in the past.

Besides, given that bishops are the main participants of the ecumenical dialogue and are tasked to recognize the dialogue's result, it is not surprising that a heavily episcopocentric ecclesiology currently dominates Orthodox concerns in the dialogue: the role of the bishop of Rome, regional and local primacies, validity of orders from the perspective of apostolic succession, etc. But from the lay perspective, these themes are less important, as baptismal unity supersedes the lack of episcopal communion. Moreover, how relevant is the structural disunity among Orthodox and Catholics compared to the union between spouses in mixed marriages, which has been blessed in the sacrament of Matrimony

90. Giuseppe Alberigo and Joseph A. Komonchak, eds., *History of Vatican II: Vol. V: The Council and the Transition: The Fourth Period and the End of the Council. September 1965–December 1965* (Maryknoll, NY: Orbis, 2006), 472–78.

recognized by both churches? A lay-experiential approach to ecumenism will differ significantly from much more abstract episcopocentric ecclesiologies.

Last, but not least, the ecumenical progress on issues of ecclesiology is impeded by what Heinrich Fries and Karl Rahner call a "tactical caution" on the part of the churches whereby "[t]hey do not really come out courageously with declarations as to what the conditions are under which they are really prepared to unite with other churches."[91] In other words, the Orthodox should take the initiative and delineate a clear and realistic plan of unity, so that other churches would know precisely what is expected of them. Unfortunately, the only clear plan thus far is one of institutional reabsorption within Orthodoxy, a plan that is neither Orthodox nor realistic. While this plan is upheld by some anti-ecumenical groups within Orthodoxy as if this is a traditionally Orthodox position, it is in fact a now-abandoned Catholic stance that influenced the thought of some Orthodox. In 1928, Pius XI declared that "the union of Christians can only be promoted by promoting the return to the one true Church of Christ of those who are separated from it, for in the past they have unhappily left it."[92] Clearly, institutional absorption is not a traditional Orthodox model, but a model that the Catholic Church has now abandoned. As Nikos Nissiotis also affirms, "The Orthodox attitude concerning return is not an appeal to the other churches to return within the Orthodox historical structure, but an appeal to all churches to find their orthodoxy in themselves, returning continually to the one tradition of the apostolic Church from which they all spring and which does not allow them to remain separate."[93]

One should not think of ecumenism as exclusively institutional, and this book will highlight mixed marriages, common actions, and theological collaborations in this sense. Moreover, during communism, Orthodox, Roman Catholics, Eastern Catholics, and Protestants suffered side-by-side under militant atheist regimes which persecuted them irrespective of denominational identity. They overcame denominational barriers even when doctrinal unity was lacking, or rather refused to give our theological quarrels more weight than they deserve. They "gave a Christian ecumenical witness by their common suffering. This kind of witness has been called, significantly, 'ecumenism behind bars' or 'ecumenism under the cross.'"[94] As communist persecutions came to

91. Heinrich Fries and Karl Rahner, *Unity of Churches: An Actual Possibility* (New York: Fortress, 1985), 9.

92. Pope Pius XI, *Mortalium Animos* (1928), par. 10.

93. Nikos Nissiotis, "Is the Vatican Council Really Ecumenical?," *The Ecumenical Review* 16, no. 4 (1964): 373–74.

94. FitzGerald and Bouteneff, *Turn to God*, 133.

an end, new challenges arose: social polarization, secularization, poverty, marginalization, discrimination, and violence. Churches can engage together in an ecumenism of solidarity not in isolation, but in collaboration. As the Lund principle (1952) states, churches should "act together in all matters except those in which deep differences of conviction compel them to act separately."[95]

Unfortunately, some segments of Orthodoxy refuse to engage in ecumenical dialogues and activities, adopting instead an *anti-ecumenical attitude*. They invoke Tradition in their arguments, but in fact misuse it by taking it out of context, quoting it selectively, without a solid historical basis. Moreover, although unknowingly, they tend to regard manual Orthodox theology as normative, when in fact manual Orthodoxy resembles more closely neo-scholastic, Western theology than the Eastern patristic tradition, so, ironically, they tend to bring Western-type arguments against the West. Although Orthodoxy contains members who are too eager to embrace everything that is new and different than the East, the present author cannot discern any impact that they might have in the life—and especially the theology—of the Orthodox Church. So, at the risk of an imbalanced approach, this book will sometimes address only these anti-ecumenical attitudes, especially when they paralyze meaningful ecumenical discussions in the context of priestly formation, attitudes of individual bishops, synodal decisions, pan-Orthodox gatherings, and even official ecumenical dialogues that take place under the terror of their reactions to any sign of ecumenical progress. Concerning the latter, I speak from experience.

Pantelis Kalaitzidis considers that the most representative anti-ecumenical body resides on Mt. Athos. The elders' 2012 "Confession of Faith" denounces ecumenism as a heresy and refers to the bishops involved in ecumenism as heretics and apostates. Hence the more rigorous—in fact the minority of—monks at Mt. Athos do not consider themselves under the obedience of these specific bishops. In Kalaitzidis' opinion, such elders have forcefully replaced the rest of Orthodoxy as the judges of Orthodoxy, in the sense that they claim an authority that was not delegated to them and is not recognized as such.[96] That is not to say that all Athonite monks are anti-ecumenical or embrace an Orthodoxy that misinterprets Tradition. On the contrary, there are numerous

95. The 1952 Third World Conference on Faith and Order in Lund (Sweden). Quoted in Kinnamon and Cope, *The Ecumenical Movement*, 463.

96. Pantelis Kalaitzidis, "Quelques réflexions conclusives au term du colloque," *Contacts* 243 (2013): 624–25. An extreme case is the Esphigmenou Monastery on Mount Athos, whose brotherhood has been declared "in schism" by the Ecumenical Patriarchate in 2002. Consequently, the monks should vacate their monastery, since no schismatics are allowed to live on Mt. Athos, but they refuse to leave, accuse the Patriarchate of heresy, and do not commemorate the Patriarch.

instances of holy life, inexpressible love, and a most profound understanding
of the Orthodox Tradition rooted in deep study and prayer life on Mt. Athos.

Anti-ecumenical attitudes are found in small pockets everywhere in the
Orthodox Church. So detrimental have been their actions, that the delegates
of all autocephalous Orthodox churches that met in 1998 in Thessaloniki
"unanimously denounced those groups of schismatics, as well as certain ex-
tremist groups within the local Orthodox Churches themselves, that are using
the theme of ecumenism in order to criticize the Church leadership and undermine its authority, thus attempting to created divisions and schisms in the
Church."[97] Similarly, the Council of Crete condemns "all efforts to break the
unity of the Church, undertaken by individuals or groups under the pretext of
maintaining or allegedly defending true Orthodoxy."[98]

Crete's strong stance against these Orthodox factions is not surprising,
since they had already condemned the council before it even took place. In
the aftermath of the Council, some few but very vocal Orthodox priests and
bishops—in Greece and elsewhere—protested the Council, gathered followers, and stopped commemorating the bishops who signed the document on
ecumenism. In response, the Ecumenical Patriarchate officially appealed to
the Greek Synod to discipline these clerics, but to no avail.[99] Since then, the
centrifugal movement intensified, even though the Council proved to have no
discernable impact on the life of the Church at grassroots level. And yet, some
condemned it as heretical (a word used very lightly by those who consider their
opinions equal in authority with the decisions of ecumenical councils), without
ever producing a shred of evidence of un-orthodoxy. Such people, who might
have an aura of holiness and may indeed live an ascetic life, do not represent
the Orthodox Tradition and create schism within Orthodoxy. On several occasions I personally felt that working with other Christians towards unity is
more attainable than achieving unity with some fellow Orthodox.

The gratuitous accusations of blasphemy and heresy are already a warning
sign that history is repeating itself and that the efforts towards intra-Orthodox
unity are more necessary than ever, so that they do not develop in full schisms.
Once schism takes hold, even the most minuscule differences become unsurpassable obstacles, and that seems to be the case between those who opposed
dialogue and the rest of the Orthodox world. Without denying the existence
of serious theological disagreements between East and West, it might lighten

97. FitzGerald and Bouteneff, *Turn to God*, 136.
98. Crete, "Relations," par. 22.
99. See Bordeianu, "Getting from Conflict to Communion," 522–23.

the tone to mention here a most ridiculous one, namely beards. In 1054, when Cardinal Humbert excommunicated Patriarch Michael Cerularius, Humbert wrote the following accusation: "while wearing beards and long hair you [Eastern Orthodox] reject the bond of brotherhood with the Roman clergy, since they shave and cut their hair." In response, the East considered the Roman practice to shave clean as "Judaizing" (let the reader discern the meaning of this accusation), violating the "apostolic institutions" and the "ancient canons," being concerned with the feminization of clergy.[100]

Often arguments against ecumenism are very abstract, creating fear that the smallest rapprochement would have catastrophic consequences. They do not stem from one's *experience of the encounter with a real other*, but from constructions of the other based on outdated arguments from books that are no longer relevant, caricatures of the other, the reduction of the other to the lowest deed that they have committed and the lowest teaching that they have taught. Sometimes, people who have no contact with living Catholics and Protestants are the most vocal anti-ecumenists.

Experiencing the other in an encounter with their true selves is much more beneficial than imposing on the other an abstract, outdated, and inimical identity. In doing the latter, we often idealize our own faith and the way we live it, while assuming the worst intentions and theological consequences of the other. That is why, as my late mentor and one of the greatest ecumenists of all time, Geoffrey Wainwright recommends, we need to compare "ideal with ideal, best with best."[101] Or, to add an acknowledgement of our fallen state, always compare best with best and worst with worst.

Our faithful experience the other as their neighbor, and do not see the connection between anti-ecumenical abstract descriptions of other churches and their experience. A 2017 Pew Research study assessed the ecumenical attitudes of Orthodox Christians throughout the world and found that, overall, the faithful from across Central and Eastern Europe see much common ground between their own faith and Catholicism. The support for restoring communion with Roman Catholics is at first sight low, with a median value of 35% among Orthodox and 38% among Catholics, although the support differs from country to country, with the highest values being in Romania among Orthodox (62%) and in Ukraine among Catholics (74%). A deeper study of the findings, however, shows that only 31% of the Orthodox oppose communion with the

---

100. A. Edward Siecienski, "Holy Hair: Beards in the Patristic Tradition," St. *Vladimir's Seminary Quarterly* 58, no. 1 (2014): 41–68.

101. Geoffrey Wainwright, *Methodists in Dialogue* (Nashville: Kingswood, 1995), 277.

Catholic Church (and thus less than the 38% who are in favor) and 38% did not know how to answer this question, meaning that they are not certain what union would entail.[102] Thus, most of the faithful are in favor of unity, but much ecumenical education is still needed, as a large segment remains uninformed.

The ecumenical task is particularly challenging in countries that have an Orthodox super-majority, but it is not impossible, as proven by the 62% of Romanians who are in favor of the restoration of Orthodox-Catholic unity, as shown above. But in general, when the faithful of these two traditions are more equally represented and live in great proximity, they experience their commonality. In Bosnia, for example, 75% of Orthodox Christians and 89% of Catholics say their religions have a lot in common. In Belarus, 70% of Orthodox Christians say this, as do 75% of Catholics."[103] Living together in love is certainly conducive to ecumenism.

Moreover, as Will Cohen shows, the life of the faithful representing other traditions often differs from what has been put on paper centuries ago. Today's Oriental (Non-Chalcedonian) Orthodox are now able to affirm chalcedonian Christology, and many contemporary Protestants use icons in their prayers.[104] While some see St. Mark of Ephesus as a champion of anti-Westernism, in fact he made a significant effort to attend the Council of Florence with the hope to listen carefully to the other and come to a consensus, writing:

> There is truly a need for much investigation and conversation in matters of theological disputation (δογμάτων ἀμφισβητήσιμα), so that the compelling and conspicuous arguments might be considered. There is profound benefit to be gained from such conversation if the objective is not altercation but truth, and if the intention is not solely to triumph over others; ... [I]nspired by the same spirit [as the apostles at the council of Jerusalem] and bound to one another by love, the goal should be to discover the truth, and we should never lose sight of the purpose that lies before us; even when its pursuit is prolonged, we should still always listen carefully to and address one another amicably so that our loving exchange might contribute to consensus (ὁμόνοιαν).[105]

102. Pew Research Center, *Orthodox Christiniaty in the 21st Century* (2017), 14–39. www.pewresearch .org.

103. Center, *Orthodox Christianity*, 41.

104. Will Cohen, "Orthodoxy and Ecumenism in View of the Upcoming Great and Holy Council" https://publicorthodoxy.org/2016/04/12/orthodoxy-and-ecumenism-in-view-of-the-upcoming-great-and-holy-council/.

105. Mark of Ephesus, "Oratio altera de igne purgatorio," par. 1, in *Patrologia Orientalis* XV (Paris: Firmin-Didot, 1927), 108–9, quoted in Cohen, "Orthodoxy and Ecumenism."

If Mark of Ephesus' efforts to attain unity have ultimately failed, his willingness to dialogue is most inspiring. In fact, another saint wrongly championed as anti-Western, namely St. Photius of Constantinople, has succeeded. Because Rome recognized his unjust deposition, Photius accused the West of heresy, especially the Filioque. But once the schism was healed, Photius restored eucharistic communion with the West without ever resolving the issue of the Filioque! His example shows that one can listen to the other's formulations of faith and find acceptable ways of receiving them, without imposing an Orthodox uniformity, but that can happen only in a climate of love and openness.

Before Photius and Mark of Ephesus, St. Basil the Great addressed Arians and Semi-Arians who denied the divinity of the Son, and some also denied the divinity of the Spirit, which are major tenets of the faith that no Protestant and Catholic denies today. And yet, Basil went out of his way to bring them back in unity:

> I think that those who serve the Lord sincerely and truly ought to have this one ambition—to bring back to unity the churches which have been severed from each other ... For, nothing belongs so peculiarly to a Christian as being a peacemaker, and therefore the Lord has promised us the greatest reward for it.[106]

If Basil wrote these words about those who did not believe that the Son and the Spirit were truly God, if Photius restored communion with Rome without solving the Filioque, and if Mark of Ephesus made such efforts to attend the Council of Florence with a genuine desire for unity, how much more open would these saints be about today's ecumenical dialogue?

Having established that Baptism marks one's entry into the Church, the *Una Sancta*, and thus all the baptized are incorporated into the one Body, it is now the time to address one last change that Baptism effects, namely consecration into universal priesthood.

THE NEW NATURE OF THE ECCLESIAL PERSON: CONSECRATION INTO BAPTISMAL PRIESTHOOD

The service of Baptism affirms that the neophyte sheds the old fallen nature, in order to put on a new nature. During the blessing of the water of baptism, the community prays:

---

106. Saint Basil the Great, "Letter 114. To Cyriacus and His Followers at Tarsus," 241.

You have bestowed upon us regeneration from on high by water and the spirit. Manifest Yourself, O Lord, in this water, and grant that he (she) that is to be baptized may be transformed therein to the putting away of the old [humanity], which is corrupt according to the deceitful lusts, and to the putting on of the new, which is renewed according to the image of Him that created him (her).

The moral aspect of Baptism reflected in this prayer does not imply that those who are baptized automatically live blameless moral lives. That remains up to each person's freedom, helped through grace that comes from within the baptized person. As Staniloae writes, the heart is the place where Christ dwells since the Baptism "as in a Holy of Holies, in a temple or a Church of the Holy Spirit."[107]

While our response to grace remains conditioned by the exercise of our freedom, the dwelling of Christ in the hearts of the baptized is something that is accomplished in the service once and for all because the newly baptized person takes on a new nature, an ecclesial one. Outwardly there is no difference between a baptized person and one who is not baptized; even ethically, sometimes people who are baptized are less moral than those who are not, so Baptism does not bring a measurable ethical change. But it changes a person beyond what it biologically and ethically observable. Zizioulas considers that there are two "modes" of human existence: "One may be called the *hypostasis of biological existence*, the other the *hypostasis of ecclesial existence*." He maintains that Baptism moves us from "biological existence" to "ecclesial existence," from the finite biological life of this world, to life in God and the Church. Baptism is the act of the Church that brings into being a Christian. In this regard, Baptism is a birth from above or regeneration. But the difference between biological and ecclesial existence is not visible. Just as when one receives Communion, it tastes like bread and wine, but it is in fact the Body and Blood of Christ, even though it is not tangibly different from unconsecrated bread and wine. In the same way, the ecclesial existence of the human being still has the same outward appearance, but it has a new way of existence.[108]

This distinction between biological existence and being truly a living being is biblical. Adam was first created out of the dust of the earth, as were the

107. Dumitru Staniloae, "Elemente de antropologie ortodoxa [Elements of Orthodox Anthropology]," in *Volumul omagial dedicat Patriarhului Nicodim [Celebratory Volume Dedicated to Patriarch Nicodim]* (Bucuresti: 1946), 242.

108. John D. Zizioulas, *Being as Communion: Studies in Personhood and the Church*, Contemporary Greek Theologians; no. 4, (Crestwood, NY: St. Vladimir's Seminary Press, 1985), 50–54.

animals and plants before him, and all of them having biological life. But Adam rises beyond biological life into spiritual life when God breathes his Spirit into his nostrils, and it is only then that "the man became a living being" (Gn 2:7). One should not imagine God initially creating an inert corpse, since what is created out of dust has biological life, as plants and animals do. But with the breath of life from God, or the Holy Spirit, Adam moves to life in God.[109] As Sandra Schneiders remarks, this act will be repeated in the renewal of humankind in Jesus. The community of disciples that will later become the Church represents a renewed humankind. Both Genesis and the Gospel according to John begin with the words, "in the beginning," but while creation ends in Genesis 2:1–2 after the creation of human beings ("... God finished ..."), in the Gospel of John, re-creation ends on the Cross, when Jesus says, "it is finished" (Jn 19:30). Immediately afterwards, Jesus hands over his spirit/Spirit, thus making the community of disciples into a renewed People of God and a new humankind that now has the Spirit. This image will be even stronger after the Resurrection, when Jesus breathes the Spirit upon the disciples, which is how Adam was created in the first place, in Genesis 2.[110] C. S. Lewis similarly writes:

> A man who changed from having *Bios* to having *Zoe* would have gone through as big a change as a statue which changed from being a carved stone to being a real man. And that is precisely what Christianity is about. This world is a great sculptor's shop. We are the statues and there is a rumour going round the shop that some of us are some day going to come to life.[111]

Returning to Zizioulas, this "ecclesial person" or "catholic person," or "whole" person is always in communion, as opposed to being isolated in individualism:

> being a person is basically different from being an individual or "personality" in that the person cannot be conceived in itself as a static entity, but only as it *relates to*. Thus, personhood implies the "openness of being," and even more than that, the *ek-stasis* of being, that is, a movement towards communion which leads to a transcendence of the boundaries of the "self" and thus to *freedom*.[112]

---

109. Speaking of the martyr as the one who truly lives by the Spirit, Irenaeus asserts that "the glory of God is a human being fully alive" (Saint Irenaeus of Lyons, *Irenaeus on the Christian Faith: A Condensation of Against Heresies*, trans. James R. Payton (Cambridge: James Clarke, 2012), IV:20.7, 116.)

110. Schneiders, Schneiders, "Whose Sins You Shall Forgive," 55–61. She does not limit the breathing of the Spirit upon the disciples to the ordained, but to the entire community.

111. Lewis, *Mere Christianity*, 159.

112. John D. Zizioulas, *Communion and Otherness: Further Studies in Personhood and the Church*, ed. Paul McPartlan (New York: T&T Clark—Continuum, 2006), 212.

Thus, Baptism does not make us members of the Church in separation from others, but, as members, we exist in relation with the others. True ecclesial being means being in communion with God, other Church members, humankind, and the cosmos. That is why Tertullian found in Baptism the image of the Church as the mother that puts us into a new relationship with our fellow baptized Christians, a relationship of brothers and sisters.[113]

From the beginning of Christianity, this renewal of humanity through Baptism, this new ecclesial being, had a strong moral component, a commitment to a "newness of life" as reflected in the Epistle reading of the service of Baptism:

> Do you not know that all of us who have been baptized into Christ Jesus were baptized into his death? Therefore we have been buried with him by baptism into death, so that, just as Christ was raised from the dead by the glory of the Father, so we too might walk in newness of life. For if we have been united with him in a death like his, we will certainly be united with him in a resurrection like his. We know that our old self was crucified with him so that the body of sin might be destroyed, and we might no longer be enslaved to sin. For whoever has died is freed from sin. But if we have died with Christ, we believe that we will also live with him. We know that Christ, being raised from the dead, will never die again; death no longer has dominion over him. The death he died, he died to sin, once for all; but the life he lives, he lives to God. So you also must consider yourselves dead to sin and alive to God in Christ Jesus (Rom 6:3–11).

This new identity of the baptized Christian or, to put it better, the identity between Christ, the Christian, and all others who were baptized into Christ, was so strong in the early Church, that it *shattered some of the most significant social conventions of the time.* Despite the perceived superiority of the Jews as the elect over Gentiles, despite the claimed superiority of free citizens over slaves or of men over women, Paul writes: "As many of you as were baptized into Christ have clothed yourselves with Christ. There is no longer Jew or Greek, there is no longer slave or free, there is no longer male and female; for all of you are one in Christ Jesus" (Gal 3:27–28).

This identity between the baptized and Christ compelled St. Cyril of Jerusalem to say to Christians: "you are rightly called 'Christs.'"[114] This is indeed the new ecclesial person: Christ. As such, any form of discrimination against our fellow Christians is discrimination against Christ. The very impossibility

---

113. Tertullian, *On Baptism* 20.
114. Cyril of Jerusalem, "Mystagogical Lectures," III:1, 168.

of this statement shows how sinful, abnormal, and irrational discrimination is: people of all genders, races, ethnicities, social status, etc. are equally Christ. Later chapters will address discrimination in all these forms, as, unfortunately, it remains a problem today, and in some cases is worse now than in the ancient world, as in the case of ethnic discrimination: unlike in the Greco-Roman world, and in the later Byzantine empire, which were composed of a multitude of ethnicities, today we see a rise in nationalism in general and, in the case of Orthodoxy, a rise of ethnophyletism in which the Christian identity—and identity with Christ—does not supersede ethnic boundaries, but is divided by national identity. At the same time, the gap between the rich and the poor grows larger and larger: "In the present, the solidarity of Christians with the joys and sorrows of their neighbors, and their engagement in the struggle for the dignity of all who suffer, for the excluded and the poor, belongs to their baptismal vocation. It is the way they are brought face to face with Christ in his identification with the victimized and outcast."[115] Orthodox Christians cannot limit themselves to singing "All those who have been baptized" at Baptisms and special feasts, forgetting the continuation of that passage: there can be no discrimination, since all are Christs, and all are one in Christ, regardless of ethnicity, social status, and gender.

Another type of division that Baptism transcends is that between clergy and the laity. As we shall see in a later chapter, there is only one priest in the Church, namely Christ. The priesthood of the Church shares in the priesthood of Christ and the former takes various forms of priesthood, based on the charisms that each member of the Church has by virtue of their Baptism. Entry into the Church and membership into Christ presuppose a prior *baptismal consecration into the universal priesthood*: "like living stones, let yourselves be built into a spiritual house to be a holy priesthood to offer spiritual sacrifices acceptable to God through Jesus Christ" (1 Pt 2:5). The early Church maintained this same awareness, as reflected in Tertullian's commentary on the baptismal rite:

> After that we come up from the washing and are anointed with the blessed unction, following that ancient practice by which, ever since Aaron was anointed by Moses, there was a custom of anointing them for priesthood with oil out of a horn. That is why [the high priest] is called christ, from chrism, which is [the Greek for] "anointing": and from this also our Lord

---

115. WCC, *Nature and Mission Church*, par. 77.

obtained his title, though it had become a spiritual anointing in that he was anointed with the Spirit of God the Father.[116]

Contemporary Orthodox theologians, too, affirm that Baptism represents a consecratory moment. Schmemann writes that "the 'priesthood' of the laity does not consist in their being some sort of priests of a second order in the Church … they are ordained into the ministry of Christ to the world, and they realize this, above all, through participation in the offering of Christ's sacrifice on behalf of the world."[117] Moreover, Afanasiev dedicates an entire chapter to "The Ordination of Laics"[118] in which he brings historical evidence that Baptism was regarded as the sacrament of consecration to the priesthood of the Church. To begin with, Afanasiev distinguishes between "lay persons" who are regarded by scholastic theology as non-consecrated and "laics," a term that he introduced in Russian to denote the consecrated character of all the baptized. In response, Afanasiev contends that all Christians are charismatics, forming the royal priesthood by virtue of their Baptism—the sacrament of ordination of laics. To support this argument, Afanasiev presents several liturgical elements that express the similarities between the early celebrations of Baptism and Ordination, showing Baptism as priestly and kingly consecration: laying on of bishop's hands, the use of the verb "to serve," the pouring of holy oil, white garments, the cap (*mitra*), tonsure, the kiss of peace, and leading of the neophyte around the altar.[119] Thus, clergy and laics are united because all ministries are charismatic. Today, this communion is not as clear as in apostolic times. According to Afanasiev, the transformation of the distinction between clergy and laics into their separation was an unfortunate historical development, perpetuated by modern manual theology. This transformation was caused by the creeping of Roman law into theology during the post-Apostolic era, as well as Byzantine theology that regarded Ordination, and not Baptism, as the sacrament of consecration.

Building upon Afanasiev's insights, it is interesting to remark that the physical structure of the church can be easily misunderstood to perpetuate the view that the clergy are the only consecrated ones, while the laity are secular and profane. The church building has three distinct areas: the altar, the nave, and the

---

116. Tertullian, *On Baptism*, #7, 17.

117. Alexander Schmemann, *The Eucharist: Sacrament of the Kingdom* (Crestwood, NY: St. Vladimir's Seminary Press, 1988), 93.

118. Afanassieff, *The Church of the Holy Spirit*, 23–31.

119. Additionally, Staniloae notes that the candidate has to confess their faith at both baptismal and episcopal consecration, both of them being now tasked with proclaiming the faith. Dumitru Staniloae, "Slujirile bisericesti si atributiile lor [Ecclesial Ministries and their Attributions]," *Ortodoxia* 22, no. 3 (1970): 468.

narthex, usually separated by walls and doors. Thus, a church would have the main doors separating the outside from the narthex, doors that separate the narthex from the nave, and the three doors of the iconostasis—two diaconal and one royal. Which doors mark the distinction between what is holy and what is worldly? In the minds of many faithful who consider the laics as worldly, the altar and its three doors accomplish this separation. The association between the altar area and priesthood and holiness are very much ingrained in Orthodox consciousness today, though it was not always so.

Baptism represents a corrective on several fronts. As shown above, paschal liturgies still imply a procession from the outside of the church to the inside, reminiscent of the times when baptisms took place outside of the church, and then the entire community processed inside the church proper; thus, the doors that separate the secular and the holy are the main doors of the church, not the altar doors. In the era of the strong catechumenate, this distinction would have been made with the doors separating the narthex from the nave, since the catechumens and the penitents participated in the first part of the Liturgy from the narthex, and then they did not attend the rest of the Liturgy reserved for baptized Christians in good standing. Thus, the door of the church makes the separation; all those who gather in the church for worship are consecrated. This image is quite potent in Tertullian, who likens the nave to the ark of Noah in which Christians are saved from the flood of sin and receive the Holy Spirit represented by the dove with the olive twig symbolizing baptismal anointing into a consecrated priesthood.[120]

ONCE BAPTIZED, ALWAYS BAPTIZED

Throughout this chapter, I have prioritized an experiential approach to Baptism based on biblical accounts that reflect the life of the early Church, the rite of the sacrament, and several Orthodox practices, especially in regard to conversion. Out of this experience arose a dynamic ecclesiology, balancing experience and theology. In this brief section, however, I will give the appearance of tilting the balance in theology's favor, only to re-balance it at the end.

Scholastic theology speaks of an ontological change that comes with Baptism: a permanent stain, or an indelible character is imprinted upon the soul of the baptized, changing them ontologically into a baptized person, regardless

---

120. Tertullian, *On Baptism*, #8, 19.

of the choices that one might make later in life. That person could decide to
become an atheist or embrace another religion. Regardless of their choice, however, they remain ontologically baptized. How does an experiential ecclesiology
address this significant question of the identity of those baptized as infants
who have later left the Church?

This question is quite complicated when one considers both one's experience of conscious rejection of the Church, but also the experience of infant
baptism described above—unaware, but no less real. The answer is that, once
baptized—always baptized. Even in the experience of denying one's membership in the Church, the point of reference is still the Church—one either embraces it or rejects it, but one can never make abstraction of it. Moreover, our
identity is not always conditioned by a conscious act or even its acceptance: we
have no choice in being born in a certain country or in a certain family; we always remain marked by that identity. So also with Baptism and membership in
the Church. One cannot refer to a baptized person who consciously renounces
their membership in the Church as a Church-member in the same way as to a
person who embraces their ecclesial identity. But even then, the voice of Baptism will cry out as a call to repentance towards God's kingdom, sometimes
with surprising results. Such positive transformations represent an ecumenical
witness for infant baptism and its benefits.

For these reasons, Chrismation is not only the rite of conversion of baptized Western Christians into Orthodoxy. Chrismation is also the rite through
which a person who has been baptized Orthodox, having left the Church for
another faith is received back into Orthodoxy. Having received a valid Orthodox baptism, they are not re-baptized, which implies the recognition of the
permanent validity of infant baptism, despite one's personal choices in life:
once baptized—always baptized.

INSTEAD OF A CONCLUSION

A brief biographical note might best sum up this chapter. I was born in communist Romania under a militant atheist regime. My parents were the first
generation born during communism and their parents taught them the faith
secretly. Having never had the freedom to exercise their faith, and facing real
danger of persecution for their religious beliefs, my parents baptized me in a
different city, where they were less known. Understandably, given the risk that
I would divulge their faith to the persecuting authorities, they did not teach me

about God, though I later learned that my mother often blessed my brother and me with the sign of the cross when we were asleep. Throughout my early childhood I do not have any memories of ever praying, hearing about God, understanding the religious symbols that peppered my country but remained meaningless to me, or even knowing that some people believed in God ... not even that. I was neither an atheist who denied the existence of God, nor an agnostic who did not know whether God exists or not. I simply did not think about God ... until I had a "conversion" moment. I was sixteen years old, two years after the fall of communism, when faith in Romania was reemerging from the underground, stronger than ever before. The overwhelming majority of the people came back to their Orthodox roots, but some were also attracted to yoga-type spiritualities. At that point in my life I found myself at a crossroads: do I practice Orthodoxy, or do I practice a far-Eastern religion? I did not linger at that crossroad, not even for a minute, for I finally realized what I was all along: a baptized Orthodox Christian. A voice cried out deep in my heart: you are already Mine.

THREE

Family

A house is a little Church

ST. JOHN CHRYSOSTOM

Ecclesial experience is closely tied to the family. A person has a Christian identity from the moment of their conception or even before that, while the parents
desire to have a child that they will baptize into the Church. Throughout their
life in the womb and up until their baptism, these children have a Christian
identity by anticipation, which we found relevant in the modern applications
of the ancient practice of baptism of desire. Even before Baptism, the community of the Church prays for these children both privately and in public worship. Once an infant becomes a member of the Church through Baptism, these
prayers continue and, as that person grows, they begin to experience worship,
to learn about the faith, and to take more and more responsibility for their
salvation. All these aspects of religious life happen first and foremost in the
family, understood, in the words of John Chrysostom, as "a little Church."[1]

As this chapter attempts to show, the family represents a domestic Church
whose origins reach back to the first chapters of the Bible. Patristic writings
and contemporary theology describe it as the point of reference for *theosis* and
for intra-trinitarian relationships. The so-called typical family, which includes
a father, a mother, and a child (or several children) will be the focus of much
of the present chapter, but several other forms of family life will be discussed

---

1. Saint John Chrysostom, "Homily 20 on Ephesians 5:22–24," in *Saint Chrysostom: Homilies on
Galatians, Ephesians, Philippians, Colossians, Thessalonians, Timothy, Titus, and Philemon*, NPNF I:XIII
(Grand Rapids, MI: Eerdmans, 1988), 148.

here, ranging from tragic distortions of family relationships in the context of abuse, to monasticism as an alternative for married life. The priestly role of the family in the upbringing of children will then continue the chapter, with special attention to the "cultural Orthodox," whose identity is connected with the Orthodox Church but are not active members, and to children who grow up in an ecumenical context. The latter will lead to an in-depth discussion of mixed marriages with their challenges and ecumenical opportunities. Orthodoxy's practices regarding Orthodox-Catholic marriages put undue pressure on the family to artificially manifest our disunity even while the spouses experience their union with Christ as one family blessed by the Church in Marriage, so the chapter will conclude with a discussion of eucharistic sharing in Orthodox-Catholic marriages in the West.

THE FAMILY AS A LITTLE CHURCH

In "An Agreed Statement on the Sanctity of Marriage" from 1978, the North American Orthodox-Catholic Theological Consultation defined Marriage as the "fundamental relationship in which a man and a woman, by total sharing with each other, seek their own growth in holiness, and that of their children, and thus show forth the presence on earth of God's kingdom."[2] Others defined marriage as "a bond forged and nurtured by love and divine grace."[3] Clearly, there are multiple ways in which one could define Marriage, and each definition remains incomplete. But these two definitions should suffice to observe that the purpose of marriage is not merely procreation, especially when considering that people past child-bearing age can be married in the Church and that some families do not have children. The purpose of Marriage is also the spiritual growth of the spouses, their emotional support, and to provide the space in which their love—with all its physical and emotional implications—grows, nourished by divine grace. Given all these considerations, Marriage is an icon of God's kingdom on this earth.

Marriage is the oldest human institution, rooted in the beginning of humankind in the Garden of Eden. The longevity of marriage as an institution poses a significant challenge to Orthodoxy: marriage existed for much longer

2. Borelli and Erickson, *The Quest for Unity*, 202.
3. Bryce E. Rich et al., "Marriage, Family, and Scripture," in *Toward the Holy and Great Council: Theological Reflections*, ed. Nathanael Symeonides (New York: Greek Orthodox Archdiocese of America, 2016), 75.

than Orthodoxy itself, and the former is not dependent on the latter. Even in the history of Orthodoxy, although blessed by the Church from earlier times, Marriage did not come to be *considered as a sacrament* until the thirteenth century. It rested more on the Genesis 2:24 mandate that "a man leaves his father and his mother and clings to his wife, and they become one flesh" than on the sacramental life of the Church. It was a fundamental human institution protected by law, that is, the civil law of a Christian empire and canon law.

For much of the first millennium, Christians simply followed the social norms of entering into a marriage relationship, reinterpreting some older customs—such as the crowning of the bride and groom—in a new Christian light. The presence of the clergy was not initially required. In the eighth century an ecclesial blessing became one of several ways in which a marriage was considered legal in the Byzantine Empire, alongside the earlier norms, namely either an agreement or the common reception of the Eucharist, the latter practice going back all the way to Tertullian.[4] Even when the crowning service later appeared, it did not exist separate from the Liturgy. Hence, a pre-Christian custom such as crowning received a new meaning, connected with holiness and the Kingdom of God. As the priest lifts the crowns from the heads of the bride and groom towards the end of the service, he prays: "Accept their crowns in Your Kingdom unsoiled and undefiled; and preserve them without offense to the ages of ages."[5] The religious service became a requirement for the legal recognition of a marriage only in late ninth century, and even then it was applied only partially.[6] This requirement became general practice in the thirteenth century, primarily under pressure from an empire that required the Church to decide the legality of marriages and thus forced the Church to

---

4. The legal collection entitled, *Epanagoge* offers three alternatives for marriage, which can be "accomplished by a blessing, or by a crowning, or by an agreement" (xvi, 1). John Meyendorff, *Marriage: An Orthodox Perspective* (Crestwood, NY: St. Vladimir's Seminary Press, 1984), 25.

5. Tertullian (*De corona* 13) rejected the use of crowns, regarding them as a pagan custom. However, later Fathers such as John Chrysostom and Symeon of Thessaloniki regarded them as symbols of virginal purity. Recently, Theodore Stylianopoulos associated the scriptural imagery of crowning with authority and honor, with the coronation of the couple as king and queen in their own house, the incorruptible crowns of the martyrs, and Paul Evdokimov connected the crowns with Jesus' crown of thorns that suggests that perfect love involves crucifixion. See Theodore G. Stylianopoulos, "Toward a Theology of Marriage in the Orthodox Church," in *InterMarriage: Orthodox Perspectives*, ed. Anton C. Vrame (Brookline, MA: Holy Cross Orthodox Press, 1997), 13–14.

6. Emperor Leo VI's *Novella* 89 (issued around 895), states that "if anyone is married without [the blessing given by the priest], this marriage is null." Even then, the law applied only to free citizens, and not to slaves who comprised more than half of the Byzantine Empire's population at that time, so this same principle needed to be reiterated in the 1177 synodal decree of Michael Anchialos. Paul Evdokimov, *The Sacrament of Love: The Nuptial Mystery in the Light of the Orthodox Tradition*, trans. Anthony P. Gythiel and Victoria Steadman (Crestwood, NY: St. Vladimir's Seminary Press, 1985), 129.

bring into existence a rite separate from the Eucharist, and which could be given to those who were not canonically in good standing.[7]

During the programmatic atheist persecution in the Soviet Union and elsewhere, a religious ceremony of crowning was a great risk, while receiving the Eucharist together was less dangerous, so the Russian Orthodox Church recognized the validity of marriages blessed in this latter manner. For this same reason, John Meyendorff laments the practice to "remarry" couples that have converted to Orthodoxy after having been married in their previous Church; Meyendorff argues that their act of receiving Communion together shows that they intend to live together in accordance with the Gospel.[8] Similarly, Alkiviadis Calivas considers that the current practice of the Greek Archdiocese in the U.S., which insists that married converts to Orthodoxy need to be remarried in the Orthodox Church, "is untenable both doctrinally and canonically. The reception of married adults into the Church through baptism or chrismation should in fact complete and validate all other aspects of their personal life."[9]

On the one hand, the non-sacramental history of marriage provides grounds for recognizing the value of civil marriages and not assuming that the increasing number of Christians who do not bless their marriages in the Church automatically have a disordered spiritual life. A recent Pew research shows that a growing number of faithful (many who identify as such) live without blessing their marriages in the Church. The same study reveals that a majority of people are not focused on what truly nurtures a good marriage, such as being a good parent, being a good role model (quite significant in the context of the family as a little church), and taking care of the material needs of the family. Instead, they focus on other aspects of marriage, which are less important, such as shared interests, sexual intimacy, and sharing household chores; sharing beliefs remains important, but it seems to be lower in their priorities.[10] The Church obviously nurtures the positive values mentioned above and provides the context in which being a good parent and a good role

---

7. Meyendorff, *Marriage*, 27.

8. Meyendorff, *Marriage*, 24–25.

9. Alkiviadis C. Calivas, "Reflections on the 'Johnstown' Pastoral Statement on Orthodox-Roman Catholic Marriages," in *InterMarriage: Orthodox Perspectives*, ed. Anton C. Vrame (Brookline, MA: Holy Cross Orthodox Press, 1997), 171.

10. When asked what is important for a successful marriage, the percentages of Americans who answered "having shared interests," "satisfying sexual relationships," and "sharing household chores" were 66, 63, and 61% respectively. Those who responded "adequate income," "shared religious beliefs," and "having children" were 46, 44, and 41% respectively. Pew Research Center, *One-in-Five U.S. Adults Were Raised in Interfaith Homes: A Closer Look at Religious Mixing in American Families* (2016), 15, 29, www.pewresearch.org.

model includes a spiritual aspect in addition to the worldly needs of the children, thus making the marriage even more meaningful than a secular marriage. And yet, many marriages remain not blessed in the Church. Sometimes their reasons include regarding the wedding as a formality to such an extent that they request significant changes to the liturgical experience (such as having the service in inappropriate venues); irreconcilable differences in religious beliefs; and not wanting to be restricted by the laws of the church, such as divorce, or, in the case of the Catholic Church, restrictions regarding the use of artificial contraception, a restriction that the Orthodox Church does not endorse.[11] In a world in which so many marriages struggle or even end up in divorce, spiritual leaders should not, under the guise of rejection of artificial contraception, demand couples to have less intimate relations. Quite the opposite, they should celebrate the love between spouses, in its physical manifestation.

To say that *Jesus' teachings about family relationships* are complicated would be an understatement. At times he seems to have renounced his own family, such as when the crowd that was listening to him announced that his mother and brothers were there and Jesus responded: "'Who are my mother and my brothers?'.... Then he looked at those seated in a circle around him and said, 'Here are my mother and my brothers! Whoever does God's will is my brother and sister and mother'" (Mk 3:33–35). Other times he even instructs those who want to follow him to forsake their family relationships for the sake of proclaiming the Kingdom: "Let the dead bury their own dead; but as for you, go and proclaim the kingdom of God" (Lk 9:60), despite the Jewish sacred obligation to bury one's family. For N. T. Wright, these texts show clearly that "Through his actions and words Jesus was calling into being a people with a new identity, a new family.... This renewed community, a 'family' formed around Jesus, included all and sundry, the only 'qualification' being their adherence to Jesus and his kingdom-message."[12] Through these provocative sayings and actions, Jesus indicated not the abolishing of family relationships, but, on

---

11. A recent document produced by a commission of twelve theologians and endorsed by the Synod of the Ecumenical Patriarchate, states: "The Church anticipates, of course, that most marriages will be open to conception; but it also understands that there are situations in which spiritual, physical, psychological, or financial impediments arise that make it wise—at least, for a time—to delay or forego the bearing of children. The Orthodox Church has no dogmatic objection to the use of safe and non-abortifacient contraceptives within the context of married life, not as an ideal or as a permanent arrangement, but as a provisional concession to necessity. The sexual union of a couple is an intrinsic good that serves to deepen the love of each for the other and their devotion to a shared life." David Bentley Hart and John Chryssavgis, eds., *For the Life of the World: Toward a Social Ethos of the Orthodox Church* (Brookline, MA: Holy Cross Orthodox Press, 2020), §24. https://www.goarch.org/social-ethos.

12. Wright, *The Challenge of Jesus*, 69.

the contrary, the extension of family relationships to the community of disciples as a reflection of the Kingdom.

One of the most prominent family relationships that characterizes the community of the Church is that of fatherhood and sonship. God the Father has only one natural Son, namely the second person of the Trinity. At the same time, all those baptized in Christ are one with Christ or, as shown in the preceding chapter, they are Christs. Hence all the baptized are adopted children of the Father. In other words, adoption results in a change that makes baptized Christians fit for a filial relationship with the Father. Orthodox Christians are constantly reminded of the importance of being able to address God as "Father," especially in the Divine Liturgy, where the Lord's prayer is introduced by the following words: "And make us worthy, Master, with boldness, without fear of condemnation, to dare call you Father ..." Terms such as "worthy," "Master," "boldness," "fear," "condemnation," and "dare" are sure indicators of how awe-inspiring is our ability to call God—Father. The Church's prayer shares in Jesus' own prayer, when he addressed God as Father, or "abba" in Aramaic (Mk 14:36; see also Rom 8:15 and Gal 4:6). Thus, all the baptized are children of God whom they address in prayer as "Father" and thus sisters and brothers among themselves—a new family as an icon of the Kingdom of God.

This parental imagery would be incomplete without references to a mother. Since the faithful are reborn in the Church through Baptism, and Jesus' response to Nicodemus that "no one can see the kingdom of God without being born from above" (Jn 3:3) was an image for Baptism, the correlation between motherhood and the Church was prominent in early Christianity. As stated earlier, Tertullian found in Baptism the image of the Church as the mother that puts us into a new relationship with our fellow baptized Christians, a relationship of brothers and sisters.[13] Moreover, Cyprian of Carthage affirms that whoever does not have the Church as his mother could not have God as his Father.[14] Thus, all members of the Church are adopted children of the Father and the Church is their mother.

Another prominent family relationship that characterizes the community of the Church is that between the husband and the wife. Again, this relationship goes back to the Genesis 2:24 mandate that "a man leaves his father and his mother and clings to his wife, and they become one flesh." The image of the

---

13. Tertullian, *On Baptism*, #20, 43.

14. Saint Cyprian of Carthage, "The Unity of the Church," in *Treatises* (Washington, DC: The Catholic University of America Press, 1958), #6, 100. See also his "Letter 74 to Pompey," in Cyprian of Carthage, *Letters*, #7, 290.

union between a husband and a wife as they "become one flesh" portrays marital intimate relationships as the means for their most perfect union—a union that hearkens back to the creation of Adam in whose flesh Eve was waiting to be created. C. S. Lewis suggests that a better modern rendition of "one flesh" is "one organism," which in turn can be illustrated with two beautiful comparisons as only this English writer could offer:

> ... a man and wife are to be regarded as a single organism—for that is what the words "one flesh" would be in modern English. And the Christians believe that when He said this He was not expressing a sentiment but stating a fact—just as one is stating a fact when one says that a lock and its key are one mechanism, or that a violin and a bow are one musical instrument.[15]

Marital love is rightly celebrated in the New Testament where Jesus repeatedly referred to himself as the Bridegroom and offered the image of a wedding banquet as an icon of the Kingdom. Jesus' self-designation as Bridegroom, however, is not rooted in his marital status—since he was single—but in the Jewish tradition that God is the husband and Israel the wife. While the Old Testament sometimes uses marital imagery to criticize the faithlessness of the people of God (most poignantly in the case of Hosea, who married a prostitute to illustrate Israel's lack of faithfulness to the covenant), more often it illustrates the love between God and his people. Marital imagery is most powerful in the Song of Songs—a book that describes in great detail the mutual longing between a man and a woman, a longing that is never consummated in the act of lovemaking, but that is ever so intense. While this book may have started as a love song or a wedding hymn that never mentions God by name, it soon came to be seen—and for this reason was included in the Jewish biblical canon—as reflecting the love between God and Israel. Rabbinic literature often emphasizes the reason why Israel is the chosen people: not because of its worthiness, not because of its faith, not because of its military power, but for no other reason than God fell in love with Israel.

The same love imagery appears in Ephesians 5:21–33 but this time reflecting the love between Christ and his Church. In his commentary on this passage, Chrysostom writes about Christ that, "having left the Father, He came down, and came to the Bride, and became one Spirit. 'For he that is joined unto the Lord is one Spirit.' (1 Cor 6:17)"[16] Moreover, the image of the Church as the Bride of Christ becomes a useful complementary image to that of the Church

---

15. Lewis, *Mere Christianity*, 104.
16. John Chrysostom, "Sermon 20," 146.

as the Body of Christ. If the latter emphasizes the already-existing union and, to an extent, identification between Jesus and the Church, the former points to the distinction between Jesus and the Church, which makes possible their longing for each other in love. While the Church longs for its full union with Christ, the Savior longs to present it spotless, holy, and blameless.

The Orthodox Marriage ceremony designates Ephesians 5:21–33 as the epistle reading, to show the relationship between Christ and the Church as the model for the relationship between husband and wife: "Husbands, love your wives, just as Christ loved the church and gave himself up for her, in order to make her holy by cleansing her with the washing of water by the word, so as to present the church to himself in splendor, without a spot or wrinkle or anything of the kind—yes, so that she may be holy and without blemish" (Eph 5:25–27). This epistle reading is also meant to impress upon the spouses that the Church is a family and the family is a little Church, as in the epigraph of this chapter.[17] Even more specifically, the service of Marriage impresses upon the spouses that *they are the priests of their own family*. Led by the book of the Gospel carried by the priest, the spouses "dance" three times around the ceremonial table while three hymns that invoke the prophets, the majesty of God, and the martyrs, are sung to remind the spouses of their prophetic, kingly, and sacrificial calling. Significantly, these same three hymns are sung at the Ordination service (in reverse order), while other clergy lead the candidate around the altar table. Thus, the service of Marriage reflects the priestly calling of the couple: to minister to one another and later to their children, if God bestows on them this gift.

It is astonishing to remark that monastic spirituality was unable to find a more suitable image for the *union between God and the soul or the Church* than the image of the union between a husband and a wife.[18] Suffice it to bring to memory "The Ecstasy of St. Teresa" by Gian Lorenzo Bernini—perhaps the most beautiful sculpture ever made. A large block of marble comes to life and takes flight upwards towards the sky, as an angel lifts up the saint to heights only describable in sexual language accompanied by the moaning sounds that the saint made during her ecstasy:

> I saw in his hand a long spear of gold, and at the iron's point there seemed to be a little fire. He appeared to me to be thrusting it at times into my heart,

---

17. Earlier on, Ephesians describes the Church as the household of God in which all members are part of the same family, a holy temple, and as the dwelling place for God by the Spirit. (Eph 2:19–22).

18. Jaroslav Pelikan, *The Illustrated Jesus Through the Centuries* (New Haven, CT: Yale University Press, 1997), 131–42.

and to pierce my very entrails; when he drew it out, he seemed to draw them out also, and to leave me all on fire with a great love of God. The pain was so great, that it made me moan; and yet so surpassing was the sweetness of this excessive pain, that I could not wish to be rid of it. The soul is satisfied now with nothing less than God. The pain is not bodily, but spiritual; though the body has its share in it. It is a caressing of love so sweet which now takes place between the soul and God, that I pray God of His goodness to make him experience it who may think that I am lying.[19]

Monastic literature has overwhelmed Orthodox spirituality, risking to create the wrong impression that the married couple was either devoid of spirituality or was spiritual only to the extent that it adopted monastic norms, with very few exceptions.[20] At a time when manuscripts were assiduously copied by hand in monasteries, perhaps it is understandable that this would be the case, although, as a married person, I would have hoped for more graciousness and pastoral attention from the monastery towards the family. But when married theologians took the lead in Orthodox theological thought and when the printing press ensured the affordability of their writings, one would think that married Orthodox theologians—as the majority of notable theologians of the nineteenth through the twenty-first centuries were and still are—would have crowded Orthodox literature with the spirituality of the married couple. These married theologians could have emulated the model of married early Christian writers such as Tertullian or Gregory of Nyssa, who commented on family spirituality probably from their own experience. Other Orthodox theologians, such as Evdokimov, have tried to apply principles of monastic spirituality to family life, thus making the former the norm. But one cannot regard monastic spirituality as the standard of Orthodox spirituality and thus disregard the complexities of married life. Regardless, both older and newer Orthodox theology largely lacks a family spirituality. There are exceptions, such as Thomas Hopko, albeit only as a marginal aspect of his works. He writes on the spiritual commitment of the spouses prior to engaging in sexual relations and about the ultimate union that they experience in the act of sexual intimacy, perfected in God, as a prefiguration of our union in the Kingdom, akin to participation in Holy Communion:

19. *Autobiography* 29:17.
20. See examples of married saints in David C. Ford and Mary Ford, *Marriage as a Path to Holiness: Lives of Married Saints* (South Canaan, PA: St. Tikhon's Seminary Press, 1999).

Orthodox Christianity contends that sexual intercourse can only be what God willed it to be within an unconditionally committed, completely faithful, and everlastingly enduring marriage of complementary love between a man and a woman—a marriage that combines charity (*agape*), friendship (*philia*), affection (*storge*), and the desire for chaste and holy union (*eros*) in God's service. Such love never begins with sexual activity. Nor is it defined by it, sustained by it, or perfected by it in itself. The act of sexual union between a married man and woman is always rather the climactic completion of their mutual love for one another in spirit and truth, which is ultimately perfected in God. The sexual act is the act that reveals and seals the authenticity of their mutual faith and love in oneness of mind and heart, a oneness that is ever more perfectly fulfilled in the unending delight of communion with God through Christ and the Holy Spirit in the age to come. In this sense, godly conjugal union in this age is, paradoxically, a symbol and foretaste of humanity's conjugal union with God in the age to come ... In this perspective, the sexual communion of love in marriage is like the participation in Holy Communion at the Church's Divine Liturgy. The fulfillment of the total conjugal commitment enables sexual union to be, like a worthy participation in Christ's Body and Blood in the Holy Eucharist, "for the forgiveness of sins, the healing of soul and body, and everlasting life" for those who partake "in a worthy manner." And it is "unto condemnation and judgment" for those who partake unworthily.[21]

Such lofty words are no exaggeration to couples married faithfully, whose love is permeated by divine grace. The family is an icon of the Kingdom, a eucharistic reality, a communion with God, and a community of people blessed by Christ. Hence, Chrysostom's words are likewise no exaggeration: "the house is a little Church." As a matter of fact, in the same twentieth sermon on Ephesians, from which the epigraph of this chapter comes, John Chrysostom, too, emphasizes the eucharistic nature of marital relationships; as he explains the Genesis mandate quoted in Ephesians 5:31, that the two spouses shall become one flesh, the two spouses become one flesh and they beget a third that is also one flesh with them, and these family relationships resemble our relationship with Christ, with whom we become one flesh by participation in Holy Communion.[22] Similarly emphasizing the union between the spouses, but this time by use of trinitarian language, Theodore Balsamon concludes that the

21. Thomas Hopko, *Christian Faith and Same-Sex Attraction: Eastern Orthodox Reflections* (Ben Lomond, CA: Conciliar Press, 2006), 46, 74.
22. John Chrysostom, "Sermon 20," 146.

two spouses united in Matrimony are "more or less the same soul, which is perceived in two hypostases."[23]

Another way in which the family is a little Church is by making Christ present in their midst. In this sense, Clement of Alexandria comments on Jesus' promise that "where two or three are gathered in my name, I am there among them" (Mt 18:20): "Who are the two or three who gather in the name of Christ with the Lord in their midst? By three does he not mean husband, wife, and child?"[24] Implied here, of course, is the idea that a church is the dwelling place of God, which is appropriate since Jesus is God and the two or three form a temple.[25]

Before going any further, it is important to acknowledge that up to this point the family has been understood as a father, a mother, and children who live in harmony with one another. Most theological writings about the family assume this model and project it on the Church. While this is indeed the reality in numerous families and the Church, for many faithful, *the experience of the family differs from this pattern*. From the earliest centuries of the Church until today, some Christians lived their faith apart from, or even against the wishes of their families. For example, the third century martyr Saint Pelagia of Tarsus was denounced by her mother and condemned to be burned alive. Similarly, the fourth century great martyr Saint Irene of Thessalonica was denounced by her father; as a result, she was condemned to be trampled underfoot by horses.

Another important variation from the idealized family model is divorce and remarriage. Statistics differ in this regard, but around 50% of marriages in America end in divorce. This number includes those who got divorced for a second, third, or fourth time, so one could say that significantly less than half of U.S. adults are divorced. And yet, this number does not consider those couples who cohabitate without marriage (not even civil marriage), sometimes even having children, and yet later ending up in separation. Without those precise statistics, it is fair to estimate that half of the total number of adults in the U.S. have experienced either divorce or separation after living together with their partners. If one also considers the children that are involved in these divorces and separations, the percentage of Americans that are affected

23. Quoted in A.G. Roeber, *Mixed Marriages: An Orthodox History* (Yonkers, NY: St. Vladimir's Seminary Press, 2018), 68.

24. Clement of Alexandria, "Stromateis, Book Three," in *Stromateis, Books 1–3*, Fathers of the Church (Washington, DC: The Catholic University of America Press, 1992), 10:68 (1), 298, PG 8, 1169 B.

25. Jesus's saying is parallel to Rabbi Hananiah ben Teradion's later remark that, "where two sit together and words of the Law are spoken between them, the Shekinah rests between them" (Mishnah *Aboth* 3.2.; cf. 3.8.). Quoted in Wright, *The Challenge of Jesus*, 114.

first-hand by such situations is even higher, which means that more than 160 million citizens of the U.S. have been affected by divorce or separation. When considering children in such situations, one needs to acknowledge that most live not only with one of their biological parents, but also with a stepparent. Numerous children have tragically experienced abandonment by one or maybe both parents; they are either raised by a single parent, or in adopted families, or in foster care. Unfortunately, the situation is equally worrisome, if not more so, in traditional Orthodox countries. And so, the contemporary family can hardly be represented by the model of mother, father, and child (or children) as theology and church documents often characterize them.

Instead of such an oversimplified and unrealistic image of the family, theology needs to acknowledge the suffering of those in abusive or destructive situations, and to praise the parents who adopt, who provide foster care, or those who are good stepparents. After all, the Righteous Joseph is a model for stepparents and, if one considers that Jesus's "brothers and sisters" might be Joseph's children from a previous marriage, then Virgin Mary was their stepmother. Similar contemporary situations certainly deserve to be treated with due respect.

Special pastoral care is required for the victims of domestic abuse—most often women and children. A 2013 World Health Organization report indicates that globally, 38% of all women who were murdered were murdered by their intimate partners, and 42% of women who have experienced physical or sexual violence at the hands of a partner had experienced injuries as a result."[26] When women and children have suffered abuse at the hand of a husband or father, church communities cannot continue to impose on them outdated patriarchal models of unconditional subordination. Nor can we ask a person who has suffered such trauma simply to get in line with everybody else in referring to God as Father. While for most Orthodox it is beneficial to address God as "Father" for the reasons explained above, for those who have suffered trauma at the hands of an abusive father or husband, such a practice goes against the intention of Jesus's prayer to God and becomes yet another reminder of patriarchal structures of oppression. Perhaps for such victims, other biblical alternatives are advisable ways to address God in prayer.

Besides divorce, separation, abandonment, abuse, adoption, and foster care, several other situations challenge the so-called traditional model of the family. One must acknowledge that the picture-perfect image of a father, a mother,

---

26. http://www.who.int/mediacentre/news/releases/2013/violence_against_women_20130620/en/

and children (and a dog) is a Western model that is at odds with other tradi-tions. Sometimes Christians in Africa are engaged in polygamous marriages; while this might come across as shocking to Western ears, one needs to con-sider the cases when an Orthodox woman is married to a husband who is the adept of traditional African religions, which allow him to later take another wife, thus putting his first Orthodox wife into a polygamous marriage. Other times, a person who is in a polygamous marriage converts to Orthodoxy later in life, a situation in which the priest can merely advise the convert to live with the other spouses "as brothers and sisters," which in fact is not a realistic request and a divorce would be unjust towards the spouses who need support. The Bible, of course, is replete with polygamous marriages, especially in the Old Testament. Even in the New Testament, one also thinks of Jesus's debate with the Sadducees about levirate marriage, in which a man who may already be married also takes on the wife of his deceased older brother (Mt 22:23–26). In fact, this so-called traditional model does not even reflect the situation in the global West when one considers that many couples cannot have children even when they desire to be parents.

Another important challenge to the so-called traditional family model comes from contemporary Western society itself, with its religious pluralism and increase in marriages that are only civil and not ecclesiastical. Several Or-thodox theologians wrote in this regard:

> expressing a desire to investigate the acceptance of civil marriages contract-ed between an Orthodox and non-Orthodox Christian or non-Christian would indicate that the Church of the 21st century like the Church of the 1st century is unwilling to cut itself off from the wider society. Willingness to investigate this particular issue based in part on the Church's acceptance of civil marriages during the first 1000 years of the Christian empire (see for example Justinian's *Institutes* 1.10) would also attest to the Church's care and love for these couples and their children. This gesture of pastoral care might also witness to the Church's desire to draw into its transfiguring life the Or-thodox believer and his/her non-Orthodox or non-Christian spouse who, because of canonical restrictions, find themselves cut off from the body of Christ.[27]

Moreover, many countries have legalized gay marriages, often with size-able support among their citizens. The historic sources that condemn same-sex sexual relations attest to the existence of same-sex attracted persons throughout

27. Rich et al., "Marriage, Family, and Scripture," 78.

the history of the Church.[28] And yet, in today's society, the Orthodox Church cannot simply have a condemnatory attitude towards the persons involved. It also needs to defend all members of society and uphold consistently the dignity of the human person. The silence of religious people when they witness the deprivation of civil rights, violence, persecution, and discrimination of the LGBTQ+ community is deafening. Secular society seems to teach compassion and respect for one's fellow neighbor better than the Church, and these values cannot be compromised regardless of one's understanding of homosexuality. But how prepared are Orthodox parishes to minister to their own spiritual children who are gay or lesbian, while being guided by the principle that the Church is a family and the family is a church? A pastoral approach is necessary and slowly Orthodox authors are gradually addressing this need while maintaining the connection with the tradition; Thomas Hopko's book on *Christian Faith and Same-Sex Attraction: Eastern Orthodox Reflections* stands out in this regard.

MONASTICISM[29]

The earlier considerations about the new type of family relationships that Jesus inaugurated as an icon of the Kingdom of God would be incomplete if we only focused on the spouses and their children. A later manifestation of these new family relationships became monasticism. A monk or a nun is a person who takes on the vows of poverty, chastity, and obedience; they can live either in a monastery or alone in the wilderness. While monasticism is a vast subject, in an experiential account on the family one can only limit the discussion to the relationship between the parish and the monastery, between people living in the world and monastics, as they form one family—the Church.

---

28. The Orthodox Church practiced the rite of "brother-making" (*adelphopoiesis*) that involved the liturgical joining together of two persons of the same sex. Thus, if two monks struggled ascetically together, or if two lay people wanted to strengthen their bond and have their relationship blessed by the Church, they would become brothers or sisters. As Claudia Rapp has shown, this practice cannot be regarded as the Orthodox Church's way of blessing homosexual marriages. See Claudia Rapp, *Brother-Making in Late Antiquity and Byzantium: Monks, Laymen, and Christian Ritual.* (New York: Oxford University Press, 2016).

29. It would be a mistake to believe that American Orthodoxy lacks a monastic tradition. When considered proportionally to the small number of Orthodox in the U.S. (under 800,000), it is actually impressive that there are 79 canonical monasteries with 573 monks and nuns. The first monastic presence was established in 1794, when ten monks from the Russian monasteries of Valaam and Konevits established a monastery on the island of Kodiak, Alaska (at that time Russian territory). Alexei Krindatch, ed., *Atlas of American Orthodox Christian Monasteries* (Brookline, MA: Holy Cross Orthodox Press, 2016), vi, xii.

In the first three centuries of persecution, Christians lived a martyred life in testimony to the Kingdom; in contrast, the Constantinian era brought a significant degree of secularization in the Church. Christianity became a comfortable religion and even a state religion, giving rise to a new type of martyrdom—that of the monastics who protested the secularization of the Church, which had become too closely associated with the empire, with power, and with the world. While initially monastics escaped into the wilderness, they soon returned to the world and the Church. Monastics like Basil the Great cared for the world in charitable institutions that provided shelter for abandoned women, schools for young girls, and hospitals for the sick. Other times, monastics offered to the Church a saint like Maximus the Confessor—a simple monk who was never ordained even though he was promised the see of Constantinople in exchange for his silence towards the emperor and the hierarchy who imposed theological compromises. At the age of 82, Maximus' right hand and tongue were cut off so that he would cease to write and speak, and thus he ended up a martyr of his own Church. Shortly thereafter, monastics strongly defended the veneration of icons again against the leaders of their own Church and empire.

These historical acts of resistance against the secularization of the Church and heresies that arose even at the highest levels of the hierarchy cannot constitute precedents for the spiritual stratification of the Church. Monastics do not stand above the rest of the Church and the hierarchy. Monasteries that embody the ideals of Orthodox monasticism commemorate and remain obedient to the local hierarch, are respectful of parish life and marriage, do not place a heavy emphasis on sins of sexual nature in Confession, and do not regularly banish the faithful from receiving Communion. To do otherwise based on a negative view of human sexuality, married life, and living in the world, would resemble Manichaeism more than the ideals of Christian monasticism. In general, one discerns within Orthodoxy a healthy relationship between the monastery and the parish, for the benefit of both.

A significant *monastic contribution to the rest of the Church* is its life structured around liturgical services. If one's life is organized around work, childrearing, hobbies, etc., then Church services tend to be interruptions of daily routines. Monastic life, however, is punctuated by services and all the other activities take place in-between prayer, which helps monastics focus on the worship even when doing other activities.[30] For monks and nuns, "focusing on

---

30. I am grateful to Mother Christophora, the Abbess of the Transfiguration Monastery in Ellwood City, PA for her suggestions on the relationship between the parish and the monastery.

Christ" means being fully present in the liturgical life of the Church and their personal spirituality. This type of life centered on Christ in turn inspires the other members of the Church to be focused on Christ.

The impact of monasticism upon the rest of the Church is also palpable regarding the three monastic vows of poverty, chastity, and obedience. The rest of the Church looks at monastics as reminders that all Christians are called to a life of perfection, as Christ demanded of all his followers: "Be perfect, therefore, as your Father in heaven is perfect" (Mt 5:48).[31] Soon after the rise of monasticism, poverty, chastity, and obedience became regarded as "counsels of perfection," meaning that regular Christians have a different standard of Christian living compared to monastics who alone seek perfection and to whom these counsels apply. These monastic super-Christians patterned themselves after Christ, but the reverse is also true: they patterned Christ after themselves, referring to Christ the monk who lives in perfect poverty, chastity, and obedience.[32]

A life without material possessions is indeed a radical proposal. It was a radical attitude in Jesus' times, when land was the most precious possession and selling it meant renouncing an earthly kingdom for the Kingdom of heavens. It is thus not surprising that early Christians, for a brief time, "had all things in common; they would sell their possessions and goods and distribute the proceeds to all, as any had need" (Acts 2:44–45). As David Bentley Hart argues, this lifestyle represented the Kingdom of God:

> local churches in the Roman world of the apostolic age were essentially small communes, self-sustaining but also able to share resources with one another when need dictated. This delicate web of communes constituted a kind of counter-empire within the empire, one founded upon charity rather than force—or, better, a kingdom not of this world but present within the world nonetheless, encompassing a radically different understanding of society and property.[33]

It is true that monasteries live a life similar to that of the early Christians, but some monasteries in fact possess significant wealth, whether in land, rental properties, or other sources of income. It is understandable why St. Francis

---

31. The larger context of Mt 5:48 refers to imitating God in his perfect love for all: righteous and sinners, those who love us and those who do not love us. But because Matthew also uses the word "perfect" in relation to selling one's possessions (19:21), poverty became regarded as a counsel of perfection.

32. Pelikan, *Illustrated Jesus*, 117–29.

33. "Are Christians Supposed to be Communists?" (This essay originally appeared in the New York Times Sunday Review) https://publicorthodoxy.org/2017/12/15/christian-communists/

of Assisi proposed the radical idea that not only individual monks, but also monasteries had to embrace the vow of poverty. Orthodoxy has its own version of St. Francis in St. Nil Sorsky, who argued that monasteries should not get entangled into worldly cares and accumulate wealth, not even for the purpose of helping the poor, but remain poor themselves.[34]

In the larger context of his teachings on family relationships, Jesus also spoke about those "who have made themselves eunuchs for the sake of the kingdom of heaven. Let anyone accept this who can" (Mt 19:12). He was talking primarily to his disciples, some of whom were married. Peter, for example, left his family in order to follow Jesus throughout Israel, showing that "let anyone accept this who can" refers not only to those who embraced a celibate life (such as Jesus and John the Baptist), but also to those who embrace celibacy while on missions for the Kingdom. Temporary celibacy is an aspect of a life of chastity that mandates no sexual relations outside of marriage. For those who will never get married, or for people who are not yet married, chastity means total abstinence. But while sexual relations are a healthy manifestation of married life, married people must live in abstinence while away from their spouse, including on missions for the Kingdom.

Christ perfectly modeled obedience to God: "he humbled himself and became obedient to the point of death—even death on a cross" (Phil 2:8). This obedience is reflected in human relationships both in the monastery towards the abbess or the abbot, and in the world towards spiritual fathers, the clergy, or spouses among themselves: "be subject to one another out of reverence for Christ" (Eph 5:21). This was a markedly countercultural prescription at a time when only wives obeyed their husbands, and not the other way around. And so, it is not only the male who represents Christ and is thus due obedience, but also the female: the wife in the family and the abbess in the monastery. As such, monastics represent an important reminder that the entire Church is called to a life of perfection in poverty, chastity, and obedience.

Having established that monasticism and married life are simply two different vocations of being a member of the Church that complement and celebrate each other, it is important to acknowledge *a third vocation, that of single life*. Historically, this has not been considered a viable option largely because childhood used to be followed immediately by adult married or monastic life, as opposed to young adulthood. Today, however, single life is ubiquitous—even

---

34. Ware, *The Orthodox Church*, 104–08.

if not considered for the entirety of one's life[35]—given how late people get married, the median age being 30 for men and 28 for women.[36] Monasticism gives a significant testimony in this regard: one can be both emotionally healthy and live a life of abstinence. Young people who are not dating or are dating without engaging in pre-marital sex should be encouraged in their path.

The Church is thus a family in which Christians who are either single, monastics, married, or widowed form a community of love reflecting the Kingdom, and all these lifestyles are equally worthy as they are all different callings.

CHRISTIAN UPBRINGING

From an experiential perspective, parents who raise their children in a Christian household accomplish a priestly role that is an extension of their consecration as family priests in the service of Marriage.[37] The spouses remain priests for one another and add a new priestly role—that of parents. A child's introduction to the faith happens when the parents teach them the faith, pray for them and with them, and lead them to salvation by offering that child a religious upbringing.[38] The parents thus have the calling of prophets, priests, and kings, bestowed on them at their baptismal consecration and during the Marriage rite.

Another indication of the priestly character of parenthood is the Orthodox ritual of *the churching of an infant*. Forty days after birth, following the example of Righteous Joseph and Virgin Mary who brought Jesus to the Temple in

---

35. In what might be the only quasi-official Orthodox acknowledgement of single life as a calling, the document entitled *For the Life of the World: Toward a Social Ethos of the Orthodox Church*, endorsed by the Synod of the Ecumenical Patriarchate, states in §20: "As an Orthodox Christian enters adulthood, he or she will begin to follow one of three possible paths: married life, monastic life, or single life. While the three paths may differ in expression, they share the Christian calling in essence as the radical acceptance of love and sharing. Traditionally, Orthodoxy has tended to recognize only two states—the monastic and the married—but it would be a profound dereliction of pastoral responsibility for the Church to fail to acknowledge that, while the single life was very much a rarity in earlier generations, cultural and social changes in the modern age have now made it considerably more common. Some persons may tread more than one of these paths in the course of his or her life; for instance, a widowed man or woman might elect to take monastic vows. For most, however, there is only one path to follow, and it is upon that path that he or she is called to serve God's Kingdom and to seek union with God."

36. https://www.census.gov/content/dam/Census/library/visualizations/time-series/demo/families-and-households/ms-2.pdf

37. See the above discussion of the ritual circling of the sacramental table, while intoning the hymns from the Ordination rite.

38. For an excellent resource on Christian upbringing, see Philip Mamalakis, *Parenting Toward the Kingdom: Orthodox Principles of Child-Rearing* (Chesterton, IN: Ancient Faith Publishing, 2016).

Jerusalem, the parents bring their child to their home parish to be "churched."
After several prayers for the mother and the child that take place in the narthex,
the priest takes the baby in his arms and carries the baby inside the church
saying, "the servant of God [name] is churched in the name of the Father and
of the Son and of the Holy Spirit," consecrates the baby at the altar, and then
recites the prayer of Symeon: "Master, now let your servant depart in peace ..."
(Lk 2:28–32). The parents' offering of their new-born child to God is clearly
a priestly offering, and the image of the priest holding the baby while bringing them into the church and altar, and then reciting Symeon's prayer shows
that the baby is none other than Jesus and that all Christians "are rightly called
'Christs,'" as Cyril of Jerusalem wrote.

It is unfortunate that such a powerful ritual was wounded by either confusion or prejudice against women, or both. The majority of the prayers are
actually about the purification of the mother at forty days after birth and in
some—though not all—Orthodox dioceses the priest takes only the male babies inside the altar, while he blesses the girls outside the altar area. Regarding
the purification of the mother, Vassa Larin points out the historical factors
that led to the current custom of regarding women as ritually impure for forty
days after giving birth and thus their forbiddance to receive Communion and
come to church. While rooted in the Old Testament, the custom of regarding the female body as impure in relation to menstruation and childbirth was
challenged by Jesus, Paul, and several Fathers of the early Church; for example,
the Syriac *Didascalia* instructs menstruating women to receive Communion
as the woman with the flow of blood touched the edge of Jesus' garment and
received forgiveness of sins. But from early on in Church history, under the
influence of Stoicism, Middle Platonism, and Montanism (that had negative
views about the body and sexual intercourse), as well as Egyptian Christianity
that stayed closer to the Semitic heritage that continued to emphasize purity
laws, ritual impurity—applied exclusively to women, not to men!—became
part and parcel of Orthodox Canon law and liturgical life, also reflected today
in the ritual for churching.[39] The custom of churching only baby boys and not
girls is equally unsatisfactory: some argue that girls cannot later become priests
and so they cannot be brought inside the altar, when in fact most of the boys
do not become priests, either, and this service is about dedication to God and
not a precursor to Ordination. Both women's ritual impurity and the refusal to

---

39. Vassa Larin, "What is 'Ritual Im/Purity' and Why?," St. *Vladimir's Theological Quarterly* 52, no.
3–4 (2008): 276–87.

dedicate baby girls inside the altar are misconceptions regarding ritual purity. It is now time to consider the risk of sacralizing the sin of sexism if it remains incorporated into worship.

And yet, the churching of a baby impresses strongly upon the parents that as faithful members of the Church they have the responsibility of Christian upbringing of their children, of offering them to God and the Church. Parents reinforce this offering of their children to God every time they prepare their children to go to church. The "Sacrament of the Assembly" that Schmemann described[40] is the gathering of all the people of God for the celebration of the Liturgy. While Christians today do not process around the city in order to enter the church, but rather get their children ready and drive to church, the family's arrival for the Liturgy maintains an eucharistic character: it is the "Sacrament of the Assembly" that constitutes the Body of Christ in worship. As opposed to a view of the family as worldly or secular, such considerations present the family as a eucharistic "little Church" that brings the children as an offering to God and worships together. Moreover, the parental act of bringing children to church has a liturgical character, if that is any consolation to parents who struggle to get their families ready for Sunday worship.

While both parents are equally equipped to exercise their priestly calling of parenthood, recent studies about religious life in the U.S. show that four-in-ten adults say that their parents did not exercise this calling equally, one bearing more responsibility than the other. In most cases, the more responsible parent was the mother. The gap is even larger in families where the parents belong to two different religions, in which case mothers are almost seven times more responsible for the religious upbringing of their children than fathers. The same study concludes,

> adults from religiously mixed backgrounds are more likely to adopt their mother's faith than to follow in their father's religious footsteps. Fully 48% of those whose parents had different religious identities now identify with their mother's religion, while 28% identify with their father's religion and 24% identify with neither. Among those from mixed religious backgrounds who say their mother was mainly responsible for their religious upbringing, roughly six-in-ten (59%) now identify with their mother's faith.[41]

In other words, the most effective priest in the family is the mother. This reality will be crucial to future reflections on Orthodox family spirituality,

40. Schmemann, *The Eucharist*, 11–26.
41. Pew Center, *Interfaith Homes*, 8.

parish ministry, as well as the sacramental and administrative structures of the Orthodox Church. For example, how is ministry in the parish supposed to look today, when there is a clear need to support mothers in their priesthood towards the family? How do we account for the complex family dynamics when fathers and mothers do not fit the older family patterns and when many families take the "non-traditional" forms mentioned above? These themes are too important to be treated only in passing here, so they are best left for future studies.

What is significant at this point is that church communities need to have in place ministries geared towards parents to equip and support them as they minister to one another and to their children. Perhaps this is a deeply meaningful way to be intentional about *cultivating family values*. Insistence on the priestly role of parents is a much more relevant "family value" than other topics that consume contemporary public discussions about the family. Unsustainable work schedules for parents, as well as extracurricular activities and undue curricular burdens that our children face are among the significant factors that put stress on the family, and it is precisely in this context that the Church must place the emphasis on the family values that are most relevant today.

When Christian upbringing is central to a family's understanding of itself as "a little Church," children are more likely to retain their parent's religion when they grow up to be adults, whether this is the religion that both parents shared in common or the religion of the parent most responsible for their upbringing. The statistics are simply astounding: among those who grew up Catholic, if religion was important to their family growing up, 73% identify as Catholics today; but if religion was not important, that number drops drastically to 38%. The corresponding numbers for Protestant families are 89% and 67% respectively.[42] In other words, the parents' dedication to their faith and to the Christian upbringing of their children has a significant effect on the children's religious lives into adulthood. Conversely, there are parents who consider that the decision to be religious or not should be left to the children when they grow up, but that is certainly a misunderstanding. In fact, by choosing not to raise their children in the Church, some parents actively choose that later in life their children would most probably not be members of the Church, since there is such a sizable difference in Church membership between those adults for whom religion was important growing up and for those for whom it was

42. Pew Center, *Interfaith Homes*, 24.

not important. The latter are most likely to identify as "nones" later in life.[43]

A category that bridges active church members and the "nones" is that of "cultural Orthodox." In the sense discussed in the previous chapter, a person is permanently baptized Orthodox (once baptized—always baptized) and thus belongs to the Orthodox Church. Despite their choices later in life, they cannot change the fact that they have been baptized in the Orthodox Church, have been raised in varying degrees as Orthodox, and thus they maintain a permanent connection with Orthodoxy, even if only a cultural one. I propose to designate this category as "cultural Orthodox" as the equivalent of what others referred to as "cultural Catholic." Since only the latter has been studied sociologically, it is necessary first to understand what cultural Catholics are, and then apply the pertinent data to the Orthodox Church.

A 2015 Pew Research Center study identifies a significant portion (9%) of the total U.S. population who do not regard themselves as active members of the Catholic Church, but either belong to a different religious group or are religiously unaffiliated, and yet consider themselves Catholic in another way. Most commonly, they were raised Catholic and, even though Catholicism is no longer their religion, they still regard themselves as Catholic by culture, ethnicity, or family tradition.[44] More than a third of cultural Catholics observe Lent, occasionally go to Mass, and would want the sacrament of the anointing of the sick if they were very ill. Interestingly, 43% are open to returning to the church someday, in contrast with those who identify as ex-Catholics and who overwhelmingly (89%) say they cannot imagine themselves ever returning to the church. Moreover, 63% of cultural Catholics and 46% of ex-Catholics say that they sometimes participate in Catholic Mass, baptisms, weddings, funerals, feast days, or other events, even if they do not believe in them, because it is important to their family or friends.[45]

The statistics about the openness to return to the church and participation in liturgical services at the invitation of family members are quite relevant for outreach, providing information about both the addressees and the effective means of reaching out to family members who are no longer active. That, of course, should not degenerate into proselytism when the cultural Catholics

43. Among Americans who were raised either by a single parent who had no religious affiliation or by two "nones," 62% identify as "nones" today. When one parent was religiously affiliated but the other was unaffiliated, the percentage drops to 38. Pew Center, *Interfaith Homes*, 5.

44. A smaller number of cultural Catholics regard themselves as such because they are married to a Catholic, attended a Catholic school, or have an affinity for Catholic beliefs, morality, and liturgy.

45. Pew Research Center, *U.S. Catholics Open to Non-Traditional Families: 45% of Americans Are Catholic or Connected to Catholicism* (2015), 12–50. www.pewresearch.org.

are active members in other religious groups, but it refers primarily to cultural Catholic who are religiously unaffiliated and open to returning to the Church.

These considerations about cultural Catholics show how important family ties and Christian upbringing are, as well as the legitimacy of regarding the Church as a family and the family as a "little Church." Many of the aspects listed above apply to cultural Orthodox. Even if they are not active members of the church, they are still a part of the family, and thus cannot be treated as outsiders. On the contrary, the active members of the family have the duty to invite them to baptisms, weddings, Liturgies, and other liturgical rites, and provide a positive experience of Church-family life. Cultural Orthodox might be the most immediate focus of outreach, since they still consider themselves Orthodox by culture, ethnicity, or family tradition and have an affinity with Orthodox beliefs, morality, and liturgy. Many observe Orthodox traditions and occasionally attend Orthodox services, being even open to the possibility of returning as active members of the Church someday. When they do, they return to the home to which they always belonged—the Church-family and the family as a little Church.

MIXED MARRIAGES[46]—ECUMENICAL CHALLENGES AND OPPORTUNITIES

There are significant advantages to marriages between two faithful of the same Church. As Tertullian writes in *To His Wife,*

> Whence are we to find (words) enough fully to tell the happiness of that marriage which the Church cements, and the oblation confirms, and the benediction signs and seals; (which) angels carry back the news of (to heaven), (which) the Father holds for ratified?... What kind of yoke is that of two believers, (partakers) of one hope, one desire, one discipline, one and the same service? Both (are) brethren, both fellow servants, no difference of spirit or of flesh; nay, (they are) truly "two in one flesh." Where the flesh is one, one is the spirit too. Together they pray, together prostrate themselves, together perform their fasts; mutually teaching, mutually exhorting, mutually sustaining. Equally (are they) both (found) in the Church of God; equally at the banquet of God; equally in straits, in persecutions, in

46. "Mixed marriage" refers to couples in which one of the spouses is Orthodox and the other one is not. Other alternative terms are: "intra-Christian," "intra-Church," "inter-Church," "ecumenical," "inter-creedal," "cross-denominational," or "interfaith."

refreshments.... Between the two echo psalms and hymns; and they mutually challenge each other which shall better chant to their Lord. Such things
when Christ sees and hears, He joys. To these He sends His own peace.
Where two (are), there withal (is) He Himself.[47]

Here Tertullian convincingly argues that marriages in which both spouses
are members of the same Church and thus can partake "equally of the banquet of God" (i.e. receive Communion together) benefit from several advantages compared to marriages between a Christian and a non-Christian who
could not commune together. Tertullian's situation was certainly different from
contemporary intra-Christian marriages, where both spouses are Christians
but belong to separate churches. And yet, most of the benefits of Tertullian's
spirituality of the homogenous marriage spirituality apply to mixed marriages
today, since both spouses belong to the *Una Sancta*, though differently. The
only notable exception is participation in the Eucharist, which requires further
analysis.

Before discussing intercommunion in mixed marriages, it is necessary to
highlight some of the *difficulties that interfaith couples are forced to face* due to
our churches' disunity. In the case of an Orthodox married to an Evangelical Christian whose tradition recognizes only adult baptisms, the issue of the
children's upbringing faces the crucial question of whether their babies should
be baptized, which is much more difficult than other mixed couples' difficult
decision of where to baptize their children. Moreover, the presence of icons in
the home might be a point of contention if the Evangelical spouse vehemently
rejects icons as idols. The same applies to devotion to Virgin Mary and the
saints. All mixed marriages also have to face the question of involvement in
church activities such as Bible studies, charitable ministries, or financial support for both of the spouses' churches. Mixed couples should be financially
prepared to support their two churches unequally if one has a capital cam-
paign or simply greater needs. Moreover, Orthodoxy has a calendar that differs from Western churches. The celebration of Easter and Christmas on a
different date can be particularly challenging if the mixed couple attends these
celebrations in the Western family not only by attending church services, but
also by interrupting the fast out of respect for their Western hosts. The issue
of the calendar was supposed to be addressed at the 2016 Council of Crete, but
the decades of pre-conciliar preparation proved that Orthodoxy is far from

---

47. Tertullian, "To His Wife (Ad Uxorem)," in *Tertullian, Part Fourth; Minucius Felix; Commodian; Origen, Parts First and Second*, transl. S. Thelwall, ANF IV (Grand Rapids, MI: Eerdmans, 1885), Book II.8, 48.

reaching a solution in this regard, so the topic was removed from the agenda. While the calendar might be a less stringent issue in traditionally Orthodox countries, it is a thorny issue for Orthodox living in the West, especially in mixed marriages.[48]

Clearly, mixed marriages come with inherent disadvantages, and that is why studies show that in the U.S. the spouses currently in religiously mixed marriages are less religious compared to homogenous marriages. When comparing frequency of worship attendance, prayer, belief in God, and self-description of the importance of religion in one's life, between 51–54% are highly religious in the first group, compared to 77% in the second category. Moreover, mixed couples discuss religious matters less frequently than religiously-matched marriages.[49] Hence it is not surprising that, as Dean Hoge shows, mixed families are also less happy and have a higher rate of divorce, sometimes due to conflicts regarding the religious upbringing of the children, other times due to pressures from the extended family.[50] Other stressors specific to mixed marriages include the religious differences that might put distance between the spouses and the different values that religion nurtures. Once again, disunity among our churches has palpable effects in daily life and the ecumenical impetus is stronger in the case of mixed marriages.

By making religion a factor of separation, we also force parents not to talk about faith with their children in order to avoid disagreeing in front of them. The same Pew study quoted above shows that if parents do not share their faith with their children, the children's chance of remaining in the church drops by an average of 50%.[51] As institutions, we are responsible for this decrease in membership. By being married to a person of a different faith, the spouses are clearly ready to move past religious differences for the sake of love. Such an attitude is not reflective of a weak spirituality, but of a commitment to surpass differences. Institutional churches lack this commitment to unity, and our man-made regulations make it harder, not easier, to have strong marriages. When family life is already hard as it is, the Church has the duty to accompany families along their journey and support them, rather than impose undue burdens on them.

---

48. The autonomous Orthodox Church of Finland celebrates Easter on the Western calendar. Moreover, Ecumenical Patriarch Meletios Metaxakis proposed in 1923 that all Christians should celebrate Easter together on the third Sunday of April. http://www.oikoumene.org/en/resources/documents/wcc-commissions/faith-and-order-commission/i-unity-the-church-and-its-mission/towards-a-common-date-for-easter/celebrating-easter-together

49. Pew Center, *Interfaith Homes*, 11, 26.

50. Hoge, "Sociological Research," 90–93.

51. Pew Center, *Interfaith Homes*, 17, 24.

Rather than being focused exclusively on homogeneous marriages, an experiential approach starts from the reality that the Church is in schism and
Christians of different denominations fall in love, get married, and have a rich
family life. It is true that 75% of Christian marriages in the U.S. are homogeneous. Out of the 25% of the U.S. population that is in a mixed marriage, 9%
are marriages between two spouses that are of different religious affiliation,
while 15% are between one spouse that is religiously affiliated and the other
who is not.[52] These numbers are particularly illustrative of mixed marriages
as opportunities to bring people to the (Orthodox) faith, since most often the
Orthodox spouse is married to a person who is not affiliated, and therefore
missions through mixed marriages does not become a means to take away
members from other faiths.

The number of mixed marriages is only going to grow. Fully one-quarter of
young adults in the Millennial generation (27%) say they were raised in a religiously mixed family. Fewer Generation Xers (20%), Baby Boomers (19%) and
adults from the Silent and Greatest generations (13%) say they were raised in
such a household.[53] But within smaller groups like the Orthodox in the U.S.,
the percentage of mixed marriages is considerably higher, namely 69%! Clearly,
mixed marriages are the norm in American Orthodoxy.

The question now becomes, *what does family spirituality look like in interfaith
marriages,* given that the Orthodox family already has an ecumenical and even
multi-religious character? The importance of this question cannot be overstated. Children growing up in ecumenical families today will be the parents who
raise their children in a spirit of openness stemming from the dialogical nature
of Orthodoxy. The effort to educate the faithful about their religion and to be
welcoming to those members of their families who are not Orthodox is more
imperative than ever.

As Dean Hoge shows from a sociological (and thus experiential) perspective, some interfaith marriages result in the conversion of one of the spouses,
and represent a missionary opportunity for the Orthodox Church, particularly
when the faith of the Orthodox spouse is the strongest. And yet, such marriages can also be a challenge, since sometimes (or actually, more often), either
both spouses convert to a "neutral" denomination or simply lose interest in religion altogether. Approximately half of interfaith marriages result in conversion
to either the denomination of one of the spouses or to a "neutral" alternative.

---

52. Pew Center, *Interfaith Homes,* 10.
53. Pew Center, *Interfaith Homes,* 3–4.

Most conversions take place either at or near the time of marriages, or before
the first child is ten years old—a strong indicator that the children's faith upbringing is a strong motivator for the conversion of the parents.[54]

Instead of an inviting attitude, some Orthodox jurisdictions *create unnecessary difficulties*, based on an exclusivist ecclesiology that ascribes little to no
grace outside of Orthodoxy. That is certainly not the position of the Orthodox
Church when addressed as a separate, ecclesiological question, but it is the
case when applied to the experience of the lived faith in mixed marriages. The
unnecessary difficulties that Orthodoxy creates range from outright prohibition of mixed marriages to the exclusion of the non-Orthodox spouse from
significant aspects of Church life, especially the Eucharist. The harsh words of
Stylianopoulos are unfortunately warranted: "The Church as an institution is
sometimes selfishly strict in such matters not because it cares so much about
the welfare of a couple but because of strategic reasons—not to lose members
to another Church. But this is a moral and spiritual failure with regard to the
pastoral attitude of the Church."[55]

The strictness to which Stylianopoulos alludes here is the ahistorical and
artificial application of ancient canons to contemporary intra-Christian relations. Our pluralistic context is significantly different from the contentious-
ness that marked the interactions between Orthodox and either heretics or
other religions when these canons originated, so their application today is not
warranted.[56] Lewis Patsavos explains that there are five canons that prohibit
the marriage of an Orthodox with a non-Orthodox, with varying degrees of
intensity. Of these five, canon 72 of Trullo has the highest authority and refers
specifically to the marriage of an Orthodox man or woman to a heretic. At that
time, such a marriage was an impossibility, since marriages took place within

---

54. Hoge, "Sociological Research," 90–93.

55. Stylianopoulos, "Theology of Marriage," 28.

56. Regarding this strict application of outdated canons and the need to return to the practice of the
early Church regarding inter-religious marriages, Demetrios Constantelos writes: "We no longer live in
Justinian's Christian *Oecumene* and most people today do not subscribe to the principle of unity in uniformity…. With more than half of all marriages among the Orthodox in the United States being mixed
marriages, with mixed marriages among Orthodox Christians and Muslims in the Near East, Orthodox
and atheists (pagans) in Russia and elsewhere, how can we faithfully apply the canons of Laodicaea,
Carthage, Chalcedon, and Constantinople?… As the Church stands now, no solemnization of a marriage
between a Greek Orthodox and a non-Christian is possible. It is my opinion that the Church should act
and allow the blessing of such a marriage provided the Orthodox member wants it and the non-Christian
has no objection to such a blessing. The practice of the early Church, which believed that the unbeliever is
sanctified through his/her union with the believer, should come back in to practice." Demetrios Constantelos, J., "Mixed Marriage in Historical Perspective," in *InterMarriage: Orthodox Perspectives*, ed. Anton C.
Vrame (Brookline, MA: Holy Cross Orthodox Press, 1997), 69–70.

the Liturgy and involved the common reception of the Eucharist. But then—under imperial pressure—marriage became a separate rite precisely to make such interfaith marriages possible. Furthermore, Patsavos and other Orthodox canonists argue, these canons do not prohibit marriages with schismatics, but only with heretics (who were regarded on the same level with the pagans), so they cannot apply to today's Catholics and Protestants.[57]

The ahistorical application of such canons to intra-Christian marriages, as well as the lack of recognition of Protestant and Catholic marriages brings to the fore a deeper ecclesiological problem: are today's Catholics and Protestants members of the Church? The previous distinction between the charismatic and canonical boundaries of the Church has to apply not only to the mutual recognition of Baptism, but also to mixed marriages, especially considering that for most of the first millennium marriages did not constitute a sacrament. To put it differently, Catholics and Protestants are members of the Church *Una Sancta*, and therefore mixed marriages between them and Orthodox are permitted, and marriages contracted in Catholic and Protestant churches are valid, as intra-Church marriages.

The issue of inter-religious marriages is more complicated, since, as Patsavos mentioned, marriage did not originate with Christianity and, throughout the ages, the Church has made significant adjustments to allow such marriages, thus recognizing its sacramental character for the Orthodox spouse and the blessing that marriage is for the non-Christian spouse. Demetrios Constantelos writes about the experience of inter-religious marriages:

> Even though Islam, too, advocates endogamous marriage between fellow Muslims, marriage between Christians and Muslims was not an exceptional phenomenon. For example Theodore Balsamon, Patriarch of Antioch, writes that the Orthodox Georgians were not disturbed that their daughters married Muslims. And John Zonaras commenting on Photios' *nomocanon* writes: "I myself know that the Iberians (Georgians) who have accepted all from us give their daughters in marriage to Agarenes (Muslims). I wonder why the bishops, who know the Church canons, do not prevent such marriages." During the Ottoman period it was not unusual for one spouse to convert to Islam and the other to remain faithful to Orthodoxy; mixed marriages of Muslim men and Orthodox women whether in Syria, Asia Minor, or Cyprus were not uncommon. Some marriages were

---

57. Lewis J. Patsavos, "The Canonical Response to Intra-Christian and Intra-religious Marriages," in *InterMarriage: Orthodox Perspectives*, ed. Anton C. Vrame (Brookline, MA: Holy Cross Orthodox Press, 1997), 72–75.

contracted with the permission of ecclesiastical authority.... However, the marriage of a Christian man with a Muslim woman was impossible. The penalty was death.[58]

These considerations about marriages between Orthodox and non-Christians in various contexts show how divergent Orthodox practices regarding marriage are. The idea of a uniform Orthodox pastoral practice is nothing more than a fictional account that provides justification for restrictive practices and a lack of boldness to fully support mixed marriages.

ORTHODOX-CATHOLIC MARRIAGES: A CASE STUDY IN CHRISTIAN UNITY?

While the previous section addressed the possibility of mixed marriages in the Orthodox Church in general, in order to take the discussion even further and to speak more boldly, it is more productive to focus on Orthodox-Catholic marriages in the North-American context. They provide a special opportunity on the way to Christian unity, as this section attempts to show.

The Catholic Church regards a marriage between an Orthodox and a Catholic that is performed in an Orthodox Church as valid.[59] Instead of issuing a reciprocal statement, most Orthodox Churches have taken advantage of the Catholic position and have asked that *the marriage should always take place in the Orthodox Church*. If, however, the marriage takes place in the Catholic Church without a second celebration in the Orthodox Church, the good standing of the Orthodox spouse is compromised. One such example is the Greek Orthodox Archdiocese, which stipulates that "a baptized Orthodox Christian whose wedding has not been blessed by the Orthodox Church is no longer in good standing with the Church, and may not receive the Sacraments of the Church, including Holy Communion, or become a Sponsor of an Orthodox

---

58. Constantelos, "Mixed Marriages," 67.

59. Canon 1127.1 reads, "if a Catholic party contracts marriage with a non-Catholic party of an Eastern rite, the canonical form of the celebration must be observed for liceity only; for validity, however, the presence of a sacred minister is required and the other requirements of law are to be observed." (http://www.vatican.va/archive/ENG1104/__P41.HTM) This canon is almost identical to a stipulation in Vatican II's *Decree on the Catholic Churches of the Eastern Rite* (*Orientalium Ecclesiarum*) (November 21, 1964), par. 18, in Flannery, *Vatican Council II Documents*, 447–48. In other words, the Orthodox marriage is valid as long as the Orthodox norms are observed; the Catholic party only needs to ask for dispensation from their bishop regarding the canonical form (e.g. the presence of a Catholic ordained minister) for liceity purposes only, and even if the Catholic party fails to ask for such dispensation, the Orthodox marriage is still valid.

Marriage, Baptism or Chrismation,"[60] serve on the parish council, and some priests might even take it as far as to refuse an Orthodox burial to a person who was not married in the Orthodox Church. The underlying principle behind this regulation is that the marriage that took place in the Catholic Church is not valid and since the couple is not yet married, the celebration of the full service of Marriage in the Orthodoxy Church is necessary.

Most Orthodox jurisdictions follow similar regulations. Fortunately, however, the Patriarchate of Moscow and the Church of Poland recognize the validity of the sacrament of marriage performed by Roman Catholic priests, provided that the Orthodox bishop gives his prior permission.[61] In the same spirit, the OCA considers that marriage in the Catholic Church affects the good standing of the Orthodox spouse, but to a much lesser degree: their restoration to full communion requires only the sacrament of Confession. If an additional blessing of the marriage is required, it does not involve the full Orthodox Wedding service, as in Greek practice. Instead, there is an alternate service of blessing an already-existing marital union, since the marriage in the Catholic Church is considered valid. For example, instead of praying for the couple as "now being united in the community of marriage," the OCA liturgical text asks for "God's protection over their life together," without implying that they are not already married.

Patsavos similarly argues that, since marriage did not begin with the Christian revelation and its essential element is marital consent, marriages outside the Church should not automatically jeopardize one's standing in the Orthodox Church. He recommends that the Greek Archdiocese follow the practice of other jurisdictions (such as the OCA) to consider a marriage contracted outside the Orthodox Church as "a violation of canonical discipline, not necessarily an empty form without substance. As such, restoration to communion of the Orthodox partner necessitates an act of contrition, not a celebration of the marriage rite as if there had never been a marriage."[62]

It is important to remember that while the Orthodox and Catholic churches were united, their understanding of marriage did not constitute a dividing point. Throughout most of the first millennium, neither East nor West had a clear understanding of Marriage as a sacrament. When they later started articulating their respective understandings of Marriage—including whether the

60. *2019 Yearbook* – "Pastoral Guidelines" 272. https://s3.amazonaws.com/goa-yearbook/2019-yearbook.pdf

61. Borelli and Erickson, *The Quest for Unity*, 214.

62. Patsavos, "Canonical Response," 79–80.

emphasis falls on the contractual aspect of Marriage, on the priest or bishop as celebrants, or on the consent of the couple—they regarded these differences as diversity-in-unity. Such was the case well into the second millennium, and neither of the two churches made any major changes in the meantime. What did not constitute grounds for lack of recognition then, should not divide now. Certainly, they should not compromise the good standing of the Orthodox spouse.

Another important aspect of mixed marriages is *the faith in which the children should be raised.* Until recently, Orthodox churches used to require the Catholic spouse to promise, verbally or even in writing, to raise their children in the Orthodox Church.[63] Most parishes have today abandoned this practice. In some cases, the subject of the faith of the children can cause significant conflicts, as, for example, when the parents are Orthodox and Baptist, respectively. If the former regards Baptism as entry into the Church and thus insists on baptizing their babies, the latter considers infant baptism as invalid and thus opposes baptizing their babies in either church. But Orthodox-Catholic marriages are certainly different because of the mutual recognition of infant Baptism and the mutual recognition of each other's status *as Church.* In this case, the conviction that the children will be raised in a *Church* alleviates the tensions inherent in deciding the ecclesial upbringing of the children. For this reason, both the North American Orthodox Theological Consultation in 1980 and the Joint Committee of Orthodox and Roman Catholic bishops in 1990 recommend that the decision of the children's church membership should rest with the parents. When it is clear that one parent will be more committed to their faith than the other, the children should be raised in the tradition of the parent who is most committed to their faith. Acknowledging that this decision is more difficult when both parents are committed to their respective faiths and that children might be raised in both churches, both of these dialogues conclude that the decision of the parents is made in good conscience given that both Orthodox and Catholics regard each other *as Church*: "This is possible because of the proximity of doctrine and practice of our churches, which enables each to a high degree to see the other precisely as *Church* [emphasis in the original]."[64]

This important ecclesiological statement is yet another example of the ben-

63. For example, the pastoral guidelines of the OCA read: "It is indeed possible for a Catholic to marry in the Orthodox Church without converting but agreeing to raise the children in the Orthodox Faith." https://oca.org/questions/sacramentmarriage/inter-faith-marriage

64. Borelli and Erickson, *The Quest for Unity,* 207–8, 41.

efits of an experiential approach to ecclesiology, stemming from the experience of unity in mixed marriages, which emphasizes the essential aspects of doctrine and practice that Orthodox and Catholics share. Unity is much more prevalent in such an experiential ecclesiology than in a purely theoretical approach.[65] Indeed, given our separate history and cultural contexts, *some theological differences between the Orthodox and Catholic understandings of marriage remain*, such as the celebrant of the sacrament: the priest or bishop in Orthodox practice, and the couple as witnessed by a bishop, priest, or deacon in Catholic practice; and yet, both traditions require an ecclesial intervention.[66] While acknowledging these differences, the North American Orthodox and Catholic bishops have declared together in Johnstown (1990):

> We do not wish to underestimate the seriousness of these differences in practice and theological explanation. We consider their further study to be desirable. At the same time, we wish to emphasize our fundamental agreement. Both our churches have always agreed that ecclesial context is constitutive of the Christian sacrament of marriage. Within this fundamental agreement, history has shown various possibilities of realization so that no one particular form of expressing this ecclesial context may be considered absolutely normative in all circumstances for both churches. In our judgment, our present differences of practice and theology concerning the required ecclesial context for marriage pertain to the level of secondary theological reflection rather than to the level of dogma.[67]

As a result of their study, the Orthodox and Catholic bishops made several significant recommendations, which some Orthodox jurisdictions (especially the OCA) already practice, while others are still awaiting implementation:

> We recommend that when an Orthodox and Catholic marry there be only one liturgical ceremony in which either one or both priests are present, with the rite being that of the officiating priest. The guest priest, normally dressed in cassock, would be invited to greet the bride and groom and to offer a prayer toward the end of the ceremony. We recommend that such marriages be recorded in the registries of both churches. We recommend

---

65. See for example the previous discussion on the Council of Crete's hesitation and inconsistency regarding the Orthodox recognition of other Christians as Churches.

66. In (highly) exceptional cases, the Roman Catholic Church allows a man and a woman to marry without the blessing of a clergyman. For example, if a priest is absent for more than one month, they can marry in the presence of two witnesses, but must obtain the blessing of a clergyman as soon as practically possible. This practice is not acceptable in other *sui generis* Catholic churches, such as Byzantine Catholic.

67. Borelli and Erickson, *The Quest for Unity*, 239–40.

that in the case of marriages celebrated in the past, if it should be decided that some supplementary liturgical action is needed for a member to be readmitted to full eucharistic communion in one's church, care should be taken that this liturgical celebration avoid the impression of being another marriage ceremony thereby implying that what had already taken place was not a marriage.[68]

Presently there is a great diversity of practices among Orthodox jurisdictions and such recommendations might seem unattainable for some. But the task of theology is to study the tradition carefully, to be sensitive to the pastoral needs of the faithful, and to make recommendations even when they seem bold. Nothing short of the spiritual well-being and salvation of souls is at stake. In this spirit, it is now inevitable to address the subject of *eucharistic sharing in Orthodox-Catholic marriages in the West.*[69]

Most Orthodox would say that they do not recognize or share the sacraments with other Christians. In actuality, such a statement is incorrect on both counts: the Orthodox recognize the validity of non-Orthodox sacraments and even go beyond simple recognition, to offering Orthodox sacraments to non-Orthodox. As shown above (and leaving anti-ecumenical groups aside), most Orthodox recognize others' baptisms as valid. At various times in history, if a Catholic person wanted to become Russian Orthodox, they were not chrismated, but received through Confession; so (at least Russian) Orthodox Christians also recognize the sacrament of Chrismation in the Catholic Church. If a Catholic priest becomes Orthodox, he is not re-ordained, but simply appointed into a parish, because we share in the sacrament of Ordination. As stated in this chapter, some Orthodox jurisdictions also recognize Catholic marriages, so the Orthodox spouse shares in a Catholic sacrament. It is noteworthy that, when a mixed marriage takes place in an Orthodox parish, the Orthodox Church offers this sacrament to both spouses. In this case, Marriage involves the administration of an Orthodox sacrament to another Christian, not simply mutual recognition of a Catholic sacrament, as in the case of Baptism, Chrismation, Priesthood, and Marriage. A similar argument for administering Orthodox sacraments to non-Orthodox can be made for Confession and Holy Unction in cases of pastoral necessity, as is sometimes the practice. The Orthodox priest should not be like the priest and the Levite from the parable

68. Borelli and Erickson, *The Quest for Unity*, 243.
69. A similar version of this section was published in Radu Bordeianu, "Eucharistic Hospitality: An Experiential Approach to Recent Orthodox Theology," *Journal of Ecumenical Studies* 54, no. 1 (2019): 5–24.

of the Good Samaritan, who refused to anoint and care for the person who was in need. Such attitudes that are contrary to the spirit of the Gospel stem from the misconception that the Orthodox do not share the sacraments with other Christians, which does not correspond to reality.

It is also surprising to see the insistence of those who refuse the sacraments to Western Christians, given that the majority of most patristic literature did not accept the designation of the seven sacraments as we do today. As I have argued elsewhere, while the East first designated the seven sacraments in the thirteenth century, this designation became commonplace only much later, with the manual tradition. More recent Orthodox theology has accepted the differentiation of the seven sacraments from the other rites of the Church under the influence of the West, in an exercise of open sobornicity understood as the acceptance of valid theological insights from other theological traditions, in this case the Catholic tradition.[70] Parts of the Orthodox tradition add to the number seven for sacraments important rites such as the anointing of a Church, burial, and tonsure into monasticism.[71] It is both ironic and tragic that the strict separation between the seven sacraments from the other rites of the Church is a Western influence, and yet it represents the basis for refusing all sacraments to Western Christians.

Sharing the Eucharist (or intercommunion) is a complex topic to which we shall return in a subsequent chapter. Suffice it to say here that, while the Orthodox recognize the validity of the Catholic Eucharist, they generally reject intercommunion. Some Orthodox, however, speak openly about the ecumenical practices in their specific context, which involve a common religious life and intercommunion. For example,

> In Lebanon and Syria it is not uncommon for Orthodox to marry Christians of other denominations, particularly Melkite Catholics or Maronites. Ancient custom obliges the woman to follow the religion of her husband, and the children likewise. The clergy of all three churches accept this custom without question and almost without exception. The result is that in

---

70. Bordeianu, *Dumitru Staniloae*, 27–30, 33–38.

71. For example, Theodore Studite omits three modern sacraments: anointing, confession, and marriage. The Byzantine adoption of seven sacraments first occurred at the Synod of Cyprus (1260), followed by the profession of Emperor Michael VIII Paleologus after the Synod of Lyons (1274). But the issue was far from being settled. For example, in the fifteenth century, Joasaph of Ephesus lists the dedication of a church, the rite of those who died in the Lord, and tonsure into monasticism in addition to the seven sacraments. Moreover, Symeon of Thessalonica bifurcates marriage into monastic tonsure and the marriage. Christiaan Kappes, "A New Narrative for the Reception of Seven Sacraments into Orthodoxy: Peter Lombard's *Sentences* in Nicholas Cabasilas and Symeon of Thessalonica and the Utilization of John Duns Scotus by the Holy *Synaxis*," *Nova et Vetera* 15, no. 2 (2017): 467–83.

those villages or cities where all three churches are present, the congregations of each are intimately interrelated with the others.... Among the earlier generations, and among the recent immigrants, young people tend to
marry exclusively within the Arabic community even though they do not
discriminate among the three churches.... Also, these families sometimes
practice religion in both churches to varying degrees. Because of immediate
family ties, Orthodox are often called upon to be god-parents and best-men
in Roman Catholic ceremonies.... At funeral and wedding masses as well,
Orthodox in these family situations feel comfortable communing in the
Catholic Church. Sometimes, whole Orthodox families make a habit of attending mass with their Roman Catholic relatives on the greater Holy Days,
especially Christmas and Easter and communing there as well.... Once
again, even though official written policy of the Archdiocese forbids such
[practices, they do] occur to varying degrees in older, "ethnic" parishes.[72]

Without ignoring the fact that in the above example the wife converts to
the faith of the husband, Orthodoxy in the Middle East seems to be much
more prepared to embrace a pastoral attitude towards the extended Orthodox and Catholic families, that even after conversion the spouses commune in
the other church, and that such open practices are the norm, rather than the
exception.[73]

At the other side of the spectrum, Orthodox jurisdictions in the U.S. do
not allow intercommunion. Having had their marriage blessed in the Orthodox Church, mixed families regularly worship together at the Orthodox parish
and Catholic spouses refrain from receiving Communion altogether, since they
rarely attend Catholic parishes. The Catholic spouse often gets involved in the
outreach ministries of our Orthodox parishes, attends Bible studies, sends
the children to Sunday School and youth groups. As an Orthodox priest, I can
say that, practically, these Catholics belong to us ... until it comes to some inevitable aspects of pastoral life. When they get sick, we visit them in the hospital,

72. Edward Hughes, "Reflections on Mixed Marriage in the Context of Parish Ministry," in *Inter-Marriage: Orthodox Perspectives*, ed. Anton C. Vrame (Brookline, MA: Holy Cross Orthodox Press, 1997), 152–54. On the other hand, John Meyendorff rejects intercommunion or mixed marriages. He propos-es that intra-Orthodox marriages be celebrated as part of the Divine Liturgy with the couple receiving Communion together, while mixed marriages as well as second and third marriages take place outside the Liturgy with a different rite, thus showing that such marriages are not the first choice of the Orthodox Church. Meyendorff, *Marriage*, 50–54.

73. In regard to Orthodoxy's relationship with Oriental Orthodox Churches, the 2001 "Pastoral Agreement Between the Coptic Orthodox and Greek Orthodox Patriarchates of Alexandria" states that "each of the two Patriarchates shall ... accept to perform all of its other sacraments to that new family of Mixed Christian Marriage," presumably inclusive of the Eucharist. Quoted in Roeber, *Mixed Marriages*, 202–03.

and yet we are not allowed to anoint them with Holy Unction but only use blessed oil ... because they are not Orthodox. We are not allowed to offer them the sacrament of Confession but only listen to them and counsel them ... because they are not Orthodox. When their parents die, we are not allowed to have a Memorial service with kollyva, but only a Trisagion service ... because they are not Orthodox. The list could, unfortunately, continue even further, but these elements are sufficient to show that, after many years of attending an Orthodox church, they do not call a Catholic priest; they simply remain devoid of sacramental care, even though that care is available in *their own* Orthodox parish that nonetheless has to live according to the misconceived principle that "the Orthodox Church does not share its sacraments with other churches." Acting otherwise could be extremely dangerous for the parish priest who could be disciplined severely, with significant consequences for his family.... But it need not be so.

Could the Orthodox Church living in the West extend eucharistic hospitality to a Catholic spouse married to an Orthodox? A later chapter will address extensively the interruption of eucharistic sharing between Orthodox and Catholics. At the heart of the division stood papal primacy and infallibility. Having already spilled quite a lot of ink on this issue,[74] I do not want to diminish the importance of this theme *for theologians and hierarchs*. But when taking an experiential approach, trying to understand what papal primacy means to ordinary Catholics and how it affects the spirituality of Orthodox faithful, one concludes that papal primacy and infallibility are not Church-dividing at *grassroots levels*. So, there is a disconnect between the theological and experiential approaches. Again, it need not be so.

A good place to start is by looking at Orthodox-Catholic marriages in the West, from the prism of *oikonomia*. When a Catholic and an Orthodox are married in either one of our churches, we bless their union of love in the Church and they become "one flesh," one organism in Christ. If the family is a "little church," as St. John Chrysostom contended, then in the sacrament of Marriage, the two become one church, while remaining Orthodox and Catholic, respectively. Interfaith marriages transcend our divisions. In their "little church," the Church is one. And since "the Eucharist makes the Church,"[75] the "little church" of mixed couples should manifest the unified eucharistic being of the Church by engaging in eucharistic sharing. In other words, Orthodox

74. Radu Bordeianu, "Primacies and Primacy according to John Zizioulas," *St. Vladimir's Theological Quarterly* 58, no. 1 (2014): 5–24.
75. See chapter five.

bishops located in the West should allow Orthodox priests to offer the Eucharist to Catholic spouses who attend their parishes.

It is inconsistent to affirm the eucharistic nature of the Church, the union in Christ of the two spouses, to bless that union in the Orthodox Church, but then to deny the Catholic spouse the Eucharist. It is self-contradictory to bless Catholic-Orthodox marriages and then ask the spouses to manifest our disunity in their marriages, to transform their "little church" into a "disunited little church." When the children are baptized Orthodox, the Catholic spouse can never commune with their children! This experience of disunity at the level of the family becomes even more tragic when considering the reason invoked by the Orthodox for refusing eucharistic sharing, namely papal primacy and infallibility. Again, this topic is important for bishops and theologians, but we need to discern the impact of our theological quarrels on the mixed marriages in our communities. In this sense, A. G. Roeber asks rhetorically (and later suggests a positive answer) whether Orthodox-Catholic marriages could

> ... include sharing in the Eucharist as part of the rite? Does not the bishop who so blesses such a marriage become pastorally responsible for the non-Orthodox partner who lives on the frontier, so to speak, with one foot in both sheepfolds? Can the Eucharist be shared on the anniversary of such a marriage to ensure the "medicine of immortality" (to use St. Ignatius' description) be given to ensure the health of the specific family involved in a mixed marriage without causing scandal or altering the reality of the separation of [the Orthodox and Catholic churches]? [In the case of Orthodox-Catholic marriages, could we] conclude that since the Orthodox Church already recognizes an "ecclesial reality" beyond its own frontiers, it might treat access to the Eucharist in the same manner that it has done so historically with regard to baptism?[76]

Once more, I would like to emphasize that my proposal has a pronouncedly localized character: it only refers to Orthodox-Catholic families in the West, and it is not meant to be prescriptive for other Orthodox churches. As stated above, a uniform Church is nothing more than the fantasy of those who want to impose their own views upon the rest of the Church. We live in a polycentric Church, in which Christian unity is localized. The Church is incarnate in specific contexts. It is not a relativistic Church, but one that pays attention to context, one that rejoices in the rich ways in which the Church is incarnate in various contexts. Mixed families in the West live Christian lives differently

76. Roeber, *Mixed Marriages*, 189, 206–7.

than families in the East. Church authorities in the East, often referred to as mother churches, need to have the humility not to impose their own spirituality upon married couples in the West and a motherly attitude that fosters the spiritual growth of children.

Already in the current stage of the ecumenical dialogue between Orthodox and Catholics, the Orthodox bishops in North America could decide to nurture mixed marriages in both churches. Concretely, that would involve: mutual recognition of the marriage ceremony, regardless in which Church it took place; allowing the couple to receive Communion in both churches at least occasionally; allowing the couple to baptize their children in either Church; and allowing their children to receive communion in either Church. This way, we both set the foundation of a family by blessing their marriage in the Church and nurture its growth with the most exulted means gifted to the Church, namely the Eucharist. Such proposals are already ratified in Catholic theology and canon law and Catholic bishops are willing to ensure that mixed marriages that take place in Catholic parishes are presided over by the priest, and not the deacon. Catholic bishops are ready, simply waiting for the Orthodox to respond. How will Orthodox bishops respond? Such Orthodox and Catholic episcopal guidance would represent a meaningful exercise of episcopal authority for the faithful entrusted to them right here, right now.

It is important to emphasize the local character of this proposal and thus argue that this is a measure by *oikonomia*—a principle that "illustrates Orthodox Christianity's long commitment to justice and mercy, as well as its reliance upon pastoral discretion to address difficult cases in order to manifest the *philanthropia* of God,"[77] a principle that allows for a pastoral and more lenient approach to the canonical tradition, as opposed to *akribeia*, which applies canons with strictness. As St. Nikodemos the Haghiorite observes, the choice to use either *oiknonomia* or *akribeia* should be motivated by the salvation of souls and the attraction of the person to the Church.[78] Nothing less is at stake here.

---

77. Roeber, *Mixed Marriages*, 228.

78. Using these canonical principles of St. Nikodemos to argue for Orthodox-Catholic intercommunion for mixed couples in the United States is surprising to say the least, given that he enunciated these principles in his attempt to explain why Latins should be rebaptized when being received into Orthodoxy, despite the lack of consensus in the Eastern canonical tradition. He writes in his *Enchiridion on Baptism*: "In order to have an easily understandable solution to this perplexity, it is necessary for one to know beforehand that two kinds of government and correction are employed in the Church of Christ. One is called strictness (*akribeia*) and the other is called economy (*oikonomia*) or moderation (*sunkatabasis*). With these, at times using the one, at times the other, the stewards (*oikonomoi*) of the Spirit promote the salvation of souls. Thus, the fact is that the holy apostles in their aforesaid canons, and all the saints who have been mentioned, employed strictness, and for this reason they reject the baptism of heretics

One might challenge the appropriateness of applying *oikonomia* in the case of the mixed marriages discussed here, since in the Middle East and in North America the majority of the faithful are in mixed marriages and a practice that is generalized cannot be considered by *oikonomia*. This is a valid observation: a generalized rule cannot be treated as *oikonomia*. But this valid challenge can be answered in a twofold manner: first, compared to the plenitude of Orthodoxy, the Middle East and North America represent rather small minorities, numerically speaking, so the practice of localized intercommunion does not imply a generalized restoration of Eucharistic communion between Orthodox and Catholics. Second, most marriages in North America are indeed interfaith, but we simply lack the data to show whether the majority of these mixed marriages are between Orthodox and Catholics. Thus, a localized Orthodox-Catholic intercommunion does not represent the norm applied to all denominations or to all Catholics (meaning those who are not in a mixed married with an Orthodox), but remains the exception and thus can be considered *oikonomia*. Moreover, when one ponders the impressive number of Catholics in North America, the majority of which is not married to an Orthodox spouse, intercommunion is by no means generalized. Lastly, intercommunion should happen only on special occasions and only as the Catholic spouse expresses a desire in this regard.

Here, of course, I speak as an individual theologian, since this is not the authoritative position of the Orthodox Church in North America. As an ordained priest I could not preach these principles from the pulpit or enact them pastorally precisely because they are not the proclaimed teaching of the Church. But there are numerous instances between these two poles that would warrant such discussions: personal catechesis, book discussions in parish settings, the pastoral discretion of the parish priest (which already happens sporadically), and the education of clergy in seminaries, retreats, and other instances of continuous education. Given that this is not simply a theoretical, academic proposal, this practice needs to have at least the tacit approval of the local bishop, which would in turn later generate an explicit, local synodal sanction—an experience that should have greater effects on our churches elsewhere in the world. True, the focus on the Eucharist within a kingdom-centered ecclesiology and the experiential

completely, while, on the other hand, the two ecumenical councils employed economy and accepted the baptism of the Arians and the Macedonians and of others, but refused to recognize that of the Eunomians and of still others.... For thanks to this economy those [whose baptisms were received] became more gentle toward the Orthodox Christians and returned to piety to such a degree that within the space of a few years they either disappeared completely or very few of them remained." Quoted in Erickson, "Cusp of Modernity," 60–62.

approach advocated here stand in tension with theological official positions. But through earnest ecumenical efforts, church life will reflect more truly theology at its best and theology will reflect more truly church life at its best.

In conclusion, the mutual recognition of Catholics and Orthodox *as Church* results in the conviction that mixed marriages represent a "little Church" consecrated as such in either one of these churches. In specific contexts, such as Orthodox parishes in the West, by *oikonomia*, the larger disunity between Orthodox and Catholics need not be manifested in the family, where the spouses and their children should engage in eucharistic sharing. The members of this "little Church" should partake of the full blessing of a marriage, including—as Tertullian wrote—partaking "equally of the banquet of God," or the Eucharist.

FOUR

Parish

─────

When you come together, each one has a hymn,
a lesson, a revelation, a tongue, or an interpretation.
Let all things be done for building up.

I COR 14:26

The term "Church" is one of the vaguest terms that people use in daily conversations. "What do you think about the Church?" I often ask this question not so much to see whether people have a positive or negative view about the Church, as to see what they mean by "Church." Some respond with their views about the hierarchy, others about intra-Orthodox international squabbles, others about Church-state relations. Others identify the Church with the clergy or with an undefined teaching authority with clearly defined answers to every modern question imaginable. The Church—especially for theologians—also means the diocese, the ethnic jurisdiction that is parallel to other ethnic jurisdictions in an area (usually in the so-called "diaspora"), the national church, the entire Orthodoxy, Christian denominations, all of Christianity, or even the cosmos as it celebrates a cosmic Liturgy and affirming the sacramentality of non-human creation.

All these are important aspects of Church life, but they can also create a certain distance between a believer and their Church. A more profitable approach to the way in which a faithful person views the Church is through their own parish. The richer the parish life, the more a person is inclined to think of the Church as their local parish, understood as both community and building. That is where they gather with other members of their community to pray, to exercise their charisms, to serve the others, and to build up the Body of Christ, as the epigraph of this chapter suggests. Of course, this is not a parochial approach: at their best, parishes interact with one another, understand their place in larger structures (such as the diocese), and get involved in pan-Orthodox ministries such as FOCUS (which provides Food, Occupation, Clothing, Understanding, and Shelter), IOCC (International Orthodox Christian Charities), OCF (Orthodox Christian Fellowship), or OCMC (Orthodox Christian Mission Center).

After clarifying several meanings of the term "church," this chapter focuses on its most immediate sense, namely the parish. While today's theology leaves the parish largely devoid of ecclesiological content, a brief historical analysis opens up new ways of speaking about the parish and its ministries. They all build up the Body of Christ, to arrive at the measure of the full stature of Christ through *theosis*—an ecclesiological endeavor. The chapter ends with a discussion of the four marks of the Church: one, holy (including sin in/of the Church), catholic, and apostolic.

MEANINGS OF THE TERM "CHURCH"

The New Testament refers to the Church in a wide array of images such as People of God, Bride of Christ, Temple of the Spirit, and Pilgrim People.[1] Each of these images emphasizes a different aspect of the Church. For example, to define the Church as the Body of Christ is to say that the Church *is* Christ in the Holy Spirit. As Paul McPartlan explains, the Apostle Paul's encounter with the resurrected Christ on the road to Damascus could explain why he adopts this image. Jesus' question, "Why do you persecute me?" taught Paul that Jesus was alive, "not at a distance but somehow in his followers, to such an extent that to lay violent hands on *them* was to lay violent hands upon *him*."[2] Furthermore, Hebrew anthropology regarded the body not as a part of the person, but as the whole outward expression of the person, so when Christ took the bread at the last supper and said, "this is my body," he was essentially saying, "this is myself."[3] Hence, the Body of Christ refers to Christ in his

1. Frank J. Matera, "Theologies of the Church in the New Testament," in *The Gift of the Church: A Textbook on Ecclesiology in Honor of Patrick Granfield, O.S.B.*, ed. Peter C. Phan (Collegeville, MN: Liturgical Press, 2000), 19–20.

2. Paul McPartlan, "The Body of Christ and the Ecumenical Potential of Eucharistic Ecclesiology," *Ecclesiology* 6, no. 2 (2010): 152.

3. McPartlan, "Body of Christ," 156.

earthly incarnation, the eucharistic Christ, and the Church. Similarly, to give just one contemporary example, for Staniloae the Church represents "the social extension of the Risen Christ" or "the communitarian Christ"[4] filled with the Spirit and made living by the Spirit.

The living Church is more encompassing than those who are alive on earth, as Orthodox prescriptions for painting the interior walls of a church illustrate. The Church is the communion of the living worshipping in the pews and being censed as living icons, the saints depicted on the walls and symbolizing all the departed, the angels, Virgin Mary, and Christ who has authority over all (Pantocrator). Being depicted in the dome of the church, Christ is represented as the head of the Church—one community that unites heaven and earth. The Church on earth prays for those who are deceased and to the saints, while the saints pray for the living and all worship God, in a communion that surpasses the boundaries of time and space in Christ.

The community of the Church extends beyond human beings. Orthodox theology has consistently affirmed that the cosmos is a sacrament created to manifest God's presence and a church that celebrates a cosmic Liturgy.[5] Of course, presently, the universe is not fully a Church; though redeemed, it is on its way to perfection. In the eschaton, however, nature will be fully the medium of God's manifestation, when God will be "all in all" (1 Cor 15:28). In other words, the universe that will have become a Church, will be God's all-encompassing sacrament, or, to be precise, the only sacrament.[6] But even on this side of the eschaton, as Elizabeth Theokritoff writes, "We praise God *for* all creation, ... but we equally praise him *with* all creation, animate or inanimate. And in a certain sense we offer praise also *on behalf of* all creation."[7] This imagery of humans offering praise for, with, and on behalf of all creation hearkens back to Maximus the Confessor, according to whom the entire universe was created to celebrate a cosmic Liturgy and be transformed into a Church through the priestly

4. Dumitru Staniloae, "Sinteza ecclesiologica [Ecclesiological Synthesis]," *Studii Teologice* 7, no. 5–6 (1955): 267–68.

5. Bordeianu, *Dumitru Staniloae*, 145–55.

6. Dumitru Staniloae, *Teologia Dogmatica Ortodoxa* [*Orthodox Dogmatic Theology*], Second ed., vol. 3 (Bucharest: EIBMBOR, 1997), 11. Dumitru Staniloae, "Creatia ca dar si Tainele Bisericii [Creation as Gift and the Sacraments of the Church]," *Ortodoxia* 28, no. 1 (1976): 28.

7. Elizabeth Theokritoff, *Living in God's Creation: Orthodox Perspectives on Ecology* (Crestwood, NY: St. Vladimir's Seminary Press, 2009), 157–58. Similarly, Abraham Heschel writes: "All Thy works praise Thee (Ps 145:10): We are not alone in our acts of praise. Wherever there is life, there is silent worship. The world is always on the verge of becoming one in adoration. It is man who is the cantor of the universe, and in whose life the secret of cosmic prayer is disclosed." Abraham Heschel, *Man's Quest for God: Studies in Prayer and Symbolism* (New York: Scribner, 1954), 82.

mediation of the human being.[8] The exact expression, "cosmic liturgy" does not appear in Maximus, but it was coined by Hans Urs von Balthasar, who writes:

> The liturgy is ... an effective transformation of the world into transfigured, divinized existence. For that reason, in Maximus' view ... the liturgy is ultimately always "cosmic liturgy": a way of drawing the entire world into the hypostatic union because both world and liturgy share a christological foundation. This is something new and original and must be regarded as Maximus' own achievement.[9]

Pushing its boundaries even beyond human beings, material creation, and angels, the Church surpasses the created world. Patristic sources consistently affirm that the Church existed before all times. The second vision of *The Shepherd of Hermas* describes the Church as being represented by an aged woman, symbolizing that "she was created before all things; therefore is she aged, and for her sake the world was framed." Saint Gregory the Theologian also speaks of "the Church of Christ ... both before Christ and after Christ" (PG 35:1108–9). Saint Epiphanius of Cyprus writes, "The Catholic Church, which exists from the ages, is revealed most clearly in the incarnate advent of Christ" (PG 42:640). Similarly, Saint Clement of Rome writes that the Church was "established before the sun and moon;" and a little further on, "the Church is not of the present time, but existed from the beginning."[10]

In all these instances of ecclesiology, the Church is an all-encompassing reality, namely the universal Church—the one, holy that the Creed confesses, or the *Una Sancta*. At the same time the Church is localized; it is the parish that has memorial services for the dead, blesses the waters and other elements of creation, portrays angels in its iconography, and enters God's eternity when it celebrates the Divine Liturgy, as it will be shown later. Being catholic, the universal Church is local, and the local church manifests the universal.

---

8. Maximus the Confessor, "*Mystagogia*," chapters 3 and 6. Lars Thumberg, *Man and the Cosmos: The Vision of St. Maximus the Confessor* (New York: St. Vladimir's Seminary Press, 1985), 119–21, 26.

9. Hans Urs von Balthasar, *Cosmic Liturgy: The Universe According to Maximus the Confessor*, trans. Brian Daley, Communio Books (Ft. Collins, CO: Ignatius Press, 2003), 322. The Orthodox Church regards itself as a leader of the ecological movement and so the Crete Council affirms: "The ecological crisis, harnessed to climate change and global warming, makes it incumbent upon the Church to do everything within her spiritual power to aid the protection of God's creation from the consequences of human greed.... the Orthodox Church emphasizes the need to protect God's creation by means of inculcating responsibility in the human person for the God-given environment, by means of discovering the value of the virtues of moderation and self-limitation." *The Mission of the Orthodox Church in Today's World* 6:10, in Council of Crete, *Official Documents*.

10. Saint Clement of Rome, "The So-Called Second Letter of St. Clement," in *The Apostolic Fathers*, Fathers of the Church (Washington, DC: The Catholic University of America Press, 1947), #14, 74.

Most Orthodox theologians understand the local church to be the diocese, emphasizing the leading role of the bishop. In pan-Orthodox contexts, the expression "local church" also refers to the national church, such as the Serbian, Bulgarian, or Romanian Orthodox Church; these are also sometimes referred to as regional structures. In ecumenical contexts, local church can also mean a denomination (e.g. Methodist, Lutheran), but Orthodox delegates do not condone this use.[11] There is, however, one notable exception to the Orthodox refusal to apply the term, "local churches" to denominations. Afanasiev proposed a model for Orthodox-Catholic unity in which each would be regarded as local churches of the same Church, precisely because each enjoys ecclesial fullness in their administration of sacraments for salvation, which is the purpose of the Church.[12] Of all the usages of "local church" mentioned here, however, the diocese is the most common.

All these senses refer to the church as a community. But in an even more concrete sense, visibly, *the church is also a building*. Not every community has a building and not every building has a community. Addressing the latter, Michael Plekon writes that in places that used to have thriving industries those active communities built large cathedrals. As the population has relocated elsewhere when those industries closed down, the large cathedrals remained in great need of maintenance and repairs. The remaining small and aged parishes are directing all their resources towards repairs, but many churches (understood as communities) end up abandoning their buildings. In Plekon's words, "the church has left the building."[13]

There is a certain tension between the two understandings of the church as community and building, and this tension accompanied Christianity from its beginnings. In biblical times it was impossible to have a Christian church building, separate from the Jewish synagogue or the household church within someone's property. And yet, early Christians seem to have longed for a building

11. The Inter-Orthodox Consultation held in Agia Napa / Paralimni in Cyprus (2011) lamented that this document uses the term "churches" to mean denominations, and they fear the branch theory or denominationalist ecclesiology implied in this usage, hence their appeal to more clarity. (Inter-Orthodox Consultation, *A Response to the Faith and Order Study: The Nature and Mission of the Church: A Stage on the Way to a Common Statement (Faith and Order Paper 198, 2005 WCC)*, Agia Napa / Paralimni, Cyprus, 2–9 March 2011 (2011), par. 11. http://www.ec-patr.org/docdisplay.php?lang=en& id=1310&tla=gr.) See also Radu Bordeianu, "The Church: Towards A Common Vision: A Commentary in Light of the Inter-Orthodox Consultation at Agia Napa in Cyprus," *Exchange: Journal of Missiological and Ecumenical Research (Brill)* 44, no. 3 (2015): 238–39.

12. Afanassieff, "Una Sancta," 20.

13. Michael Plekon, *Saints as They Really Are: Voices of Holiness in our Time* (Notre Dame, IN: University of Notre Dame Press, 2012), 221–45.

or at least spiritually transposed the unique temple in Jerusalem upon their own gatherings. In this sense, the New Testament affirms that, by the power of the Holy Spirit, believers grow into "a holy temple in the Lord" (Eph 2:21–22), into a "spiritual house" built with "living stones," namely each member of the Church (1 Pt 2:5).

When Christians were later allowed to worship freely, despite these biblical references to a community that replaces the need for a temple, Christian architecture and iconography developed exponentially. Church Fathers such as Maximus compared the church—especially Hagia Sophia in Constantinople—with the universe, visible and invisible, all centered around Christ: "Likewise the world is a church since it possesses heaven corresponding to a sanctuary, and for a nave it has the adornment of the earth."[14] At the same time, the church building presents the world as it will be at the end; Staniloae affirms that the church as temple, "as liturgical space, is for the faithful another world, or a created world transfigured, or in the process of transfiguration.... This experience of the temple is significantly enhanced by its icons."[15] In the icon, a transfigured cosmos finds its peace and harmony, singing a hymn of triumph, and the faithful experience the eschatological Kingdom in the sacred, liturgical space of the local parish.

Medieval European cities built their churches in the city-center, making the church equally accessible to all by their inhabitants. Moreover, the church had a large space in front, where merchants sold their products, people were entertained, and citizens gathered. In modern cities, people have to drive to church, sometimes considerable distances, so their participation in church life during the week is limited by distance. Schedules are also increasingly full, so people do not shop and are not entertained in the same places, which makes it difficult to form a community, but having a church easily accessible by foot, with multiple aspects of life close to it, would create a stronger sense of community— something that new urbanism takes into consideration and new church building projects should keep in mind.

Communism brought another challenge to the relationship between the building and the community. Militant atheist authorities demolished a vast number of Orthodox churches. Parishes that retained their churches gathered in them at great risk. Consequently, during communism, much of the faith took refuge inside the home and became privatized in personal spiritualities.

14. Maximus the Confessor, "*Mystagogia*," #3, 189.

15. Dumitru Staniloae, *Spiritualitate si comuniune in Liturghia Ortodoxa* [*Spirituality and Communion in the Orthodox Liturgy*] (Craiova: Editura Mitropoliei Olteniei, 1986), 79, 81.

Many people believed without gathering as a community, for fear of persecution. And many people—myself included—did not believe. And yet we were all a Church. A Church without a building, without a community, and yet a Church that instantly came into the open after the fall of the Iron Curtain. To this day, there are places around the world (e.g. mainland China) where Orthodox Christians are not allowed to gather physically in a church, so they form underground online communities that support each other and participate in worship services streamed online from other countries.

Decades later, I find myself in an Orthodox parish in America, a parish in which the Kingdom of God is manifested in a community that is filed with the Spirit and a building that looks like heaven on earth. But the parish has moved four times in a hundred years, including because the community has moved away from a building, so we had to build a church (building) where the church (community) lived. Currently, we are trying to maintain both emphases—the local church is both building (the place of liturgical celebrations, education, and ministries) and the community (a family, home of the baptized, a place of welcome for others). These two elements are only the first ingredients in a theology of the parish.

THE PARISH

The parish is a community of the faithful gathered together around the priest for the celebration of the Eucharist and other services; for being an instrument of the Kingdom, bringing healing and proclamation of the good news to their locality and the world in general; and for exercising the various charisms of its members for the building up of the Body of Christ. Despite being the most common church structure, the parish appears to have no ecclesiological identity and theologians largely ignore it.

Almost the entirety of modern Orthodox theology understands the local eucharistic assembly to be the diocese gathered around its bishop in the Eucharistic celebration. This view is reflective of the *eucharistic ecclesiology* of Nicholas Afanasiev and its revised versions in the communion ecclesiologies of Dumitru Staniloae and Metropolitan John Zizioulas, which have dominated Orthodox thought on this issue. Complementary to this theological approach to the local church, a practical or experiential approach presents a different picture: the diocese does not gather all its faithful to celebrate a single Eucharist. The bishop celebrates the Liturgy in the parish that he visits, not in his office where most of his ministry takes place. The diocese may have a chapel at its headquarters, but it does not have a community entrusted to its pastoral ministry. The parish is the only place that is suited to be a Eucharistic celebration, while the diocese is not. Instead, the *locus* of the eucharistic celebration is the parish, which gathers the priest and the church community in order to send it on its mission to live out the Kingdom of God. An experiential approach to ecclesiology retrieves elements of eucharistic ecclesiology and focuses primarily on the identity of the parish, the ministry of the parish priest, and the communion between clergy and the laics in the parish, all of which shed a new light on the role of the bishop.

As a preamble to this discussion, it is important to recall the main tenets of eucharistic ecclesiology and their evolution into communion ecclesiology. A particular area of concern for eucharistic ecclesiology is the relationship among the local church, the Eucharist, the episcopal office, and other local churches. Afanasiev considered the ecclesiology of the Orthodox Church today to be the successor of the universal ecclesiology of Cyprian of Carthage, who affirmed that the universal Church is constituted of the sum of the local churches, which are parts of the whole but do not have fullness, and that the unity of the universal Church stems from the unity of their bishops. In contrast, the eucharistic ecclesiology of the first two centuries considered that the eucharistic assembly of the local church contained the fullness of the Church, the *Una Sancta* that we confess in the Creed. Local churches were autonomous, but at the same time they related to other local churches through their bishops, through the acceptance of other local churches' ecclesial life, and—most importantly— through mutual identity, as they each represented the fullness of Christ's presence in the local eucharistic assembly. Consequently, Afanasiev arrived at the heart of his eucharistic ecclesiology:

> The Church is where the eucharistic assembly is. It is also possible to formulate this in another way. Where the Eucharist is, there is the Church of God, and where the Church of God is, there is the Eucharist. It follows that the eucharistic assembly is the distinctive, empirical sign of the Church. [...] The actual limits of the Church are determined by the limits of the eucharistic assembly.
>
> In affirming that the eucharistic assembly is the principle of the unity of the Church, the thesis that the bishop is the distinctive empirical sign of the local church is not excluded, because the bishop is included in the very concept of the Eucharist. According to its very nature, the eucharistic assembly could not exist without its president or, according to the terminology

established by usage, without the bishop. The foundation of the ministry of the bishop is the eucharistic assembly.[16]

Thus, according to Afanasiev, the church *Una Sancta* is fully manifested in each local eucharistic assembly, which, in the early church, meant the diocese around its bishop—not the parish. Moreover, the unity of the church depends primarily on the same Eucharist being celebrated in different local churches, not on dogmatic uniformity and episcopal communion as in universalist ecclesiology. Having said this, however, it is important to note that Afanasiev included dogmatic unity (not uniformity) and the role of the bishop in the celebration of the Eucharist, the latter being the preeminent sign of the Church.

John Zizioulas' main criticism of Afanasiev is that churches cannot have eucharistic communion without communion among bishops, even when two separate churches celebrate their valid Eucharists. Alternatively, Zizioulas proposes communion ecclesiology, which emphasizes the relationships among bishops gathered in synods and in communion with one another. He identifies the bishop with the entire local eucharistic assembly and therefore concludes that the unity of the Church is not simply eucharistic but also hierarchical.[17] As a result of Zizioulas' reaction to Afanasiev, communion ecclesiology—which emphasizes the ministry of the bishop in the eucharistic celebration—became the norm within Orthodox ecclesiology. It also solidified the assumption that the celebrant of the Eucharist is the bishop in the local diocese, and not the parish priest in the parish. Despite these variations, all recent Orthodox theology converges around the following points: the Church is eucharistic in nature, the local church is the diocese, and the bishop is the celebrant of the Liturgy.

My proposal to retrieve eucharistic ecclesiology and apply it to the parish affirms the importance of the community gathered in one place for the celebration of the Eucharist. Additionally, it incorporates (1) the aspects of church life that are not included in the Eucharist, (2) the parish as the natural place of the eucharistic celebration, and (3) the reality that parishioners generally experience the Eucharist as presided over by the priest.

The term, "parish," derives from the Greek term, *paroikía*, which, in biblical literature, refers to a dwelling in a strange land, such as the Jewish people's stay in Egypt (Acts 13:17). As the entire Christian life is supposed to be akin to an exile, Christians in this world are in a *paroikía*—a temporary adaptation while

16. Afanassieff, "Una Sancta," 14.

17. John D. Zizioulas, *Eucharist, Bishop, Church: The Unity of the Church in the Divine Eucharist and the Bishop During the First Three Centuries*, trans. Elizabeth Theokritoff (Brookline, MA: Holy Cross Orthodox Press, 2001), 116.

sojourning (cf. 1 Pt 1:17). The etymology of the term, parish, thus suggests that the parish is an impermanent structure, a temporary adaptation as the Church pilgrims toward the eschatological Kingdom where it truly dwells.[18] Centuries later, *paroikía* began to designate the local eucharistic community—a pilgrim community toward the eschatological Kingdom—but without clear correspondence to the original communities. In the earliest centuries of the Church, the eucharistic community was the gathering of the local church under the leadership of a bishop. If one places the emphasis on the bishop, then today's equivalent of the ancient eucharistic community is the diocese, that is the church governed by the bishop. However, if the emphasis falls on the gathering of the local church, then the ancient eucharistic community is today's parish. Of these two possibilities, the New Testament suggests that the emphasis fell on the community, not on its leaders. Churches such as Corinth, or Ephesus, were extremely small by today's standards—around forty or fifty members.[19] No community was too small for its leaders, just as it was not too small for Christ: for where two or three are gathered in my name, I am there among them" (Mt 18:20). Hence, the successor of the early Christian community is today's parish, rather than the diocese.

Gradually, churches gained more members, but their growth was rather limited. Sociologist Rodney Stark estimates the total number of Christians in the world to be around 1,000 by the year 40 and 7,530 by the year 100.[20] It is likely that these communities remained relatively small, certainly not in the thousands as it is the case of today's dioceses and even some parishes. Thus, early Christian communities, though they were headed by bishops, resembled quite closely today's regular parishes. Afterwards, the East had city bishops (Metropolitans), as well as country bishops (*chorepiscopoi*) in an attempt to have a bishop lead each and every Eucharist. Quite early on, this situation proved unsustainable; when communities grew in number, priests became their leaders. As Zizioulas writes,

> the first indications concerning the appearance of the parish should be placed around the middle of the third century. The parish appeared at that time *as a result of necessity*. The rapid rise in the number of Christians in the cities and perhaps also in the rural interior, and the lengthy absence of the Bishops from their Churches which followed obliged the Church to entrust the leadership of the Eucharist to the Presbyters on a more permanent than usual

18. "For here we have no lasting city, but we seek the city that is to come" (Heb 13:14).
19. Harrington, *The Church*, 51.
20. Harrington, *The Church*, 129.

basis and to break up the one Eucharist under the leadership of the Bishop into several assemblies centered on Presbyters. So at this period, for the first time, Presbyters appeared attached individually and permanently to communities of their own. This was the original form of the parish.[21]

While Zizioulas's analysis of the necessities that led to the emergence of the parish have their own merit, one can also concur with Olivier Clément who considers it an enigma why parishes were not "episcopalized," or led by bishops.[22] The emergence of the parish should be studied more in-depth both historically and theologically. Because of the lack of complete identification between the situation in the early Church and today's ecclesial structures, Orthodox ecclesiology tends to attribute no ecclesiological significance to the parish. As Schmemann contends, "the process which transformed the original 'episcopal' structure of the local church into what we know today as parish ... although it represents one of the most radical changes that ever took place in the Church, remained, strange as it may seem, virtually unnoticed by ecclesiologists and canonists."[23] On this subject, Western theology is almost as quiet as Eastern. The Council of Trent, in its attempt to eliminate conflicts over priests' jurisdiction (and thus income), required the establishment of clear parochial boundaries, leading to a geographical understanding of the parish.[24] Meanwhile, the biblical translations of the Reformers rendered the Greek word *ekklēsia* in terms that suggested local community—Luther chose *Gemeinde* and Tyndale *congregation*. Their renewed focus on the local community led the Catholic Church to move in the opposite direction, overemphasizing the universal Church. Hence, the 1917 Code of Canon Law described the parish as a territorial section of the diocese or its administrative sub-unit, and a source of income for the priest (cc. 451, 1409–1488).[25]

How important are these historical norms? Though not addressing the

---

21. Zizioulas, *Eucharist, Bishop, Church*, 216–17.

22. Olivier Clément, *You Are Peter: An Orthodox Theologian's Reflection on the Exercise of Papal Primacy* (New York: New City Press, 2003), 13. Zizioulas proposes the same solution, of having bishops of the heads of much smaller dioceses to replace today's parishes and thus restore the pastoral role of the bishop. Zizioulas, *Being as Communion*, 251, n. 6.

23. Alexander Schmemann, "Towards a Theology of Councils," *St. Vladimir's Seminary Quarterly* 6, no. 4 (1962): 177.

24. To this day, parishes in the Catholic tradition are not constituted voluntarily, but based on territory. A Catholic person joins a parish by moving into its territory, not by voluntarily establishing membership. Francis Cardinal George, "The Parish in the Mission of the Church," in *What is a Parish? Canonical, Pastoral, and Theological Perspectives*, ed. Thomas A. Baima and Lawrence Hennessey (Chicago: Hillenbrand Books, 2011), 34–36.

25. Brett C. Hoover, "A Place for Communion: Reflections on an Ecclesiology of Parish Life," *Theological Studies* 78, no. 4 (2017): 827.

question of the parish but writing about history in general, Georges Florovsky writes that "Christianity is a religion of historians.... Christianity is basically a vigorous appeal to history, a witness of faith to certain particular events in the past."[26] Indeed, converts to Orthodoxy often state that one of the greatest points of attraction to Orthodoxy is its sense of Tradition: the same faith has been preserved since biblical times. In their quest to find the church that the Apostles have left behind, they find the Orthodox Church. This apostolic spirit has been preserved and enhanced from the Patristic era until today, when the Church still acts in the spirit of the Apostles and—to use Florovsky's expression—"the mind of the Fathers."[27]

But this same sense of Tradition can become crippling to Orthodoxy if it degenerates into traditionalism: Tradition is not supposed to be fixed, immovable, uncreative in all regards. It becomes detrimental to long for an idealized earlier century and geographical space, rather than be contextual, responding to present needs. It is equally problematic to become fixed on a certain century and ignore the subsequent historical development. The Holy Spirit did not abandon the Church after the second century. And yet, it seems that Zizioulas leans that way. He even insists that the emergence of the parish was an *anomaly* or, in his words, a "rupture in its own eucharistic ecclesiology. For it was no longer possible to equate every eucharistic celebration with the local Church."[28] The same goes for the bishop's absence from most eucharistic celebrations.

In the life of the Church, *anomalies sometimes become the norm.*[29] First of all, not one single model encompasses all Tradition. In fact, history presents so many models of church existence that the normative statement that emerges is that there is no norm.[30] Within this plurality of traditions, some become

---

26. Georges Florovsky, "The Predicament of the Christian Historian," in *Christianity and Culture; Collected Works, vol. 2* (Belmont, MA: Nordland, 1974), 31.

27. Georges Florovsky, "St. Gregory Palamas and the Tradition of the Fathers," in *Bible, Church, Tradition; Collected Works vol. 1* (Belmont, MA: Nordland, 1972), 105–8, 44, 20.

28. Zizioulas, *Being as Communion*, 251. Turcescu considers that the emergence of the parish actually exposes a weakness of eucharistic ecclesiology, rather than being a lamentable historical development. Lucian Turcescu, "Eucharistic Ecclesiology or Open Sobornicity?," in *Dumitru Staniloae: Tradition and Modernity in Theology*, ed. Lucian Turcescu (Palm Beach, FL: Center for Romanian Studies, 2002), 95.

29. The discussion of the relationship between anomaly and the norm was inspired by Hahnenberg, who writes: "The Church exists within a broader tradition that is not only *normal* but also *normative*.... [The theologian] sets out to examine ministerial anomalies not in order to undermine these doctrines or to propose new ones but rather to ask how previous understandings are confronted or complicated by reality. The norm of past tradition is rarely abandoned, but it is often bent, as individuals and groups work creatively with the norm, applying, adapting, and transcending it—sometimes even transforming the anomaly into the exemplar." Hahnenberg, "Learning from Experience," 174–75.

30. Hahnenberg, "Learning from Experience," 162.

the norm, and others are regarded as anomalies. That is why, while remaining within the normative Tradition, theology needs to recognize the adaptive work of the Spirit in the Church. The entire community discerns those anomalies that do not necessarily go against the norm, but may be an unusual way of living the norm and eventually become the new norm. That is how tradition renews itself. Sometimes in order to remain the same, one has to change.

Cyril Hovorun considers that the Church must change "in order to correspond more truly in its human and historical dimension to what God wants it to be."[31] He compares ecclesial structures with scaffolding, which is temporary and designed to be moved around as new needs arise. Such "work of deconstruction does not seek to destroy the structures but rather to keep them open so they can be readjusted to their original meaning,"[32] namely communion with God. Closer to our theme—how could the Church remain eucharistic by nature, when the diocese no longer celebrated the unique Eucharist with the bishop as the presider? The parish emerged and the priest became the presider. This is why Schmemann recommends that Orthodox theology addresses this reality, rather than bemoan it:

> Because of this *real* situation, all attempts simply to return to the "episcopal" experience of the Church in its second or third century forms (*episcopus in ecclesia et ecclesia in episocopo*) will remain the domain of academic wishful thinking as long as we ignore the reality of the parish and the position of the priest in it. We must admit that many of the characteristics of the early "episcopal" community have been assumed by the parish, just as the priest has been given many of the bishop's functions. Today, the priest is the normal celebrant, pastor and teacher of the Church, all functions which in the early Church were fulfilled by the bishop.[33]

Thus, an experiential ecclesiology of the parish earnestly considers the transition from the eucharistic assembly led by the bishop in the diocese to the Liturgy presided over by the priest in the parish. Furthermore, recent decades have transformed Western parishes in regards to the means of recognizing membership, ethnicity, the number of congregations, and ecumenical composition. All of these factors offer several *qualifications regarding contemporary parishes*.

Orthodox parishes in the United States tend to have a *congregationalist* form of organization. This characterization is not intended to be pejorative. It is rather

---

31. Hovorun, *Scaffolds of the Church*, 12.
32. Hovorun, *Scaffolds of the Church*, 181.
33. Schmemann, "Theology of Councils," 179.

descriptive of the voluntary nature of membership and self-identification along ethnic lines, rather than geographical belonging to a community. A geographical distribution of parishes is, on the one hand, constrictive, and forces the faithful to attend a certain community simply because of where they live. In cities that are rather segregated racially, financially, and ethnically, the parish does not challenge the sinful character of segregation. On the other hand, if a parish covers a larger area that encompasses a diverse group of people, such a geographical distribution of parishes has the advantage of transcending the divisions extant in society and forces parishioners who would otherwise not interact with one another to form a community in Christ, in whom "there is no longer Jew or Greek, slave or free, male or female" (Gal 3:28).

How does the typical American join a parish? Usually, after "shopping around" for a suitable parish based on musical preferences, quality of sermons, characteristics of the community such as ethnicity or age, the faithful register as members, which illustrates their intentional and financial commitment to a particular parish. But the number of registered members is far greater than the number of faithful who regularly attend services and are involved in ministries. An even greater number is that of adherents who identify as Orthodox, whether they are registered or not. Thus, a recent study of American Orthodoxy shows that the total number of adherents is slightly under 800,000, of whom 209,000 attend regularly. That means that only 26% of adherents attend church with some regularity,[34] while the rest do so only on special occasions, fitting under the designation of "cultural Orthodox," as discussed previously. This rate compares unfavorably to the rest of American Christianity, since 51% of Americans attend church regularly.[35] Thus, the Orthodox attendance rate represents half the national average that considers all Christians. Although this rate of attendance is still much greater than in traditionally Orthodox countries, American Orthodoxy has a significant (even urgent) impetus for internal missions, since about three quarters of its faithful do not attend church regularly.

The size of the parish partially explains the gap between overall membership and the 26% rate of regular attendance. When a parish is under 25 members, church attendance is close to 70%; when a parish has more than 2000 members, church attendance is around 15%. The most significant drop in church attendance happens when a parish grows above 150 members. But the size of the parish is not always a reliable indicator for church attendance, which varies greatly

34. Alexei Krindatch, *Eight Facts about Church Attendance in US Orthodox Christian Churches* (http://assemblyofbishops.org/news/research 2010), 2.
35. Pew Center, *Choosing New Church*, 7.

from jurisdiction to jurisdiction. In parishes of all sizes, attendance in Greek and Serbian churches is much lower than Antiochian and OCA parishes.[36] Ecclesiologically, this situation calls into question the understanding of the parish as a tightly knit community in which all are part of a larger family. Instead, if a parish is an extremely large group of people where attendance inevitably goes down, or if the priest cannot be the spiritual father of all parishioners because the community comprises of more than 2,000 parishioners, then the parish becomes a system set up for failure in regards to its sense of community. Breaking it down into sub-units that can create a sense of community might be an answer, one however that is complicated by the shortage of priests and financial considerations regarding the viability of a parish.

One way to break the mold of one community with one priest and one building is to look at various situations in the Orthodox world. Some parishes have only one church building, while others have several. In Greece, for example, where the number of church buildings abounds, the community uses them in turn. Elsewhere, where communities are too small to be self-sufficient financially, they form a cluster of churches or a community of communities, gathering several congregations under one umbrella, with one single priest, who serves them in turn. That is especially the case of mission churches that depend on a larger parish for resources, including for their eucharistic life. A variation on the practice of *fermentum* exist today. Some of my students served Nigerian Catholic parishes that have twenty satellite communities; the priest consecrates the Eucharist in the main parish and sends seminarians to distribute it in the satellite communities, even though seminarians are neither ordained nor a minor order. The Orthodox version in the Antiochian diocese is that, when the priest is absent from the parish, the community gathers for a Reader Service or Typika, and the deacon distributes the Eucharist that has been previously consecrated in a regular Liturgy presided by the priest.

Shortages of priests and financial considerations will certainly force the Church to adapt. And yet, it is difficult to ignore a significant transformation that is taking place in our understanding of the Eucharist as consecrated apart from the community. The liturgy is not a magical act. The liturgy is the gathering or work of the people, serving together. It is the common worship of the local community. So, when the distribution of pre-consecrated communion becomes the norm, we revive the neo-scholastic or manual theology that was centered around the role of the priest and the "transubstantiation" of the elements

---

36. Krindatch, *Eight Facts about Church Attendance*, 5–6.

(to use the language of a previous era), while the rest of the Liturgy and of the community were incidental at best. Twentieth century theologians, especially Afanasiev and Schmemann, have vehemently criticized such an approach, with transformative effects upon Orthodox parishes worldwide. And yet, that approach is coming back not for theological reasons, but because of practical considerations surrounding financial hardships and shortages of priests. If the Liturgy cannot be celebrated regularly, how will the Church remain eucharistic in nature?

Furthermore, some parishes are *ethnic in character*, while others are multi-ethnic. Most often, Orthodox parishes in America started out as a direct outgrowth of early immigrant cultural and fraternal organizations such as the Society of Athena, the Sts. Cyril and Methodius Brotherhood, the Soudie Syrian Brotherhood Society, etc. These immigrants then established churches that corresponded to their national, political, and regional loyalties, often in close proximity to other Orthodox parishes that differed in these three regards: national identity, political convictions, and regional provenance within the same country. Consequently, these secular criteria took precedence over the identity of the Church understood as a community of faith shared by people of all nationalities. Initially, national identity even determined church membership, but more recently Orthodox jurisdictions in America have eliminated the link between parish membership and ethnicity.[37] Ethnic parishes in which the majority of the faithful are second or third generation immigrants have seen the perils of artificially holding on to one's ethnic background and the benefits of ministering to their faithful in a language that is meaningful to them and to their families.

A pronounced ethnic character attracts immigrants, but their children do not display the same understanding of the language and appreciation for ethnic traditions. These, of course, should be cultivated and are strongly desirable. But the mission of the Church is not to maintain the cultural heritage of a certain community. This is a rather controversial statement, and for good reasons: in traditionally Orthodox countries, the Church has contributed significantly to the development of culture. But in the diaspora, where parents are unable to teach their children their native language, they should not expect the parish to do so, especially in the context of the Liturgy or of Sunday School—and thus at the expense of worship and catechesis. How will these youths be able to give testimony

37. John H. Erickson, "Organization, Community, Church: Reflections on Orthodox Parish Polity in America," in *The Orthodox Parish in America: Faithfulness to the Past and Responsibility for the Future*, ed. Anton C. Vrame (Brookline, MA: Holy Cross Orthodox Press, 2003), 68–76.

to their faith in front of their peers in the West, if they are unable to understand the material taught in Sunday School in the language of their parents? And even if they understand these languages, they remain unable to defend their faith in the language of their peers. Most importantly, they will have to explain their faith to their spouses because, as stated earlier, they will likely get married with a person who is not Orthodox. Historically, this has proved an extremely difficult task, and Orthodoxy has lost a significant number of faithful who were unable to speak to their spouses about the beauty of Orthodoxy, ending up converting to the faith of their non-Orthodox spouse.

When a parish is incarnate in its surrounding culture—even while maintaining an ethnic identity that does not stifle its Orthodoxy—that parish is likely to *include converts*. Some parishes are ecumenical in character, while others are closed-in. Given the prevalence of mixed marriages in American Orthodoxy, the identity of the parish—and the very meaning of the word "parish"—differs from majority Orthodox countries. If in the latter context a parish is the community of believers who share the same faith and the fullness of liturgical life, in American Orthodoxy the parish is more than the body of communicants with the same beliefs.[38] In varying degrees of commitment, Catholic and Protestant members of Orthodox parishes refer to their parish and their priest as being the Orthodox.[39] More often than not they are involved in the charitable and educational aspects of parish life, attend services, and for all pastoral purposes belong to the Orthodox parish. They often donate their time, treasure, and talents generously, and yet leadership positions and most sacraments (with the exception of Marriage) are out of their reach. While sometimes the non-Orthodox members of a parish remain in their faith, other times they convert. The *history of conversions into Orthodoxy in America* is highly relevant for what constitutes an ecumenical parish.

Oliver Herbel shows that those who have now become iconic and normative in the history of conversions to Orthodoxy in America fit into a unique Eastern model of restorationism, understood as the re-embodiment of an ancient faith. They used the American context of religious choosing and religious novelty-creation to make the un-American choice in favor of the unbroken Eastern Orthodox Tradition. In doing so, they have challenged the norms of

---

38. Having said this, the official acts of various Orthodox jurisdictions in America still define the parish as the local body of communicants of the Church in a given locality. Erickson, "Organization, Community, Church," 67–68.

39. Emmanuel Gratsias, "The Effect of Mixed Marriage on the Parish," in *InterMarriage: Orthodox Perspectives*, ed. Anton C. Vrame (Brookline, MA: Holy Cross Orthodox Press, 1997), 146–47.

American Christianity, including in its social, religious, and political aspects. Thus, Alexis Toth and his followers converted to Orthodoxy in response to Latin Catholics' abuse of Eastern Catholics. Raphael Morgan was a Jamaican who found the Orthodox tradition as a means for addressing the racial struggles of African American Christians. Orthodoxy was attractive to him for predating the tradition of racial segregation, an experience that was confirmed during his trip to Russia and in his interactions with Greek Orthodox clergy in the U.S. Although a relatively small number of faithful followed him, Morgan inspired the later work of Patriarch McGuire of the independent African Orthodox Church, which led to numerous conversions to Orthodoxy in Africa and their entry into the larger Eastern Orthodox family through the Patriarchate of Alexandria.[40]

Similarly, Moses Berry saw the connections between Eastern Orthodox and African American spiritualities, converted to Orthodoxy together with numerous followers, and founded the Brotherhood of St. Moses the Black—a pan-Orthodox organization that connects African Americans with Eastern spirituality. And yet, as the namesake of his brotherhood, he had to endure racism at the hand of Orthodox clergy: when visiting a parish in St. Louis, he was forbidden to enter the church (even though it was open) and asked to inquire into the Coptic Orthodox Church. But he did not lose heart; instead, he inspired fellow African Americans to connect with Eastern Orthodoxy as a way to reach out to their African ancestors and to pre-slave African Christianity.[41]

Peter Gillquist was instrumental in the conversions of many Evangelicals in the 1970s and 80s, who burned with zeal for the apostolic faith (whose study was their main reason for conversion) and the evangelization of nonbelievers. Unlike other converts, they were not immediately received into Orthodoxy, even suffering a last-minute refusal to meet with Ecumenical Patriarch Demetrios despite Bishop Maximos of Pittsburgh's support. Among the reasons

---

40. D. Oliver Herbel, *Turning to Tradition: Converts and the Making of an American Orthodox Church* (New York: Oxford University Press, 2014), 2–14, 67–84.

41. Herbel, *Turning to Tradition*, 93–95. Herbel's remarks should not give the impression that the Eastern tradition is free of racism. To give an example from the patristic tradition, at the ordination of St. Moses the Black, the Archbishop said to him, "See, Abba Moses, now you are entirely white." The Archbishop—and here the text sanitizes the archbishop's racism by claiming that it was a test—instructed the priests to drive Abba Moses out the sanctuary to hear what he says. History then records the following: "So the old man came in and they covered him with abuse, and drove him out, saying, 'Outside, black man!' Going out, he said to himself, 'They have acted rightly concerning you, for your skin is as black as ashes. You are not a man, so why should you be allowed to meet men?'" *The Sayings of the Desert Fathers: The Alphabetical Collection (Rev. Ed.)*, trans. Benedicta Ward (Collegeville, MN: Liturgical Press, 1984), 136–39. The racism recorded in this encounter, including the attempt to sanitize it as a test of Abba Moses' humility, are beyond appalling.

for the refusal was the suspicion that the new converts would not integrate into Greek Orthodoxy and would not promote the values of Hellenism; as will be discussed in the last chapter, ethnophyletism prevailed over missions. But the new converts persisted, until about 2,200 members joined the Antiochian Archdiocese in 1987, and formed the Antiochian Evangelical Orthodox Mission (AEOM). Many followed later, maintaining some Western liturgical practices.[42]

These briefly described examples show that an ecumenical parish has to embrace converts who sometimes leave their cradle faiths because of conflict, injustice, or because they are dissatisfied with churches that do not continue the life of the Church of the New Testament. Imposing a certain liturgical and cultural heritage on them and persisting in unjust practices will turn them away. And in America, the alternatives are endless, because Orthodoxy is not above the "spiritual marketplace of expanding religious diversity and individual choice-making that has marked the post-World War II American religious landscape," according to Amy Slagle.[43] In a context in which about half of adult Americans have changed their religious affiliation at least once in their lifetime, some choose Orthodoxy for theological reasons, or liturgical motivations, or for being in a mixed marriage, or being part of a certain community, or a combination of these factors. They usually arrive at the doorsteps of Orthodoxy after they have already experienced, evaluated, and criticized other church traditions. While converts certainly adopt collective objectives when they embrace Orthodoxy, the individual motivations typical of American Christianity remain prominent: interior growth, fulfillment, and psychological comfort. They are willing to accept, cherish, and even adopt some aspects of the parish's ethnic heritage, since Orthodoxy is so intrinsically coupled with ethnicity, but the onus is upon the rest of the community to embrace people of diverse ethnic and racial backgrounds without making ethnic heritage a precondition or an obstacle to belonging in the community.[44] All the elements addressed in this analysis of conversion are crucially important for forming an ecumenically-minded Orthodox community.

42. Herbel, *Turning to Tradition*, 103–25.
43. Amy Slagle, *The Eastern Church in the Spiritual Marketplace: American Conversions to Orthodox Christianity* (DeKalb, IL: Northern Illinois University Press, 2011), 5.
44. Slagle, *Spiritual Marketplace*, 38–60, 84–104, 24–42.

MINISTRIES FOR BUILDING UP
THE BODY OF CHRIST

Experientially speaking, a church has numerous ministries, and most often, a church bulletin that includes numerous activities throughout the week denotes a vibrant church. But, counter-intuitively, the number of ministries is not directly proportional to the vitality of a church. Focusing on the less important ministries, at the expense of the more effective ones, can deter from the role of the church. A 2017 *Young Adults in Orthodox Parishes* study lists in descending order of their importance the six most effective and attractive ministries for which the American Orthodox youth thirst: "Fellowship groups; Theology and contemporary issues study groups/classes; Scripture study groups/classes; Prayer groups, spiritual retreats; Community service activities; and Mission trips, travel groups."[45] Given their emphasis on building up the Body of Christ into a community that is an icon of the Kingdom, and given their orientation towards healing and proclamation, these ministries characterize a Kingdom-centered ecclesiology.

As the New Testament emphasizes repeatedly, ministries are gifts from God, or charisms with which God has endowed the members of the Church as instruments through which God works. As such, they are not for an individual to boast, but for the benefit of the Body of Christ and for its growth into Christ: "The gifts he gave were that some would be apostles, some prophets, some evangelists, some pastors and teachers, to equip the saints for the work of ministry, for building up the body of Christ, until all of us come ... to maturity, to the measure of the full stature of Christ" (Eph 4:11–13). Similar passages such as the epigraph of this chapter and 1 Corinthians 12–14 emphasize the same idea, that all members of the church are charismatics, endowed with gifts for the building up, or edification of the Body, until the community is transformed into Christ or, as later Orthodox theology would say, until the church attains *theosis*.

Because the Spirit is ever-present in the Body of Christ, a multitude of charisms abound in Orthodox parishes, especially those Orthodox parishes

---

45. Alexei Krindatch, *Young Adults and Young Adult Ministries in American Orthodox Christian Parishes* (http://assemblyofbishops.org/news/research 2017), 21. Similarly, a study commissioned by the US Episcopal Assembly indicates that the most effective ministries are the ones that focus on the values of the Kingdom, namely proclamation and healing (learning about the faith and reaching out into the wider community), and that social activities are less effective, including sports, premarital groups, parenting classes, etc. Alexei Krindatch, *Orthodox Christian Churches in 21st Century America: A Parish Life Study* (http://assemblyofbishops.org/news/research 2018), 70.

located in the West. Hopefully those in office are also charismatics, but there are a *multitude of ministries* that, although not ordained (such as priest) or officially delegated (such as parish council), are no less real and no less crucial. Dumitru Staniloae was instrumental in placing all charisms within the priesthood of Christ and of the Church, with ordination being one of those ministries.[46] All charisms contribute to the edification of the Body of Christ in general and the parish in particular.

Although in traditionally Orthodox countries the parish council exists, in practice its function varies greatly, often being almost inexistent. Schmemann offers a historical explanation for this phenomenon, relating it to the loss of the proper ministries of governing for the presbyters who surrounded the bishop once the structure of the first Christian centuries evolved:

> the parish, deprived of the conciliary government which the "episcopal" church had in the presbyterium, it lost for several centuries even the rudimentary forms of conciliary life, ceased to be "council" in any real meaning of this word. It was thus forced, first, into a purely passive understanding of the *laos* as completely subordinated to the hierarchy, and then, the progress of democratic ideas helping, into a lay rebellion *against* the hierarch.[47]

Especially in the West, however, this conciliar nature of the parish resurfaced, manifested especially in the communal exercise of ministries. There are a multitude of other male and female ministries that build up parishes, so suffice it to list here some ministries that women lead: visitation of the sick and elderly, Sunday school teachers and coordinators, spiritual mothers, members of the parish council thus participating in church governance, greeters, youth coordinators, tour guides, readers at liturgical services, iconographers, secretaries, presbyteres (i.e. priest's wife), they sing in the choir,[48] lead Bible studies or other educational activities especially as many are theologians or serve in other academic positions, counseling, fundraising, care for liturgical vestments, and they bake liturgical items including the bread that becomes the body of Christ. All these ministries are indispensable to parish life. Of course, were the order of deaconesses to be fully restored in the Orthodox Church, some women

---

46. Dumitru Staniloae, "Temeiurile teologice ale ierarhiei si ale sinodalitatii [The Theological Foundations of Hierarchy and Synodality]," *Studii Teologice* 22, no. 3–4 (1970): 176–77.

47. Schmemann, "Theology of Councils," 178.

48. Vassa Larin shows that in the first millennium, Byzantine Christians (men and women) actively participated in the Liturgy through congregational singing. However, seventeenth century parochial choirs in Russia were reserved exclusively for men. Women were allowed to join these choirs only in the nineteenth century. Vassa Larin, "'Active Participation' of the Fatihful in Byzantine Liturgy," *Saint Vladimir's Theological Quarterly* 57, no. 1 (2013): 73–74.

would be able to minister even more meaningfully by offering an official prayer of the church instead of praying informally when they visit the sick, and by giving Communion when they go into women's prisons or visit the shut-ins. Deaconesses would also offer Communion in parishes, teach authoritatively in the public worship of the Church, and re-include our charitable activities into the ordained ministry of the Church, after the model of the deacons of the early centuries.

A middle way between lack of public recognition of ministries and ordination to diaconate is what Richard Gaillardetz terms, "installed ministries." He observes that in the early Church, all ministries were recognized with a blessing or ordination, and that no ministry lacked a public recognition and commissioning. Gaillardetz then proposes that a ministerial installation—not to be confused with ordination—would still re-position a specific person in the community of the Church.[49] Perhaps a practical way of implementing this suggestion in Orthodox parishes is to discern which lay ministers should be blessed (cheirothesia) by the bishop into one of the minor orders, as close as possible to the ministries at hand. For example, a person who is a Sunday School director or leads a Bible study should be blessed as reader—catechist, or someone who visits the shut-ins as subdeacon or sub-deaconess.

Committed to the values of the Kingdom, each parish should have a visitation ministry, in which not only the priest and the deacons visit the sick and the elderly, but also the faithful who are called to this ministry of healing. Frequent visits to the sick provide the opportunity for the church "to be there" in times of need. The friends of the paralytic are the model for having such a strong faith, that Jesus heals (Mt 9:2). Notably, the paralytic did not suffer alone, and his friends do not say anything in this specific episode, because "being there" is all that is needed. Markus Zusak, in his famous novel, *The Book Thief*, introduces a word that perfectly describes the role of the Church in its ministry of healing, namely "thereness."[50] Zusak defines thereness as the ability to be next to someone in need, soothing them, loving them, simply staying there to kill the aloneness, holding someone, and reassuring them. Thereness. In this sense, the Church is "there" to heal. The healing takes place as a manifestation of the Kingdom because Christ is there through the Spirit. "Where two or three gather in my name, there am I with them," (Mt 18:20), promised Jesus,

---

49. Richard R. Gaillardetz, "The Ecclesiological Foundations of Ministry within an Ordered Communion," in *Ordering of the Baptismal Priesthood*, ed. Susan Wood (Collegeville, MN: Liturgical Press, 2003), 44–46.

50. Markus Zusak, *The Book Thief* (New York: Knopf, 2005), 36.

who is "there" in the midst of those who gather in his name, so the mission of the Church is to make Jesus present through healing and proclamation as manifestations of the Kingdom.

As these examples show, the Orthodox laity in the West, especially women, are very involved in parish life to a level that is rarely experienced in majority-Orthodox countries. In Orthodox churches in the United States, the Eucharist is of course central to the life of the Church, but many parishes go beyond once-a-week participation, being active seven days a week thanks to their liturgical, educational, and charitable ministries. Their parish life is Kingdom-oriented. Acts 2:44–45 presents an early Church in which "all who believed were together and had all things in common; they would sell their possessions and goods and distribute the proceeds to all, as any had need." Although the sharing of resources today takes the form of stewardship, contemporary parishes follow the example of the early church and minister to those in need by building homes, paying utility bills and medical expenses, or establishing networks for the redistribution of goods. Interestingly, this aspect of parish life is not liturgical in nature and transcends denominational and physical boundaries, well beyond the local parish.

If many of the ministries discussed in this section are geared primarily toward the parish, the parish as a whole also ministers to the world around it. John Wesley, the founder of Methodism, said that the world was his parish,[51] which contrasts to those pastors for whom the parish is their world. There are some parishes that are so enclosed onto themselves that their own community is their whole world. An *outward-looking parish*, however, regards the whole world as its responsibility. Such a parish is the local church inserted into a certain neighborhood because it has a mission towards the place in which it functions, for the growth of the Kingdom, as many parables suggest.

A Kingdom-centered approach to parish life, of course, has financial implications. Each parish, family, and individual needs to look carefully at their finances and see how these reflect their priorities. They should not spend well over 95% of their income on their own needs and very little on furthering the Kingdom by giving to others. The Bible commands tithing (Ex 14:18–20; Nm 18:21; Mal 3:8), although tithing should not be done without remembering the weightier matters of the law (Mt 23:23). Forcefully imposing a 10% tithe on

---

51. As testified by his *Journal* ch. 3, John Wesley preached not only in churches, but also in the fields, which encroached on other pastors' parishes. When he was criticized for his practice, he responded: "seeing I have now no parish ..., I look upon all the world as my parish." The words "the world is my parish" became a motto of Methodists engaged in missions.

families and communities of all incomes goes against mercy—a weightier matter of the Law. For a poor family, 10% is too difficult, and the Rabbinic tradition
prescribes a limit to giving alms to the poor, namely one cannot impoverish
one's own family and thus make them a burden on others. At the same time,
for a rich family 10% may be neither meaningful nor sacrificial giving. And yet,
recent studies show that in American Orthodoxy, higher income households
are less generous than lower income households when it comes to percentage
of giving, averaging 2.5% and 3.75%, respectively. Moreover, a median Orthodox
household gave $2,000 to its local parish in 2014, as well as other smaller con-
tributions to other religious organizations and nonprofits. The Antiochian and
OCA jurisdictions are the most generous (about $3,000), while the GOA is
the third, at $1,500. Furthermore, converts to Orthodoxy support tithing more
than cradle Orthodox. The greatest predictors of generosity are involvement in
parish life and the parish's outward orientation—doing the work of the Kingdom outside its boundaries.[52]

When looking at the community rather than the individual, on average,
Orthodox parishes spend 82% of their income on personnel, office supplies, and
building occupancy. A high percentage of their other expenditures, sometimes
far exceeding 10% annually, goes towards their larger administrative body, such
as an Archdiocese or a Metropolis, that assesses their parishes as a means for
raising funds for ministries but also as a condition for their recognition as parishes in good standing. This spending practice is certainly too inward-looking.
A Kingdom-centered budget should include a larger portion for others, according to the financial abilities of each parish: wealthier parishes should give more,
while struggling parishes can give less, but they need to give nonetheless. Again,
at both family and parish levels, giving should be meaningful and sacrificial.
Only then does the Church become a means towards a Kingdom, rather than
a self-serving community.

Focusing on the Church itself is detrimental to the Church, while focusing
on other human beings is constructive for the Church. That is not to say that
it is not important to have a strong community and to strengthen a church
from the inside. But more and more we are discovering that we need to look at
the outside in order to be strong on the inside. True, sometimes parishes are
forced to become inward-looking because of extenuating circumstances. Especially in the northeastern United States, in old Pennsylvania mining towns or

52. Alexei Krindatch, *Exploring Orthodox Generosity: Giving in US Orthodox Parishes* (http://assem-
blyofbishops.org/news/research 2015), 1–4.

Ohio industrial cities, parishes are dying out because most of the people that used to populate these places have moved away, in search for new jobs. A small community of senior citizens still exists in these cities and all their efforts are directed to fundraisers that would repair the roof of an old church building. Their main purpose is to be financially viable enough to have a part-time priest until they all die out, because there are no prospects of growth. But most other times, communities become inward-looking because they lack a proper purpose: instead of being there to manifest the Kingdom of God to the world, they gather as a community focused on personal friendships or ethnicity. Other times, communities choose to be inward-looking because they want to insulate themselves from an outside world that is regarded as evil; this attitude is prevalent among those who do not want to "get their hands dirty" with ministry to the world and think that prayer alone is their purpose.

The elements mentioned above are all ingredients of a healthy ecclesiology, and realistically no parish can have them all. It is only natural that some communities will focus on one of these elements; parishes have each their own charisms. Developing parishes will focus on church building in their beginnings, but their financial efforts should go beyond church architecture. Friendships and ethnicity are important for building up the community and welcoming new immigrants, but they are stumbling blocks when visitors are not welcome because they are outsiders and of a different ethnic background. There are times when the only way to preserve one's Orthodoxy is to be set apart, separate, and this is what being holy truly means: have strong moral convictions when others have abandoned them, observe the fast when others do not, and love when others hate. But if we isolate ourselves completely from the world, how are we going to be a testimony to the beauty of our faith? If we dismiss the others as lost or heretics, how are we going to find a common language to express the truth? Indeed, hearing the word of God duly proclaimed within the Church is a manifestation of the Kingdom, but a partial one, if not paired with the proclamation of the gospel to the world and the healing of the world from poverty, suffering, and sin.[53]

---

53. In this sense, Pope Francis writes: "I prefer a church which is bruised, hurting and dirty because it has been out on the streets, rather than a church which is unhealthy from being confined and from clinging to its own security ... a poor Church for the poor [in which the bishops and priests have] the smell of the sheep." *Evangelii Gaudium / The Joy of the Gospel*, par. 49, 24.

"UNTIL ALL OF US COME ... TO THE MEASURE
OF THE FULL STATURE OF CHRIST":
THEOSIS AS ECCLESIAL ENDEAVOR

The gifts he gave were that some would be apostles, some prophets, some evangelists, some pastors and teachers, to equip the saints for the work of ministry, for building up the body of Christ, until all of us come to the unity of the faith and of the knowledge of the Son of God, to maturity, to the measure of the full stature of Christ. (Eph 4:11–13)

The previous section mentioned this passage from Ephesians as it described a multitude of ministries at work in the parish, emphasizing human actions and human responsibility. This passage, however, also emphasizes the divine work in the Church. It describes ministries as the work of God through the members of the Church. A ministry is gift, or a charism that God bestowed on each member of the Body of Christ, so that these members would become vehicles through whom Christ himself works. In other words, Christ works through the members of his Body. The result of their work is the building up of the Body of Christ, spiritual growth, up to the point where the community emulates Christ's maturity. In Orthodox language, this maturity, the full stature of Christ, bears the name, divinization, deification, or *theosis*. It means becoming god by grace, noting the small "g" in "god," since the creature does not become Creator.

Theosis has been a constant presence in Orthodox spirituality, although not in Orthodox theology. Norman Russell notes that it was uncommon in later Byzantine writers. Gregory Nazianzus and Maximus the Confessor refer to it in the sense presented above, but the majority of patristic literature understands *theosis* as baptismal adoption by grace or blessed life in the eschatological Kingdom. Later on, Gregory Palamas retrieved older patristic writings and the practice of the hesychasts and defined *theosis* as a personal experience attainable in this life through contemplative prayer.[54] He argued that humans be-

---

54. Norman Russell, "Theosis and Gregory Palamas: Continuity or Doctrinal Change?," *Saint Vladimir's Theological Quarterly* 50, no. 4 (2006): 357. Elsewhere, Russell writes that *theosis*, or divinization, or deification "refers first to a broad theological theme concerning the divine Economy, a theme encapsulated in the so-called 'exchange formula:' the Word 'was made human that we might be made divine' (Athanasius, *Inc.* 54). It refers also to a cluster of spiritual teachings: the incorporation of the believer through Baptism and the Eucharist into the new humanity hypostasized by Christ ... the ascent of the soul through the ascetic life from the image to the likeness of God ... and the participation of the hesychast in the divine energies through the practice of noetic prayer ... These different ideas have all grown out of a single patristic insight, namely, that the 'gods [and] children of the Most High' of *Psalm* 82:6 are to be identified

come "gods by grace" (χάριτι θεοί)[55] and participate in the energies of the Holy Spirit to the point to which "the saints are the instruments of the Holy Spirit, having received the same energy as He has [as proved by their] charisms of healing, the working of miracles, foreknowledge, the irrefutable wisdom ...."[56] In other words, the energies (i.e. activities or operations) of God become the energies of the saints. When taken collectively, all those who are "gods by grace" form the Church, and the Church manifests God's energies into the world. In the same sense, Maximus had previously said that the energies of God are at work in the Church, rendering the Church as an "icon and figure of God."[57]

It is true that sometimes spiritual literature presents *theosis* as a goal attainable only by a spiritual elite, but more often it is an ecclesial endeavor: the whole Church, living as an icon of God, becomes god by grace. The exercise of ministries represents the occasion for God to act through all the members of the Church as the Body of Christ.[58] That is because the Church is the extension of the incarnation, as Florovsky and Staniloae affirm,[59] and the members of the Church are "rightly called 'Christs,'" in the words of Cyril of Jerusalem.[60] Applying *theosis* to the Church in this way, means that the ministries of the Church in fact extend Christ's salvific work into the world. Hence, Palamas regards charisms as instruments of God:

> Anything taken hold of by somebody outside itself, sharing in the energy but not the essence of the one acting through it, is his instrument. As David declared through the Holy Spirit, "My tongue is the pen of a ready writer." The pen is the writer's instrument, sharing in the energy, though obviously not the essence, of the writer, and inscribing whatever he wishes and is able to write.[61]

with those who, according to Paul, are by adoption siblings of and fellow heirs with Christ (Rom 8:15–17)." Norman Russell, "Deification," in *The Cambridge Dictionary of Orthodox Theology*, ed. Ian A. McFarland et al. (Cambridge: Cambridge University Press, 2011), 132–33.

55. Gregory Palamas, *The Triads*, ed. John Meyendorff, trans. Nicolas Gendle (Mahwah, NJ: Paulist Press, 1983), III.II.12, 98.

56. Gregory Palamas, *The Triads*, III.I.33, 88.

57. Maximus the Confessor, "Mystagogia," #3, 189.

58. In this sense, Staniloae wrote: "the center of the Church, its leader, the one who has the initiative, is Jesus Christ, whose divine-human will extends as central will of the Church in all the eras and in each person, as member [of the Church]." Staniloae, *Jesus Christ or the Restoration of Humankind*, 381.

59. Florovsky, "The Historical Problem of a Definition of the Church," 29. Staniloae, *Jesus Christ or the Restoration of Humankind*, 392–93.

60. Cyril of Jerusalem, "Mystagogical Lectures," III:1, 168.

61. Palamas, *Hom.*, 24.8.

Centuries earlier, Maximus used the metaphor of a hot iron to explain that the human person becomes a vehicle for the "fire" of divine activity while still remaining iron.[62] Thus, *theosis* is an ecclesiological endeavor in which the community of the Church becomes god by grace, its ministries are instruments for the extension of Christ's salvific work into the world, which in turn matures the Church until it reaches "the measure of the full stature of Christ."

THE FOUR MARKS OF THE CHURCH:
ONE, HOLY, CATHOLIC, AND APOSTOLIC

As we confess in the Creed, the four marks of the Church are: one, holy, catholic, and apostolic. These four marks do not apply only to the universal Church—as most treatises of ecclesiology discuss them—or to the diocese, but *also to the parish*. Thomas Hopko has no hesitation in this regard:

> An Orthodox parish, i.e. a local community of Orthodox Christians with a priest, has only one God-given reason for being. It exists to be the one, holy, catholic and apostolic Church of Christ…. We say that a parish must be *the* Church of Christ, and not simply *a* church, because, according to the Orthodox faith, every local community of Orthodox Christians with a priest must be—and theologically understood, actually is—the one Church of Christ…. The Orthodox Christian parish must also be catholic. For the parish to be "catholic" means that it is full, complete and whole; lacking nothing to its mystical and sacramental being and life as Christ's holy Church. In an Orthodox Christian parish the whole fullness of God must dwell, as in Christ's body, with all the fullness of life and grace and truth, by the indwelling of the Holy Spirit.[63]

The first mark of the Church is *oneness*, addressed throughout the book both as an ecumenical issue and an intra-Orthodox matter, as for example in the above-analysis of the unity of ministries in the parish. The second mark of the Church is *holiness*. This topic can be treated theologically, experientially, biblically concerning Israel, and pragmatically regarding sin. From a theological perspective, the Church is holy because Christ, the head of the Church is holy, and so the Church as the Body of Christ is holy; it is a divine-human communion

---

62. See Maximus the Confessor, *Opuscula*, (PG 91:189D), quoted in Balthasar, *Cosmic Liturgy*, 258.

63. Thomas Hopko, "The Orthodox Parish in America," in *The Orthodox Parish in America: Faithfulness to the Past and Responsibility for the Future*, ed. Anton C. Vrame (Brookline, MA: Holy Cross Orthodox Press, 2003), 2–3.

that does not have a hypostasis distinct from Christ, since the Church is the extension of Christ; it is the bride of Christ; Christ gave himself up for her in order to sanctify her; the Church is endowed with the Holy Spirit and thereby has the means of salvation and communion with God; all its members are called to holiness, being justified by grace and election, adopted children of God in the Spirit, and partakers of the divine nature.

From an experiential perspective, the Church is holy because the Spirit produces fruits of grace in the lives of all the faithful; its members strive to perfect the gifts or charisms with which God has endowed them; the baptized pray for forgiveness and receive it, and they partake of the sacraments, especially the Eucharist, which sanctify them; the Church does the holy work of God when it functions as an icon of the Kingdom, through healing and proclamation; the Church has received the gift of knowing the will of God through Revelation, including the Scriptures; the Church lives not only on earth, but also in heaven, where all those who are saved dwell; and finally, holiness is manifested in the lives of the saints who have been canonized by the Church.

Each argument for the holiness of the Church listed above represents a special topic that cannot be fully addressed here. A nuanced discussion of the holiness of the Church that stems from its saints, for example, raises the question of why the holiness of a minority of spiritual champions that are recognized as saints makes the Church holy, while the ubiquitous sinfulness of the faithful does not make the Church sinful. Moreover, Zizioulas is also right to counter the conception that the holiness of the Church comes from a small minority of saints and when we refer to the Church as holy, we refer exclusively to them. On the contrary, the Liturgy affirms that the holy gifts are given to the holy (*ta agia tois agiois*—literally "the holy for the holy" sometimes translated as "the Holy Gifts for the holy people of God"). The congregation's response is that "one is holy, one is Lord, Jesus Christ," showing that Christ is the only holy one and all the saints added together are sinful compared to the holiness of Christ.[64]

The same Liturgy shows that holiness is attainable for the regular faithful, not just for the most spiritual ones. Holiness is communal and eucharistic, for after receiving Communion, the church sings, "we have seen the true light, we have received the Holy Spirit ...," which is the same uncreated light as a manifestation of the Spirit that was revealed to the disciples on Mount Tabor—a

---

64. John D. Zizioulas, *Lectures in Christian Dogmatics*, ed. Douglas H. Knight (New York: T&T Clark, 2008), 152.

sign of *theosis* as Gregory Palamas would say. Moreover, when exclaiming, "For you are our sanctification …" the eucharistic assembly of the parish confesses to be the Church that is holy. Clearly, all members of the parish are sinful, so their confession *to be holy and sanctified does not mean being sinless. Holiness means primarily being set apart, being chosen for a specific purpose.* This is how the Bible portrays Israel: set apart from all the nations, chosen to be God's holy people:

> if you obey my voice and keep my covenant, you shall be my treasured possession out of all the peoples. Indeed, the whole earth is mine, but you shall be for me a priestly kingdom and a holy nation. (Ex 19:5–6)

This text that represents God's will for Israel is significant in several respects. First, it begins as a conditional phrase because it is pronounced before God revealed the Law on Mt. Sinai and thus before the people accepted the covenant. Once Israel became a covenant people, their status as God's "kingdom of priests" became irrevocable. Second, this promise shows God's free election of the people of Israel. God could have chosen any nation upon the earth, and yet God fell in love with Israel, as later Rabbinic literature explains; so God elected Israel, not because of the people's merits, but because God fell in love with her.[65] Third, the text differentiates between what is holy and what is not: Israel is holy, while the other nations are not. That is not to say that other nations are profane, since they remain God's creation, but Israel is set apart. Fourth, unlike the common concept that in a nation only some are holy—namely the priests—and the rest are not, here the concept of holiness applies to the entire nation. Which is not to say that all will bring sacrifices or perform the duties of the priest, as only Aaron's descendants do. But it speaks in priestly terms about the entire people, including those who are not from a priestly family. As a matter of fact, being a nazirite is another form of holiness (as in making oneself separate for the Lord), and it is open to all tribes and all genders: "either men or women make a special vow, the vow of a nazirite, to separate themselves to the Lord" (Numbers 6:2).

As with most biblical texts, these passages should be read in light of other texts that might even stand in tension with them. For example, in Ex 22:31 God tells Israel, "you shall be consecrated to me" in the sense that Israel shall be holy, thus rendering holiness as a future reality. Moreover, Deuteronomy 7:6 refers to Israel as "a people holy to the Lord your God; the Lord your God has chosen

---

65. Rabbinic literature and canonical texts such as the Song of Songs consistently emphasize this point. There is, however, a notable exception. Isaiah describes the Lord's forgiveness of Egypt who will turn to the true worship of the Lord, becoming God's people, together with Assyria, with Israel as the third partner: "Blessed be Egypt my people, and Assyria the work of my hands, and Israel my heritage" (Is 19:19–25).

you out of all the peoples on earth to be his people, his treasured possession," unconditionally, even though in general Deuteronomic language is conditional.

The emphasis on separation as a means of becoming holy, of course, occurs much earlier, in the first account of creation. After God separated the light from darkness, the waters from the dry land, and so forth, at the end of creation, he set aside the day of rest. In Genesis 2:2–3, the Sabbath is holy or, as some translations put it, God hallowed it. The holiness of the Sabbath is one of the defining characteristics of Jewish practice and identity. The rabbinical tradition identifies 39 categories of work.[66] Their motivation is probably related to the building process of a temple and to daily activities. They are also meant to keep a person within the community on the Sabbath day, and thus separate from others, instead of being taken outside the community through work. From this perspective, the Sabbath is meant to create community and to separate Jews from others.[67]

This Jewish understanding of holiness as being set apart is the primary meaning for the holiness of the Church, which is described in the New Testament in the same way as Israel was described at Mt. Sinai:

> you are a chosen race, a royal priesthood, a holy nation, God's own people
> (1 Peter 2:9).

Thus, the holiness of the Church is primarily an indication that the Church is set apart, chosen by God to be a priestly people, an icon of the Kingdom. If holiness does not equate with sinlessness, what does Orthodox theology say about *sin in the Church?* Florovsky writes about the tension between the historical and eschatological church. The former contains sinful elements, but their presence does not take away from the holiness of the church that comes from its eschatological nature: "the Church is still *in statu viae* and yet it is already *in statu patriae.* It has, as it were, a double life, *both in heaven and on earth.* The Church is a visible historical society, and the same is the Body of Christ. It is both the Church of the redeemed, and the Church of miserable sinners—both at once."[68] Kallistos Ware places the holiness of the Church within the ten-

---

66. Activities that cannot be performed on the Sabbath include: sowing, plowing, reaping, grinding, baking, bleaching, dyeing, tying a knot, untying a knot, sewing, trapping or hunting, slaughtering, marking out, cutting, writing, erasing, building, demolishing, kindling a flame, carrying from private to public domain and vice versa, and putting the finishing touch to a piece of work already begun before the Sabbath.

67. Exodus and Deuteronomy present different motivations for the Sabbath: the creation of the world in six days and the liberation from Egypt, respectively. It appears that Jesus preferred the second approach by performing numerous healings on the Sabbath.

68. Florovsky, "The Church: Her Nature and Task," 68.

sion between history and eschaton, but looks at the eschaton as an imperative coming from within the very being of the Church as it exists already: "The Church on earth exists in a state of tension: it is already the Body of Christ, and thus perfect and sinless, and yet, since its members are imperfect and sinful, it must continually become what it is."[69] Boris Bobrinskoy attempts to discuss the existence of sin in the Church in a distinct section in his treatise of ecclesiology,[70] but leaves the reader with an image of a Church separated from its sinful members, isolating sin as a personal reality, separate from the ecclesial character of the sinners. In other words, because these theologians emphasize holiness as sinlessness (as opposed to being set apart), they affirm the holiness of the Church despite its sinful members. But God can use any instrument, regardless of how sinful it is, to do his work of sanctification, so there is no need to deny the sinfulness of the members of the Church in order to preserve the holiness of the Church.

By the grace of God, there will never be a time when the Church will be entirely devoid of holiness. But there were times in history when the official structures of the Church were sinful and the majority of the Church perpetuated the sinfulness of this world. Indeed, the Church will always have an Athanasius the Great or a Maximus the Confessor as islands of righteousness. But these two saints have been persecuted by their own Church: Athanasius was among the few remaining faithful to Nicaea in the East, deposed and exiled in the desert. Maximus was officially condemned by synods that preferred the way of the emperor, rather than the truth. Similar examples abound in history, iconoclasm being just one of them, when many church leaders embraced falsehood and enforced it by virtue of their ecclesial authority, often resorting to violence in the name of the Church. Such instances are not merely the sin of some individuals, or even the sin of the majority of Church members, but forms of systemic sin.[71]

It is appropriate to speak of systemic sin when sinful ideologies that originate in the darkness of the world and contradict the spirit of the Scriptures make their way into Church mentality, Church discipline, and even into Church hymnography. How else could one speak about the Church's possession of

---

69. Ware, *The Orthodox Church*, 244.

70. Boris Bobrinskoy, *The Mystery of the Church: A Course in Orthodox Dogmatic Theology*, trans. Michael Breck (Yonkers, NY: St. Vladimir's Seminary Press, 2012), 140–42.

71. Contrary to the belief that only individuals (and not collectives) can sin, Bradford Hinze points out that ideologies act as modes of consciousness that bear upon a collective's actions and beliefs, resulting in social sin and thus the need for ecclesial repentance. Bradford E. Hinze, "Ecclesial Repentance and the Demands of Dialogue," *Theological Studies* 61, no. 2, June (2000): 222–29.

slaves as late as the Middles Ages, when monasteries owned entire villages and especially marginalized populations such as the Roma? Or when disparaging cultural norms made their way into hymnography and Church practices regarding women and the Jews? The Church's hymnography and preaching sometimes fanned the flames of anti-Semitism, because the biblical texts that speak about the everlasting character of God's election of Israel, of his irrevocable promises, are drowned by hymns during Holy Week that are unworthy of being repeated here, that do not represent the richness of Orthodox theology, and that intentionally misinterpret biblical passages, taking them out of context and enveloping them in a language of hatred.[72]

Having said this, it is important to recognize that, in hindsight, the Church recognizes systematic sin and, as Church, corrects it. This is a process that will continue until the end of times, raising again the biblical question of whether holiness is a present or a future reality. As stated earlier, the Old Testament upholds both positions in regard to Israel. While the holiness of the Church in the sense of being set apart as the redeemed community of the baptized is a present reality, in the eschaton, the Church will be perfected: "Christ loved the church and gave himself up for her, in order to make her holy by cleansing her with the washing of water by the word, so as to present the church to himself in splendor, without a spot or wrinkle or anything of the kind—yes, so that she may be holy and without blemish" (Eph 5:25–27). Under the loving care of Christ, the process of perfection (or holiness in the sense of sinlessness) has already begun, even though it will be fulfilled in the eschaton. In the meantime, we affirm the holiness of the Church in the Creed without blushing because we do not mean that the Church is sinless, but that it is set apart and, as such, its members are sanctified and through them the world is sanctified. This understanding of holiness applies to the Church as both universal and local parish.

The third mark of the Church is *catholic*, a term first used by Ignatius of

---

72. Readers who might find such a strong indictment of anti-Semitism unmerited would benefit from Bogdan Bucur's analysis of various Orthodox theologians on this subject. Eugen Pentiuc recommends the revision of liturgical texts and discarding anti-Judaic statements from Orthodox hymnography, whose poetry is otherwise too sublime to be marred by such low sentiments. Bert Groen laments that, in the liturgical hymns of Holy Week, anti-Jewish rhetoric degenerates into torrents of abuse. For instance, the congregants hear constant invectives against "the swarm of murderers," "the gang of God-haters," "the lawless assembly," that "teeth-grinding, most malicious race of the Hebrews." Theokritoff considers that such hymns do not enrich our theological understanding but infuse the services with "a mood of anger and indignation." Today, they are deeply disturbing, since rhetoric of this kind has led to violence against Jews, especially around the Easter season that sometimes degenerated into pogroms. Bucur concludes that the anti-Jewish overtones are unessential to the theological message of the hymns and do not belong in Orthodox worship. Bogdan G. Bucur, "Anti-Jewish Rhetoric in Byzantine Hymnography: Exegetical and Theological Contextualization," *St. Vladimir's Theological Quarterly* 61, no. 1 (2017): 39–60.

Antioch in the second century.[73] "Catholic" means "according to the whole": the whole is present in the part and the part is according to the whole. That means that the local church is fully the Church of Christ, not just a fragment of that universal Church. It is similar to the way in which the eucharistic Body of Christ is fully present in the fragment of Communion that each faithful receives, while at the same time remaining one. When a faithful receive the body and blood of Christ, they do not receive anything less than then entire body and blood of Christ, even though to an outsider it would seem that they only receive a small part of the entire Eucharist prepared that day. But from a faith perspective, the whole is present in the part and the part is according to the whole. This eucharistic image suggests how the faithful experience their local parish, as the fullness of the Church, and not merely a partial reality that cannot be properly called Church, and thus insufficient as means for their salvation. It may seem that a small parish of twenty families is an insignificant part of a worldwide Christianity that counts 2.1 billion members, but it is not. That small parish is catholic. To say that the Church is catholic means that the Church *Una Sancta* is present in the local church and that the local church *is* the Church.

Orthodox theologians understand the catholicity of the Church according to two major lines of thinking. On the one hand, the Slavonic tradition originally translated *katholiki* with *kafolitcheskaya*, before replacing it in the sixteenth century with *sobornaya*. From the latter, Alexei Khomiakov coined the term *sobornost*, which implies synodality and solidarity, as opposed to individualism and isolationism; it also evokes ecumenicity, togetherness, communion, harmony, concord, mutuality, unanimity, oneness, and organic unity. The best way to summarize Khomiakov's view of sobornicity is with the term, "universality."[74]

On the other hand, Florovsky preferred to write about "catholicity" rather than "Sobornost" and, instead of understanding it quantitatively (i.e., universality), he emphasized the qualitative aspect of catholicity, namely its orthodoxy. If Vincent of Lérins affirmed that what is true has been held by all, in all places,

73. Ignatius writes: "Apart from the bishop, let no one perform any of the functions that pertain to the Church. Let that Eucharist be held valid which is offered by the bishop or by the one to whom the bishop has committed this charge. Wherever the bishop appears, there let the people be; as wherever Jesus Christ is, there is the Catholic Church." Ignatius, "To the Smyrnaeans," in Ignatius of Antioch (Theophorus), "The Letters," #8, 121.

74. Viorel Coman, *Dumitru Stăniloae's Trinitarian Ecclesiology: Orthodoxy and the Filioque* (New York: Fortress / Lexington, 2019), 218–20. In the same section, Coman clarifies that Khomiakov never used *sobornost* in his writings, but only the adjectival form *soborny*.

and at all times, Florovsky reacted against this Vincentian canon by pointing out that there were times in history when "Christian communities were but solitary rare islands in a sea of unbelief and paganism," or when the majority of the Orthodox faithful embraced various heresies (e.g., Arianism in the fourth century), so "'Catholic' at that time meant 'orthodox' rather than 'universal.' In that period, the true Church was persecuted and had to escape to the desert. The majority was embracing different heresies, so 'catholicity' is more a qualitative than a quantitative term."[75] Moreover,

> The universality of the Church is the consequence or the manifestation, but not the cause or the foundation of its catholicity. The world-wide extension or the universality is only an outward sign, one that is not absolutely necessary. [...] Καθολική from Καθ'όλου means, first of all, the inner wholeness and integrity of the Church's life.[76]

Florovsky's view that catholicity means orthodoxy rather than universality represents the prevalent opinion today. When one considers that there are 8 billion humans on our planet, but only 2.1 billion Christians, and the proportion of Christians compared to the rest of humankind is diminishing, it becomes impossible to speak about the universality of the Church quantitatively. But not about the fullness of the local church.

Although neither of these lines of thinking address the catholicity of the parish but that of the diocese, they both could support the affirmation that the parish is catholic. The parish displays Khomiakov's traits: a community that rejects individualism and promotes solidarity; synodal, as we shall see in a later chapter; concord; and organic unity given its ministries at work as the Body of Christ. Florovsky's considerations support the affirmation that the parish is catholic by rejecting a minimal quantitative membership as a condition for catholicity. When the true Church retreated in the desert, it lacked even the structures of today's parish, and yet it remained catholic, the parish is catholic.

The affirmation of the parish as catholic fullness of the Church is a daring proposition. Zizioulas criticizes Schmemann and Afanasiev for ascribing ecclesiological fullness to the parish.[77] As quoted in the beginning of this section, however, Hopko boldly ascribes ecclesiological fulness to the parish. In light of the arguments presented in this chapter, I consider that, when a parish remains

75. Florovsky, "The Catholicity of the Church," 39–40, 51. Florovsky, "The Historical Problem of a Definition of the Church," 33.

76. Florovsky, "The Catholicity of the Church," 39–40.

77. Zizioulas, *Eucharist, Bishop, Church*, 259. It is debatable whether Zizioulas presents Schmemann and Afanasiev's positions fairly, but Zizioulas' stance on the parish lacking ecclesiological fullness is clear.

in eucharistic, dogmatic, and synodal communion with the other parishes, the local bishop, and other local dioceses, the parish is a catholic Church, an instantiation of the fullness of the Church universal.

The fourth and final mark of the Church is *apostolic*, which means that the Church here and now is the Church that the Apostles left behind, or the Church of the New Testament. Orthodox and Catholics tend to focus on apostolicity as the uninterrupted chain of ordinations from the apostles until today, which they have faithfully preserved.[78] Protestant churches tend to understand apostolicity as having the same life of the early, apostolic Church present in them. Concretely, they read the Scriptures and preach the word of God, they perform sacraments such as Baptism, the Eucharist, and Orders. In this latter sense, the apostolicity of these churches cannot be denied ecumenically. The U.S. Orthodox-Catholic Consultation even gives priority to the latter over the former sense of apostolicity:

> (a) The apostolicity of ministry is generally seen as derived from the continuity of the community as a whole in apostolic life and faith; the succession of ministers in office is normally agreed to be subordinate to that ecclesial apostolicity. (b) Apostolicity seems to consist more in fidelity to the apostles' proclamation and mission than in any one form of handing on community office.[79]

Orthodox and Catholics are grateful to have recovered this larger understanding of apostolicity as a result of their ecumenical encounters with Protestant churches. These encounters also highlighted the historical reality that apostolic succession understood as uninterrupted chain of succession does not suffice as a condition for apostolicity. In Irenaeus of Lyon's times, Gnostics possessed such valid ordinations, but they did not guard the deposit of the true faith.[80] Consequently, Irenaeus downplays the importance of the uninterrupted chain of ordinations and emphasizes the need to read Scriptures correctly, going as far as to say that heretics should not read the Scriptures.

As a corrective to this approach that looks exclusively at the clergy, Zizioulas affirms that apostolic succession is not just about the ordained, it is also

---

78. A notable exception is Afanasiev, who points out that the apostles have not transmitted their ministry to those whom they ordained. Rather, the apostles transmitted their place at the eucharistic assembly, a place that they themselves have received from Christ. Thus, Afanasiev prefers a topological understanding of apostolic succession. Afanassieff, *The Church of the Holy Spirit*, 248–51.

79. "Apostolicity as God's Gift in the Life of the Church [1986]" in Borelli and Erickson, *The Quest for Unity*, 127–28.

80. Borelli and Erickson, *The Quest for Unity*, 127.

about the laity. Recognizing the apostolicity of a church cannot be limited to its bishop, but has to extend to the entire community. That is because the bishop is never separate from the community.[81]

Another factor that adds to the complexity of apostolicity is that the church as we experience it today is the living experience of the eschaton, informed and nourished from the end of times. If that is the case, how can Protestant churches not have apostolicity? The eschatological Church manifests itself in their life today, thus making them apostolic in this eschatological sense. Orthodox theologians cannot simply look backwards in history in order to judge apostolicity, but also forwards to the Kingdom to come, as Zizioulas writes, and this eschatological approach is most relevant in ecumenical relations.[82]

When Orthodox and Catholics condition unity on apostolic succession understood as uninterrupted chain of ordinations, some Christians are willing to oblige for the sake of unity. For example, some Methodists do not believe in the need for such an uninterrupted chain of ordinations (so they do not regard themselves as lacking something in this regard), but they are open to having a bishop in unquestioned uninterrupted apostolic succession present at their future ordinations. In several cases, British Methodists accepted episcopal ordinations that included the participation of Anglican bishops, for the sake of unity with the Church of England, which claims the kind of historic succession discussed here. Worldwide Methodism, in its responses to WCC's *Baptism, Eucharist, and Ministry (BEM)*—the convergence document approved at Lima—affirmed its willingness to accept historic episcopal succession in BEM's understanding as "a sign, though not a guarantee, of the continuity and unity of the Church" a phrase that should be acceptable to the Orthodox, given Irenaeus' contention that Gnostic apostolic succession did not guarantee apostolicity.[83]

Thus, apostolicity involves several aspects of church life: the uninterrupted chain of ordinations that Orthodox and Catholics have preserved, and which some Protestants are willing to take on in the future; the holistic understanding of the Church as clergy and faithful together, without exclusive reference to the clergy; the continuity between the Church of today, with both the past and the eschatological Kingdom; and the preservation of apostolic life in the

81. John D. Zizioulas, "The Theological Problem of 'Reception,'" *One in Christ* 21, no. 3 (1985): 191–93. Zizioulas, *Being as Communion*, 166, 93.

82. Zizioulas, *Being as Communion*, 178.

83. Wainwright, *Methodists in Dialogue*, 54.

Church. In all these regards, apostolicity applies not only to the Church universal and the diocese, but also to the parish.

—

In conclusion, when considering the designation of the Church as the Body of Christ, the identification of Christ with the members of the Church, or *theosis* as an ecclesiological endeavor, the Church *is* Christ in the Holy Spirit. Its membership encompasses the living, the saints, all the departed, the angels, Virgin Mary, the entire cosmos as the sacrament that celebrates a cosmic Liturgy, and even extends beyond the created world, since the Church existed before all times and Christ is its head. Theologians tend to refer to the Church as the diocese, the ethnic jurisdiction, the national church, the entire Orthodoxy, Christian denominations, and all of Christianity, while and experiential approach to the Church focuses on the parish.

Despite being the most common church structure, the parish appears to have no ecclesiological identity and theologians largely ignore it. In contrast, an experiential ecclesiology of the parish earnestly considers the transition from the eucharistic assembly led by the bishop in the diocese to the Liturgy presided over by the priest in the parish. The parish is a community of the faithful gathered together around the priest for the celebration of the Eucharist and other services; for being an instrument of the Kingdom, bringing healing and proclamation of the good news to their locality and the world in general; and for building up the Body of Christ by exercising the various charisms of its members— divinized extensions of Christ—showing *theosis* as an ecclesiological endeavor.

The local church is both the building (the place of liturgical celebrations, education, and ministries) and the community (a family, home of the baptized, a place of welcome for others). Furthermore, recent decades have transformed Western parishes in regards to the means of recognizing membership, ethnicity, the number of congregations, and ecumenical composition. For example, if in majority Orthodox countries a parish is the community of believers who share the same faith and the fullness of liturgical life, in Western Orthodoxy the parish is more than the body of communicants with the same beliefs. In varying degrees of commitment, Catholic and Protestant faithful are members of Orthodox parishes and the parish welcomes a significant number of converts and faithful who do not share the same ethnic background as the majority.

The parish is not simply an administrative unit of the diocese. Rather, the parish, too, is the one, holy, catholic, and apostolic church. The parish is one in its ministries, for example. It is holy not in the sense that the Church is sinless (since there is sin in the Church), but that it is set apart, chosen by God to be a priestly people, an icon of the Kingdom; as such, its members are sanctified and through them the world is sanctified. The parish is catholic as an instantiation of the fullness of the Church universal. The apostolicity of the entire Church—clergy and laity alike—refers to the continuity between the Church of today with the life of the Church of the Apostles, the past, and the eschatological Kingdom, as well as an uninterrupted chain of ordinations.

FIVE

Liturgy

It is time for the Lord to act.

With these words proclaimed by the deacon in the beginning of the Divine Liturgy, the worshipping Church professes that the Lord is the ultimate celebrant of the Liturgy. The Greek word employed here is *kairos* (sacred time), not *chronos* (regular time). This is not merely a reminder that the time to start the Liturgy has arrived, although habitual latecomers should heed it in this sense, too. *Kairos* is God's sacred time bursting open into our own time, eternity manifested in our age. As the Liturgy begins with the words, "Blessed is the Kingdom," we get a glimpse of that eschatological Kingdom here and now.

The Liturgy is an inexhaustible source for theology, so, to stay within the confines of this project, numerous eucharistic themes will remain unexplored. This chapter will focus on one main thesis: in the past, ecclesiology has been the cause of lack of eucharistic communion; today, however, ecclesiology should be the main reason for eucharistic communion between Orthodox and Catholic churches, as we experience the Kingdom of God here and now in the Liturgy. This thesis involves unpacking several subthemes. First, I address the liturgical assembly as it gathers to do "the work of the people"—the meaning of the Greek term, *leitourgia*—followed by a presentation of the clergy and the people as con-celebrants, which implies an active participation of the laity and an eschatological approach to the work of God in this present age. The chapter will then focus on the Eucharist as boundary marker and the issue of intercommunion, ending with the ethical implications of the Liturgy.

THE LITURGICAL ASSEMBLY

The communion that the faithful experience in the Liturgy presupposes the act of gathering together in one place. The previous chapter identified the normative gathering as the parish church building. This statement was already qualified by the reality that some communities have several places of worship, others do not have one at all, and that persecutions affect Christians' ability to gather in one place, forcing them to retreat underground and, most recently, into online communities.

To further qualify the act of gathering into one place, it is important to note that an increasing number of parishes stream their *services online* to respond to the needs of those who are shut in or are unable to come to church for reasons of physical and emotional health, occupation (some jobs requiring their presence away from the church), or travel to places without a church. If these cases are usually in the minority, during the pandemic that began in 2020, online worship became the norm for the majority of Christians. In all these situations, the physical gathering of the entire body of faithful in one place is impossible. Instead, the faithful join the assembly of the Church virtually, in a community that extends beyond the normative physical space of the parish into the online space. This is an unprecedented ecclesiological reality, in which the faithful participate in the prayers of the Church, hear the proclamation of the word of God, and donate their treasure, time, and talents to the Church online. Virtual worship is not a substitute for normative forms of worship,[1] for the body of Christ is a visible reality, but the expansion of the liturgical assembly into the virtual realm has already become normative and, in exceptional cases such as during a pandemic, it is the only way to participate in worship.

Throughout its history, the Church had to counter the perpetual temptation of retreating away from the physical world, whether it was reacting against Gnostic dualism that rejected the goodness of the material world, or the view of the true Church as an invisible reality, or a spiritual elitism that still remains a perpetual temptation in the Church. Instead, locality and place are manifestations of an incarnate Church, gathered around the body and blood of Christ, understood not in a dematerialized sense, but as flesh tabernacling among us and made present in the Spirit of God. A sacrament remains in need of matter: bread, wine, water, oil, all of which cannot be substituted in an online

1. Long before the 2020 pandemic, exclusively online worship involved the avatar of the minister and other avatars populating virtual pews, participating in worship and receiving virtually the bread and the wine. See http://liturgy.co.nz/virtual-eucharist. Such examples stray far from the Orthodox experience.

community. When they are not dictated by necessity, disembodied forms of worship do not create community, but border a magical understanding of sacraments and a gnostic anthropology that rejects the goodness of the body. Extending the community of the faithful who gather in one place to the online realm is a positive adaptation to the practical needs of our time, but exclusively virtual gatherings cannot supplant the community that shares the same physical space of the church building and the sacraments. Instead, the members of the Church gathered in the parish building have the duty to visit the sick and the shut-ins in their homes with the sacraments of Communion and Holy Unction and to bring them to church whenever possible, as the communion of the Church is manifested in the worshippers assembled around the Eucharist, as an icon of the Kingdom—a Kingdom that is manifested visibly in the sacred space of the church building.

For this reason, *church architecture* is relevant beyond its esthetic value or its practical purpose of offering the space for the community to gather. The church temple represents a tangible representation of the Church—icon of the Kingdom. Of course, biblically speaking, the need for sacred spaces goes all the way back to the beginnings, and Orthodox theology is remarkably similar to the Jewish tradition in this regard. The first account of creation presents a world that is ordered concentrically, as an ancient temple that contained the image of the god in the middle or, in this case, with the human being as the image of God created at the end of creation. The human being lived in the garden of Eden, often portrayed in Orthodox iconography as the Kingdom of God and vice versa: the eschatological paradise has the tree of life (Jesus) in its central point. Eden is the place where God is present, and the tree of knowledge of good and evil and the tree of life are (or, is, since this is one and the same tree) in the middle of the garden.[2]

Later Orthodox architecture will look at the altar area as the garden of Eden, with the Cross in the middle, symbolizing the tree of life. Orthodox hymnology interprets biblical references to the tree typologically, as images for the Cross, since the Greek word *xilos* could mean both tree and wood, associated more specifically with the wood of the Cross. While Adam received from the tree of knowledge of good and evil the fruit that brought death, we receive from the tree of life (the Cross) the fruit of life, namely the Body and Blood of Christ, sacrificed on the wood (tree) of the Cross. No cherubim with a flaming

2. For an illustration of this idea, see the front cover of this book, which reproduces an icon from the St. George chapel of my home parish, Holy Trinity Greek Orthodox Church in Pittsburgh.

sword keep us from partaking of the tree of life (Gn 3:24), but together with the cherubim, humans now enter into God's presence. The altar as an image of Eden is thus the place where humans and God are in communion / Communion. That is not to say that the faithful who are in the nave or the narthex are further away from God than those who are inside the altar, since according to Maximus the Confessor, Christ has abolished the separation between Eden and the rest of the world.[3] Orthodox architecture suggests the closeness between all those present in the church and God, as humankind before the fall in the Garden of Eden.

Looking at the Garden of Eden and the entire earth as the place in which God's presence is manifested challenges the need for a building that represents a sacred space. At the same time, however, ancient Israel also longed for a physical place in which God was present to a greater extent. While Israel wandered in the desert, the LORD was present in a special way in the Ark of the Covenant, the tent, and the court, all of which were not simply human creations, but resembled heavenly realities and were made under inspiration. The LORD has filled the workers "with the Spirit of God, with skill, intelligence, and knowledge ... to do work done by an artisan" (Ex 35: 31–34), a clear reference to God's act of fashioning the world (again, created as a temple). Thus, humans who build sacred spaces imitate God, and the resulting temple for God's presence becomes patterned after the heavens.

When the first temple was built in Jerusalem, it became the dwelling place of God, but at the same time Solomon had the awareness that God cannot be limited to a temple built by human hands: "will God indeed dwell on the earth? Even heaven and the highest heaven cannot contain you, much less this house that I have built!" (1 Kings 8:27). So, on the one hand God remains un-circumscribable, while on the other hand God dwells mysteriously in the Temple. To use biblical language, "the glory of the LORD filled the house of the LORD" in the form of a cloud and "then Solomon said, 'The LORD has said that he would dwell in thick darkness. I have built you an exalted house, a place for you to dwell in forever'" (1 Kgs 8:10–13). Hence, Hebrews going to the temple of Solomon and Orthodox Christians going to church do not simply enter a building; they enter God's dwelling place, built after the heavenly pattern.

When Solomon's temple was destroyed, "the glory of the Lord" was again

3. Saint Maximos the Confessor, *On Difficulties in the Church Fathers: The Ambigua*, trans. Nicholas Constas, 2 vols. (Cambridge, MA: Harvard University Press, 2014), 41:4, vol. 2, p. 107. See Adam G. Cooper, *The Body in St. Maximus the Confessor: Holy Flesh, Wholly Deified*, The Oxford Early Christian Studies, (Oxford, NY: Oxford University Press, 2005), 104.

lifted up and, carried away by cherubim, traveled to Babylon with the people, now become again a wondering nation (Ez 10:3–19). But God does not become absent when his dwelling place is destroyed. Similar to Israel, Orthodox Christians know that all too well, since God dwelt with his people even when communists bulldozed churches or transformed them into dancing clubs with fake ceilings covering the iconography, or filled them up with trash, thus implicitly recognizing their sacred character when trying to desecrate them. Communism fell and these churches were restored to their former glory because God is king and he conquers evil.

Israel, too, returned from Babylon and began to rebuild the Jerusalem Temple, but never finished it and the glory of the Lord did not dwell in it. But, from a Christian perspective, an even greater presence tabernacled in the world— Jesus Christ, the Son of God, who was the presence of God and a walking temple, the temple of his body (Jn 2:21). Moreover, Matthew portrays Jesus entering Jerusalem triumphantly on two animals—the donkey and its colt (Mt 21:1–10). Despite the difficulty in visualizing Jesus riding two animals (though iconography was quite creative in this regard by having Jesus sit on the donkey and resting his feet on the colt), the evangelist suggests that the glory of the Lord has returned to Jerusalem, in a reversal of its departure when cherubim carried it away into exile. Because of the ambulatory character of God's dwelling place in the body of Christ, early Christians understood their own identity as Body of Christ (i.e., Church) as not being bound to an earthly temple. The community itself was a temple. They met in house churches, even while they continued to go to the Jerusalem temple until its destruction in AD 70. *A persecuted community cannot have permanent places of worship*, so early Christians gathered in homes and around the relics of the martyrs. The veneration of the martyrs and the act of gathering around their relics shows that there is one Church in heaven and on earth, with heaven feeding the earth: Ignatius of Antioch describes his own bones and flesh being crushed like grains and becoming bread for Christ and a eucharistic sacrifice: "I am God's wheat; I am ground by the teeth of the wild beasts that I may end as the pure bread of Christ."[4] After being devoured by beasts, when only his bones were left, his relics were conveyed to the Church of Antioch "as an inestimable treasure left

---

4. Ignatius, "To the Romans," in Ignatius of Antioch (Theophorus), "The Letters," #4, 109. The prayer of St. Polycarp of Smyrna carries the same eucharistic connotations: "I bless Thee, because I may have a part, along with the martyrs, in the chalice of Thy Christ, unto resurrection in eternal life, resurrection both of soul and body in the incorruptibility of the Holy Spirit. May I be received today, as a rich and acceptable sacrifice." "Martyrdom Polycarp," #14, 158.

to the holy Church by the grace which was in the martyr."[5] But the martyr continued to be present in the community:

> some of us saw the blessed Ignatius suddenly standing by us and embracing us, while others beheld him again praying for us, and others still saw him dropping with sweat, as if he had just come from his great labour, and standing by the Lord. When, therefore, we had with great joy witnessed these things, and had compared our several visions together, we sang praise to God, the giver of all good things, and expressed our sense of the happiness of the holy [martyr]; and now we have made known to you both the day and the time [when these things happened], that, assembling ourselves together according to the time of his martyrdom, we may have fellowship with the champion and noble martyr of Christ.[6]

In times of persecution such as these, the dwelling place of God naturally transfers into the hearts of Christians. Some even receive the name of Theophorus (i.e., bearer of God), as Ignatius of Antioch did, and Ignatius describes the others as temples: "as though He were dwelling within us—we as His temple and He within as our God."[7]

The association between Ignatius's martyrdom and the eucharistic sacrifice, the assembling of the community (presumably in Liturgy) to commemorate his martyrdom, the veneration of relics, and the hearts of the martyrs as temples show the intrinsic connection between martyrdom and the Eucharist as a substitute for a temple in which the eucharistic sacrifice takes place. This connection becomes even more relevant in times of persecution when the celebration of the Eucharist is impossible and the faithful find other ways of being a eucharistic Church. Similar to baptismal ecclesiology, which considers as full members of the Church not only those baptized through regular Baptism with water, but also those who received "baptism by blood," perhaps we can speak similarly of "*Eucharist by blood*" in places where Christianity is persecuted. To give a later example, Orthodox faithful incarcerated in communist prisons could not celebrate the Eucharist proper.[8] But they never ceased to be a eucharistic Church. In fact, they may have been even more vibrantly Church,

5. "The Martyrdom of Ignatius," in *The Apostolic Fathers, Justin Martyr, Irenaeus*, transl. Alexander Roberts and James Donaldson, ANF 1, (Grand Rapids, MI: Eerdmans, 1885), #6, 131.

6. "The Martyrdom of Ignatius," #7, 131.

7. Ignatius, "To the Ephesians," in Ignatius of Antioch (Theophorus), "The Letters," #15, 93.

8. In the exceptional cases, benevolent guards provided these modern-day martyrs with the necessary elements to celebrate the Liturgy, obviously without any of the other liturgical elements such as icons, vestments, or incense, and yet those Liturgies were more glorious than most.

compared to the years of having the freedom to celebrate the Eucharist and then freely abstaining from receiving it.

Perhaps we can also speak about "Eucharist of desire" in contexts devoid of clergy, liturgies, and church buildings, where the Eucharist cannot be celebrated, such as in women's monasteries devoid of priests, mission communities, etc. When the desire to celebrate the Eucharist is strong, and yet it cannot be fulfilled for objective reasons, then the same motivation that supported "baptism of desire" in the early Church should now support "Eucharist of desire": the faithful yearn to partake of these sacraments, but it is objectively impossible for them to do so, and thus the rest of the Church community regards them as nothing less than full members of the Church who partake of the sacraments "by desire" in ways known only to God.

Returning to the fourth century, when Christianity was given freedom, the concept of *sacred space saw an unprecedented development*: places associated with the life of Jesus became the sites of glorious churches, and places associated with martyrs and various saints were marked by churches that gave a new meaning to the concept of sacred space, usually enhanced by developing these sacred spaces into sites for pilgrimages—a significant departure from the practice of the earlier centuries that did not have sacred geography and pilgrimages.[9] Moreover, some ancient pagan temples were rebuilt as churches, but these temples were usually built with numerous interior columns and could not accommodate a large number of worshippers. Hence, Christians adopted the architectural model of the basilica—the ancient building where the work of the *basileus* (the emperor) was being carried out. Citizens used to wait on the sides, behind the columns, until their time came to proceed down the large middle aisle to the front, where their case was heard. Similarly, Christians attended the service on the sides and came down the aisle to receive Communion—the Body and Blood of the King of Kings. Such is the Orthodox practice to this day.

The Orthodox worship space is patterned after the Jerusalem Temple with narthex, nave, and altar corresponding to the antechamber, the holy place, and the holy of holies ... but not exactly. According to Schmemann, the iconostasis that stands between the nave and the altar is not meant to separate the congregation from the priests; rather, the entire church structure is thought of as the holy of holies in which the entire priestly people of God serves the Lord.[10] The place where the faithful attend (the nave) and the place where the priests

9. Schmemann adds that "The Church itself was the new and heavenly Jerusalem: the Church *in* Jerusalem was by contrast unimportant." Schmemann, *For the Life of the World*, 20.

10. Schmemann, *The Eucharist*, 20–21.

lead the service (the altar) are in fact one space because at Jesus' crucifixion, the temple curtain separating the holy from the holy of holies was torn into two from top to bottom, signifying that the abolishing of the distance between the holy and the holy of holies was God's doing, not ours, which would have been symbolized by the tearing of the curtain from bottom to the top. That is also why earlier Orthodox churches did not have icon screens.

The iconostasis started out as a small demarcating structure that allowed full visibility into the altar, and then developed considerably after the crisis of iconoclasm, in order to reinforce the central role of icons in Orthodoxy. Perhaps the iconostasis' most rapid development took place from the thirteenth to the fifteenth centuries in the East, while at the same time a similar development was taking place in the West, namely the development of the "rood screens"—an ornate structure that partitions the chancel from the nave.[11] Unlike the West, where this structure allows visible access, the icon screen blocks it. It has become so elaborate, that in most contemporary Orthodox churches it practically separates the congregation and the priests, in a sense reinforcing clericalism. In the Greek tradition the Divine Liturgy (and most services) take place with the royal doors open, giving the faithful visual access to the altar. In the Slavonic tradition, however, the royal doors are mostly closed and—despite the tearing of the curtain of the Jerusalem temple at Jesus' crucifixion—there is even a curtain that is closed at various points throughout the services, thus impeding any visual contact between the congregation and the clergy. It would be a return to earlier—more communal—Orthodox traditions to build future Orthodox churches with smaller icon screens that do not block the visual access between the altar and the congregation.

Such a change would uncover a very important icon that is traditionally painted on the apse of the altar: that of *Virgin Mary—image of a priestly people of God*. Women are neither allowed to be ordained to the priesthood in the Orthodox Church, nor to be altar servers.[12] And yet, Orthodox iconography commends that Virgin Mary be portrayed above the altar, to show that not only the ordained, but all the members of the Church are priests. Nikos Nissiotis describes Virgin Mary as "the image of the Church in continual prayer … a representation of the praying community."[13] Similarly, Golitzin refers to

11. Diarmaid MacCulloch, *Christianity: The First Three Thousand Years* (New York: Penguin Books, 2009), 484.

12. While the prohibition of women to be altar servers is the norm, nuns are allowed to serve in the altar of their own monasteries.

13. Nikos Nissiotis, "The Main Ecclesiological Problem of the Second Vatican Council and the Position of the Non-Roman Churches Facing It," *Journal of Ecumenical Studies* 2, no. 1 (1965): 51–52.

Virgin Mary as "the outstanding type or icon of the church," pointing that the prescribed Old Testament liturgical readings for Marian feasts refer to God's presence in liturgical settings such as the temple, throne, ark, mercy seat, holy of holies, tabernacle, temple, paradise, candlestand, vessel containing manna, bridal chamber of light, holy table, etc., all of which become images for the Church that—as the Virgin Mother—holds Christ.[14] St. John of Damascus implies that Virgin Mary is the one who contains Christ and the one from whom Christ has been revealed, just as God was present in the burning bush and spoke from it. Actually, Christ was most present among humans in Virgin Mary, just as in the Temple God was most present in the holy of holies. As John of Damascus observes,

> The [burning] bush is an image of the Divine Mother, and God said to Moses when he was about to approach it, "loose the sandals from your feet, for the ground, on which you stand, is holy ground." If, therefore, the ground on which the image of the Mother of God was seen by Moses is holy ground, how much more is the image itself? For not only holy, but, dare I say it, also the holy of holies.[15]

As the holy of holies where only the priests of the Old Testament entered, of course is it most appropriate that Virgin Mary should be portrayed above the altar.

The act of assembling took various forms throughout history. In times of persecutions—old and new—gathering as a Church was a confession of faith made at great risk. In times when Orthodoxy was the religion of the *polis*, it was a communal endeavor to express the religious identity of the citizens. In times of secularism, it is a public act that refuses to relegate religiosity to the private domain, but regards public worship as an act essential to its identity as a Church. Schmemann opens up his book on *The Eucharist* with a chapter on "The Sacrament of the Assembly," an expression that originates with Pseudo-Dionysius and that shows the importance of gathering together "as a church" (1 Cor 11:18). In other words, the Church is the assembly of those gathered together in one space.

The act of gathering for worship precedes Christianity. In ancient Athens, for example, the people would gather from all over the city, climb up the Acropolis, circle around the Parthenon, and then begin their worship. Later on, the citizens of Constantinople would go around the city in procession, reading

---

14. Golitzin, "Scriptural Images of the Church," 260–62.

15. Saint John of Damascus, *Three Treatises on the Divine Images* (Crestwood, NY: St. Vladimir's Seminary Press, 2003), II:20, p. 77.

Psalms and singing antiphons (as Orthodox do today in the first part of the Liturgy), after which they all entered the church.[16] Thus, the sacred space that they entered was not only the altar, but the entire church building. Orthodox Christians still follow this tradition at Pascha, when the entire community, after proclaiming the resurrection outside, enters the church in procession. A similar typikon is prescribed for the consecration of a new church, but both examples are rather rare occurrences, with the notable exception of the New Skete monasteries, where the entrance still takes its ancient form.[17] Typically, however, the Orthodox experience the "entrance" to be the procession with the Gospel that is carried from the altar table to ... the altar table (irreverently called "the liturgical U-turn with the Gospel"). The priest still recites the prayer, "grant that holy angels may enter with us, that together we may celebrate and glorify Your goodness." One might wrongly get the impression that the angels (symbolized by altar servers) enter together with the clergy into the sacred space that is the altar. But when looking at the practice of the early Church, the "sacrament of the assembly" culminated with the entrance of the entire Church (clergy and the people) into the sacred space (the entire church, not just the altar), to celebrate the divine Liturgy together with the angels. Orthodox iconography supports this interpretation: the faithful gather in the nave and look up at the dome, where angels are portrayed surrounding Christ.

Once the community has ascended into the church, it finds itself in the presence of God who is surrounded by the angels. So it is most appropriate that what follows is the hymn that the angels sing to God, as Isaiah describes his vision when he ascended into heaven and entered the glory of God: "Holy, Holy, Holy" (Is 6:3). In its Orthodox form, this hymn is "Holy God, Holy Mighty, Holy Immortal, have mercy on us." These liturgical considerations present a church gathered in the temple, uniting heaven and earth, ascending to the glory of God, and singing the angelic hymn. Later in the Liturgy, the Cherubic hymn expresses this communion between heaven and earth even more clearly: "We who mystically represent the cherubim, sing the thrice holy hymn ..." Kallistos Ware explains that the word "represent" does not capture the fact that we on earth do the same thing that angels in heaven do, as the

16. To this day, when the bishop celebrates a hierarchical Liturgy, he plays no significant role prior to the small entrance.

17. At the New Skete monasteries in Cambridge, NY, the Liturgy begins with the gathering of monks, nuns, clergy, and laypeople outside the church. At the Small Entrance, the assembly enters into the nave, the clergy remaining in the middle of the church, surrounded by laypeople. Only later do the clergy enter the altar, demarcated by a low iconostasis, which permits seeing inside, as was the case at Hagia Sophia in Constantinople. Krindatch, *Atlas of American Orthodox Christian Monasteries*, 112–13.

Greek term *iconizomen* suggests. He prefers to translate the hymn as, "We who in this Mystery are icons of the cherubim ..."[18]

WORK OF THE PEOPLE: *LEITOURGIA*

The entire Church—laity and clergy, heaven and earth—gather together to serve the Lord, or to do "the work of the people," which is the meaning of the Greek term *leitourgia*. Afanasiev and Schmemann have tirelessly advocated for a return to the earlier understanding of the entire Church, clergy and the people, as celebrants of the Liturgy, as opposed to the neo-scholastic manual theology that regarded the priest as the celebrant of the Liturgy and the faithful as passive spectators of a magical act done for them.[19] The key to the return to earlier traditions is the understanding of Christ as the ultimate celebrant, and the entire Body of Christ as manifesting visibly Christ's priesthood or, in other words, both clergy and the faithful in mystery being icons of Christ the Archpriest. That is why, during the Cherubic hymn, the priest recites a prayer that acknowledges Christ as both the sacrifice and the priest: "For you, Christ our God, are the Offerer and the Offered, the One who receives and is distributed." Moments later, the assembly will say (through the priest who lifts up the gifts of bread and wine), "we offer to you in all and for all." The offering of the Church is actually the offering of Christ through the entire Church, clergy and the people. The "work of the people" (*leitourgia*) is thus an icon of the work of Christ.

This argument is multi-layered and unpacking it will lead into several directions: sometimes the priest acts as an icon of Christ, other times as the leader of the community; it is the Spirit who makes the offering to the Father possible; the entire community is priestly, not just the ordained; clericalist practices that have drawn an edge between the clergy and the faithful include rare communion of the faithful; and active participation of the faithful as an antidote to clericalism.

18. Kallistos Ware, "The Holy Spirit in the Liturgy of St. John Chrysostom," in *It Is the Spirit Who Gives Life: New Directions in Pneumatology*, ed. Radu Bordeianu (Washington, DC: The Catholic University of America Press, 2022), 118. Maximus emphasizes the eschatological character of the union between heaven and earth, lived here and now in the Liturgy, the eschaton piercing in time in the Liturgy: "The triple exclamation of holiness which all the faithful people proclaim in the divine hymn represents the union and the equality of honor to be manifested in the future with the incorporeal and intelligent powers." Maximus the Confessor, "Mystagogia," 202, 10.

19. See the second chapter.

John Chrysostom famously wrote that "the priest simply lends his tongue and [provides] his hand"[20] to Christ, the ultimate Priest. Orthodox and Catholic theologians write about the priest acting *in persona Christi*, or in the person of Christ, which they complement with the act of the priest in the person of the congregation (*in persona ecclesiae*).[21] When the priest faces towards the East, in the same direction as the congregation, the priest acts in the person of the congregation, and so the entire liturgical assembly is an icon of Christ—clergy and the people.

As Ware observes, "it is incorrect to speak of the priest as consecrating the Holy Gifts. The consecration is performed by God the Father, *acting through the Holy Spirit*. In the words of the author of the best-known Byzantine liturgical commentary, St. Nicolas Cabasilas (*c.* 1322–*c.* 1397), 'It is the Spirit who, through the hand and the tongue of the priests, consummates the mysteries.'"[22] This pneumatological dimension should come as no surprise, since the Spirit is also concelebrating with the Body of Christ (i.e. the Church gathered for the Eucharist), as the dialogue between the priest and the deacon after the Great Entrance makes clear:

> *Priest:* The Holy Spirit shall come upon you, and the power of the Most High shall overshadow you.
> *Deacon:* The Spirit himself will concelebrate with us all the days of our life.

The genius of Christianity was to affirm that not only the ordained, but *all the members of the People of God are offering the sacrifices, being priests*. The ancient world regarded the offering of sacrifices as the privilege of the few—the priests. In contrast, early Christianity regarded all the baptized as "a holy priesthood to offer spiritual sacrifices acceptable to God through Jesus Christ" (1 Peter 2:5). This idea that the entire people can bring sacrifices did not arise in a vacuum. As Judaism found itself without a temple after the year 70, its priesthood became devoid of purpose. And yet, the priestly character of all Israelites was not totally lost. For example, Philo of Alexandria, a Jewish writer contemporary with the writing of the New Testament, notes that on Passover, each Jew was allowed to sacrifice the lamb, without the priest and the temple:

---

20. Saint John Chrysostom, "Homily 86 (John 20.10–23)," in *Commentary on Saint John the Apostle and Evangelist, Homilies 48–88*, Fathers of the Church (Washington, DC: The Catholic University of America Press, 1959), 457.

21. Bordeianu, *Dumitru Staniloae*, 169–77.

22. *Commentary on the Divine Liturgy* 28, 2, in Ware, "The Holy Spirit in the Liturgy," 106.

In this festival [Passover] many myriads of victims from noon till eventide are offered by the whole people, old and young alike, raised for that particular day to the dignity of the priesthood. For at other times the priests according to the ordinance of the law carry out both the public sacrifices and those offered by private individuals. But on this occasion the whole nation performs the sacred rites and acts as priests with pure hands and complete immunity.... On this day every dwelling-house is invested with the outward semblance and dignity of a temple.[23]

Philo's words could be repeated verbatim and applied to early Christians, to show the dignity of the entire people of God who bring sacrifices in their house-churches. The significant difference is that, if in Israel such sacrifices were permitted only once a year on Passover, Christians who celebrate the Eucharist can do so any time of the year. The *Didache* makes this connection explicit,[24] and the tradition continues uninterrupted in the Orthodox Church even today: when the entire people of God gather, even in the smallest of parishes, they do what priests have always done—offer sacrifices:

We offer to you this spiritual worship, without the shedding of blood and we ask, pray, and entreat you to send down your Holy Spirit upon us and these gifts here presented and make this bread the precious Body of your Christ (congregation: amen) and that which is in this cup the precious Blood of your Christ (congregation: amen), changing them by your Holy Spirit (congregation: amen, amen, amen).

The congregation's response with the "Amen" in this consecratory prayer from the Liturgy of St. John Chrysostom is a practice attested much earlier in 1 Cor 14:16, which describes a liturgical context in which the people say the "Amen" to the thanksgiving—a clear eucharistic reference. Justin Martyr testifies to the same understanding that the prayer of the celebrant is not complete until the congregation says the "Amen," giving also other details about early Christian worship including the order of Baptismal Liturgies, the kiss of peace, the role of the deacons in the distribution of the Eucharist both in the church and to those absent, as well as Baptism and orthodoxy as the conditions for receiving Communion:

At the conclusion of the prayers we greet one another with a kiss. Then, bread and a chalice containing wine mixed with water are presented to the

---

23. Philo, "Special Laws" 2:145–46, quoted in Spinks, *Do This in Remembrance of Me*, 6–7.
24. Spinks, *Do This in Remembrance of Me*, 22.

one presiding over the brethren. He takes them and offers praise and glory
to the Father of all, through the name of the Son and of the Holy Spirit,
and he recites lengthy prayers of thanksgiving to God in the name of those
to whom He granted such favors. At the end of these prayers and thanksgiving, all present express their approval by saying 'Amen.' This Hebrew
word, 'Amen,' means 'So be it.' And when he who presides has celebrated the
Eucharist, they whom we call deacons permit each one present to partake
of the Eucharistic bread, and wine and water; and they carry it also to the
absentees. We call this food the Eucharist, of which only he can partake
who has acknowledged the truth of our teachings, who has been cleansed
by baptism for the remission of his sins and for his regeneration, and who
regulates his life upon the principles laid down by Christ.[25]

It is thus unfortunate that in many parts of Orthodoxy, the kiss of peace is
reserved exclusively for con-celebrating clergy as opposed to a gesture building
up the communion of the entire gathering and that consecratory prayers are
said silently, by the priest alone, without the participation of the people. In
rare cases when a deacon serves, the latter gives the "Amen," but the congregation is not even aware that this dialogue is taking place. Under Schmemann's
influence, more and more parishes say the consecratory prayers out loud and
the congregation gives the "Amen," because the Holy Spirit is invoked not only
on the gifts and the priest (who would be using the plural of majesty), but the
"us" of the prayer quoted above refers to all those who bring the sacrifice: clergy
and the people—the entire priestly people of God. In this sense, as Afanasiev
and Schmemann affirm, the clergy and the people co-serve or concelebrate the
Liturgy.[26]

Schmemann boldly characterizes the practice of silent prayer and the congregation's exclusion from priestly acts as *clericalism*. The most obvious result of
clericalism was that, at the beginning of the twentieth century, the laity received
the Eucharist only four times a year, although the Catechism allowed even as
little as once a year. Schmemann writes about the "clericalization" of the Orthodox Church in the sense of the "great distancing of the clergy and laity from
each other," adding that

entry to the altar, approach to the sanctuary came to be forbidden to the laity, and their presence at the Eucharist became passive. It is accomplished on
behalf of them, for them, but they do not take part in its accomplishment. If

25. Justin Martyr, "First Apology," #65–66, 105.
26. Schmemann, *The Eucharist*, 14.

earlier the line separating the Church from "this world" embraced the laity, it now excluded them.[27]

Schmemann's words might sound harsh; I have certainly perceived them as such in the past.[28] But I now believe that his words are justified, especially when they are contrasted with the practice of the early Church to offer the Eucharist often and not to differentiate between clergy and the people regarding the reception of Communion. I used to be a priest who kept the faithful away from the Eucharist. When I was first ordained in Romania, the faithful had to fast at least three days in a row and go to Confession each time before receiving Communion. The result was that very few adults received the Eucharist outside the four Lenten periods. I remember distinctly being a young priest and celebrating the Divine Liturgy at the chapel of the seminary where I was teaching. At the appropriate moment, I came out with the chalice and said (or, rather, Christ issued the invitation), "With the fear of God, faith, and love, draw near." But no one came. My students told me that they have never seen me as sad as at that moment. With pure hearts, they decided to take turns, fast more than the Church has prescribed by fasting three days in a row outside the Lenten fasts, go to Confession, and thus at least one seminarian received Communion every Sunday. But I was not respecting the same rules as they did, because I was ordained. They had to fast three days in a row to receive Communion; I did not, but I ate meat on Saturdays and received the Eucharist on Sundays. They had to go to Confession before each Communion; I did not, but went to Confession at larger intervals. Shouldn't it be the exact opposite? Shouldn't it be harder for me, as a priest, than for them, as laity? Or was I like "the scribes and the Pharisees [who ...] do not practice what they teach. They tie up heavy burdens, hard to bear, and lay them on the shoulders of others; but they themselves are unwilling to lift a finger to move them" (Mt 23: 1–4)?

Schmemann was right: these systemic practices of claiming that the Liturgy is the Kingdom of heaven on earth yet at the same time excluding the faithful from the prayers of the Liturgy, forbidding the laity to commune at every Liturgy while the clergy commune without following the same rules as the laity, and hiding the priests who secretly recite prayers behind the curtain of the altar amount to clericalism.[29] These clericalist practices are, of course, unfaithful to the tradition of the Orthodox Church. John Chrysostom teaches:

27. Schmemann, *The Eucharist*, 232.
28. Bordeianu, *Dumitru Staniloae*, 179.
29. Schmemann, *The Eucharist*, 230–32.

All things are equal between us and you, even the very chief of our blessings. I [as bishop] do not partake of the holy Table with greater abundance and you with less, but both equally participate of the same. And if I take it first, it is no great privilege, since even among children, the elder first extends his hand to the feast, but nevertheless no great advantage is gained thereby. But with us all things are equal.[30]

Schmemann has the great merit of having brought the Eucharist back to the center of Orthodox life, especially in America; it is no exaggeration to call him "the Father of Eucharistic renewal," even though he is rooted in the thought of Afanasiev and the Slavophil movement. One would be hard pressed to find a theologian whose scholarship has had a greater impact on the life of the Orthodox Church by restoring the tradition (or better, Tradition) of frequent communion.

The means to return to Tradition and counter clericalism is the *active participation* of the faithful in the liturgical life of the Church. This expression was consecrated at Vatican II, which affirmed that

all the faithful should be led to that full, conscious, and active participation in liturgical celebrations which is demanded by the very nature of the liturgy, and to which the Christian people, "a chosen race, a royal priesthood, a holy nation, a redeemed people" (1 Pt 2:9, 4–5) have a right and obligation by reason of their baptism.[31]

Vassa Larin shows that the active participation of the faithful is not an exclusively Roman Catholic question, but that the East, too, needs to focus on it, since most often in her own Slavonic tradition, contemporary liturgies are characterized by

the almost complete absence of congregational singing, with the people's responses replaced by a complicated, polyphonic repertoire sung by church choirs, the central prayers delegated to the silent recitation by the priest alone, the lack of understanding by many of the faithful of the archaic liturgical language, and the general dearth of catechetical instruction in the liturgy.[32]

---

30. John Chrysostom, "Homily 4 on 2 Thessalonians 2:6–9," in *Saint Chrysostom: Homilies on Galatians, Ephesians, Philippians, Colossians, Thessalonians, Timothy, Titus, and Philemon*, NPNF I:XIII (Grand Rapids, MI: Eerdmans, 1988), 392.

31. Vatican Council II, *Sacrosantum Concilium* (December 4, 1963), par. 14, in Flannery, *Vatican Council II Documents*, 7–8.

32. Larin, "Active Participation," 68.

The earliest Christians actively participated in the Liturgy, including through congregational singing. Byzantine liturgies of the first millennium had a vibrant tradition of congregational participation in sung services, and these traditions continued (although in a diminished form) into the subsequent centuries, even while the choir sang the more complex hymns such as the Cherubic hymn and the *Axion Estin*. The diminishing of active participation in the Liturgy disproportionately affected women. Larin writes about "the constant effort to *segregate* and even *hide* the female members of the congregation during liturgy" in Byzantine parishes, including designating special areas for women and the introduction of curtains to hide them. Moreover, seventeenth century parochial choirs in Russia were reserved exclusively for men; women were allowed to join these choirs only in the nineteenth century.[33]

The twentieth century saw an unprecedented liturgical revival—one of the fruits of ecumenism. Nicholas Denysenko documents "the cross-pollinating exchanges between the Orthodox and Catholic Churches."[34] These were informal exchanges between Orthodox and Catholic theologians such as Afanasiev, Schmemann, and Congar, who influenced each other as they studied together the Liturgy. Their agreement on the communitarian nature of lay and ordained priesthoods rooted in their common Baptism is what gave rise to Vatican II's call for the faithful's active participation. [35] Vatican II's stature, in turn, influenced several liturgical reforms in the Orthodox Church. It became common to change from liturgical prayers said silently to being read out loud; from laborious church architecture and Byzantine-style iconography to more simple, modern architecture and modest iconography; from prominent roles assigned to the priest and the cantor to active participation of all the faithful who practice

33. Larin, "Active Participation," 73–74, 82.

34. Nicholas E. Denysenko, *Liturgical Reform After Vatican II: The Impact on Eastern Orthodoxy* (Minneapolis: Fortress Press, 2015), 9.

35. Henri de Lubac's wrote that "the Eucharist makes the Church." Henri de Lubac, *Corpus Mysticum: The Eucharist and the Church in the Middle Ages*, trans. Gemma Simmonds and Richard Price (Notre Dame, IN: Notre Dame Press, 2007), 88, 260. Later on, Vatican II affirmed the constitutive role of the Eucharist for the Church, stating that the eucharistic celebration led by the bishop represents the fullness of the Church, and that it is by the Eucharist that the Church exists and grows, since the community becomes the Body of Christ (i.e. the Church) by partaking of the Body of Christ (understood as the Eucharist). *Lumen Gentium* 26; *Sacrosanctum Concilium* 41. The roots of Vatican II's eucharistic ecclesiology extend beyond the Catholic tradition to include Afanasiev, who was present as an Orthodox observer and interacted richly with the bishops and the *periti*. Emmanuel Lanne, "La Perception en Occident de la participation du Patriarcat de Moscou à Vatican II," in *Vatican II in Moscow (1959–1965): Acts of the Colloquium on the History of Vatican II. Moscow, March 30–April 2, 1995*, ed. Alberto Melloni (Leuven: Library of the Faculty of Theology K.U. Leuven, 1997), 125. Mauro Velati, *Separati ma fratelli: Gli osservatori non-cattolici al Vaticano II (1962–1965)* (Bologna, Italy: Il Mulino, 2014), 107. Alberto Melloni, Federico Ruozzi, and Enrico Galavotti, eds., *Vatican II: The Complete History* (Mahwah, NJ: Paulist Press, 2015), 278.

frequent Communion. On the other hand, looking favorably to the role of the Spirit in the Orthodox Liturgy, Catholicism revived the split epiclesis, added three new eucharistic prayers, and emphasized the role of the Spirit in the sacrament of Confirmation. Catholics experienced a renewed role of the laity in the Liturgy, including assistance with the distribution of Communion, frequent reception of Communion, and prayer in vernacular languages.[36] As both Orthodox and Catholics struggled with clericalism, they found its antidote in "the cross-pollinating exchanges" that determined them both to revive the active participation of the faithful, which is "the work of the people" (*leitourgia*).

WORK OF GOD: "IT IS TIME FOR THE LORD TO ACT"

As the Liturgy is about to begin, the deacon proclaims that "it is time for the Lord to act" (Ps. 119:126). The Greek term *kairos*, translated here as time, refers to God's eternity interrupting our time, making eternity present in time. While the term could be translated in a secular sense as "opportune moment," "period of time," or "season" (the latter appears in a petition during the Great Litany), it also has a religious sense of "God's time." Given the liturgical context in which it occurs here, as well as its biblical origin, the primary meaning of *kairos* is that the eternal God pierces through the Liturgy and makes the Kingdom manifest here and now. Paul Tillich describes *kairos* as "the qualitative time of the occasion, the right time," distinct from *chronos*, which is "the quantitative time of the clock."[37] Finding ourselves in the presence of God, we forget our earthly cares, the distractions that are temporal (*chronos*). But that does not mean that we become indifferent to the needs of the world, since immediately after these words we begin to pray for the authorities, the captives, those who are sick and those who travel. *Kairos* does not mean indifference to *chronos*, but using time as means towards the eschatological Kingdom. As Florovsky writes, "the *eschaton* does not mean primarily *final*, in the temporal series of events; it means rather *ultimate* (decisive); and the ultimate is being realized within the stress of historical happenings and events."[38]

Orthodox theologians tend to emphasize the eschatological character of the Liturgy. Since this is a study in ecclesiology and not in liturgiology or

36. Denysenko, *Liturgical Reform*, 357–65.
37. Paul Tillich, *A History of Christian Thought: From Its Judaic and Hellenistic Origins to Existentialism* (New York: Simon and Schuster, 1968), 1.
38. Florovsky, "The Church: Her Nature and Task," 68.

eschatology, it should suffice to present here some brief *eschatological consider-ations* that connect God's eternity present in the *kairos* of the Liturgy with the Kingdom and the Church. Most prominently, Schmemann writes:

> ... we can now affirm that the Church's worship was born and, in its ex-ternal structure, "took shape" primarily as a *symbol of the kingdom*, of the Church's ascent to it and, in this ascent, of her fulfillment as the body of Christ and the temple of the Holy Spirit. The whole newness, the unique-ness of the Christian *leitourgia* was in its eschatological nature as the pres-ence here and now of the future *parousia*, as the epiphany of that which is to come, as communion with the "world to come." ... [I]t is precisely out of this eschatological experience that the "Lord's day" was born as a *symbol*, i.e. manifestation now of the kingdom.[39]

In the same vein, Zizioulas affirms that "the divine Eucharist is the revela-tion of the Kingdom of God and quite simply the revelation of ultimate reality. The Eucharist reveals this reality [of the Church] which is future to us in the form of the present ... the penetration of the future into time."[40] Similarly, Hugh Wybrew refers to the Eucharist as a foretaste of the Kingdom,[41] and Staniloae considers that the Church gathered in the Liturgy "is the anticipated Kingdom of the Holy Trinity."[42] Ware also writes:

> Just as the Spirit unites past with present, so equally he unites present with future. As an eschatological Spirit, the Spirit of the age to come, he ... trans-forms the Divine Liturgy not only into a re-enactment of the Last Supper but also into the Feast of the Kingdom, into the Messianic Banquet of the Eighth Day. It is noteworthy that, in the eucharistic *anamnesis* or 'calling to mind' that comes in the consecratory prayer between the narrative of the Last Supper and the *epiclesis* of the Holy Spirit, we "remember" not only the Cross, Resurrection and Ascension of Christ, but also his "Second and Glorious Coming again." The Holy Spirit enables us to *remember the future*.[43]

If the eschatological character of the Liturgy might appear abstract when expressed in theological language, perhaps a historical narration will illustrate it better with the help of esthetics: eschatology is experienced as beauty. The *Primary Chronicle* describes how the Kievan Prince—Saint Vladimir ordered

39. Schmemann, *The Eucharist*, 43.

40. Zizioulas, *Lectures in Christian Dogmatics*, 137–38, 55.

41. Hugh Wybrew, *The Orthodox Liturgy: The Development of the Eucharistic Liturgy in the Byzantine Rite* (Crestwood, NY: St. Vladimir's Seminary Press, 2001), 16.

42. Staniloae, *Spirituality and Communion*, 6.

43. Ware, "The Holy Spirit in the Liturgy," 95.

the conversion of his people to Christianity in 988. His decision was reinforced by the visit of his envoys to various places of worship in Islam and Judaism, culminating with the church of Hagia Sophia in Constantinople. Upon their return, they reported:

> We knew not whether we were in heaven or on earth, for surely there is no such splendor or beauty anywhere upon earth. We cannot describe it to you: only this we know, that God dwells there among humans, and that their service surpasses the worship of all other places. For we cannot forget that beauty.[44]

Indeed, such words describe the union between heaven and earth in the Liturgy through the most appropriate category that remains beyond words, apophatic even: beauty. These instances of Orthodox theology and history (and the list is by no means exhaustive) affirm that the Church gathered in the Eucharist is not merely a communion in time (*chronos*), but a piercing of God's eternity in this special moment (*kairos*) in which the Church is most clearly an icon of the eschatological Kingdom. Lofty words! When compared with the beauty of Orthodox Liturgy and with the mystery that takes place in it, these words are not lofty enough. But when compared with the reality of schism in the Church, they are exceedingly lofty. An excursus into the services of *Proskomide and the Divine Liturgy* will emphasize both these aspects.

The Proskomide is the service dedicated to the preparation of the gifts of bread and wine to be offered during the Divine Liturgy. The pieces of bread arranged on the paten show Christ as the center of the Church, surrounded by Virgin Mary, nine different categories of angels and saints, the living and the dead, constituting an icon of the entire Church (see fig. 1). When cutting out the part for Jesus Christ, or the Lamb (*Amnos*), the celebrant pierces it and then pours wine and water into the chalice. The sacrifice on the Cross and the piercing of Christ's side are taking place at that time without taking away from the Divine Liturgy proper as a sacrifice. It is tempting to separate neatly the moments of the Liturgy, to delineate precisely what exactly happens with each gesture, and to say that this is not the eucharistic sacrifice. But an eschatological orientation, where the eschaton pierces all throughout the Liturgy allows us to see all the acts of the Liturgy, together, collectively, as the sacrifice of Christ. The words of Alexander Schmemann are relevant in this sense: "The Eucharist can be interpreted correctly only in eschatological categories. Performed *in*

44. MacCulloch, *Christianity*, 506.

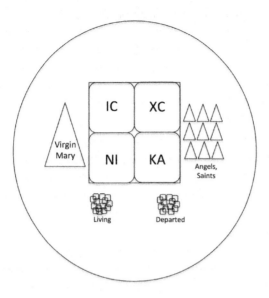

FIG. 1 Proskomide

time (*not outside* of time), the Liturgy reveals *in time*; anticipates and gives the Kingdom of the age to come; so that the Sacrament of the Eucharist, although consisting of a series of actions, is one, undivided sacrament."[45]

The eschaton is again revealed shortly after the prayer "Our Father," in which we pray, "Thy Kingdom come." Indeed, the Kingdom comes; the celebrant breaks the Lamb and sets the four portions on the outer sides of the disk (see fig. 2). If during the Proskomide the Church was represented with Christ in the middle, Virgin Mary, angels, saints, living and the dead around Christ, now we see the Kingdom of God in which Christ encompasses all. Christ is all in all (Eph 1:23); God is "all in all" (1 Cor 15:28). The eschaton is now manifested on the paten. The space between the four portions of the Lamb is not an empty space, but includes all who now constitute visibly the Christ, so that Christ encompasses all (see fig. 3). For this reason, in the Liturgy, the second coming is not a remote, future event, but it is something we remember, as we do in the Anaphora of St. John Chrysostom: "Remembering, therefore, this command of the Savior, and all that came to pass for our sake, the cross, the tomb, the resurrection on the third day, the ascension into heaven, the enthronement at

---

45. Juliana Schmemann, ed., *The Journals of Father Alexander Schmemann 1973–1983* (Yonkers, NY: St. Vladimir's Seminary Press, 2000), 275.

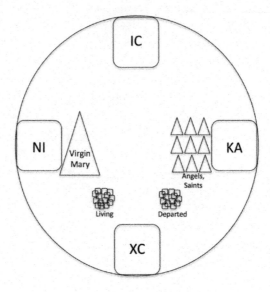

FIG. 2 The Divine Liturgy

The Lamb of God is broken and distributed; broken but not divided. He is forever eaten yet is never consumed, but He sanctifies those who partake of Him.

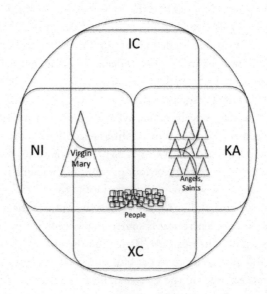

FIG. 3 The Eschaton

The Church is Christ's "Body, the fullnes of him who fills all in all" (Eph. 1:23) God will be "all in all" (1 Cor. 15:28)

the right hand of the Father, and *the second, glorious coming,* we offer to You these gifts from Your own gifts *in all and for all.*"[46]

It is most surprising that all the members of the Church need to grow into Christ until the end of times; this includes not only the living and the dead commemorated, but also Virgin Mary, the angels, and the saints. All grow into "the measure of the full stature of Christ" (Eph 4:13), as when *theosis* was previously described as an ecclesiological endeavor. It is in this sense that the Church prays in the Liturgy of St. John Chrysostom[47] not only *to* Virgin Mary, the angels, and the saints, but also *for* them:

> Again, we offer this spiritual worship *for* those who repose in the faith, forefathers, fathers, patriarchs, prophets, apostles, preachers, evangelists, martyrs, confessors, ascetics, and for every righteous spirit made perfect in faith.
>
> Especially *for* our most holy, pure, blessed, and glorious Lady, the Theotokos and ever virgin Mary.
>
> *For* Saint John the prophet, forerunner, and baptist; *for* the holy glorious and most honorable Apostles, *for* Saints(s) (*Names*) whose memory we commemorate today; and *for* all Your saints, through whose supplications, O God, bless us. Remember also all who have fallen asleep in the hope of resurrection unto eternal life. (*Here the priest commemorates the names of the deceased.*) ... Again, we ask You, Lord, remember all Orthodox bishops who rightly teach the word of Your truth, all presbyters, all deacons in the service of Christ, and every one in holy orders. We also offer to You this spiritual worship for the whole world, for the holy, catholic, and apostolic Church, and for those living in purity and holiness. And for all those in public service; permit them, Lord, to serve and govern in peace that through the faithful conduct of their duties we may live peaceful and serene lives in all piety and holiness.
>
> Above all, remember, Lord, our Archbishop (*Name*) ... Remember also, Lord, those whom each of us calls to mind and all your people.
>
> Remember, Lord, the city in which we live, every city and country, and the faithful who dwell in them. Remember, Lord, the travelers, the sick, the suffering, and the captives, granting them protection and salvation. Remember, Lord, those who do charitable work, who serve in Your holy churches, and who care for the poor. And send Your mercy upon us all.

These considerations about the experience of the eschaton in the Liturgy, the ever-expanding membership of the Church, and the needs of the world for which

---

46. Emphases added.

47. In the corresponding moment in the Liturgy of St. Basil, the community prays to be united with one another and *with* the saints, although there, too, they pray *for* Virgin Mary.

the Church prays stand in tension with several contemporary liturgical practices.

To those who do not recognize ecclesial reality outside of the canonical boundaries of Orthodoxy, these images of the Proskomide and the Liturgy represent the Orthodox Church in exclusivity: the parts commemorating the living and the dead refer exclusively to Orthodox Christians. Since they consider that the Church Una Sancta coincides with the canonical boundaries of the Orthodox Church, they refuse to commemorate the names of those who are not Orthodox, both living and dead, both at the Proskomide and at Memorial Services, which include *kollyva*—a symbol of the resurrection! There are even cases of convert priests who do not commemorate their own extended family that remained Protestant or Catholic, as if their own family are completely devoid of any ecclesial reality and as if a Christian can neglect to pray for their family. Besides the argument presented in previous chapter, the liturgical-eschatological considerations discussed here show that such a view is incorrect. The paten is meant to be an icon of the entire Church (which includes non-Orthodox), and of the eschatological Kingdom, which is larger than the Orthodox Church. If there will be non-Orthodox in the eschatological Kingdom of God (and yes, "many will come from east and west and will eat with Abraham and Isaac and Jacob in the kingdom of heaven"—Mt 8:11), then numerous pieces of bread commemorating the living and the departed should represent non-Orthodox persons.

To put it unequivocally, in light of the eschatological perspective described here, there are significant reasons to commemorate non-Orthodox faithful at the Proskomide and to have memorial services (with *kollyva*) for non-Orthodox faithful who have living Orthodox relatives in our parishes. Can the same unequivocal tone refer to the reception of the Eucharist—the pinnacle of human-divine Communion? The previous considerations about intercommunion for mixed Orthodox-Catholic couples in the West would suggest that the answer is significantly more timid in this regard.

INTERCOMMUNION: THE EUCHARIST AS A BOUNDARY MARKER AND CREATOR OF UNITY[48]

From the outset it must be said that a discussion of intercommunion is abnormal. Florovsky used the expression "theology of the abnormal" to describe any ecclesiology written in the context of the paradoxical, antinomical, and

48. Excerpts from this section have appeared in Bordeianu, "Eucharistic Hospitality," 5–24.

abnormal situation in which Christianity is divided among "separated brethren" while also being one Church.[49] On the one hand, Christians are "brethren" by being members of the one Church. On the other hand, they are separated, since the Church is divided into churches. Schism is against the will of Christ for his Body, and so it is impossible to justify it theologically. The concept of intercommunion struggles with this reality of schism: on the one hand, the Eucharist is a sign of unity, but the Church is disunited and thus the lack of eucharistic sharing becomes a sign of our disunity. On the other hand, Christians (and this section deals primarily with Orthodox and Catholics) are united in a real sense, and sharing in the Eucharist enhances their unity, just as each Church also regards the Eucharist as means towards (internal) unity. From this *purely theoretical ecclesiological perspective*, it is impossible to arrive at a consistent conclusion regarding intercommunion. An experiential—liturgical—eschatological approach, however, bears more fruit.

From a *liturgical perspective*, it is more likely that intercommunion should be encouraged, albeit with some qualifications. Being a memorial of Christ's sacrifice on the Cross and Resurrection for the salvation of humankind and not only for the Church—or even more narrowly for the salvation of the Orthodox Church—the Eucharist encompasses the entire assembly of the parish, and so all should commune. Being an eschatological event, the Liturgy also extends beyond a certain denomination. Looking back at the eschatological image on the paten described above (see again fig. 3), the sacrificed and broken Christ encompasses all those who are saved. The Orthodox Church has never claimed that there will be only Orthodox in the eschatological Kingdom. If the Eucharist is indeed a piercing of the eschaton into our time and an experience of the end-times, then God's eschatological presence in all should be manifested in the *kairos* of the Liturgy by sharing the Eucharist with those who are not Orthodox. An eschatological, Kingdom-centered perspective commands such openness, while the "not yet" aspect of the Kingdom and the fact that Christians are still in schism forbid it. Since the latter is the dominant view within Orthodoxy, it must be stated with humility that, because we do not share the Eucharist with those who will be part of the eschatological Kingdom of God, in our Liturgy we do not fully experience the eschaton. And that is not God's doing, but our own doing—the work of the people.

The *experiential ecclesiology* proposed here unites the two approaches—

---

49. Georges Florovsky, "St. Cyprian and St. Augustine on Schism," in *Ecumenism II: Collected Works* vol. 14 (Belmont, MA: Nordland, 1989), 50.

purely theoretical ecclesiology and liturgical, in an attempt to remain true to the ancient principle articulated by Prosper of Aquitaine, that the rule of prayer should lay down the rule of faith—*lex orandi lex credendi*.[50] After an analysis of the role of the Eucharist as boundary marker and of the two main attitudes towards intercommunion in modern Orthodox theology, I return to the previous chapter's proposal for limited intercommunion for Orthodox-Catholic families residing in the West and its benefits. Such a solution remains imperfect (still a "theology of the abnormal"), but it is a first step towards surpassing the stalemate caused by the two opposing approaches described here.

One final caveat before dealing with the subject of intercommunion: while the Catholic Church has spent much energy identifying criteria for a true Eucharist (including priesthood in apostolic succession defined narrowly as uninterrupted chain of ordinations), the Orthodox Church did not officially formulate such criteria. Nor do Orthodox theologians spend considerable amount of thought on this topic. The Orthodox are mainly concerned with a different set of questions: in which church are we allowed to receive Communion and whom should we allow to receive our Communion? The Orthodox have consistently recognized the validity of Catholic Eucharist, and yet Orthodox faithful are not allowed to receive the Catholic Eucharist, although practically they were allowed to receive it under special circumstances in Anglican churches.[51] At the same time, pre-Chalcedonians are allowed to receive the Orthodox Eucharist in most jurisdictions in the West, at least. In Orthodox theology, sharing in the Eucharist is primarily dependent on ecclesial communion, and not on the validity of the Eucharist. After all, if the Orthodox did not ascribe any eucharistic value to Protestant liturgies, it would be incomprehensible why Orthodox faithful would be forbidden from receiving the "simple/unconsecrated bread and the wine" in such Protestant liturgies. But the very act of forbidding intercommunion recognizes a eucharistic character to Protestant liturgies.

From the earliest Christian centuries, the Eucharist functioned as a *boundary marker* related to doctrine, morality, and religious belonging.[52] Often quoted

50. Jaroslav Pelikan, *The Christian Tradition: A History of the Development of Doctrine. Vol 1: The Emergence of the Catholic Tradition (100–600)* (Chicago: University of Chicago Press, 1971), 339.

51. At the 1931 Joint Anglican-Orthodox Theological Discussions at Lambeth, the Orthodox representatives considered that only pan-Orthodox consensus has authority to declare general intercommunion, but in the meantime "the practice of the Orthodox receiving Holy communion from Anglican priests in case of need and where no Orthodox priest was available, might continue, provided that an Orthodox authority did not prohibit such a practice." Kallistos Ware, "Intercommunion: The Decisions of Vatican II and the Orthodox Standpoint," *Sobornost* 4, no. Winter (1966): 266.

52. Bryan Spinks shows that, despite the open character of many of Jesus' meals with sinners, the Last Supper was reserved to the Twelve, 1 Corinthians excludes those who would participate unworthily from a

in this regard is Irenaeus's famous saying, "our view [i.e., teaching] accords with the Eucharist, which in turn establishes our view."[53] In his context, Gnostics considered that the flesh does not partake of life and so the Eucharist is futile; Irenaeus urges Gnostics to change their opinion and receive the Eucharist, thereby receiving life in our bodies through matter (bread and wine) and showing the consistency between eucharistic practices and orthodox doctrine.[54] At Irenaeus' urging, bishop Victor of Rome (189–199) produced the first historical instance of excommunication based on difference of faith. Victor ended the custom of sending consecrated Eucharist to a variety of Christian communities in Rome, particularly Gnostics who challenged the importance of material creation (including the eucharistic elements), Montanists whose charismatic manifestations led them away from the structures of the Church, and Monarchians who contended against the distinctions between the Father and the Son and the Holy Spirit, considering them as modes of the same person.[55]

Since eucharistic practices and orthodox doctrine need to be consistent, and thus eucharistic sharing is conditioned upon agreement in the truth, it is crucial to ask, what constitutes orthodox doctrine? The ecumenical movement has been trying to draw the line between church dividing issues and matters of legitimate diversity, with significant eucharistic consequences: when two churches disagree on church-dividing issues (in other words, when one of them falls from the truth), they interrupt eucharistic communion. That is not to say that sharing in the truth means uniformity. On the contrary, unity is found in diversity. For example, the East uses leavened bread in the Eucharist, while the West uses unleavened bread. This difference cannot be regarded as Church-dividing issue, despite the attempts of many to exaggerate its importance. According to the Synoptics, Jesus and the disciples ate unleavened bread at the Last Supper (hence the Western practice), while according to John, Jesus was crucified on Passover, so the night before, at the Last Supper, he used leavened bread (hence the Eastern practice). If the early Church, in deciding the scriptural canon, accepted this type of diversity, we cannot consider today's yeast-related practices as Church-dividing. Throughout history, the line that demarcated Church-dividing issues has shifted considerably.

The most significant shift in the line that demarcated Church-dividing

---

moral perspective, and the Didache allows only the baptized, concluding that the Eucharist was from the beginning a boundary marker. Spinks, *Do This in Remembrance of Me*, 28–29.

53. Irenaeus of Lyons, *Against Heresies*, IV.18.5, III.

54. Spinks, *Do This in Remembrance of Me*, 36.

55. MacCulloch, *Christianity*, 136.

issues occurred in the context of twentieth-century dialogues between Eastern and Oriental Orthodox Churches, which proved that, despite centuries of alienation, mutual condemnation at the highest level (i.e., ecumenical councils in the East), and terminological confusion, the two churches actually share the same Christological faith! This most important accomplishment of ecumenical dialogue is already bearing fruit in pastoral life in some jurisdictions not only in the Middle East, but also in Western Europe and North America, where members of the two churches share in the Eucharist.[56] This *unofficial, localized occurrence of intercommunion* remains confined to the grassroots level, but is no less real than if it had full official recognition.[57] And this is where we find again a distinction between official theology and the concrete existence of the Church, between theoretical and experiential approaches to ecclesiology. Although he did not put it in these terms, this tension saddened Emmanuel Lanne. After observing how much more open the Orthodox are to eucharistic communion with the Oriental Orthodox than with Catholics, he asked rhetorically whether there is not greater unity of faith between the Eastern Orthodox and the Roman Catholics—identical Christology, the seven ecumenical councils, the veneration of Virgin Mary, and so on—than with the Oriental Orthodox.[58] In other words, since the Eastern Orthodox tradition is closer to the Catholic than to the Oriental Orthodox traditions, Lanne would like to see intercommunion between Orthodox and Catholics, thus closing the gap between theoretical and experiential.

It is justifiable to question today the decisions to interrupt eucharistic communion that both Orthodox and Catholic churches made in the past. At a

---

56. The "Statement of the Orthodox Church of Antioch on the Relations between the Eastern and Syrian Orthodox Churches, November 12, 1991" forbids accepting conversions from one church to another; encourages joint synods; allows for episcopal concelebration at baptisms, funerals, and weddings; and, most importantly, states that "#9 in localities where there is only one priest, from either Church, he will celebrate services for the faithful in both Churches, including the Divine Liturgy, pastoral duties, and holy matrimony ..." (https://orthodoxjointcommission.wordpress.com/2014/06/27/statement-of-the-orthodox-church-of-antioch-on-the-relations-between-the-eastern-and-syrian-orthodox-churches/) Although this latter stipulation does not explicitly mention intercommunion, it clearly allows for eucharistic hospitality in situations where there is only one priest.

57. In and of itself, an unofficial, localized occurrence of intercommunion is not automatically an indication of truth. As stated above, ideally, the rule of prayer should lay down the rule of faith but, when these two elements are not in harmony with one another, one needs adjustment. Incorporating the results of the theological dialogue between the Eastern and Oriental Orthodox traditions that points to their shared theological legacy, the adjustment of "the rule of prayer" becomes necessary. This process takes an inordinate amount of time at an official level, but this localized occurrence of intercommunion bears witness that the process of readjustment has already begun.

58. Emmanuel Lanne, "Quelques questions posées à l'Église orthodoxe concernant la 'communicatio in sacris' dans l'eucharistie," *Irénikon* 72, no. 3–4 (1999): 435–52.

time when the two churches regarded each other with suspicion due to worldly reasons, even the tiniest dogmatic diversity was exaggerated into a Church-dividing issue. Perhaps the East-West schism was initially quite similar to recent intra-Orthodox schisms that are motivated by jurisdictional and political reasons. Sometimes the cessation of eucharistic communion applies only to Patriarchs, as was the case of the schism between the Patriarchs of Jerusalem and Romania, now resolved. Other times it applies to all bishops, clergy, and even some of the faithful, as is the case in the conflict between the Patriarchates of Jerusalem and Antioch. This latter conflict even had repercussions upon the 2016 Council of Crete, which Antioch refused to attend, explaining that it could not engage in a Council with the Church of Jerusalem when the two churches could not share in the Eucharist, thus bringing to the fore the Irenaean connection between doctrine and Eucharist. A most significant recent cessation of eucharistic communion happened in 2018 between the Patriarchates of Moscow and Constantinople over their conflict regarding the autocephaly of the Orthodox Church of Ukraine. It is noteworthy that only Moscow refuses to commune with Constantinople, but the reverse is not true: Constantinople is willing to commune with Moscow. This schism is so tragic because of the immense number of faithful that it affects, since it refers not only to Patriarchs and bishops, but also to priests and the faithful. The words of Archbishop Anastasios of Albania are no exaggeration: the Eucharist has been "used as a weapon."[59]

If the Eucharist can be (ab)used as a boundary marker, it can also become a means towards a greater unity, such as when various communities that previously were in schism re-establish eucharistic communion, even if at first timidly and on a limited basis. Such could be the case when communities discern that intercommunion would be beneficial to the faithful out of pastoral necessity, or when the limits of Church-dividing theological issues are redrawn, or when churches realize that their division was for canonical or disciplinary reasons and not for divergence from the truth. Could either (or all) of these be the case of *Orthodox-Catholic relations*?

When Vatican II had barely started, Nicholas Afanasiev wrote: "We believe that the hour is near when the Catholic Church, after having transcended human passions, would extend a fraternal hand to the Orthodox Church, and that this hand would not remain suspended in the air."[60] Two years later, Pope

---

59. Anastasios, Archbishop of Tirana, Durres, and All Albania, in *Letter to Patriarch Kirill of Moscow and All Russia* no. prot. 796/18, Nov. 7, 2018.

60. Afanassieff, "Una Sancta," 27.

Paul VI surprised the participants at Vatican II with his intention to promulgate *The Decree on the Catholic Churches of the Eastern Rite*, which in that draft version allowed for intercommunion between Orthodox and Catholics. One of the Orthodox observers, the Romanian monk André Scrima, protested the decision to establish *communicatio in sacris* as unilateral, without Orthodox consultation.[61] Stating that Orthodoxy does not allow eucharistic hospitality even in extreme circumstances, Scrima and the other Orthodox observers convinced Yves Congar to influence the Pope and freeze the decree's approval process. Hence, a new phrase was inserted, stating that eucharistic sharing with the East can occur only "after consultation also with the hierarchs of the separated churches."[62] The Orthodox observers did not close the door to this astounding invitation, since they anticipated the possibility that Orthodox hierarchs would give their approval. It has not yet happened. To use Afanasiev's imagery, the Catholic hand remains suspended in the air and officially it might remain as such for a while. But practically, it need not be so.

The Irenaean dictum, "our view [i.e., teaching] accords with the Eucharist, which in turn establishes our view," certainly does not apply to Orthodox-Catholic relations today. Out of respect for the Fathers and their context, no one should put contemporary Orthodox-Catholic disagreements on the same level with the Gnosticism, Montanism, and Monarchianism of the past. Today's Catholics or Orthodox are not the heretics of the first millennium, so applying uncritically this eucharistic principle to today's divisions is inappropriate. And if we agree on the truth, then "the Eucharist [should] in turn [confirm] our opinion," meaning that we should express our unity in the Eucharist.

Throughout most of our history, Orthodox and Catholics shared in the Eucharist. It is unfortunately ingrained in contemporary Orthodox mindset to consider that in 1054, East and West split and interrupted their eucharistic communion, when in fact the two anathemas referred only to the heads of the

---

61. Ware has a more conciliatory view of this development, considering that Vatican II's motivation was both pastoral (economy) and to further the cause of Christian unity. Ware, "Intercommunion," 262–63.

62. *Orientalium Ecclesiarum* par. 29, *Unitatis Redintegratio* par. 15. To this day, given the close degree of communion between the Orthodox and Catholic Churches and the recognition of Orthodox sacraments (especially Eucharist and Ordination), the Catholic Church allows and encourages intercommunion, while also recognizing that the Eastern discipline is more restrictive and should be respected. Moreover, in cases of necessity or when "a genuine spiritual advantage suggests," a Catholic person is allowed to receive the sacraments of penance, Eucharist, and anointing of the sick from an Orthodox clergy. Catholic clergy may administer these same three sacraments to Orthodox faithful, while giving due consideration to Orthodox discipline and avoiding any suggestion of proselytism. Pontifical Council for Promoting Christian Unity, *Directory for the Application of Principles*, 122–25. http://www.christianunity.va/content/unitacristiani/en/documenti/testo-in-inglese.html.

churches of Rome and Constantinople. Even after the 1204 sack of Constantinople by the Crusaders, East and West continued to share in the Eucharist. Thirteenth-century Greek and Latin monks at Mt. Athos shared communion. Moreover, even as late as 1484, the Church of Constantinople was still forbidding sharing the Eucharist with Latins, which shows that intercommunion was nevertheless happening. At that time, the Patriarchate of Constantinople was under pressure from the Ottomans who wanted to ensure that the Orthodox remain estranged from the Catholics for a simple political reason: if Orthodox and Catholics were close, they might seek military alliances. If they remained separated, then the Ottoman grip on the East would remain strong.[63] Despite this fifteenth century forbiddance of eucharistic sharing, historical evidence suggests that intercommunion occurred until much later in history. Ware points out that in December 1969, when almost all Catholic parishes in the USSR had been closed, the Synod of the Russian Orthodox Church decided to allow Catholics to receive Communion in Orthodox parishes.[64] Moreover, in the previous chapter we encountered the practice of intercommunion among Christians in the Middle East, so the schism was never total.

It is not the place here to exhaustively treat the history of eucharistic sharing between Orthodox and Catholics, but these historiographical considerations are sufficient evidence that intercommunion existed throughout the entire history of the Church. So, whenever somebody claims that "this is what the Holy Fathers have always taught," it is important to point out both that most Fathers lived in the first millennium of unity (so their divisions with those who challenged essential dogmas were much more significant than ours), and that history contains numerous inconsistencies and thus one cannot simply over emphasize one aspect and ignore the larger picture. Naturally, inconsistencies do not automatically become norm, but at least they point out that certain practices are very recent, certainly dating after the age of the Fathers, and that exclusivist practices often have non-theological motivations. Thus, the Eucharist remains a boundary marker, but the boundaries of the early Church do not

63. George E. Demacopoulos, "Crociate, Memoria e Perdono Nella Construzione dell'Identità Cristiana," in *Misericordia e Perdono* (Bose, Italy: Qiqajon Comunità Bose, 2016), 337–54.

64. The Church of Greece rejected Moscow's decision. But, as Ware wisely points out, "It would be presumptuous for Orthodox who do not live under conditions of persecution to pass judgment about the pastoral problems of the Orthodox Church within the USSR." Moreover, prominent hierarchs of the Ecumenical Patriarchate agreed with Moscow's decision and took it further by considering the Catholic person who comes to commune as practically Orthodox and admitting that Orthodox faithful participate in Catholic and Anglican eucharists in cases of necessity. Timothy (Kallistos) Ware, "Church and Eucharist, Communion and Intercommunion," *Sobornost* 7, no. 7 (1978): 560–62.

coincide precisely with the boundaries of today, and the boundaries that the Eucharist marks are porous. This complexity is also reflected in recent Orthodox theology.

Twentieth century Orthodox theologians are astoundingly diverse on the topic of eucharistic sharing. According to John Jillions, recent Orthodox theologians display one of two main attitudes: mainstream or prophetic.[65] In what follows, I use Jillions's framework and supplement it with other examples of Orthodox theologians.

The foremost proponent of *the mainstream view* was Florovsky, whose vision has been adopted in all Orthodox ecumenical statements in a surprisingly consistent manner: the purpose of ecumenical discussions is to bring other Christians into the fullness of Orthodox faith and life, since the Orthodox Church is the true Church (although not yet the perfect Church); in the meantime, there can be no intercommunion.[66]

Those who oppose dialogue criticize ecumenists as though the latter have brought about changes and compromises in the Orthodox faith, but—to their likely surprise—I am placing ecumenists under the mainstream position. Orthodox participants in the ecumenical movement consistently reject eucharistic hospitality. As early as 1937, the Orthodox delegates at the Faith and Order conference in Edinburgh affirmed that intercommunion "must be considered the crowning act of real and true Reunion which has already been fully achieved by fundamental agreement in the realm of Faith and Order and is not to be regarded as an instrument for Reunion."[67] According to this line of thinking, the Eucharist is a sign of unity and only within a united Church can it become a means to strengthen that unity. In today's divided Christendom, the inability of the Orthodox Church to share in the Eucharist with other churches is *the sign* of our disunity. (The tragic irony of this statement is difficult to ignore and represents a call to earnest ecumenical engagement.)

Staniloae spoke in no uncertain terms against intercommunion without doctrinal unity: "I cannot understand how communion in the Holy Eucharist

65. John A. Jillions, "Three Orthodox Models of Christian Unity: Traditionalist, Mainstream, Prophetic," *The International Journal for the Study of the Christian Church* 9, no. 4 (2009): 295–311.

66. Florovsky's claim that the Orthodox Church is the true Church led him to say that he had no confessional loyalty (since Orthodoxy is not simply one among many confessions), but that his loyalty solely belongs to the *Una Sancta*. Therefore, "Christian reunion is just universal conversion to Orthodoxy." 285–286. Georges Florovsky, "Confessional Loyalty in the Ecumenical Movement," in *The Patristic Witness of Georges Florovsky: Essential Theological Writings*, ed. Brandon Gallaher and Paul Ladouceur (London: T&T Clark, 2019), 285–86.

67. Limouris, *Orthodox Visions of Ecumenism*, 16.

can somehow compensate for non-communion in faith."[68] He contended that orthodoxy does not result from the Eucharist, but that the true Eucharist results from orthodoxy, so that eucharistic communion can only take place within the context of sharing in the same faith.[69] This conclusion stems from the order of the Divine Liturgy, where the community first confesses its common faith and then the epiclesis takes place.[70] But Staniloae did not intend to imply that the Catholic Church has fallen so much from the true faith that its Eucharist is not valid. He recognized that the Catholic Church professes the presence of the Body and Blood of Christ in the Eucharist.[71] Moreover, he affirmed that the Catholic Church, just like the Orthodox Church, has preserved the faith in the Trinity and in Christ, even if it has also added to the Church's ancient faith the dogma of papal primacy, papal infallibility, the Filioque, and purgatory. Among these, only the dogmas of papal primacy and infallibility are obstacles for communion,[72] or church-dividing—a statement that is quite encouraging when noting that the Filioque is not church-dividing, in Staniloae's estimation.

Bobrinskoy, too, rejects intercommunion without unity in faith, adding: "Unanimity in the faith constitutes the perpetual miracle of Orthodoxy insofar as we have no formal or magisterial structure that imposes doctrinal unity."[73] This is a memorable statement: Orthodox unanimity in faith is a miracle. Without a formal magisterial structure endowed with power to decide in matters of faith, God bestows the gift of doctrinal unity upon Orthodoxy, obviously, not in the sense of absolute uniformity in all details, but as unanimity in the truths that are essential for salvation, leaving room for diversity, creativity, and continuous discernment. One could take Bobrinskoy's words in a different direction and ask, does a self-imposed magisterium that says that Catholics and Orthodox do not have unity of faith have any authority to keep us separate? Why would this self-imposed authority drown the numerous voices that advocate intercommunion all throughout history, as shown above? Have we simply accepted uncritically the rhetoric of differentiation?

Zizioulas has criticized the term "intercommunion" as "inept," since sharing in the Eucharist can only take place within a united church, not between churches that are not in full union. He contends that "orthodoxy is unthinkable

68. Quoted in Ware, "Church and Eucharist," 558.
69. Staniloae, Spirituality and Communion, 398–99.
70. Staniloae, Spirituality and Communion, 399.
71. Staniloae, Spirituality and Communion, 81–82.
72. Staniloae, Spirituality and Communion, 401–2.
73. Bobrinskoy, The Mystery of the Church, 129.

without the Eucharist" and that "the Eucharist without orthodoxy is an impossibility;" in the present state of Christian disunity, there can be no eucharistic sharing, even though this situation is tragic and unnatural.[74] If here Zizioulas emphatically rejects intercommunion, elsewhere he stresses the tragic and unnatural character of our divided Christianity by questioning the very idea of denominationalism and denouncing the existence of separate denominational cultures in the same locality, where the Eucharist is supposed to strengthen unity.[75]

In contrast with the mainstream view of intercommunion, Jillions points to *the prophetic view*. Between 1933–1935, Sergius Bulgakov called for partial intercommunion among members of the Fellowship of St. Alban and St. Sergius, mainly Anglicans and Orthodox. Bulgakov noted that the members of the Fellowship shared the same faith more deeply than members of the congregations of either church, so he did not advance a minimalist proposal. Bulgakov then added a structural aspect: based on the model of autocephalous Orthodox churches, he advocated a union between Orthodoxy and other churches that would preserve their historical character. For Bulgakov, intercommunion does not need to wait for the solution of all dogmatic differences and offers a favorable climate for common growth into Orthodox doctrine and life.[76] Even more boldly, Bulgakov asked rhetorically: "May it not be that Christians sin now by not heeding the common eucharistic call?"[77] Bulgakov's proposal was supported by some members of the Fellowship, both Anglican and Orthodox such as Lev Zander, Anton Kartashev, and Nicholas Zernov, but most members did not support it. The Fellowship decided to shelve Bulgakov's call for partial eucharistic intercommunion and instead "preferred the more restrained concept of spiritual intercommunion at two chalices, rather than at one."[78]

Bulgakov's proposal interwove the theological and the experiential approaches: theologically, intercommunion came after agreement in doctrine, and experientially this agreement already existed within the Fellowship. He did not advocate for a generalized Orthodox-Anglican sharing in the Eucharist, but for an exceptional and localized intercommunion. Bulgakov brought up another very important question when he highlighted how the members of

74. Zizioulas, *Eucharist, Bishop, Church*, 133, 257–58.

75. Zizioulas, *Being as Communion*, 259–60.

76. Jillions, "Ecumenism and the Paris School of Orthodox Theology," 155–58.

77. Sergius Bulgakov, "By Jacob's Well," in *Tradition Alive: On the Church and the Christian Life in our Time: Readings from the Eastern Church*, ed. Michael Plekon (Lanham, MD: Rowman & Littlefield, 2003 [orig. 1933]), 64.

78. Brandon (Anastassy) Gallaher, "Bulgakov and Intercommunion," *Sobornost* 24, no. 2 (2002): 15–16.

the Fellowship shared the same faith more deeply than members of the congregations of either church: how much more important is canonical belonging to a church, compared to charismatic belonging (in the spirit)? There are many nominal Orthodox and nominal Anglicans in our parishes, and we treat them more hospitably than we treat those who are Orthodox and Anglicans in spirit, without bearing that name. Perhaps an informed, pious Anglican is more Orthodox than a complacent Orthodox.

Afanasiev's eucharistic ecclesiology holds a prominent place in the prophetic category. He claimed that, although Catholics and Orthodox are separated canonically, they celebrate the same Eucharist. The same ecclesial reality is present in both of them, and therefore they have never been essentially disunited. Afanasiev recommended that the Orthodox Church and the Catholic Church work toward manifesting their still-existing unity by renewing their communion, sharing in the Eucharist, and postponing the solution of dogmatic divergences (including with regard to papal primacy) for the time when they would be able to address them in the spirit of love.[79] Afanasiev understood the division between Orthodox and Catholics as being "merely canonical,"[80] which is quite a statement coming from a professor of Canon Law. Despite their relatively frequent occurrence, canonical dissentions are not Church-dividing. That is not to say that there are no cessations of eucharistic communion for canonical reasons, as explained above in relation to the Patriarchates of Jerusalem, Romania, Antioch, Moscow, and Constantinople. But to regard the Orthodox-Catholic schism on the same level as these intra-Orthodox quarrels is a significant ecumenical advancement that Afanasiev proposes and that considers papal dogmas as non-Church-dividing issues, but rather pertaining to the canonical order. While Afanasiev's eucharistic ecclesiology represented a significant ecumenical advancement, some aspects of his own proposal and— to a larger degree—subsequent Orthodox eucharistic ecclesiologies reversed Afanasiev's advancements regarding intercommunion and cast a negative light upon non-eucharistic aspects of Church life. As John Behr explains,

> Whether the sacrament of the Kingdom, already celebrated in anticipation by the Church *in via*, can be used to define the boundaries of the one true Church is a very serious question. This is, of course, how the "eucharistic ecclesiology" espoused by many Orthodox theologians during the twentieth century views the matter. This has undoubtedly contributed to an increased

79. Afanassieff, "Una Sancta," 27–28.
80. Afanassieff, "Una Sancta," 25.

ecclesial awareness, but it has also had a deleterious effect in two respects. First, the "eucharistic revival" that has accompanied such ecclesiology has emphasized participation in the eucharist to such a point that it often overshadows, if not obscures, the perpetual baptismal dimensions of Christian life; baptism is regarded as the necessary preliminary step into body which celebrates the eucharist. Taken to its extreme, this results in a community of, in John Erickson's phrase, "eucharisticized pagans"—members of the Church who participate in the eucharist but do not otherwise have any consciousness of the life in death that is the Christian life in this world. Secondly, it results in a view that sees life outside the Orthodox Church, defined as coextensive with participation her celebration of the eucharist, in uniformly negative terms:... In this perspective, not only do the Orthodox regard themselves, rightly, as belonging to "the one true Church," but they deny the designation "Church" to any other body gathering together in the name of Christ: outside the Orthodox Church, "humanity is ruled by alien powers."[81]

Thus, Afanasiev rightly belongs among the prophetic Orthodox theologians who advocated for intercommunion, even though his theology represented the springboard for exaggerations such as diminishing the pilgrim character of the Church; absolutizing Orthodox liturgical life, rather than regarding its eschatological characteristics as imperatives from the future; the relegation of morality to the outskirts of ecclesial life, content with a rich liturgical experience; the diminishing of baptismal ecclesiology;[82] a judgmental attitude and even an epistemological certainty regarding the damnation of the other, certainly uncharacteristic of Orthodox apophatism. But none of these unintended consequences should take away from the merits of Afanasiev's theology.

As Jillions shows, other theologians from the School of Paris advocated intercommunion before the solution of all dogmatic divergences: Zernov proposed that Christians submit their ecumenical impasses to divine arbitration and allow God to bring them into unity, as opposed to trying to build that unity by human efforts. Zander considered that other churches did not have the fullness of the faith, so prohibiting Orthodox participation in Western sacraments was understandable to him; but he proposed that the Orthodox invite others to share in the Orthodox fullness of the faith and its sacraments, trusting the

81. John Behr, "The Trinitarian Being of the Church," *Saint Vladimir's Theological Quarterly* 48, no. 1 (2003): 82–83.

82. Paul Meyendorff, "Liturgical Life in the Parish: Present and Future Realities," in *The Orthodox Parish in America: Faithfulness to the Past and Responsibility for the Future*, ed. Anton C. Vrame (Brookline, MA: Holy Cross Orthodox Press, 2003), 148.

mystical power of the Spirit to act in the hearts of all Christians—a significant argument that cannot be justly analyzed here. Kartashev predicts that if inter-communion would start in just one place as an instance of ecumenical heroism, then it would spread to the entire Church.[83] These theologians are all saying that the Orthodox have good reasons to embrace intercommunion; all that is needed is courage, trust, faith, and good will.

Other Orthodox theologians embrace such prophetic attitudes. Ion Bria remarks that Orthodoxy's conciliar tradition embraces polyphony and a va-riety of creedal formulas. Moreover, the order of the Liturgy indicates the pre-conditions for communion: since the Creed is recited before communion, we should commune (by *oikonomia*) with those who confess the Creed. Bria considers that a priest has the authority—without episcopal approval or for-mal conversion—to give communion to Oriental Orthodox, Roman Catholics, and Old Catholics, and that this step would not derail the process of arriving at full eucharistic communion.[84] Bria's last remark is important because one argument against intercommunion is that if eucharistic hospitality happened before the solution of dogmatic divergences, we would not have the incentive to seek full communion. But this argument does not hold water for either Af-anasiev or Bria, or myself, for that matter. I cannot understand how we could reconcile better when we live in distant, deep trenches, than when we live in the same household. Having said this, and in line with the pragmatic approach of this study, it is important to acknowledge how difficult it could be to put Bria's proposal into practice. Bria recommends intercommunion only based on the authority of the priest and without episcopal approval. Practically, however, that authority rests with the local bishop. If the latter did not have the neces-sary degree of openness, he would not hesitate to exercise his oversight in the parish. The priest would then have to face the sanctioning of the bishop in the form of suspension or even defrocking, so eucharistic hospitality requires at least a tacit, if not explicit, episcopal approval.

Ware belongs in the prophetic category as well. He writes about Ortho-dox faithful—particularly Greeks—who frequently received Communion in Anglican parishes both in England and in America in mid-twentieth century. Ware then adds: "and viewing the matter purely from a pastoral viewpoint, it is entirely understandable that they should do so."[85] He acknowledges that hier-

---

83. Jillions, "Ecumenism and the Paris School of Orthodox Theology," 169–74.

84. Ion Bria, *The Liturgy after the Liturgy: Mission and Witness from an Orthodox Perspective* (Geneva: WCC Publications, 1996), 26, 29.

85. Ware, "Intercommunion," 265–66.

archical approvals for intercommunion were only informal, with one exception, when Syrian Orthodox bishop Raphael of Brooklyn issued an encyclical letter in 1910, stating that in cases of need his people might receive Communion from Episcopal clergy. Other Orthodox churches in America protested this letter and forced bishop Raphael to retract it.[86]

Olivier Clément and Paul Evdokimov wrote an *Appeal to the Church* to transcend its internal dissensions in order to respond to the needs of humankind. They unequivocally called for the restoration of unity between the Eastern and Oriental Orthodox Churches. Regarding the relationship with the Catholic Church, they acknowledged that in general the Eucharist is not a means towards unity. But, as the dialogue progresses, they appealed to sharing the Eucharist based on the principle of "economy" (*oikonomia*) so that the theological dialogue would be nourished by the dialogue of charity and by the occasional assistance of common celebrations, which on a regular basis would not imply intercommunion, but the principle of economy could be applied occasionally.[87]

This survey adopted Jillions's categories of mainstream and prophetic attitudes towards intercommunion, but went beyond the theologians that he discussed. It has established that most Orthodox theologians reject *generalized* eucharistic hospitality. And yet, mainstream theologians acknowledge that the Eucharist is not only a boundary marker, but it also calls us to transcend those boundaries. The disunited state of Christianity is abnormal and we cannot remain complacent in our divisions. Prophetic theologians consider that intercommunion is allowed *on a limited basis*, by *oikonomia*, based on the faith that we share in its most significant aspects and due to pastoral necessities. The prophetic attitude represents a healthy reminder that we should not place so much emphasis on theological dialogue that we overlook the action of the Spirit, the common life in Christ that we already share, and the possibility of new forms of Christian unity. The merit of the mainstream position is that it compels us to continue our dialogue towards the goal of unity in faith.

The topic of intercommunion necessitates some *further liturgical remarks*. First, the patristic mind did not clearly separate the moments of the Liturgy, but regarded the entire celebration as a single act. In this sense, the first part of the Liturgy (of the word) is not completely devoid of eucharistic connotations, evidenced by the dismissal of catechumens after the readings from the Scriptures and the sermon, with the understanding that they departed with Christ.

---

86. Ware, "Intercommunion," 265–66.
87. Olivier Clément, *Orient-Occident: deux passeurs, Vladimir Lossky et Paul Evdokimov*, Perspective orthodoxe; no 6, (Genève: Labor et Fides, 1985), 205.

The sacred words brought Christ in people's hearts to such an extent that Origen wrote about "spiritual communion" as partaking of the Word by listening to Scriptures; his intent was to highlight the importance of the Church's proclamation of the Good News, without focusing exclusively on the reception of the Eucharist. In the same tradition, Maximus the Confessor affirmed that even in the Old Testament there was a partaking of the Word through Scripture, similar to the Eucharist.[88] Both of these Fathers used eucharistic language in reference to the Scriptures. In other words, the words of Scripture have a "eucharistic effect," which calls into question the practice to refuse Communion to those who are baptized and share in the most important aspects of the faith (as Catholics and Orthodox do), even while being canonically in schism.

Second, the theologians analyzed above draw conflicting conclusions from the order of the Liturgy that places the Creed before the reception of the Eucharist: Staniloae requires full dogmatic unity, while Bria considers the Creed sufficient for intercommunion. In the Orthodox Liturgy, the priest comes out with the chalice saying, "With the fear of God, with faith, and love draw near," while facing the people, so he represents Christ who invites them to receive Communion. This is not merely an invitation, but also a commandment: "Do this in remembrance of me." But of all biblical commandments, "do this in remembrance of me" is probably the least respected when the Orthodox themselves do not receive Communion and do not permit others, either. This practice cannot be defended eschatologically. In the Kingdom there will be no Orthodox, Catholics, Protestants, but all will be one in Christ. Refusing to allow others at the table does not reflect that Kingdom. So, again, Orthodox theologians should humbly and realistically admit a sad reality: when we do not share the Eucharist with those who will be part of the eschatological Kingdom of God, in our Liturgy we do not experience the eschaton. And after we admit this, let us repent and seek a Kingdom-centered ecclesiology in which our churches reflect our theologies at their best and our liturgies at their best.

As the fourth side of the table is open in Rublev's *Trinity* icon as an invitation to the viewer to participate in the heavenly banquet of the eucharistic chalice, and as the Scriptures testify that many will come to this heavenly banquet from the East *and the West* (e.g. Mt 8:11), opening up Communion on a limited basis would be a step in the right direction. In the case of Orthodox-Catholic faithful, intercommunion would mean that the Orthodox do

88. Dumitru Staniloae and M. A. Costa de Beauregard, *Mica dogmatica vorbita: dialoguri la Cernica* [*Brief Spoken Dogmatics: Dialogues at Cernica*], trans. Maria-Cornelia Oros (Sibiu: Deisis, 1995), 125.

not recognize papal primacy and infallibility as common dogmas, but at most as *theologoumena* applied only in the West. As far as the Orthodox Church is concerned, there are no church-dividing dogmas between us, even though the Catholic Church officially affirms them as dogmas *de iure divino* beginning with the promulgation of *Pastor Aeternus* in 1870. This being the case, even without episcopal communion (as with the non-Chalcedonians), Orthodox faithful should be allowed to receive Communion in the Catholic Church and Catholics in the Orthodox Church, as Catholic discipline already allows it. The Orthodox Church should not excommunicate itself for its lack of recognition of a (late) Catholic dogma. This is even more so the case since, as mentioned above, Vatican II's *Decree on the Catholic Churches of the Eastern Rite* allows for intercommunion despite the Orthodox rejection of papal dogmas. As Afanasiev puts it, the Catholic hand remains suspended in the air—but this section has shown that it need not be so.

The main *benefit of intercommunion* is a deeper unity within the parish. In a previous chapter I have advocated for *limited* intercommunion for Orthodox-Catholic couples, and here I am extending this proposal to other members, as well. And yet, the following remarks do not apply primarily to larger Church bodies, but to the community of the parish, formed by members of different faiths. In fact, most writings of early Christianity do not deal with universalizing aspects of the Church, but with concrete communities formed by a small number of faithful.

The first to address the unity stemming from the common reception of the Eucharist is the Apostle Paul, who writes to a very diverse community of Corinth, one that even experiences schisms within itself (1 Cor 1:10). And yet, he compares them to the people of Israel who were united in their partaking of the sacrifices, and so Christians who receive of the same cup and of the same bread are one in Christ: "The cup of blessing that we bless, is it not a sharing in the blood of Christ? The bread that we break, is it not a sharing in the body of Christ? Because there is one bread, *we who are many are one body, for we all partake of the one bread*" (1 Cor 10:16–17).[89] Clearly, for Paul, unity stems from partaking of the one bread together. This motif of the bread being one and creating unity will reverberate in subsequent writings. One of the oldest descriptions of Christian liturgies, *The Didache*, describes the benefits of the

---

89. Augustine interprets this Pauline passage in Sermon 226: "If you have received worthily, *you are what you have received,* (italics mine) for the Apostle says: 'The bread is one; we though many, are one body.'" Augustine, *St. Augustine: Sermons on the Liturgical Seasons*, trans. Sister Mary Sarah Muldowney R. S. M. (Washington, DC: The Catholic University of America Press, 1977), 195–96.

community receiving the Eucharist together, growing into unity. Notably, the limitation that this text imposes upon those who receive the Eucharist is that they all be baptized:

> As this broken bread was scattered upon the mountain tops and after being harvested was made one, so let Thy Church be gathered together from the ends of the earth into Thy Kingdom, for Thine is the glory and the power through Jesus Christ forever. But let no one eat or drink of the Eucharist with you except those baptized in the name of the Lord, for it was in reference to this that the Lord said: "Do not give that which is holy to dogs."[90]

Cyril of Alexandria also writes about the Eucharist creating unity:

> For by one Body, that is, His own, blessing through the mystery of Eucharist those who believe on Him, He makes us of the same Body with Himself and with each other. For who could sunder or divide from their natural union with one another those who are knit together through His Holy Body, which is one in union with Christ? For if we all partake of the one Bread, we are all made one Body; for Christ cannot suffer severance. Therefore, also the Church is become Christ's Body, and we are also individually His members, according to the wisdom of Paul. For we, being all of us united to Christ through His Holy Body, inasmuch as we have received Him Who is one and indivisible in our own bodies, owe the service of our members to Him rather than to ourselves.[91]

All the faithful gathered in the Liturgy owe their service to Christ, whose members they are, and all of them, baptized into the Lord, are to grow in their unity by partaking by the one bread and the one cup that gather what is scattered, that make one what is separate.

ETHICAL IMPLICATIONS

Eucharistic ecclesiology has its undeniable merits, and this chapter has highlighted several ways in which "where the Eucharist is, there is the Church of God, and where the Church of God is, there is the Eucharist," as Afanasiev puts it.[92]

90. "The Didache or Teaching of the Twelve Apostles," in *The Apostolic Fathers* (Washington, DC: The Catholic University of America Press, 1947), #9, 179.
91. Saint Cyril of Alexandria, "On the Gospel according to John," trans. T. Randell, Library of Fathers 44, vol. 2 (London: Walter Smith, 1885), book 11, #11, 550.
92. Afanassieff, "Una Sancta," 14.

But as already stated above, it would be reductive to regard the Eucharist as comprehensive of all aspects of the Church, such as its work of healing and proclamation—the values of the Kingdom. Eucharistic ecclesiology cannot become constrictive by overshadowing baptismal ecclesiology, charitable ecclesiology, or mission-centered ecclesiology—in other words, Kingdom-centered ecclesiology. Staniloae is a good example of an Orthodox theologian who not only upheld the eucharistic nature of the Church, but also went further to contend that Christ is present in the Spirit through the Eucharist, the other sacraments, the "prayers, proclamation, and the good and pure deeds of the faithful,"[93] all of which constitute the Church and have the Church as their premise. Obviously, the latter elements in this enumeration apply directly to proclamation and being a healing presence in the world.

A parish community cannot retreat into the Divine Liturgy at the expense of the "Liturgy after the Liturgy." The latter refers to the Church's service to those who are vulnerable, a service that results from participation in the Eucharist.[94] John Chrysostom speaks about two altars: one is in the church, adorned with golden vessels and vestments, and we rightly revere it. The second altar is the poor, those who lack clothing, food, or a roof over their heads, and this one we wrongly ignore. While adorning God's house, we cannot overlook our brothers and sisters, who are more properly God's temple.[95] But both are sacred altars, and both are necessary for a full parish life. Maximus the Confessor writes in this sense in his treatise on the Church gathered in the Liturgy that

> … nothing is either so fitting for justification or so apt for divinization, if I can speak thus, and nearness to God as mercy offered with pleasure and joy from the soul to those who stand in need. For if the Word has shown that the one who is in need of having good done to him is God … and if the poor man is God, it is because of His condescension in becoming poor for us and in taking upon himself by his own suffering the sufferings of each one.[96]

Thus, the community of the Church as a whole and its members individually, cannot retreat into a false spirituality that does not care for the poor and does not heal those who suffer. God *is* those who hunger, and God *is* those who need healing, and serving the Lord means serving at their altar, too. In this sense, Zernov writes that "the Eucharist is … the source which inspires all the

93. Staniloae, *Spirituality and Communion*, 82.

94. Bria, *Liturgy after Liturgy*.

95. Saint John Chrysostom, "Homily 50 on Mt 14:23–24," in *St. John Chrysostom, on the Gospel of St. Matthew*, NPNF I:X (Grand Rapids, MI: Eerdmans, 1888), #4–5, 303.

96. Maximus the Confessor, "Mystagogia," 211–12.

social activity of the Christians, all their endeavours to fight against poverty, injustice, disease and death, and it confirms their hope in the ultimate victory of good over evil.[97] Along similar lines, Kallistos Ware interprets the concluding words of the Liturgy, "Let us depart in peace," to mean that

> "The Liturgy is over; the Liturgy after the Liturgy is about to begin." So far from being merely a comforting epilogue, a signal of release, these words are rather a command and a challenge: "Go out into the world, and impart to all around you the eucharistic life and hope with which you yourselves have been filled. You have received the Holy Gifts: gifts are intended to be shared with others." Doxology must now become evangelization. The Eucharist makes us apostles. In our missionary witness, we shall not necessarily be speaking *about* the Liturgy, but all that we say will be *from* the Liturgy.[98]

Clearly these Orthodox authors consider that the Church's mission to proclaim the good news and heal stem from the Eucharist and that missions are intrinsic to the eucharistic aspects of the Church. If that is the case, the Church cannot be defined exclusively in eucharistic terms but, at the same time, *there remains a strong connection between missions and the Eucharist*: the Eucharist enables the Church to go into missions, and missions oftentimes lead to a eucharistic celebration in a new local church, which will then have its own missions going outwards.

The relationship between the Eucharist and the Church's outward movement marked the Church from the first days of its existence. Jesus' meal with the two disciples at Emmaus is the eighth meal-scene in the Gospel of Luke, whereas the Last Supper was the seventh, leading N. T. Wright to comment: "the week of the first creation is over, and Easter is the beginning of the new creation. God's new world order has arrived."[99] This new order consists in the Church walking with people in the wrong direction (towards Emmaus when they should stay in Jerusalem), listening to them, so that the Church can reveal to them the love of God, teach them the good news, feed them, and heal them. It is because of the Resurrection which inaugurates God's Kingdom, always renewed in our Liturgical celebrations, that the Church becomes the means through which God brings healing, forgiveness, peace, and abundance. These connections are highlighted in the Paschal Homily of John Chrysostom, which is read in Orthodox churches at the Easter celebration:

---

97. *St. Sergius—Builder of Russia* (London: SPCK, n.d. [c.1939]), 105.
98. Ware, "The Holy Spirit in the Liturgy," 120–21.
99. Wright, *The Challenge of Jesus*, 164.

Enter then, all of you, into the joy of our Lord.
First and last, receive alike your reward.
Rich and poor, dance together.
You who fasted and you who have not fasted, rejoice together.
The table is fully laden: let all enjoy it.
The calf is fatted: let none go away hungry.
Let none lament his poverty;
for the universal Kingdom is revealed.
Let none bewail his transgressions;
for the light of forgiveness has risen from the tomb.
Let none fear death;
for death of the Savior has set us free.

...

O death, where is your sting?
O hell, where is your victory?

Thus, the manifestation of the Kingdom and the celebration of the Resurrection in the Liturgy do not allow Christians to be exclusively focused on the individual (without the community), the spiritual (without the material), and the eschatological (without the present). It is tempting to believe that being in the *kairos* of the Liturgy could be a substitute for fulfilling one's duty to the *chronos*. *Attending Liturgies is not a substitute for caring for the poor, bringing healing to the world, and proclaiming the good news.* Paradoxically, only by focusing on the *chronos* does a church enact the values of *kairos*, thus representing both a presence and an instrument of the Kingdom of God—an icon of the Kingdom. The Liturgy itself testifies to this, as Maximus the Confessor interpreted the kiss of peace as an experience in this world of the eschatological harmony: "The spiritual kiss which is extended to all prefigures and portrays the concord, unanimity, and identity of views which we shall all have among ourselves in faith and love at the time of the revelation of the ineffable blessings to come."[100]

One of the pressing ways in which the Church needs to care for the *chronos* in order to lead into the eschatologically-harmonious *kairos* is to fight for *racial and social justice*.[101] The image of Archbishop Iakovos, leader of the Greek Archdiocese of North and South America, marching to Selma on March 15,

---

100. Maximus the Confessor, "*Mystagogia*," 202.
101. See the programmatic *The Kairos Document. Challenge to the Church: A Theological Comment on the Political Crisis in South Africa* (1985–1986). https://www.sahistory.org.za/archive/challenge-church-theological-comment-political-crisis-south-africa-kairos-document-1985. This document condemns racial and socio-economical discrimination and has since become an aspect of liberation theology.

1965 with Dr. Martin Luther King Jr. to protest racial injustice is so powerful, that it almost functions as an icon of the Kingdom, especially since he was the only white bishop who agreed to join the march. At that point in history, most churches in fact exacerbated the racial divide. As Martin Luther King Jr. said, "eleven o'clock [on Sunday morning] is the segregated hour in Christian America."[102] Parishes, even within the same denomination, were segregated along racial lines. Unfortunately, these words still ring true today. I once was even faced with racism after death: I was invited to celebrate a Memorial service for a deceased Orthodox person in a small town in North Carolina. I was not familiar with the area, so I got directions to the funeral home, not even considering that such a small town could have more than one funeral home, but I was soon surprised to find out that it did. To my dismay, one was "the black funeral home," where I first went, while the other was "the white funeral home," where I was supposed to do the Memorial service. It is a perversion of the Gospel to call ourselves Christian and act as if segregation continues after death, as if our racial divides rise up to the Kingdom of heaven.

A 2015 Pew Research Center study concluded that 81% of Orthodox parishes in the U.S. are white, with a diversity index of 4.2, which is below the median[103] and could be partially explained by the countries of origin of numerous parishioners making up American Orthodoxy. But one cannot simply dismiss racial issues as being outside the purview of American Orthodox parishes. As George Kasamias observed, in the Western hemisphere, even saints from North Africa are generally depicted in icons as white. Moreover, after marching along Martin Luther King Jr., Archbishop Iakovos received hundreds of death threats from Orthodox Christians in the U.S. And yet, Kasamias also points out that Orthodoxy has the potential and the historical background to be at the forefront of the fight for racial justice. Originating in the East, Orthodox history has not been tainted by the slave trade and the racism that confronted the West, and has been present for the past two millennia on the African continent, especially in Egypt and Ethiopia.[104] The road ahead is still long, but a

---

102. Martin Luther King Jr. Sermon "A Knock at Midnight" (June 5, 1963). In fact, MLK is paraphrasing here Helen Kenyon, an official of the National Council of Churches, who more than a decade earlier labeled eleven o'clock on Sunday morning as "the most segregated time" in the United States ("Worship Hour Found Time of Segregation," *New York Times*, Nov. 4 1952). Both references: https://kinginstitute. stanford.edu/king-papers/documents/knock-midnight.

103. Pew Research Center, *The Most and Least Racially Diverse U.S. Religious Groups* (2015). www .pewresearch.org.

104. George Kasamias, "Orthodoxy and Race in Light of Trump's Inauguration," https://publicorthodoxy.org/2017/01/19/orthodoxy-and-race-after-trump/

Church that lives according to the values of the Kingdom and that experiences that Kingdom in its Liturgy cannot take any part in the sinfulness of racism.

Also noticeable are divisions along social lines—divisions that go back to the beginning of the Church. The Corinthian community was so divided in different social classes, that they ate separately before partaking of the Body and Blood of Christ, to the dismay of the Apostle Paul who instructed them to eat together (1 Corinthians 10–11). The Apostle's commandment bore fruit and, as Zizioulas notes, early Christian communities that gathered together many social classes stood in stark contrast to other organizations in the Greco-Roman world, which gathered according to ethnicity or social class. Early Christian communities were unique in that they offered the Eucharist to all the members of the community, transcending their sociological boundaries.[105]

Hearkening back to the early Church's Eucharist that challenged sociological divisions and also to the time when the bishop was the celebrant of the unique Liturgy that gathered all the members of the diocese, it is relevant to consider the example of Archbishop Oscar Romero. Despite the objection of the papal nuncio, Romero designated a specific Sunday on which his entire church in San Salvador would celebrate a single Eucharistic liturgy. Wealthy Salvadoran Catholics of the land-owning class refused to attend, under the pretense that they would be unable to hear the Mass and thus to fulfill their Sunday obligation. They also invoked the distance that they would need to travel, even though they had the ability to drive to the Cathedral. Instead, the poor who did not have the luxury of such means of transport all gathered around the Archbishop, standing in the sun for the Eucharistic liturgy.[106] Romero's intention to gather the entire diocese into a single Liturgy shows the power of the Eucharist to transcend social divisions—a power too hard to bear for the rich Salvadoran landlords.

Highlighting the unity that the Eucharist commands and creates is a suitable way to end a chapter that argued that in the Divine Liturgy we have the opportunity to experience the end times, when Christ will be all in all, when he will encompass the entire creation and transcend our divisions. This gift comes from the one who infuses our times with a glimpse of eternity by the work he does through the Church: "it is time for the Lord to act."

105. Zizioulas, *Being as Communion*, 151–52.

106. Jon Sobrino, *Witnesses to the Kingdom: The Martyrs of El Salvador and the Crucified Peoples* (Maryknoll, NY: Orbis, 2003), 20–24.

SIX

Priesthood

*It is no longer the layman who stands in
need of definition but the priest.*

YVES CONGAR[1]

What is a "priest" or *iereus*? A third century Christian would respond that, for their fellow citizens of the Greco-Roman world who worshipped the gods, the term "priest" was a narrow cultic designation of those who offered sacrifices in a temple. Attentive to their Jewish roots, that same Christian would say that the term "priest" in Israel had a similar, sacrificial meaning referring to those descendants of the tribe of Levi who served at the Temple of Jerusalem. A notable exception for this narrow description of priesthood happened at the foot of Mount Sinai, when the entire People of God was designated as "a kingdom of priests" (Ex 19:6 JPS), which is a better translation than "a priestly kingdom" (NRSV).[2] These words were then quoted verbatim in 1 Pt 2:9–10, which applied Israel's attributes to all the members of the Church—a kingdom of priests, sharing in Christ's priesthood. Moreover, Acts 6:1–7 refers not to the ordained alone, but to the entire Christian community as priests (*iereon*). Other passages explicitly connect Christian life and priestly sacrifices in Christ, the Priest: "like living stones, let yourselves be built into a spiritual house to be a holy priesthood to offer spiritual sacrifices acceptable to God through Jesus

---

1. Congar, "Path-Findings," 182.
2. The Hebrew *mamlechet kohanim* implies a kingdom that is populated with priests, while "a priestly kingdom" (NRSV) is closer to the Septuagint *basileion hierateuma*, where the direct object is not the kingdom, but priesthood, which is extended throughout the kingdom.

Christ" (1 Pt 2:5). Of course, the early Church knew the distinction between those ordained and the rest of the baptized, but the ordained were never called priests exclusive of the rest; instead, they were called deacons, presbyters, and overseers. Thus, third century Christians would say that the word "priest" refers to pagan and Jewish servants who bring sacrifices, the people of Israel, Christ himself, and to all members of the Church.[3]

Beginning with the fourth century and up to today, the question "what is a priest?" receives a different answer from most Christians: a priest is the ordained leader of a parish.[4] The priesthood of Christ and that of the entire people of God no longer represent the central aspects of the faithful's experience of priesthood. That is why it is important to retrieve the sense that the entire people of God—which includes the clergy—is a priestly icon of Christ and that all the baptized, not just the ordained, constitute the priestly Body of Christ, while maintaining, of course, the distinction between those ordained and those who are not ordained. Based on this communitarian foundation, ordained priesthood becomes even more meaningful.

Numerous Orthodox icons illustrate *the priesthood of Christ* by portraying him vested as a bishop, even though Jesus did not have a role similar to the early bishops nor was he a temple priest. There are exceptional traditions according to which Jesus was from the tribe of Levi, but in fact neither Jesus nor the Apostles belonged to levitical priesthood, and thus Christianity started out as a lay movement, albeit with a priestly calling.[5] Hence, far from implying that only bishops share in the priesthood of Christ, these iconographic representations of Jesus the High Priest point out that not only those who are officially designated as clergy, but the entire community of the Church shares in Christ's priesthood.

As stated in the previous chapter, when the Liturgy is about to begin, the Church acknowledges that its Liturgy is ultimately God's own work: "it is time for the Lord to act." Later on, during the Prayer of the Cherubic Hymn, Christ is confessed as both Priest and Sacrifice: "You are the Offerer and the Offered, the one who receives and is distributed, Christ our God." John Chrysostom further develops the idea that God is the priest in his famous passage: "Father and Son and Holy Spirit direct everything. The priest simply lends his tongue

---

3. Pelikan, *Illustrated Jesus*, 28.

4. In the case of a monastery, the priest is the celebrant of the Liturgy or the father confessor.

5. Afanasieff acknowledges a minority tradition represented by Hippolytus of Rome, Ambrose of Milan, and Hilary of Poitiers, who harmonize the genealogies in Matthew and Luke in a way that present Jesus as descending also from Levi because the tribes of Levi and Judah had merged, but this tradition never received a wide acceptance. Afanassieff, *The Church of the Holy Spirit*, note 7 on p. 278, 12.

and [provides] his hand."[6] But since the Liturgy is at the same time "the work of the people" and since God needs the visible hand and tongue of the priest, it follows that Christ *the* Priest works visibly through a priestly people (the Church) in which some members (the ordained celebrant) offers the sacrifice on behalf of Christ and preaches Christ to the community, lending his hand and tongue to Christ. The priest is never alone in his priesthood. He does not offer the sacrifice in isolation but together with the community, and he preaches not his own opinions but the living word of God to which the people give their "Amen."

Thus, the priesthood of Christ is manifested and represented iconically as the priesthood of the entire Church, clergy and laity—the consecrated people of God. No attempt to explain the distinction between the clergy and the people can take away the full participation of both the ordained and those who are not ordained in the priesthood of Christ. That is why Zizioulas writes that there is no ministry in the church that is not Christ's ministry.[7] His mentor, Florovsky, likewise wrote that the Church is "the extension ... of the Holy Incarnation [which means that Christ] is Himself the only true Minister of the Church. All others are but stewards of His mysteries."[8] As such, far from rendering obsolete *the priesthood of the clergy and the laity*, the priesthood of Christ represents their foundation.

First, a terminological clarification regarding the terms designating those who are ordained and those who are not ordained. Schmemann considered that the Greek term *laïkos* denotes the belonging of all Christians to the People (*laos*) of God (cf. 1 Peter 2:9).[9] On the contrary, Hans Küng avoids the term "laity" because in the ancient Greek world it referred to the uneducated masses and in the Jewish tradition to one who was neither priest nor Levite.[10] For the same reason, Afanasiev constructed a term that did not previously exist, namely *laic*. Another possibility is to use the oft-repeated liturgical term, "faithful," as well as "the people" as when the community prays "for the clergy and the people," *tou klerou kai tou laou*. In the present volume, I have used all these terms interchangeably with the assumption that the term laity does not carry negative connotations and that the terms "faithful" and "people" do not exclude the clergy from the People of God or from among those who have faith. Moreover,

---

6. John Chrysostom, "Homily 86," 457.

7. Zizioulas, *Being as Communion*, 210.

8. Florovsky, "The Church: Her Nature and Task," 64–68.

9. Schmemann, *The Eucharist*, 232. Afanassieff avoided this term and invented a word that did not previously exist in Russian, namely "laics."

10. Hans Küng, *The Church* (Garden City, NY: Image Books, 1976), 492–94.

after the fourth century, one can refer to the leader of the parish as the priest, who is the successor of the earlier elder or presbyter.

If terminology raises so many questions, the theology of the laity, predictably, is even more susceptible to misunderstandings. Catholic theology has for a long time defined the laity by negation: "all the faithful except those in holy orders and those in a religious state sanctioned by the Church" (LG 31). This negative definition of the laity as neither ordained nor monastics (in other words, what they are lacking) was then given content, under the influence of Yves Congar, and the Second Vatican Council also defined the laity positively, as the baptized who share "in the priestly, prophetic, and kingly functions of Christ" (LG 31). The second chapter of the present volume argued that through Baptism and Chrismation, all the faithful are consecrated into the priesthood of the Church, sharing in the priesthood of Christ. Chapter four further differentiated between the priesthood of all the baptized and (within it) the priesthood of the ordained from the perspective of their diverse ministries within the community, all working together for the edification of the Body of Christ. Chapter five argued that both clergy and laity celebrate the Liturgy and the Liturgy after the Liturgy together. Those arguments need not be repeated here and they provide enough responses to the question, "who are the laity?" It is now time to ask the next logical question, namely "who are the clergy?" This latter question will be the focus of the present chapter.

The main motivation for raising this question is experiential. Theology needs to *respond to concrete challenges and opportunities* that Orthodox parishes face today. Some of these challenges have already turned into opportunities of growth, and they include the following, in no particular order of importance: first, all over the world there are numerous parishes that are not financially viable; they cannot cover their operational expenses, maintain their existing buildings, and cannot afford to pay the salary of a full-time priest who works exclusively in ministry. That is why an increasing number of priests are bi-vocational. They are dedicated to their ministry in the parish but, in order to support their families, they also need a secular job or they teach religion in public schools (in traditionally Orthodox countries) or in universities. This situation is not ideal when the priest cannot preside at services because of his secular job. And yet, in many cases especially in North America, it is the only way in which a parish can have a priest. Other parishes respond to this challenge by consolidating into a cluster of communities that are served by one priest, who presides at the Sunday Liturgy on a rotating basis in those parishes, or who substitutes the Sunday service for a Saturday Liturgy, as it sometimes happens especially with mission churches until the latter become financially viable and can afford a full-time priest.

Second, Orthodoxy in North America as well as in some traditionally Orthodox countries faces a shortage of priests. Especially in the U.S., the number of seminary graduates who are ordained (many are not ordained upon graduation) is lower than the number of priests who exit ministry for various reasons, such as retirement, sickness, or divorce. One of the reasons for inadequate seminary enrollment is that in the past, conflicts arose between priests and their parish councils. We are now paying a hefty price: fewer and fewer talented men enroll in seminary, being discouraged to heed their priestly calling by their parents who try to protect them from such conflicts. The relationship between the priest and parish leadership is significantly improved now and hopefully we will see a resurgence in the number of priestly vocations as a result. Another factor determining low seminary enrollment might be a shift in what the contemporary world considers "success," namely financial gain. Even in those jurisdictions in which priests earn good salaries, their earnings are lower than those of professionals with comparative levels of education. Here the Church has an important mission: impress upon its members that in the Body of Christ there are different ministries, and God calls each person to a different vocation. Happiness comes from faithfully fulfilling that vocation, not from large earnings. Happiness and fulfillment are more important than material wealth. Parishes, on their part, should ensure a comfortable standard of living and a peaceful atmosphere for its ministers.

Third, and related to the previous challenge, priests in the U.S. are overburdened in their ministry. They work very long hours, with less time for recreation compared to other professions, and are in worse health than the general population.[11] Very few parishes, even large ones, can afford to hire an assistant priest or a lay assistant. The sheer number of services, visitations, and other ministries, sometimes render the priest a liturgical operator. A healthy communion between ordained ministries and lay ministries is necessary for the flourishing of a parish, avoiding the situation where the priest retreats in the liturgical aspect of the parish, while lay ministries are the only ones entrusted with teaching and administration, youth activities, etc. A healthy parish realizes that many ministries are lay vocations that respond to its needs better than an overburdened

11. Up until 1959, clergy lived longer and healthier than non-clergy in the U.S. Since then, however, the rates of obesity, heart problems, diabetes, etc. among the clergy are higher than the general population. Rae Jean Proeschold-Bell and Patrick J. McDevitt, "An Overview of the History and Current Status of Clergy Health," *Journal of Prevention and Intervention in the Community* 40, no. 3 (2012): 177–79.

priest. Moreover, parishes need to nurture other ordained ministries, especially bi-vocational priests and permanent deacons with secular jobs. As the present chapter will show, this challenge can seamlessly become an opportunity for a greater role of permanent deacons. Orthodoxy needs to respond to the need for clergy, without whom its parishes cannot remain eucharistic.

Last but not least, an honest discussion of priesthood needs to tackle the subject of clericalism. Either because of older theologies that emphasize an ontological change conferred at Ordination, or as a counter-reaction to con-gregationalism, some Orthodox parishes suffer from the disease of clericalism. This term refers to the pretension of the clergy to be a privileged class that is not responsible to the rest of the Body but only to itself. An emphasis on com-munion among the clergy and laity in both theology and the lived experience of the parish acts as an antidote to the temptation of clericalism.

All these challenges are in fact opportunities to retrieve forgotten elements of the Orthodox tradition. Looking back at the role of deacons and especially deaconesses in the Early Church uncovers a wealth of theology and practices that can respond to the need for ordained ministers in today's parishes. More-over, regarding once again the leader of the community not as a despot, a litur-gical machine, or a person who replaces all ministries, but as a father, offers a historical precedent that can be recovered and further nurtured to strengthen the communion between the clergy and the people and thus participate more fully in the priesthood of Christ.

To respond to theological and practical challenges outlined above, this chapter will point in *two main directions*, namely the ministries of various or-ders in Orthodox parishes (with special insistence on the diaconate—male and female), and the communion between clergy and laics. It will not even attempt—much less claim—to offer a full account of ordained priesthood, so Congar's words from the epigraph of this chapter will remain true to the end: "It is no longer the layman who stands in need of definition but the priest."[12]

ORDINATION

The second chapter argued that, in Baptism, all the members of the Church are consecrated—a concept associated with the priesthood of all believers who all share in the priesthood of Christ. The priesthood of all believers does not

---

12. Congar, "Path-Findings," 182.

mean the priesthood of every believer. This statement, of course, uses two distinct senses of "priesthood": while all members of the Church are part of a priestly people of God, not all members are priests in the sense of being ordained. According to Staniloae, Ordination is

> the act through which Christ, in a visible form, chooses and invests these men as instruments through whom, when they celebrate the sacramental actions, He Himself will celebrate them invisibly; when they teach and pastor in His name, He Himself will teach and pastor through them. But through this act of consecration, they are not only enabled for this purpose, they are also laid under obligation. This means that they are invested with a "charism" or a "gift" so that they can officiate these works with seriousness, responsibility, and as an obligation, so that what they officiate Jesus Christ may officiate through them. Priests are ... visible instruments of [Christ's] invisible priesthood.[13]

Zizioulas defines ordination as "assignment to a particular 'ordo' in the community."[14] He considers that ordination puts the clergyman in a new relationship with the rest of the community. In his new state, the ordained person is no longer conceived in himself, but his existence is determined by communion. The pastor is the minister of a community.[15] To better explain this new relationship, Zizioulas refers to Maximus the Confessor's term, "co-divided"—a relational reality that differentiates the community into multiple ministries, without creating division between clergy and laity.[16] Moreover, Michael Spence compares the change that the priest undergoes at Ordination to the changing of the bread and the wine into the Body and Blood of Christ: "The priest is a sacrament of Christ to the Church ... in this way, the life of the priest is Eucharistic—taken, blessed, broken, and shared, which happens through the

---

13. Dumitru Staniloae, *The Experience of God: Orthodox Dogmatic Theology—The Sanctifying Mysteries*, trans. Ioan Ionita and Robert Barringer, vol. 5 (Brookline, Mass.: Holy Cross Orthodox Press, 2013), 140–41. Summarizing Staniloae's understanding of ordination, Rosu defines ministerial priesthood as "being *bidirectional-representative*: taken from among the general priests (i.e., those baptized), and ordained by the bishop with the participation of the community, the priest *typologically* represents Christ inside the community, and, at the same time, the congregation before Christ." Alexandru Rosu, "Fr. Dumitru Staniloae's View on Laymen's Participation in the Infallibility of the Church," *Ecumenical Review Sibiu / Revista Ecumenica Sibiu* 6, no. 1 (Apr. 2014): 37.

14. Zizioulas, *Being as Communion*, 216.

15. Zizioulas, *Being as Communion*, 226.

16. Zizioulas, *Being as Communion*, 220. Influenced by Zizioulas, Gaillardetz proposes a shift to a "relational ontology" in which attention is drawn not to the isolated individual who receives special powers at ordination, but an "ecclesial re-positioning" understood as "the reconfiguration of the person into a new ministerial and ecclesial relationship that requires that empowerment by the Holy Spirit necessary for that ministry." Gaillardetz, "Ecclesiological Foundations," 36.

activity of the Holy Spirit. As at the epiclesis, the Holy Spirit enables something (bread/wine, a human being) to become something it is not (the Body/Blood of Christ, the person of Christ)."[17]

Through the imposition of the hands of the ordaining bishop(s), a candidate is placed in one of the three major orders: deacon or deaconess, priest, and bishop. Within the rite of ordination, the ancient "Divine Grace" formula stands out:

> The Divine Grace, which always heals that which is infirm and supplies what is lacking, appoints the [designated order] N., beloved by God, as [designated order]. Let us pray therefore that the grace of the Holy Spirit may come upon him.[18]

Although there is a single sacrament of Ordination, each of these orders have their own specific character, as opposed to being degrees of participation in the ministry of the bishop who would presumably have the fullness of Ordination, while the priest would share in that ordination to a lesser degree and the deacon to an even lesser degree, as Afanasiev believes.[19] Rather than possessing different degrees of fullness of ordination, these orders should be regarded as different roles. The specific ministries of each of these three orders are abundantly attested in the New Testament, despite the interchangeable terminology that the apostolic Church used for them. For example, 1 Pt 5:1–5 uses the term "elder" or "presbyter" for what we would call today a bishop as the leader of a church.

Church structures developed gradually and by the second century, local churches combined the conciliar model characteristic of the Jewish synagogue led by a council of elders with the Roman model in which the *pater familias* led the household.[20] Thus emerged a new normative church structure that in-

---

17. Michael Spence, *Priest Acting in Persona Christi" The Mystery of Faith: Reflections on the Encyclical Ecclesia de Eucharistia* (Blackrock: Columba Press, 2005), 173–89.

18. Paul Bradshaw, *Rites of Ordination: Their History and Theology* (Collegeville, MN: Liturgical Press, 2013), 86.

19. Afanassieff, *The Church of the Holy Spirit*, 219–20. At the polar opposite, Thomas Aquinas denies that the episcopate is at a higher degree than priesthood, since the Eucharist presided over (or, in his words, confected) by the bishop is equal to the Eucharist presided over by the priest, each presiding over the fullness of the Eucharist. (*Summa Theologiae Suppl.* Q.37, A. 2. in Thomas Aquinas, *Summa Theologiae, Complete English Edition in Five Volumes*, trans. Fathers of the English Dominican Province (Allen, TX: Christian Classics, 1981). Two centuries later, two papal rescripts granted abbots (who were not bishops) in England and Germany the authority to ordain men to the priesthood. See Robert Christian, "Bonds of Communion among Parishes and among Priests," in *What Is a Parish? Canonical, Pastoral, and Theological Perspectives*, ed. Thomas A. Baima and Lawrence Hennessey (Chicago: Hillenbrand Books, 2011), 137.

20. Harrington, *The Church*, 162.

cluded the one bishop (monoepiscopate), surrounded by a council of elders or *presbyterium* whose role was consultation and administration, assisted by deacons entrusted with social-charitable responsibilities and the distribution of the Eucharist, and all the faithful with various charisms. Such a structure can be seen for example in the writings of Ignatius of Antioch who describes the local church as being led by "one bishop with the [presbyters] and deacons;"[21] "apart from these there is nothing that can be called a Church."[22] To give one more example from this era, the *Apostolic Constitutions* state the differences between the three orders, their functions and rites of ordination:

> We command that a bishop be ordained by three bishops, or at least by two; but it is not lawful that he be set over you by one; for the testimony of two or three witnesses is more firm and secure. But a presbyter and a deacon are to be ordained by one bishop and the rest of the clergy. Nor must either a presbyter or a deacon ordain from the laity into the clergy; but the presbyter is only to teach, to offer [the Eucharist], to baptize, to bless the people, and the deacon is to minister to the bishop, and to the presbyters, that is, to do the office of a ministering deacon, but not to meddle with the other offices.[23]

Since the ministry of the parish priest and that of the bishop have already been addressed in previous chapters, including their historical development, in this section I focus on the diaconate and, at greater length, on the female diaconate.[24]

The Deacon

Male Diaconate   I served as a deacon less than 24 hours. I was ordained a deacon on a Sunday and a priest the next day, on Monday. While some of my seminary colleagues may have remained deacons for a few weeks longer, ours is a rather typical journey: a candidate who graduates seminary with the intention of becoming a priest cannot be ordained directly into the priesthood, so he is first ordained a deacon. For most priests, the experience of the diaconate is nothing more than a stepping-stone towards the priesthood.[25] For the laity, the

21. Ignatius, "To the Philadelphians," in Ignatius of Antioch (Theophorus), "The Letters," #4, 114.

22. Ignatius, "To the Trallians," in Ignatius of Antioch (Theophorus), "The Letters," #3, 103.

23. *Constitutions of the Holy Apostles* [*Apostolic Constitutions*], trans. James Donaldson (Grand Rapids, MI: Eerdmans, 1886), Book III:20, 432.

24. For a detailed historical analysis of the evolution of orders throughout history, as well as the pastoral implications of these developments, see Paul Bernier, *Ministry in the Church: A Historical and Pastoral Approach*, Second ed. (Maryknoll, NY: Orbis, 2015).

25. When Ordination into the diaconate takes place, a candidate goes through the ranks of the minor

diaconate is veiled in mystery. In traditionally Orthodox countries, deacons are rather rare, almost exclusively surrounding the bishop. It is thus not surprising that Orthodox theologies of Ordination do not focus on the diaconate, content to describe it as a partial share in the ministry of the bishop, twice removed behind the priest, and not as a ministry in its own right. In the United States, however, more and more parishes have permanent deacons, who usually have secular jobs and are not supported financially by the parish, hence *a theology of the permanent diaconate is much needed today.*[26]

The early Church's experience with the diaconate provides both an understanding of how we got to the present situation and a model for the revival of the permanent diaconate. In biblical times, the diaconate appeared as a response to a practical need described in Acts 6:1–7: when some members of the Church were "neglected in the daily distribution [*diakonia*] of food," the Twelve asked that seven men would be chosen to "wait on tables" [*diakonein trapezais*] so that the Twelve would be able to devote themselves "to prayer and to serving the word [*diakonia tou logou*]." The community of disciples "had these men stand before the apostles, who prayed and laid their hands on them" (Acts 6:6), and thus the first seven deacons were ordained to distribute food to the hungry and the Eucharist to the community of the Church (Acts 6:7). They were to be servants (*diakonoi*), after the model of Jesus who came "not to be served, but to serve [*diakonesai*]" (Mt 20:28).

As Ignatius of Antioch and *The Didascalia* testified above, by the second century, when the tripartite orders of bishop, priest, and deacon were more clearly established, the role of the deacon was to assist the bishop. At that time the bishop was still the father of the community and the diocese represented the local community, gathered around a unique Eucharist. But as the role of the diocese as eucharistic assembly led by the bishop transferred to the level of the parish led by the priest (see chapter 4), the deacons became less and less present in parishes,

---

orders without skipping any ranks; similarly, someone being ordained as a priest has to first be a deacon, and someone who is ordained bishop has to first be a priest. Historically, the Church of Rome has used a similar *cursus honorum*: porter, lector, exorcist, acolyte (these being part of the minor orders), sub-deacon, deacon, presbyter, and bishop (major orders). In the twentieth century, Pope Paul VI suppressed the minor orders, although he restored lectors and acolytes, both of which remain stepping stones to ordination into the diaconate. It is important to note that the sequence of ordination reflected in *cursus honorum* was not firmly into place until the Middle Ages; in the earliest Christian centuries, bishops were sometimes ordained from among the baptized or the deacons, without first being ordained as presbyters. Richard R. Gaillardetz, *Ecclesiology for a Global Church: A People Called and Sent* (Maryknoll, NY: Orbis, 2008), 67, 140.

26. See for example John Chryssavgis, *Remembering and Reclaiming Diakonia: The Diaconate Yesterday and Today* (Brookline, MA: Holy Cross Orthodox Press, 2011).

remaining instead as assistants to the bishop. Today, while that is generally still the case, in American Orthodox parishes the situation is rapidly changing.

In North America, the presence of permanent deacons is becoming more and more common, especially in Antiochian and OCA parishes. The explanation for this growth is partially practical. In the Orthodox Church, only an ordained person can distribute the Eucharist. In countries where the faithful do not receive Communion frequently, one parish priest suffices to distribute Communion effectively, even in large parishes. If until the mid-twentieth century the norm used to be that most American Orthodox faithful would commune only between one and four times a year (and thus one chalice was sufficient), as a result of the eucharistic revival spearheaded by Schmemann, most American Orthodox churches today practice frequent communion, meaning that the majority of the faithful present at any given Liturgy receive the Eucharist. Besides the recovery of the traditional practice of frequent communion, a second factor contributes to the need to have more ordained clergy who can distribute Communion, namely the multitude of large parishes served by only one clergyman who cannot distribute Communion in a timely fashion. Since the number of seminarians (and thus candidates for priesthood) remains gravely insufficient in the United States, the only remaining practical solution is to encourage the permanent diaconate.

In response to the faithful who have a vocation for ordained ministry and to the needs of so many parishes, there are programs of diaconal education that have an online component as well as a residency requirement for practical-liturgical education. Men whose calling has been discerned clearly in their parish and who benefit from the mentoring of their parish priests, receive the necessary education for ordination into diaconate. At the end of such programs, a candidate can be ordained as a deacon and appointed into his parish of provenance without the possibility of later being ordained to the priesthood, unless that person obtains an M.Div. degree from a seminary.

When the deacon is a common presence in the parish, it becomes clear that the diaconate is not a stepping-stone towards the priesthood, just as priesthood is not a stepping-stone towards the episcopacy. Being ordained in one rank does not mean automatically a future ordination into a superior rank. Thus, the diaconate is a ministry in its own right. It is a ministry of eucharistic distribution and outreach.

Having already discussed the eucharistic needs of the Church today, it is now important to emphasize the second aspect of the diaconate, namely outreach. For too long Orthodoxy has retreated (or communism forced it to retreat) within the walls of its churches, without a role in the larger society. But *a Kingdom-centered approach* that places the Church in the midst of the world to minister to its needs, represents Orthodoxy at its best. A truly traditional Orthodox stance would be to revitalize the order of permanent deacons because they are a much-needed ministry as the Church ministers to society by proclaiming the Kingdom and bringing healing to the world.

As stated in the previous chapter, Justin Martyr combines the two roles of the deacon: distribution of the Eucharist in the church and outreach to those who are absent presumably sick at home, in the hospital, or in prison: "they whom we call deacons permit each one present to partake of the Eucharistic bread, and wine and water; and they carry it also to the absentees. We call this food the Eucharist."[27] Justin's words remind us that the Liturgy continues with the Liturgy after the Liturgy, and serving at the altar in the church continues with the service at the altar of the poor, as Chrysostom wrote. Thus, the ministry of the deacon continues (or better, finds its fulfillment) beyond the Divine Liturgy, into the charitable ministry of the Church.

In North America, people in need often look to parishes to help with utility bills, unexpected car repairs, or temporary lack of medication, and churches provide the necessary relief that enables families to keep their home, workers to get to work and maintain their jobs, or sick people to transition to a stable situation. Often these ministries are coordinated by parish priests in collaboration with women's ministries, when in fact the deacon should coordinate them. Churches that have a more developed charitable ministry, led by a deacon, are able to establish more efficient ways to help as well as networks of redistribution of goods.[28]

When the ministry of the deacon is not purely liturgical, it transcends the physical boundaries of the parish, reaching out to those in need not only within the community, but also to the larger society. That is when the ministry of the deacon also transcends denominational boundaries, resembling the ministry of Jesus the Servant, who came to serve not only the community of disciples, but the entire world. This is the sense in which St. Ignatius of Antioch writes that "in the same way all should respect the deacons as they would Jesus Christ, just as they respect the bishop as representing the Father and the priests as the council of God and the college of the Apostles. Apart from these there is

27. Justin Martyr, "First Apology," #65–66, 105.
28. See for example the St. John the Merciful Outreach Ministry in Raleigh, NC http://www.st-johnmerciful.org

nothing that can be called a Church."[29] Thus, a Church cannot exist without the deacons who exercise the servant ministry of Christ who was sent by the Father, just as the deacon is sent by the bishop to serve. As in the ancient world the *diakonos* was not simply a social worker, but a person commissioned by his superior to act in the latter's name, so deacons are commissioned by the bishop and the parish priest to serve to the needs of the world through healing and proclamation. Deacons are thus much more than "first-class altar boys or second-class priests."[30]

Having said this, it is necessary to be realistic about the role of the diaconate in the Orthodox Church, including in the U.S. Most seminary graduates will indeed be ordained as deacons, but eventually they will go on to be ordained priests. This section will hopefully make the diaconate a meaningful first phase of their journey into ministry, and not merely a stepping-stone towards priesthood; not simply learning liturgical rubrics, but being a vital part of the Church's manifestation of the Kingdom through proclamation of the good news, charity, and distribution of Communion both in the church and in hospitals, nursing homes, and prisons.

This section on the male diaconate remains quite short because many roles of the deacon will be further highlighted in the following section, on the female diaconate.

Female Diaconate Women deacons have been a continual presence in Orthodox history, although with different degrees of intensity. They are much needed in today's parishes and perhaps even more urgently in nuns' monasteries, so it is necessary to look into the history of the order of deaconesses, address their role, and propose ways in which their ministry would benefit today's Orthodox Church.

The *history of female diaconate* begins in the New Testament. Besides the indirect references to the women who ministered to Jesus and the disciples (such as the Myrrh-bearing women), there are direct references to women deacons. While some translations refer to Phoebe as "servant" for the Greek, *diakonon* (Rom 16:1), the more direct translation is "[female] deacon," or "deaconess." She was a great benefactor to Paul and to many others. Moreover, 1 Tm 3:8–13, which deals with the qualifications of deacons, refers to both males and females

---

29. Ignatius, "To the Trallians," #3, 102–03.

30. On November 16, 2019, Pope Francis said. "Move the deacons away from the altar.... They are the custodians of service, not first-class altar boys or second-class priests." https://www.vaticannews.va/en/pope/news/2019-11/pope-francis-dicastery-family-laity-life-plenary.html

within the same context—a clear indication of the existence of deaconesses in the early Church. A careful reading of the New Testament also reveals a much more prominent role for women in the early Church than what we would call "deaconesses" today. For example, some are identified as Apostles, such as Junia who was esteemed among the Apostles (Rom 16:7). Moreover, in his Epistle to the Romans, Paul greets Prisca before greeting her husband, Aquila, and mentions "the church in their house," implying that there is a community that assembles in their house, giving Prisca a prominent role in the Roman Church (Rom 16:3–6). Similarly, the church in Laodicea meets in the house of Nympha (Col 4:15), without a reference to a husband, so it is quite possible that Nympha alone had a leadership role in her Church. Clearly, women in the early Church were deaconesses, apostles, and leaders of local communities.[31]

Shortly after these New Testament references, the second century *Didascalia* describes in great detail the role of deaconesses and deserves to be quoted at length:

> Wherefore, O bishop, appoint thee workers of righteousness as helpers who may co-operate with thee unto salvation. Those that please thee out of all the people thou shalt choose and appoint as deacons a man for the performance of the most things that are required, but a woman for the ministry of women. For there are houses whither thou canst not send a deacon to the women, on account of the heathen, but mayest send a deaconess. Also, because in many other matters the office of a woman deacon is required. In the first place, when women go down into the water, those who go down into the water ought to be anointed by a deaconess with the oil of anointing; and where there is no woman at hand, and especially no deaconess, he who baptizes must of necessity anoint her who is being baptized. But where there is a woman, and especially a deaconess, it is not fitting that women should be seen by men but with the imposition of hand do thou anoint the head only. As of old the priests and kings were anointed in Israel, do thou in like manner, with the imposition of hand, anoint the head of those who receive baptism, whether of men or of women; and afterwards—whether thou thyself baptize, or thou command the deacons or presbyters to baptize—let a woman deacon, as we have already said, anoint the women. But let a man pronounce over them the invocation of the divine Names in the water. And when she who is being baptized has come up from the water,

---

31. While the calendar of the Catholic Church mentions only deaconesses (servants) Phoebe and Apollonia, the Orthodox calendar is replete with a great number of deaconesses. See more in Kate Cooper, *Band of Angels: The Forgotten World of Early Christian Women* (New York: Overlook Press, 2013), 6–10.

let the deaconess receive her, and teach and instruct her how the seal of baptism ought to be (kept) unbroken in purity and holiness. For this cause we say that the ministry of a woman deacon is especially needful and important. For our Lord and Saviour also was ministered unto by women ministers, Mary Magdalene, and Mary the daughter of James and mother of Jose, and the mother of the sons of Zebedee [Mt 27.56], with other women beside. And thou also hast need of the ministry of a deaconess for many things; for a deaconess is required to go into the houses of the heathen where there are believing women, and to visit those who are sick, and to minister to them in that of which they have need, and to bathe those who have begun to recover from sickness.[32]

This passage explains *the ministry of the deaconess as being both dictated by necessity and reaffirmed by its fruitfulness.* The deaconess is "especially needful and important" for reasons of propriety. At a time when the larger population was unfamiliar with Christian ministries, a male deacon visiting a Christian woman in a pagan household might be misunderstood or even generate accusations of inappropriate contacts. But a deaconess would not raise such suspicions. Moreover, during the ritual of Baptism, the minister must anoint the person who is being baptized. For reasons of propriety, a male minister could anoint only the head of a woman being baptized, but no other part of her body. It would, however, be proper for a woman to offer a complete anointing. Of course, a person would customarily be baptized completely naked, and this is why these considerations of propriety are so important and dictate by necessity that women should be baptized with the assistance of women deacons.

The *Didascalia* also reaffirms the female diaconate because of its fruitfulness. While Christian women benefited from the ministry of male deacons in many regards, this passage indicates that "the ministry for women" in the community is best done by women in many respects. For example, as the newly baptized woman emerges from the water, the deaconess receives her and embarks on a journey of instruction into the Christian way of life—"how the seal of baptism ought to be (kept) unbroken in purity and holiness." Moreover, the *Didascalia* demonstrates the fruitfulness of the female diaconate regarding those who are sick. Their needs were both spiritual (presumably encouragement, anointing with oil, prayer, receiving Communion) and physical, including help with bathing as the Christian woman recovers from her sickness. While

32. *Didascalia Apostolorum*, trans. R. Hugh Connolly (Oxford: Clarendon Press, 1929), #xvi [iii.12], 70–71.

today the physical needs of the sick fall primarily under the responsibility of medical personnel, the spiritual needs of newly baptized women and women in sickness would certainly benefit from the ministry of deaconesses.

Deaconesses remained prominently *present in the life of the Church in subsequent centuries*, even though the practice of adult baptism became more and more rare, thus showing that the ministry of the deaconess was not exclusively linked to adult female baptism. In the seventh century, several dozens of deaconesses were still serving at Hagia Sophia in Constantinople. It is actually quite humorous that in 612, Patriarch Sergius was concerned that there were too many ministers serving at Hagia Sophia, so he reduced their number to (the still impressive count of) 80 priests, 150 deacons, 40 deaconesses, and numerous other ministries.[33] If forty deaconesses survived this drastic reduction in personnel, clearly their ministry remained both necessary and fruitful.

A similar historical testimony comes from the Quinisext Council in Trullo, held in 692, whose fortieth canon states the minimum age at which deaconesses can be ordained and highlights the fruit that their ministry has already borne: "the sacred canons have decreed that a deaconess shall be ordained at forty, since they saw that the Church by divine grace had gone forth more powerful and robust and was advancing still further, and they saw the firmness and stability of the faithful in observing the divine commandments." Later on, an eighth century *Euchologion* (Gr. 336) provides the ordination prayer recited by the bishop during the Liturgy, at the altar: "Send down upon her the rich gift of your Holy Spirit. Preserve her in the Orthodox faith, that she may fulfill her ministry in blameless conduct according to what is well pleasing to you."[34] Afterwards, the newly ordained deaconess received a stole and a chalice, and communed with the clergy inside the altar. Besides the responsibilities listed earlier in the *Didascalia*, now deaconesses also took communion to those who were unable to come to church, participated in processions, and assisted the bishop with the philanthropic mission of the Church.[35]

These historical considerations show that the deaconesses were not simply appointed through *cheirothesia*, as if they were simply blessed for their social work. Rather, deaconesses were received into the rank of the clergy through

33. MacCulloch, *Christianity*, 431.
34. The St. Phoebe Center for the Deaconess: Thoughts on Our Mission https://publicorthodoxy .org/2017/12/06/a-dialogue-on-the-mission-of-st-phoebe-center-for-the-deaconess/.
35. AnnMarie Mecera, Caren Stayer, Gust Mecera, Teva Regule, Carrie Frederick Frost, and Helen Theodoropoulos. "Towards a Reasoned and Respectful Conversation about Deaconesses" https://public orthodoxy.org/2018/04/17/conversation-about-deaconesses/.

cheirotonia (ordination). They were ordained into the major orders at the same moment in the Liturgy as male deacons, in the altar area before the altar table, following the same rubrics, receiving the *orarion* (or the diaconal stole), and receiving Communion inside the altar with the clergy.[36]

Deaconesses remained a continual presence in the Orthodox Church until modern times. Albeit drastically reduced compared to the first eight centuries, they never totally fell out of existence. In 1911, one of the most revered contemporary Orthodox saints, Nectarios of Aegina (1846–1920), ordained two deaconesses for the nuns' monasteries where he lived. Also *in Greece*, in 1986, then-Metropolitan Christodoulos of Demetrias (later Archbishop of Athens) ordained a nun as deaconess, using the ancient ordination rite mentioned above. Throughout his ministry, the Archbishop remained a tireless advocate for the restoration of the female diaconate. Shortly thereafter, the Inter-Orthodox Symposium, "The Place of the Woman in the Orthodox Church" took place in Rhodes in 1988.[37] It spoke strongly against women's ordination to the priesthood, but affirmed the exact opposite regarding the diaconate, recommending that "the apostolic order of deaconesses should be revived."[38]

Merely six years later—which in Orthodox time is the blink of an eye—on October 8, 2004, the Synod of the Church of Greece met under the leadership of the same Archbishop Christodoulos of Athens. The majority of the 64 bishops present decided to restore the order of the diaconate for women, acknowledging the relative sense of the term "restore" since the order of deaconesses has been a continuous presence in Orthodox history. This historic decision was the result of an extensive discussion regarding the theological, liturgical, canonical, and ministerial aspects of the order of deaconesses raised at the 1988 Rhodes Symposium.

While the Greek Synod's decision to rejuvenate the female diaconate is

36. Inter-Orthodox Symposium, "The Place of the Woman in the Orthodox Church," in Gennadios Limouris, ed., *The Place of the Woman in the Orthodox Church and the Question of the Ordination of Women: Inter-orthodox Symposium, Rhodos, Greece 30 October–7 November 1988* (Katerini: Tertios, 1992). One of the foremost authorities on the issue of the deaconess' ordination is Evangelos Theodorou who, since the 1930's, has argued that women deacons were ordained to the higher orders of the clergy. For his responses against those who argue that deaconesses were only consecrated, and not ordained, see Evangelos Thedorou, "Service of God and Service of Man," in Θεολογια no. 3 (1997): 424–428.

37. This symposium was preceded by an International Orthodox women's gathering at the monastery of Agapia (Romania) in 1976. While the Rhodes symposium was comprised mostly of men, women were in the majority at Agapia. Behr-Siegel describes this gathering "as more or less the birthplace of a specifically Orthodox feminism." Elisabeth Behr-Sigel, "The Ordination of Women: Also a Question for the Orthodox Churches," in *The Ordination of Women in the Orthodox Church*, ed. Elisabeth Behr-Sigel and Kallistos Ware (Geneva: WCC Publications, 2000), 32.

38. Rhodes #8.

momentous and (considering the opposition that any discussion of gender issues provokes today, even) prophetic, its practical implementation remains quite disproportional to the enthusiasm that it initially generated. To this day, we do not have concrete information about any ordinations that might have followed this decision, and thus we cannot speak convincingly about the experience of the ministry of deaconesses in Greece today.[39]

The opposite is true on the African continent. In November 2016, *the Synod of the Patriarchate of Alexandria and All Africa* decided to revive the institution of deaconesses. In less than the blink of an eye in Orthodox time,[40] the Patriarchate of Alexandria announced in February 2017 that it had ordained five deaconesses. They were consecrated at the Missionary Centre of Kolwezi with the mandate to help with missionary efforts such as adult baptisms, marriages, and catechism. Orthodox liturgists and other theologians enthusiastically supported this development.[41] As expected in the current climate of internal divisions, this decision was also criticized through unofficial channels. As a result, the Patriarchate of Alexandria clarified that the five women were "blessed" as sub-deacons, rather than "ordained" as deaconesses, and that they would mostly function as catechists, even while they will maintain the title of "deaconess," in the hope that in the future they would take pre-sanctified Communion to those in need.

As a general rule, the catechist is part of the minor orders, while the deaconess is considered among the major orders. And yet, this "clarification" goes even further than the initial announcement about the ordination of deaconesses, since in Africa the catechist has more responsibilities than the deacon. The total population of Africa grew 313% in the last fifty years, and so did the needs of all Christian churches.[42] While numerically speaking the African continent offers an impressive number of seminarians and new clergymen, proportionally speaking—that is, the number of faithful that a priest ministers—there remains

---

39. Deaconess Maria Spyropoulou (1933–2022) is a partial exception to this lack of visibility of Greek deaconesses. She was tonsured (or blessed) as a deaconess in the Orthodox Cathedral of St. Nicholas in Seoul on September 24, 1978 with a prayer reserved for deaconesses and was appointed to fulfill the duties of a deaconess. Shortly thereafter, her name and title "deaconess-teacher" appeared in the official "Ecclesial Register" of the Church of Greece. Athanasios N. Papathanasiou, "Maria Spyropoulou, the Semi-Transparent Deaconess," https://publicorthodoxy.org/2022/06/24/maria-spyropoulou-the-semi-transparent-deaconess/#more-11419.

40. See above, where an Orthodox "blink of an eye" took six years.

41. Statement by Evangelos Theodorou, Alkiviadis Calivas, Paul Meyendorff, George Filias, Panagiotis Skaltsis, Stelyios Muksuris, Nicholas Denysenko, Phillip Zymaris, and John Klentos. https://pan orthodoxcemes.blogspot.com/.

42. In the same period Catholic population grew 708%, significantly outgrowing the general demographic and religious growth on the continent. Gaillardetz, *Ecclesiology Global Church*, 154.

a significant shortage of priests. This shortage, coupled with the insufficient means of transportation, results in a situation in which many parishes do not see a priest on a regular basis. A Kenyan Orthodox bishop shared with me his dream to provide each one of his priests with a motorcycle to be able to visit all the parishioners entrusted in his care. Similarly, one of my past doctoral students, an African priest, used to serve twenty-three parishes, which made it impossible to visit each of them more than twice a year. In the absence of the priest, the catechist is the de facto leader of the parish, being responsible not only with the teaching of the Church (as traditionally catechists would), but also with the sacramental needs of the parish, such as baptisms, funerals, and weddings. In the case of marriages, when the priest eventually comes into the parish, the wedding is blessed by the priest; but the couple already begins their married life with the blessing of the catechist. A catechist, however, cannot lead the Eucharistic service, resulting in what Elochukwu Uzukwu calls a "eucharistic famine" that Christians in Africa experience across denominations and which can only be averted by giving local ecclesial bodies the authority to re-imagine ministry.[43] Otherwise, how do we define the church eucharistically in the absence of the Eucharist for extended periods of time? Certainly, the Patriarchate of Alexandria's proposal to allow deaconesses to distribute pre-sanctified Communion is a step in the right direction and other churches should respect Alexandria's authority to decide in such matters within its jurisdiction. A "eucharistic famine" can only be averted by allowing local Church authorities to reimagine ministry according to their pastoral context.

Given the special role of catechists in Africa, the five women ordained in the Patriarchate of Alexandria have a ministry comparable to a deaconess, not to be situated into the ranks of the lower clergy (despite the Patriarchate's forced retraction), and possibly even exceeding traditional diaconal roles. Ideally, the African experience will grow and, seeing its fruits, other Orthodox churches will follow suit. A pan-Orthodox decision is not necessary in this regard; it is up to each individual bishop to assess the qualifications of the person he ordains. Hopefully, more and more bishops will stop considering femaleness as an impediment for ordination into the diaconate.

There is a great need for the female diaconate today and we have reasons to believe that this ministry will be fruitful. From the earliest times in Christian

---

43. Elochukwu E. Uzukwu, "Ministry with 'Large Ears'—Approaches to Dynamic African Patterns of Reform and Renewal in the Church Today, in *Ecclesia semper reformanda : Renewal and Reform beyond Polemics*, ed. Peter De Mey and Wim François, Bibliotheca Ephemeridum Theologicarum Lovaniensium (Leuven: Peeters, 2020), 347–48.

history until today, the female diaconate remained both a necessity and a ministry that bears fruit. This traditional approach is the main motivation for the
restoration of female diaconate, and not misplaced agendas.

The sad reality is that most *female monasteries* do not have a permanent
priest. Retired, traveling, or neighboring priests usually respond to the liturgical needs of the nuns, but most weekday services take place without a priest.
Services would be much more complete if a deaconess would read the Gospel,
cense fully (as opposed to the partial censing that nuns offer), and distribute
pre-sanctified Communion. That is not to say that no one receives Communion in the absence of a priest. In cases of necessity, the mother abbess com-
munes a sister in need with pre-sanctified Communion from the tabernacle
situated on the altar table. Such actions are not permissible to an Orthodox
person who is not ordained, not even in case of necessity. Monasticism is not
equivalent to ordination, so currently such actions are solely dictated by necessity. The Church has the opportunity to respond to these practical needs and
normalize these practices by ordaining deaconesses.

Likewise, other practices being performed by women, such as Confession,
could be sacramentalized through the restoration of the female diaconate.
The mother abbess listens to the Confessions of the nuns and, when a priest
is available, he gives them the absolution. Ordaining the abbess as deaconess
would bring this experience closer to its sacramental nature, with two qualifications: first, Confession does not fall into the attributes of the deacon but
of the priest or the bishop, and second, there is a longstanding Orthodox tradition that monks and nuns are allowed to listen to Confessions and give absolution. St. Symeon the New Theologian was asked whether it is proper to
confess one's sins to monks who are not ordained to the holy order, or whether
the power to bind and to loose was given only to priests. The saint answered
that Confession is primarily about the admission of our debts and the awareness of our failings, and all the baptized who keep the commandments and are
filled with the Holy Spirit possess the riches that enable them to forgive sins.
Moreover, since monks who were not ordained have listened to Confessions
since ancient times, what matters more is not the ordination itself, but the
gift of the Holy Spirit that abides in some who are not ordained, but who
can forgive sins.[44] Symeon's answer justifies the practice for abbesses to listen
to nuns' Confessions and to be spiritual mothers to other Christians. Moreover, one should also consider that Orthodoxy is not strictly technical in its

---

44. Symeon the New Theologian, "Letter 1: On Confession" 1–3, 10–16.

liturgical theology regarding the celebrant of sacraments or about the precise moment when forgiveness happens (these being typically scholastic questions), but rather sees the entire act of repentance as imparting forgiveness. Thus, the deaconess would respond properly to the need to listen to Confessions if (and only if) her special charism as a spiritual mother has been recognized by the Church. The ordination to the female diaconate is clearly a necessity first and foremost in nuns' monasteries. Perhaps that is why I have not yet encountered a nun who opposes the female diaconate in monasteries.

These considerations are also relevant to *parish life*. If women already have such ministries in Orthodox monasteries because the Church has discerned that some women (who happen to be nuns) have the special charism of spiritual motherhood, then the same should apply to married women in the parish whose charisms have been similarly discerned. Moreover, just as nuns in their monasteries lead a service without a priest and would benefit from receiving Communion, a similar need exists in the parish. In American Orthodoxy, occasionally parishes have readers' services that take place without priests who may be absent from the parish for blessed reasons. When a male deacon is present, he is permitted to read the Gospel, preach the sermon, and distribute the pre-sanctified Eucharist to the faithful. In communities that do not have a male deacon, these same roles could be fulfilled by a female deacon. Clearly, the need goes beyond the social aspects of the ministry of the deaconess, well into the liturgical realm.[45] Frederick Frost points to even more contemporary needs, in this case related to the experience of womanhood:

> There are so many challenging or important situations in which I believe most women need the ministrations of a woman rather than a man, such as: domestic violence, marital problems, miscarriage, sexual abuse, rape, menstruation, childbirth, lactation, care of the elderly, and gynecological illnesses. Every priest should be trained in, say, how to compassionately counsel a woman who has miscarried; I am not suggesting that all the male clergy step away from these matters (in fact, they would benefit from having female colleagues who have direct experience with these things). However,... does it not make sense, for example, to have a trained and vetted deaconess who is overseen by her bishop and called to this work to minister to a young woman who miscarries her first pregnancy at twenty weeks?[46]

45. Limiting the role of deaconesses to social-charitable functions and excluding them from the liturgical life of the Church would perpetuate the differentiation of ministries based on sex.

46. Carrie Frederick Frost, *Women Deacons in Africa, Not in America*. https://publicorthodoxy.org/2017/03/02/alexandria-deaconesses/.

The Church has the means of sanctifying and fulfilling the mutual support that women already give each other in such contexts through its sacraments. Emotional support, though valuable, does not represent the fullness of grace that the Church has to offer. That is why a priest does not simply offer comfort to a sick person in the hospital, but also prays for them, anoints with oil, receives their Confession, and distributes the Eucharist. If the ideal pastoral care involves both counseling and sacraments, in the cases that Frederick Frost mentions, either the priest cannot offer proper counseling, or women's visitation ministries cannot offer the sacraments. I asked the women who make up the visitation ministry of my parish: What would fulfill your ministry? They answered, the ability to offer the official prayers of the Church and the sacraments. A deaconess would be able to do just that.

It is worth pointing out that the Catholic Church is—practically speaking—a step ahead: they have numerous extraordinary eucharistic ministers, the majority of whom are lay women commissioned to assist with the distribution of the Eucharist. While theologically the Catholic Church remains behind the Orthodox Church regarding the theology of ordination of deaconesses, practically, extraordinary eucharistic ministers offer a generalized solution that calls into question the qualifier, "extraordinary."

Orthodox faithful from countries that do not practice frequent Communion might not see the merit of these adaptations. But for Orthodox Christians who receive Communion at least weekly, this is a question about the eucharistic nature of the Church. Changelessness does not mean paralysis. In order to stay the same, to remain a eucharistic community, the Church has to adapt. That full eucharistic measure will come when deaconesses become a more significant presence in Orthodoxy, as in earlier centuries. One can hope that bishops will rise up to their pastoral responsibility to maintain the eucharistic character of the Church. Synodally they can recognize the changes that have already taken place and come to a common determination to rejuvenate the order of deaconesses. Individually, they would be responsible to carry out this decision and ask parishes to delegate suitable candidates for ordination, educate them, and ultimately ordain them as deaconesses.

The Priest

Orthodox theology seems insufficiently prepared to speak theologically about the identity of the parish priest. In fact, theological treatises ascribe priesthood little or no content, distinct from other major orders. They regard priesthood primarily as a partial and delegated aspect of the ministry of the bishop; only the bishop has the fullness of ordination and is therefore considered the celebrant of the Eucharist and the father of the community. This line of thought seemingly goes back to the second century, when Ignatius of Antioch wrote that, "apart from the bishop, let no one perform any of the functions that pertain to the Church. Let that Eucharist be held valid which is offered by the bishop or by the one to whom the bishop has committed this charge."[47] the latter person entrusted (or delegated) being the presbyter or, in today's terminology, the priest. Ignatius's context, however, presupposed that the bishop regularly presides over the eucharistic assembly that unites the entire diocese. Zizioulas explains that shortly thereafter, communities multiplied and, as they attempted

> to keep the presbyterocentric Eucharist in a relationship of organic and essential dependence on the one episcopal throne, a solution was found to the problem: the parish did not form a self-sufficient and self-contained eucharistic unity, but an extension in space of the one self-same episcopocentric Eucharist. The Presbyter thus, celebrated the Eucharist in the name of the Bishop who remained the only true head of this mystical body of the Church of God. The thrones of the *synthronon* were dispersed, but they did not form discrete centers of eucharistic unity. They were simply *radii* of the same circle constantly dependent on the one center which was occupied by the Bishop.[48]

From an experiential perspective, and contrary to Zizioulas' attempt to read a historically-defunct situation into contemporary parish life, the priest is no longer merely the delegate of the bishop and an extension of the bishop's ministry. As Schmemann writes,

> To explain the change in the priest's status only in terms of "delegated power," as it is done by the supporters of "episcopalism" *à outrance*, to reduce, in other words, the priest to the position of a bishop's delegate, is simply impossible. The priest is ordained to the priesthood, and not to be a "delegate," and this means that he has the priesthood of the Church in his own right. One cannot be priest, teacher and pastor by "delegation" and there can be no "delegated charism." The very transformation of his status was possible because from the beginning the presbyter was a priest, shared in the priestly functions.[49]

---

47. Ignatius, "To the Smyrnaeans," #8, 121.
48. Zizioulas, *Eucharist, Bishop, Church*, 226–27.
49. Schmemann, "Theology of Councils," 179.

What are some of the priest's functions that make his ministry not merely an extension or delegation of the bishop's ministry, but also an ordained order in its own right? The priest is *the leader of the parish*—a role that stems from the various roles that presbyters (or elders) had in antiquity.

In the Greco-Roman world, elders were not so much associated with religious life, as with justice in society regarding leases of land, taxation, hearing appeals, and disciplinary measures. In Judaism, eldership originated when seventy elders assisted Moses with administrative issues (Nm 11:16–30). Subsequently, elders were responsible for the administration of the nation and, important for our topic, of the local synagogues. They neither led liturgical gatherings, nor preached—a model that the Church of the New Testament followed closely. For example, in anticipation of a famine, the elders in Judaea received financial support from other Christian communities (Acts 11:30). Presbyters also had a leading role in the Council of Jerusalem (Acts 15:2, 16:4) and advised Paul how to navigate sensitive pastoral situations regarding circumcision and other Jewish rituals (Acts 21:18–25). While ascribing primarily advising and administrative duties to presbyters, the New Testament also uses the term *presbyteros* interchangeably with ministries that will be associated with episcopacy later on; Paul leaves the elders of Ephesus as watchers over all the flock, over which the Holy Spirit has made them overseers (Acts 20:28–29). In these historical considerations, an extremely important aspect of the ministry of today's parish priest (the presbyter) is missing, namely presiding at the Liturgy—a function that at that time belonged to the bishop and was later transferred to the presbyter as the leader of the parish, and not simply as a delegate.[50] As Thomas Hopko remarks,

> The head of the parish in its total life must be the chief parish presbyter who is ordained and assigned by the diocesan bishop. This does not mean that the parish priest functions merely as the bishop's "representative" or "delegate." It means rather that he is appointed by the bishop and accepted by the parish as the community's spiritual and sacramental leader, father and pastor.... The parish priest, properly understood in Christian Orthodoxy, is neither a domineering despot nor a servile hireling. He is neither an authoritarian "stand-in" for an almost always absent hierarch, nor a lackey at the beck and call of a secularized "board of trustees." He is rather a called,

50. For an analysis of the development of the ministries of the presbyter, as well as the bishop and the deacon, including the transfer of functions between these clerical ranks, see Kenan B. Osborne, "Envisioning a Theology of Ordained and Lay Ministry: Lay/Ordained Ministry—Current Issues of Ambiguity," in *Ordering of the Baptismal Priesthood*, ed. Susan Wood (Collegeville, MN: Liturgical Press, 2003), 195–227.

trained, tested, and ordained teacher, pastor, and priest who guarantees the presence and action of Christ in the community.[51]

The leadership role of the priest thus differs from secular models of leadership and instead focuses on coordinating various aspects of parish life, some that the presbyter had in the beginning of Christian history such as charity, counseling, administration, and pastoral activities, as well as the later additions of teaching and presiding at the eucharistic assembly.[52] In other words, the priest's calling is that of *servant leadership*. He is neither the sacrificial lamb nor the savior of the community. The priest is not a person who needs to address each and every situation arising in the parish, to the detriment of his own health, that of his family, and ultimately that of the community. Such an attitude presupposes that the priest has all the gifts—those of teaching, those of administration, festival organization, janitorial abilities, and so forth. If the priest has to address and repair all aspects of parish life, they end up being postponed. This is the bottleneck model, where the needs are great and there is only one way out: through the priest. It is a model doomed to overflow.

Instead, the duty of the priest is to identify the charisms of each member of the community, strengthen them, and guide them for the building up of the Body of Christ. The priest has the task of administering these charisms. He cannot be excluded from any aspect of church life as if administration is a secular enterprise best left to a business-oriented board of directors. Instead, the priest oversees the manifestations of these charisms and is spiritually responsible for all that goes on in the parish. At his Ordination, the bishop entrusts the Body of Christ into the hands of the priest, symbolizing that the priest is responsible for both the sacrament and the community entrusted to his care. This is the monastic model, in which all that happens in the community has the blessing of the superior of the monastery and it fits into the parish, as well.

Having said this, the priest is not a monarch in the parish, or a first-class citizen who stands above the community. The servant leadership model takes precedence over what historians call a monarchical model. Schmemann points out that even though some speak of "monarchical" episcopate, that does not mean that the bishop was a monarch in today's understanding of the term, as if the priests were merely his subordinates:

51. Hopko, "Orthodox Parish," 9.
52. In antiquity the presbyterium was regarded as a college whose functions were counseling and governing. Zizioulas, *Being as Communion*, 196.

All available evidence points to the very real importance of the *presbyterium* in the local church, the college of presbyters or elders being precisely the *council* of the bishop and an essential organ of church government. Long before their transformation into heads of separate communities the members of the "second order" existed as a necessary collective complement of the bishop's power, and early rites of ordination point to the "gift of government" as the principal charism of the presbyters.[53]

Today it is rare to find bishops who gather their priests regularly for consultation and then involve them in governing. Instead, this structure has shifted down at parish level—at least in America—where the priest is the spiritual leader, but the staff and parish council are involved with counseling, governing, and ministries. As Schmemann points out, and his words deserve to be quoted at length,

> If indeed the "power of decision," the final responsibility, belongs to the priest, in the process of reaching that decision as truly ecclesial, he needs the help of all, for his power is to express the "mind of the Church." [... T]his means that the *parish council* properly understood is not a committee of practical and business-minded men elected to "manage" the "material interests" of the parish, but the *council* of the priest in all aspects of church life.... There exists the deeply un-Orthodox opposition of "spiritual" matters to "material" ones, an opposition which contradicts and destroys the sacramental nature of the Church, where all that is "material" is transformed and spiritualized, and all that is spiritual is a power of transformation. The conciliary principle which has been "forced" on the parish need not be either rejected or "limited" by reinforcement of "clericalism." It must be *churched*. This means, on the one hand, the acceptance by the clergy of the true hierarchical principle, which is not naked "power" but a deeply spiritual and pastoral concern for the Church as family, as oneness of life and manifestation of the spiritual gifts.... this will take place only when the laity understand that the priest really *needs* them, that he needs, not their "votes," but their talents, their advice, their real "council" or, in other terms, their real participation in the life of the Church.[54]

As the parish priest coordinates ministries and nurtures charisms, he is *the spiritual father of the parish*. A monk from Mt. Athos, who shall remain unnamed, told me that the parish needs a priest who will use his God-given intellectual abilities to respect the spirit of Orthodox canon law without following

53. Schmemann, "Theology of Councils," 176.
54. Schmemann, "Theology of Councils," 178, 80.

blindly its letter. In a monastery, the abbot or the abbess has a significant authority concerning the spiritual lives of the monastics entrusted to them. Given
this role of spiritual motherhood and fatherhood, the abbess or the abbot has
traditionally made significant decisions regarding the *typikon* and the Liturgy,[55]
pastoral considerations, and the teachings professed in their monasteries. The
same authority should translate into the parish, where the priest is the spiritual
father of his community, concluded the Athonite monk. Unfortunately, priests
sometimes regard themselves merely as an extension of the bishop and the
parish as an incomplete unit of the diocese, and thus hesitate to fully take on
their role as spiritual fathers, sometimes for serious reasons, as shown below.
As a corrective to this attitude of fear and in order to ascribe the parish priest
the same authority that abbots and abbesses have in their monasteries, we need
to emphasize priesthood as a ministry based on the traditional role of spiritual
fatherhood in which the priest takes personal responsibility for his parish, with
courage, boldness, and care for his flock.

The parish priest straddles the spiritual needs of his parish and the illusional "universal" norms of Orthodox liturgy, teaching, and discipline of the larger
Orthodox Church. In a universalist worldview, one would consider the role of
the parish priest as having to embody the common Orthodox life in the local
parish community. But this universalist view raises two questions: first, how
much unity in liturgy, teaching, and discipline is there in the Orthodox Church
worldwide and through the centuries? Any cursory reading of history shows a
significant degree of diversity, which raises the second question: which of the
multiple facets of Orthodoxy in space and time should be embodied in the
local parish? The spiritual father of the parish has a significant role in discern-
ing the answers to this question, which is particularly difficult due to several
factors.

First, there has been a rise in attitudes that reduce Orthodox diversity to its
strictest, least-loving stance. Those who espouse such attitudes take historical
moments out of context, regard them as normative, and claim a uniformity that
has never existed; just because a certain community produced a written document in a certain moment in time and space does not mean that it is representative of the entire Church in all times and in all spaces. It is very detrimental
when such isolated ecclesial instances are then imposed upon the rest of the
Church today, irrespective of context. In an era of unlimited communication, it

55. Robert F. Taft, "The Byzantine Office in the Prayerbook of New Skete: A Critique," *Orientalia Christiana Periodica* 48 (1982): 338.

is not an exaggeration to speak about imposing this illusional uniformity upon the rest of the Church. These self-proclaimed "judges of Orthodoxy" regard the entire Church as their jurisdiction, even though duly appointed Church leaders have limited jurisdictions. Internet trolls misrepresent any creative exercise of pastoral ministry in a scandalous and divisive way, creating real obstacles for priests who are responsible for the spiritual growth of their communities but are afraid of being criticized online.

The second difficulty standing in the way of the parish priest is a lack of episcopal guidance at synodal level, which should provide truly pastoral guidelines, ones that would be rooted in love and a realistic understanding of parish life. Often, however, there are local bishops who exercise their prophetic charism in a bold and constructive way, even without synodal support. Episcopal pastoral guidance is necessary since Orthodoxy does not have a uniform and consistent canon law. This lack of uniformity is expressed in the canons themselves, when a certain saint prescribes a number of years of repentance for a certain sin, while another saint prescribes a different number of years of repentance for the same sin. This type of canonical tradition based on precedent and lived experience (as opposed to a codified system) allows for a responsible, bold, and compassionate spiritual fatherhood, unmitigated by fear of gratuitous criticisms.

And third, while the parish priest is entrusted with local pastoral responsibilities, the exercise of his spiritual fatherhood is limited by the ability of the local bishop to transfer priests as a measure of discipline. Excluding the cases when such ultimate measures are unavoidable (and unfortunately, they are sometimes needed), the indiscriminate practice of transferring priests can be devastating. If the priest is the spiritual father, then he cannot be uprooted from among his children at a moment's notice. A spiritual bond is formed with priests who have been in the same parish for long periods of time, where they have the opportunity to truly become spiritual fathers and build long-lasting relationships. Furthermore, since most Orthodox parish priests are married, they also have to be responsible to their own families and provide stability in their household, which sometimes undercuts their ability to confidently be the spiritual fathers of their parishes for fear of being transferred.

In light of these considerations, there should be more consultation among priests. Once aware of the diversity of practices in various parishes, the spiritual father can then have the boldness to choose the most loving and beneficial course of action for his spiritual children in his parish. Parish priests also need each other's support in this great responsibility that they bear, to be spiritual fathers.

The priest's ministry as the spiritual father of the parish is greatly enhanced by the spiritual mother of the parish, namely *the priest's wife*.[56] The priest's wife participates in the pastoral life of the parish, so it is not surprising that her title is *presbytera* (Greek), or *pani matka* (Ukrainian), or *matushka* (Russian). She is a mother-figure in the community. The spiritual leadership of the parish is not entrusted to the priest alone, but to his wife, as well. The married priest is called to be a model of Christian family life, together with his entire family, which could lead to unfair scrutiny of the priest's children, but ideally this is not the case, and the entire priestly family embraces their ministerial calling together, of one accord.[57]

In conclusion to this section, even though experientially the priest is the normative leader of the Orthodox community, the theology of priesthood is insufficient for a proper description of this important ministry. The exact opposite is true of the ministry of the bishop: his role is more clearly articulated from a theological perspective than from an experiential viewpoint. The next section attempts to present the experiential relevance of some of the theological perspectives on the role of the bishop in the Church.

The Bishop

Florovsky affirms that both individually and collectively, bishops have the duty "to secure the universal and catholic unity of the whole Church in space and time"[58] in the sense of ensuring that their diocese is in dogmatic, liturgical, and canonical unity with all Orthodox churches in the world and throughout the centuries. As such, each bishop acts as "the mouthpiece of the Church," giving voice to the authority of Christ.[59] That is not to say that ordination into the episcopacy automatically transforms a person into the authoritative voice of Christ. That is the case only when the bishop remains in communion with

---

56. Neither Catholic nor Orthodox churches allow their priests to marry. The Orthodox Church, however, predominantly chooses married candidates to priestly Ordination, while the Catholic Church—with the exception of Eastern Catholic Churches—predominantly chooses celibate candidates. When a celibate Orthodox priest is assigned to a parish, obviously, the remarks about the priest's wife do not apply.

57. DeVille observes that the *presbytera* also represents a safeguard against clerical sexual abuse in a way that a bishop who often lives far away is unable. The *presbytera* would not tolerate transferring abusers between various parishes. Adam A.J. DeVille, *Everything Hidden Shall Be Revealed: Ridding the Church of Abuses of Sex and Power* (Brooklyn, NY: Angelico Press, 2019), 109–10.

58. Florovsky, "The Church: Her Nature and Task," 66.

59. Florovsky, "The Catholicity of the Church," 53.

the entire Church in space and time, particularly his own flock. The entire ministry of the bishop can only be exercised together with those who are being ministered. Augustine expressed this reciprocal relationship between the clergy and the people with the memorable words: "Where I'm terrified by what I am for you, I am given comfort by what I am with you. For you I am a bishop, with you, after all, I am a Christian. The first is the name of an office undertaken, the second a name of grace; that one means danger, this one salvation."[60]

One way to clarify the meaning of episcopal authority in the communion of the Church is to analyze the term, *hierarchy*. Such a proposal could be surprising given that society is deeply suspicious of hierarchy, preferring instead individual charisms that are seen in opposition to hierarchy.

In a worldly sense, "hierarchy" is the opposite of "democracy" and oftentimes theologians fall into the trap of regarding the Church as either a hierarchy (understood as a monarchy) or a democracy. One of the problems with this approach is that it construes "hierarchy" as a form of organization based on rank and power, with the connotation of inequality and dominance of the superiors over the subordinated. This form of organization becomes what sociologists call "dominance hierarchy" and a hierarchical Church becomes a society of un-equals, in contrast with a democracy in which equals have coequal voices in governance.[61] The Eastern tradition proposes a different model of leadership.

Pseudo-Dionysius the Areopagite was the first to have coined the term, "hierarchy," but he meant it in a very different sense compared to our contemporary understanding of hierarchy as inequality and dominance of the superiors over the subordinated. For him, the Church is a hierarchy of sanctification mirroring celestial hierarchy in which the firsts sanctify the orders below them. Dionysius identifies in the Bible three triads of angels, for a total of nine categories of heavenly beings. The angels that are closest to God illumine those who are underneath: "Hierarchy causes its members to be images of God in all respects, to be clear and spotless mirrors reflecting the glow of primordial light and indeed of God himself. It ensures that when its members have received this full and divine splendor, they can then pass on this light generously and in accordance to God's will to beings further down the scale."[62] The same process

60. Augustine, "Sermon 340 on the Anniversary of His Ordination," in Augustine, *Sermons*, trans. Edmund Hill (Hyde Park, NY: New City Press, 1992–1994), vol. III/9 – 340:1, 292.

61. Elizabeth T. Groppe, "The Contribution of Yves Congar's Theology of the Holy Spirit," *Theological Studies* 62, no. 3 (2001): 473–76.

62. "Celestial Hierarchy" 3.2 in Pseudo Dionysius the Areopagite, *Pseudo-Dionysius: The Complete*

of sanctification from those above to those below continues into the hierarchy of the Church in which the bishops, presbyters, deacons, and laity, form a community of divine sanctification.[63]

The three ranks of the ministers first purify the uninitiated by way of the sacraments; second, they bring illumination to those whom they have purified; and third, they perfect those who have been illumined, these stages corresponding to the rites of making the catechumen, baptism, and the Eucharist.[64] Far from introducing separation, the purpose of having a hierarchy is that those below come closer to those above them. The hierarch (that is, the bishop) symbolizes this gathering of all the faithful into a divinized unity when he comes out of the altar to cense the people, and then returns into the altar.[65] All these aspects of divine, angelic, and Church life are embodied in the hierarch— "a holy and inspired man, someone who understands all sacred knowledge, someone in whom an entire hierarchy is completely perfected and known."[66] This understanding of hierarchy will dominate the Eastern theological tradition.

As Ashley Purpura has recently shown in her study of Pseudo-Dionysius, Maximus the Confessor, Niketas Stethanos, and Nicholas Cabasilas—whom she puts in conversation with modern power theorists—"Orthodox ecclesiastical hierarchy as developed and reflected by Byzantine theologians is most fundamentally and consistently rendered as the communication of divinity."[67] This understanding of hierarchy permeates significant aspects of Orthodox life, such as church leadership, liturgical rituals, and the relationship between spiritual children and their spiritual father or mother.

Authority does not reside in a certain individual in isolation. Rather, it is dependent on that person's relationality with other members of the Body of Christ to whom he communicates divinity. In light of this view of hierarchical authority, a bishop's authority is limited when the other members of the

Works, trans. Colm Luibheid and Paul Rorem, The Classics of Western Spirituality, (New York: Paulist Press, 1987), 154.

63. Alexander Golitzin affirms that "a hierarchy is … a community, a single corporate organism bound together by the exercise of a loving and mutual providence whose origins and enabling power come directly from God." Alexander Golitzin and Bogdan G. Bucur (ed.), *Mystagogy: A Monastic Reading of Dionysius the Areopagita*, ed. Bogdan G. Bucur (Collegeville, MN: Cistecian Publications, 2013), 221. Purpura defines hierarchy from a Dionysian perspective as "that which communicates divinity and brings about divinization." Ashley M. Purpura, *God, Hierarchy, and Power: Orthodox Theologies of Authority from Byzantium* (New York: Fordham University Press, 2018), 45.

64. "Ecclesial Hierarchy" 5.3 in Dionysius the Areopagite, *Complete Works*, 235.

65. "Ecclesial Hierarchy" 1.1, 3.3 in Dionysius the Areopagite, *Complete Works*, 196, 212.

66. "Ecclesial Hierarchy" 1.3 in Dionysius the Areopagite, *Complete Works*, 197.

67. Purpura, *God, Hierarchy, Power*, 17.

Church believe that he no longer communicates divinity.[68] The same applies to the authority of the spiritual father, who has to be obeyed in all things and, in the case of monastic living, even in the most minute aspects of one's life. And yet, when the spiritual father's counsel contradicts the gospel, St. Symeon the New Theologian states that the spiritual child no longer needs to obey.[69] Thus, authority and sanctification do not come only from those above to those below, but are also bestowed by those below upon those above. Recognizing a hierarchical relationship lived in this vein, men and women choose to live in monasteries, where the abbess or the abbot is not a subjugating figure, but a loving spiritual mother or father who ensures the salvation of the monastics entrusted in their care. Similarly, parishioners choose to be members of a parish led by a priest who is a servant and spiritual father, not a despot. Moreover, the principle of hierarchy determines who presides at the Liturgy, gives the blessing, and lifts up the gifts that are offered on behalf of all, and, at the same time, who gives the "Amen" that seals the prayer of the celebrant and blesses the presider by responding "and with your spirit." This is the proper sense of a hierarchical Church—a communion of sanctification in which grace circulates both downward and upward.

The two-way communication of grace that takes visible form in the liturgy could be strengthened by revisiting the *manner of deciding who can be ordained as a bishop*—a practice that has undergone significant changes throughout history and differs greatly among Orthodox jurisdictions today.[70] The later

---

68. Purpura, *God, Hierarchy, Power*, 132. Purpura's understanding of the role of the Church community in limiting the role of the bishop who no longer communicates the grace of sanctification, the essential truths of the Christian faith, and its norms of fundamental decency are not intended in the sense that the majority of the community is always right. As I show later in the book, even consensus does not guarantee orthodox doctrine and life, which are not proclaimed through plebiscites. At times, the dissenting minority was the one that remained orthodox, as was the case in the fourth century, when the majority of the East was Arian or Semi-Arian, and a small dissenting minority retreated in the desert where it kept the true faith. That small minority could also be a bishop whose authority is wrongly limited by the local community.

69. In Purpura, *God, Hierarchy, Power*, 146–47.

70. Bishops in New Testament times were married, hence the requirement that "a bishop must be above reproach, married only once" (1 Tm 3:2). Prominent bishops such as St. Gregory the Elder (the father of Sts. Basil and Gregory of Nyssa) and St. Gregory of Nyssa, were married as well. After the fourth century, however, the wealth of the bishoprics grew exponentially and episcopacy became a rather desirable career path, making it difficult to separate the personal property of the bishop and that of the Church. Hence, sixth-century Justinian legislation decreed that married persons are not eligible for the office of bishop and the Quinisext Council (692) addressed the nepotism and the inheritance of Church property by bishops' children that plagued the Church. Candidates for episcopal ordination should have been monks, but in practice they were mostly celibates who did not live in monasteries for extended periods of time. For example, out of the twenty patriarchs of Constantinople from the seventh to eighth centuries, only four were selected from among monks, the rest being dignitaries. (Peter L'Huillier, "Episcopal Celibacy in the

first-century letter, *1 Clement*, states that initially bishops were appointed by apostles who also "gave them [i.e., their offices] a permanent character" in the sense that bishops should be replaced by successors to their ministry, as opposed to the ministry of the apostles that was not replaced. Later on, bishops were appointed "by other eminent men, with the consent of the whole Church,"[71] namely by a council of elders with the approval of the entire community. Soon it became normative to elect bishops, with the input of the rest of the community. In the fifth century, Pope Celestine I (422–432) enounced the principle that "the one who is to be head over all should be elected by all. No one should be made a bishop over the unwilling; the consent and desire of the clergy, the people and the order is required."[72] That is not to say that election always followed a set procedure and it involved careful consideration of arguments. Vasile Mihai points out several notable exceptions:

> St. Ambrose, who with the help of the emperor Valentinian was elected bishop of Mediolanum (Milan) on December 7, 374, at the age of thirty, directly from lay status (remarkably, he was a catechumen, not even baptized). Another famous case is that of Nectarios, Patriarch of Constantinople; Nectarios was a lawyer in the legal department of the emperor Theodosius, who imposed his ordination when Gregory of Nazianzus resigned his position. In a matter of days Nectarios was elevated from catechumen to bishop and Patriarch of Constantinople and president of the Second Ecumenical Council. If that is not outrageous enough, the case of Flavian is most revealing of people's attachment to signs and abandonment of reason and canonical prescriptions. Flavian, a monk who happened to walk in front of St. Peter's Basilica and on whom a white dove landed, was made pope within several days, as the Holy Spirit was thought to have revealed himself through the white dove.[73]

Gradually, another change happened regarding the election of bishops, namely a reduced (or complete absence) of the role of the laity and other members of the clergy in the election of bishops, a task that was gradually relegated

Orthodox Tradition," St. *Vladimir's Theological Quarterly* 35, no. 2–3 (1991): 271–88.) Today is no different. Often celibate administrators are nominally tonsured into monasticism but do not spend a meaningful amount of time in a monastery. There are also cases where priests have been married and then became widowed. While tragic from a family perspective, such cases usually offer the opportunity for pastors with a solid understanding of family and parish life to become bishops.

71. Saint Clement of Rome, "The Letter of St. Clement of Rome to the Corinthians," in *The Apostolic Fathers*, Fathers of the Church (Washington, DC: The Catholic University of America Press, 1947), #44, 43.

72. Celestine I, *Epistolae* 4.5, PL 50:434–35.

73. Vasile Mihai, *Orthodox Canon Law: Reference Book* (Brookline, MA: Holy Cross Orthodox Press, 2014), 12.

to the episcopacy alone. But recently some jurisdictions returned in one form or another to the earlier practice to involve the laity in the election of bishops. Mihai writes that Orthodox churches in the so-called diaspora

> had to adjust the manner of electing bishops by submitting the names of a few candidates (usually three) to mother churches or to the Patriarchate of Constantinople. In some of these local churches the input of laity is mostly of an advisory nature, while in others both the laypeople and the clergymen vote in the election of their bishops.... Lay and clergy delegates to the All-American Councils of the Orthodox Church in America vote in the election of their bishops; in the American Carpatho-Russian Orthodox Diocese (where there is no synod), the priests and the laypeople elect their bishop.[74]

In an attempt to harmonize the earlier practice of lay involvement in episcopal elections and today's practice of bishops electing bishops, Zizioulas affirms that election by the people is not essential, since ordination takes place within the Eucharistic community where the laity express their consent by the acclamation, "axios," that is, "he is worthy."[75] Zizioulas refers here to the rite of Ordination when the ordaining bishop asks whether that candidate is worthy and the community responds "axios." In practice, the laity do not always know well the person being ordained and they do not have an alternative but to respond positively to the ordaining bishop's exclamation, which is no longer a question since the candidate has already been elected and consecrated. And yet, there is a parallel between the eucharistic consecration and Ordination in the sense that the laity's "axios" response is similar to their "Amen" at the eucharistic consecration; in both cases, the response of the people fulfills the consecration.

Another way in which the hierarchical relationship (in the sense of downward and upward flow of grace) manifests itself is in the process through which a bishop *appoints priests for the parishes under his jurisdiction*. A parish can neither function, nor have a priest without the approval of the bishop. The bishop ordains priests but, more importantly, he gives them the blessing to celebrate the Liturgy in his diocese. In this sense, it is highly significant that, during the Liturgy, the priest does not commemorate the bishop who ordained him, but the bishop of the local diocese.[76] The order of divine services thus indicates that the priest's ordination is not sufficient for an authentic parish life, but the commissioning of the local bishop is also necessary. Thus, the bishop is the

---

74. Mihai, *Orthodox Canon Law*, 13.
75. Zizioulas, *Being as Communion*, 218.
76. Zizioulas, *Eucharist, Bishop, Church*, 216–17.

leader of a diocese by being responsible for appointing priests and legitimizing the lives of the parishes under his jurisdiction.

Moreover, the bishop coordinates those activities that bring many parishes together. For example, the bishop appoints a youth director who organizes summer camps for the youth in the entire diocese. In this sense, the bishop is *the link between parishes* within a diocese. Furthermore, the bishop represents the diocese's *connection with other dioceses* within each autocephalous church and around the world, to ensure unity of teaching, Liturgy, and practice within Orthodoxy. Unity should not be confused with uniformity. The relationship with other dioceses cannot become a crippling limitation to the bishop's pastoral duties in his own diocese. As he acts locally, a bishop cannot stifle local charisms for fear that the other bishops in his synod—who do not know first-hand the pastoral reality of his community—will question him. This difficult reality applies particularly to bishops in the so-called diaspora, who are members of the synods of their "mother churches" and thus responsible towards the other bishops who live far away. Instead, a bishop needs the space to exercise his ministry within the diocese, while also allowing for the possibility of mutual correction within a synod. Such an approach presents the episcopacy not as a rigid institution, but as a charismatic ministry that nourishes unity and diversity.

Thus, the bishop cannot be a distant figure that demands deference, large financial contributions, and stands above his priests and laity while having limited contact with them. Rather, the faithful need to experience the ministry of the bishop as it relates directly to their spiritual lives in the parish. A good bishop understands his role as one of unity in the diocese and between the diocese and the rest of the Church, as representation of the diocese in external relations, as the one who is responsible to ordain and appoint worthy pastors in his parishes, as a defender of the truth, administrator of ministries that transcend the parish, and as a hierarch in the sense outlined above.

COMMUNION BETWEEN CLERGY AND LAITY

Recent Orthodox theology has approached the subject of the communion between the clergy and the laity from different angles, all of which try to express how the clergy and the laity are distinct yet in union as they participate together in the priesthood of Christ.[77] There is no need to address them here, except when they resonate with a Kingdom-centered, experiential ecclesiology.

77. Bordeianu, *Dumitru Staniloae*, 161–88.

A first challenge as we express the communion between clergy and laity is to state that their distinction involves a relationship of *authority, not to be confused with power*. Perhaps the churches gathered in the WCC (including Orthodox) have best articulated the nature of authority in the convergence document entitled, *The Church: Towards a Common Vision*:

> The distinctive nature of authority in the Church can be understood and exercised correctly only in the light of the authority of its head, the one who was crucified, who "emptied himself" and "obediently accepted even death, death on the cross" (Phil. 2:7–8).... Authority within the Church must be understood as humble service, nourishing and building up the *koinonia* of the Church in faith, life and witness; it is exemplified in Jesus' action of washing the feet of the disciples (cf. John 13:1–17). It is a service (*diakonia*) of love, without any domination or coercion.[78]

Authority is thus different from power, since power can be imposed unwillingly upon one's subordinates, while authority is freely accepted by those who follow their leaders. A bishop or a priest would have no authority in their relationship with the faithful if the latter did not accept their authority, which also explains why leaders of other religions have no authority among Christians.

Given this distinction between power and authority, a Christian leader cannot aspire to such a position out of a desire to dominate others. In the earlier Christian centuries, a person would not ascend to a leadership position due to thirst for power, financial gain, or sociological advantages. On the contrary, that person was most likely to be martyred due to their position of leadership, and so it was natural that Christianity emphasized servant leadership, emulating Christ's own self-emptying in order to serve. History proves abundantly that authority does not necessarily devolve into power. Such an understanding of authority, especially in its liturgical manifestation as the inspiration for all other aspects of ecclesial life, fits well with Zizioulas's affirmation that the Church finds the structure of the Kingdom in the Eucharistic celebration and then molds itself according to that structure of the Kingdom that unites all its members.[79]

Without denying that the heavenly Kingdom represents the model of the Church's structure and that it is realized as such throughout history, it is important to acknowledge that Christianity had also borrowed from the structures and terminology of the earthly kingdoms, especially the Roman empire.

---

78. WCC, *The Church: Towards a Common Vision* (Geneva: WCC Publications, 2013), par. 49.
79. Zizioulas, *Being as Communion*, 206.

Emperor Diocletian (284–305) reorganized the empire into twelve dioceses and then placed the dioceses into larger units, which would later be called by the Church, metropolises, as the Church identified its canonical territories with imperial regions and aligned the responsibilities of bishops with those of secular rulers.[80] DeVille cautions that when Church-structures mimic the power-structures of the empire and the army, they create the soil in which the sin of power may germinate in the Church. He warns particularly of the resemblance between holy orders and "the sequential advancement of office holders in the Roman army,"[81] which places ambition and power within the orders of the Church.[82]

The alignment between secular and religious structures does not automatically lead to the transformation of authority into power. As Cohen shows, regional ecclesial structures are essential to the Church's mission in each local context. Such structures enable the local bishops to respond communally to their immediate context, to address local governmental structures together, and to manifest historically and contextually the universal mission of the Church.[83] Having said this, however, there were historical instances where both East and West took this alignment of secular and religious structures to an extreme. After the fall of the Western Roman Empire, when most of the political power was concentrated in Constantinople, the only political authority that remained in the West was the Church. Bishops took on social responsibilities based on previous secular models provided in Roman law. That was particularly the case of the bishop of Rome, who held the only apostolic see in the West, with no equal among other Western bishops—a situation that contrasted with the Eastern Empire, where there was an abundance of apostolic sees. It is thus not surprising that the Pope gradually assumed political and military power.

In the East, the clearest similar development began after the fall of the Byzantine Empire under the Ottomans in 1453. The Golden Gate calculated that Byzantines would be less likely to revolt if they were administered by their own Patriarch, so the Patriarch of Constantinople became the administrator

---

80. Ecclesial and secular jurisdictions did not always coincide. For example, Alexandria belonged to the civil jurisdiction of Antioch, and yet ecclesiastically it remained independent, having several metropolitan provinces under its jurisdiction.

81. Adam A. J. DeVille, "The Sacrament of Orders Dogmatically Understood," in *The Oxford Handbook of Sacramental Theology*, ed. Hans Boersma and Matthew Levering (New York: Oxford University Press, 2015), 531–44.

82. DeVille, *Everything Hidden*, 43–44.

83. Will Cohen, "Why Ecclesial Structures at the Regional Level Matter: Communion as Mutual Inclusion," *Theological Studies* 75, no. 2 (2014): 315–17.

of the conquered territories on behalf of the Sultan, which, in fact, turned the religious authority of the Patriarch into a tool for the conquering power. This system known as *millet* entrusted the Patriarch with worldly tasks such as collecting the *jizya*—a tax imposed by Muslim conquerors upon their Jewish and Christian subjects. This situation is not without precedent in Eastern Christianity. Even before the Ottoman conquest, the Byzantine Empire used its political and military power to enforce the canons and definitions of the Church, including the decisions of the ecumenical councils that became imperial law. Worldly power thus supplanted heavenly authority because, somehow, the authority of a hierarchy that emulates the structures of the heavenly kingdom was insufficient without the power of the emperor over his earthly kingdom.

True authority never disappeared from the Church. Many hierarchs remained worthy bearers of their rank. Moreover, saints such as Francis of Assisi in the West or Seraphim of Sarov in the East were not in positions of power, and yet they had more authority than popes and patriarchs. Authority comes from the Holy Spirit, and enlivened by that same Spirit, the community discerns the authority that a Christian has within the community.

Another way to frame this opposition between power and authority is in Slavophile fashion, *opposing law and love*. One representative of the Slavophile tradition, Afanasiev, affirms that law becomes necessary only when love has been weakened. Unfortunately, he laments, our churches are too steeped into law, especially when they govern the relationship between the hierarchy and the rest of the Church.[84] Instead of this legalistic approach to Church life, Slavophiles propose that the Church lives in communion, manifesting the *sobornost* of the Russian village. In their idealized description of Russian rural life, love is at the foundation of human relationships, as opposed to law and external authorities. *Sobornost* is antithetical to relationships of power imposed through laws given by, and favoring those, in power.

These oppositions between authority and power and between love and law are not meant to suggest that clergy (especially bishops) have power and law, while charismatics have authority and love. Since all members of the Church are charismatics, *those in office have a charism* that the Church discerned and as a result placed them in an order, according to their charism. In this sense, Zizioulas laments that "one of the greatest and historically most inexplicable misfortunes for the Church came when, I do not know how, the most charismatic of all acts, namely ordination into the ministry, came to be regarded as a

---

84. Afanassieff, *The Church of the Holy Spirit*, 264–67.

non or even anti-charismatic notion."[85] Order devoid of charisms is detrimental, as are also charisms unchecked by order. History is replete with examples of charismatics that have undermined structures, caused disorder, and ultimately oppression in the Church. That was the case in Corinth, where those who spoke in tongues boasted that they were above the rest of the community whose other gifts they considered as less significant. In response, Paul argues that all charisms have a common source (the Holy Spirit), a common purpose (the building up of the Body of Christ), and that all Christians are charismatic members of the Body of Christ, which remains an ordered, hierarchical community:

> God has so arranged the body, giving the greater honor to the inferior member, that there may be no dissension within the body, but the members may have the same care for one another. If one member suffers, all suffer together with it; if one member is honored, all rejoice together with it. Now you are the body of Christ and individually members of it. And God has appointed in the church first apostles, second prophets, third teachers ... (1 Cor 12:24–28).

Charismatic groups tend to start out as highly democratic, with no visible structure. However, they eventually become extremely hierarchical (in a worldly-power sense), where the leader of the group has a special status. The history of Montanism is but one example in which the leader, Montanus, became regarded as being in hypostatic union with the Holy Spirit. Often in today's charismatic, congregational, and non-denominational mega-churches, the founding pastor similarly holds a position of unchecked authority, while some charismatic communities within mainline churches have sectarian tendencies representing a sort of *ecclesiola in ecclesia*.[86] Such models of Church leadership are too worldly, oscillating between lack of formal leadership and the unchecked leadership of one. This is why it was so important to explore in this chapter an understanding of ordination that has meaning and bears weight in the Church, while always remaining within the priesthood of the totality of the Church that shares in the priesthood of Christ. Baptismal consecration without the balance of a communitarian understanding of Ordination tends to result in relationships of dominance, as also does Ordination without baptismal consecration. Only by ascribing a proper theological meaning to both, can one experience communion in the Church.

85. Zizioulas, *Being as Communion*, 192.

86. Sarah Coakley, *God, Sexuality, and the Self: An Essay 'On the Trinity'* (Cambridge: Cambridge University Press, 2013), 161–86.

As the next chapter will reveal, the Orthodox Church provides a model of communion between the clergy and the people in Church governance (such as when the Parish Council and the General Assembly, together with the parish priest, discern the pastoral, financial, and missionary needs of the parish) and in the proclamation of Church teaching, as for example in the processes of consultation and reception.

SEVEN

Synodality

—

The apostles and the elders with the consent of the
whole church ... decided unanimously

ACTS 15:22, 25

Having just resigned in the middle of the Second Ecumenical Council because
of the participants' refusal to affirm the Holy Spirit as *homoousion* with the Father and the Son, St. Gregory the Theologian said, "Synods and councils I salute
from a distance, for I know how troublesome they are. Never again will I sit in
those gatherings of cranes and geese."[1] But Orthodox theology and Orthodox
experience looks at councils kindlier, considering synodality an essential characteristic of the Church. Our dear saint was clearly in a moment of frustration.

In the first millennium, the Orthodox Church has been synodal at all levels: parish, diocese, regional, and universal. Since then, Orthodoxy has become
less synodal at the universal level, but, in varying degrees, increasingly conciliar
at the other levels, with different levels of lay involvement. Orthodox theology
tends to associate synodality with its universal manifestations in ecumenical
and pan-Orthodox councils, often based on the pattern of the Apostolic Council in Jerusalem. The focus in these cases is on the relationships among bishops.
From an experiential perspective, however, synodality is also (or perhaps even
more) a reality in the parish, diocese, and autocephalous Orthodox Church,
with the involvement of bishops, priests, and the laity. We shall approach these
topics here after some brief terminological and historical considerations.

1. Gregory of Nazianzus, *Letter* 124, *Poems about Himself*, xvii, 91, quoted in Ware, *The Orthodox
Church*, 35–36.

The term "synod" refers primarily to a gathering of bishops who exercise their ministry together. It comes from the Greek words *syn* (with) and *odos* (way), and so suggests "walking together along the same path." Its etymology implies both that the Church remains pilgrim as it advances towards the Kingdom of God and that one cannot travel along this path in isolation. In a larger sense, "synodality" and its synonym, "conciliarity" refers not only to the episcopate, but to all the baptized members of the Church, as they exercise their responsibilities together.[2]

HISTORICAL CONSIDERATIONS

Synodality originated in *the communal character of the earlier ministry of Jesus Christ*, who called the twelve to symbolize the entirety of Israel, and not just a group of twelve, then seventy (or seventy-two) disciples, to the exclusion of Jesus' other followers. Within the community of disciples, they were to consider each other friends, to be ready to lay down their lives for each other, and Peter was to strengthen his brethren. These early roots of synodality developed and bore fruit soon after the emergence of the Church, most notably at the *Apostolic Council in Jerusalem* described in Acts 15. "Paul and Barnabas and some of the others were appointed [by the community in Antioch] to go up to Jerusalem to the apostles and the elders." These delegates consulted along the way with other communities, and when they arrived in Jerusalem, "the apostles and the elders were gathered together to consider this matter." After Peter, Paul, and Barnabas spoke, James took the role of mouthpiece for the Council. Moreover, "the apostles and the elders, with the whole church" chose representatives *omothumadon*—"with one accord" (NKJV) or "unanimously" (NRSV)—in order to disseminate the decision of the Council, which was inspired by the Holy Spirit ("it has seemed good to the Holy Spirit and to us"[3]). This Apostolic Council became the (perhaps idealized) template for future councils, with emphasis on churches designating representatives, a process of consultation, plurality of voices represented at the council, inspiration by the Holy Spirit, unanimity (or maybe consensus), a mouthpiece for the council, a conciliar decision, and its dissemination. Clearly, the Apostolic Church was synodal—a

---

2. I have explored this subject in Radu Bordeianu, "Local Synodality: An Unnoticed Change," in *Changing the Church: Transformations of Christian Belief, Practice, and Life*, ed. Mark Chapman and Vladimir Latinovic (London: Palgrave Macmillan, 2021), 341–50.

3. Acts 15:2, 6, 22, 25, and 28 respectively.

shared responsibility that included the Apostles, the elders, and all the faithful.

By the second century *local churches* canonized synodality at the level of each community. As stated earlier, church structures included the one bishop, surrounded by a council of elders, whose role was consultation and adminis-tration, assisted by deacons entrusted with social-charitable responsibilities, and all the faithful with various charisms. The church remained synodal even in times of persecution. For example, when Cyprian of Carthage was unable to consult with his church because of the persecutions, he assured his faithful of the exceptional character of his actions: "from the beginning of my episcopate, I decided to do nothing of my own opinion privately without your [that is, presbyters'] advice and the consent of the people."[4] Thus synodality remained at the heart of the local church's life.

The same was true at a *regional level*. Local churches supported each other financially, exchanged letters, strengthened each other in times of martyrdom, prayed for one another, and appealed to one another regarding doctrinal and disciplinary issues. Regional synods gradually increased in number, gathering the bishops of a certain region together, thus showing that episcopacy is a min-istry that cannot be exercised in isolation. Bishops were held responsible to both their local communities and their brother bishops. Even as the monarchi-cal episcopate became the norm in the local community, the acts of the bishop were not those of an autocrat. Rather, they were actions in communion with the bishop's flock and with other bishops gathered in synods, which counter-balanced the bishop's ultimate authority that could degenerate into abuse of power.

As local churches from larger regions (such as around Alexandria, Rome, and Antioch), and then throughout the entire Christian world faced similar challenges, synods expanded to include representatives of more metropolitan areas. Orthodoxy recognizes *seven of these councils as ecumenical*. Based on the ideals of the Apostolic Council outlined above, the seven ecumenical councils have been received as authoritative instances of the Tradition due to the im-portance of their proclamations of faith, the consultation with the faithful and theologians, the large representation of various local churches, the consensus achieved during their works, and the reception of their decisions especially in liturgical life.

Having mentioned several *criteria for recognizing a council as ecumenical*, it is important to state that Orthodoxy in fact does not have a fool-proof system

---

4. "Letter 14 to the priests and the deacons, his brethren," in Cyprian of Carthage, *Letters*, #4, 43.

of recognizing the ecumenical status of a council. Significant exceptions to the above-listed rules prove this point. For example, the rule that a council needs to represent the entire Christian world to be ecumenical is challenged in two ways. First, a council could gather a large number of bishops without being ecumenical; the Council of Hiereia (754)—which condemned the veneration of icons—boasted the participation of over 400 bishops from various parts of the Empire and regarded itself as ecumenical, but it was received neither by the Pope, the Patriarchs of Alexandria, Antioch, and Constantinople, together with their clergy, nor by the Council of Nicaea II (787). Second, a council could be convened as a regional synod, but later be received as ecumenical; such was the case of Constantinople I (381), which only gathered around 150 bishops (without representatives from Rome), but whose Creed became the primary confession of faith for all Christians.[5] In both these examples, it transpires that a council's own claim of ecumenicity is not a sufficient criterion, since Hiereia considered itself ecumenical but it was not received as such, while Constantinople did not regard itself as ecumenical, and yet it was received in this way.[6] Moreover, participation from all geographical areas is not a condition of ecumenicity, either, since Hiereia fulfilled this condition, while Constantinople did not. Nor can it be said that a council is ecumenical only if it has been affirmed by a subsequent ecumenical council, since the last ecumenical council cannot be confirmed by a later ecumenical council. Last but not least, the reception by the people of God is extremely difficult to gauge, since reception can last for centuries, as I will show below in the discussion of the reception of the third through seventh ecumenical councils among Oriental Orthodox Churches.

Among these principles of synodality, the *distinction between unanimity and consensus* is quite relevant today. The distinction is significant since unanimity requires that all conciliar bishops agree, giving veto privileges to each bishop. In the case of consensus, the majority decision moves forward while acknowledging the reservations of the dissenting minority. The Apostolic Council's mode of deciding *omothumadon*—"with one accord" (NKJV) or "unanimously" (NRSV Acts 15:25)—became a model for future councils, many synods claiming unanimity. But unanimity seems to be more an ideal than a fact. The book of Acts refers to the public opposition by those who wanted to impose

---

5. Joint Orthodox-Catholic Working Group, "Serving Communion," par. 7.10.
6. The councils of Lyons II (1274) and Ferrara-Florence (1438–1445) also regarded themselves as ecumenical, but the East did not receive them as such. The West considered them ecumenical until mid-twentieth century, when they started being counted among the "general" councils of the Catholic Church, thus differentiating them from the seven ecumenical councils of the united Church – East and West.

circumcision upon Gentile Christians, an opposition that continued after the Council. Moreover, the Pauline letters often address this issue, as for example when some Christians of Jewish origin (including Peter) refused table fellowship with Gentiles (Gal 2:11–14) or when he redefined circumcision as being a matter of the heart (Rom 2:29). Thus, the Jerusalem Council decided by consensus rather than unanimity. Moreover, the ecumenical councils went down in history as having decided unanimously, which is more a figure of speech, suggesting their inspiration (similar to the Apostolic Council), rather than a historical fact. After all, the Arians present at the First Ecumenical Council did not embrace the orthodox doctrine immediately and the Third and Fourth Ecumenical Councils resulted in the painful schism with the Oriental Orthodox Churches, so unanimity was counted only after the dissenting minority left the Council. Thus, the ecumenical councils reveal the consensus method as the traditional one.

Later on, no autocephalous Orthodox church adopted the model of unanimity concerning its internal matters, including in its election the primate who represents externally the entire autocephalous church. It was only in Crete's pre-conciliar process that the principle of unanimity was imposed in Orthodoxy. From its beginnings, it was a means for the minority to paralyze the majority. I have argued elsewhere that this tactic has a precedent when the Catholic Church invited the Orthodox Church to send observers to the Second Vatican Council. When all Orthodox churches sent representatives at Rhodes I (1961) to discern their response to this invitation, the Russian Patriarchate insisted that all autocephalous Orthodox churches should act in unison in their interaction with the West. This system of unanimity under the guise of Orthodox unity was in fact the USSR's tactic to control the entire Orthodox world. As one of the Russian delegates, Vitaly Borovoi, explained in his report to the KGB, without the Russian delegation's intervention in Rhodes, Constantinople and the other Greek churches would have sent their observers to the Second Vatican Council and the Russian church would have remained isolated in its opposition. Instead, Constantinople and the other churches that shared its vision, became unable to act without Moscow's accord. Borovoi concluded in terms that clearly show that the principle of unanimity was simply a means to control other churches: "The key to solve the problem of Orthodox observers is now in Moscow, it is not in Constantinople."[7]

7. Quoted in Adriano Roccucci, "Russian Observers at Vatican II: The 'Council for Russian Orthodox Church Affairs' and the Moscow Patriarchate Between Anti-Religious Policy and International Strategies," in *Vatican II in Moscow (1959–1965): Acts of the Colloquium on the History of Vatican II. Moscow,*

In what might be nothing more than a historical coincidence, before the opening of the Council of Crete in 2016, this distinction between consensus and unanimity again came to the forefront. Attempting to ensure that no single bishop could hold the entire council captive, some Orthodox churches proposed the consensus method, while others insisted on unanimity. The latter group of churches ended up not participating at the council.

The same national churches that found the consensus method insufficient for Crete have previously embraced it not only in their internal matters, but also in the WCC. When Orthodox participation in the WCC was called into question because Orthodox churches were regularly outvoted, the WCC adopted the consensus method, which stipulates that the majority works with the minority until the minority either fully embraces their position, or can step aside in humility, ready to support the majority decision or at least not oppose it. The minority position is acknowledged in the final document.[8]

Having said that, consensus does not guarantee orthodox doctrine and life, which are not proclaimed through plebiscites. At times, the dissenting minority was the one that remained orthodox, as was the case in the fourth century, when the majority of the East was Arian or Semi-Arian, and a small dissenting minority retreated in the desert where it kept the true faith.[9]

The above considerations raise the important question of the participation of the entire Church—not only conciliar bishops—in the process of proclaiming the faith in synods. Councils included lay participation from the beginning. The Jerusalem Apostolic Council took place in the presence of an assembly (Acts 15:12). Similarly, local synods gathered during Cyprian's time in the Church of Carthage "with a multitude of faithful present" expressing their opinions,[10] and at the First Ecumenical Council, the laity eagerly defended the party of their choice.[11] Other similar instances abound throughout history and they all stem from the conviction that the revealed truth rests in the Church

---

March 30–April 2, 1995, ed. Alberto Melloni (Leuven: Library of the Faculty of Theology K.U. Leuven, 1997), 66–67. See Bordeianu, "Orthodox Observers," 86–106.

8. WCC's Eighth Assembly in Harare (1998) also ensured that the consensus method does not give the power of veto to every single delegate by allowing an 85% majority to still call for a formal vote as a last result after earnestly considering the minority position. Historically, when a small number of members, who are known to generally cause dissension, refuse to accept the majority position, the decision moves forward without mentioning the minority position.

9. Florovsky, "The Historical Problem of a Definition of the Church," 33.

10. Cyprian, *Epistle* 13, quoted in John N. Karmiris, *The Status and Ministry of the Laity in the Orthodox Church* (Brookline, MA: Holy Cross Seminary Press, 1994), 14.

11. Socrates, *Ecclesiastical History*, 1.8, quoted in Karmiris, *The Status and Ministry of the Laity in the Orthodox Church*, 14.

in its totality, clergy and laity alike, and not in the clergy alone. Rather, before taking a position at a council, the bishop is supposed to consult with his diocese and ensure that he expresses not simply his personal opinion, but the faith of his flock.

While these instances fall under the general category of *consultation*, another way in which the communion between the clergy and the people is manifested prophetically is through *the process of reception*, in which the teachings of a council must be recognized by the entire church, especially in its liturgy. Sometimes, the process of reception took very intense forms, exciting spirits. Compared to twenty-first-century complacency, it is rather humorous to read the complaint of some Fathers of the Church about the faithful's involvement in matters of faith. Gregory the Theologian and Gregory of Nyssa were quite vocal in their dissatisfaction with the theological arguments that existed everywhere in their cities. The latter saint writes:

> The whole city is full of [debates about incomprehensible matters], the squares, the market places, the cross-roads, the alleyways; old-clothes men, money changers, food sellers: they are all busy arguing. If you ask someone to give you change, he philosophizes about the Begotten and the Unbegotten; if you inquire about the price of a loaf, you are told by way of reply that the Father is greater and the Son inferior; if you ask "Is my bath ready?" the attendant answers that the Son was made out of nothing.[12]

Reception is a communal discernment process, it can be a combative one, and it can take a very long time—more than fifteen centuries in the case of Eastern-Oriental Orthodox discernment of the decisions of the third and fourth ecumenical councils in light of recent terminological and historical clarifications; to be precise, the re-reception of these councils refers not to the doctrinal truths that they have affirmed, but to their stance against those who opposed these councils. The teaching authority of the Church lies in the reception of the entire Church, and not in ecumenical synods alone, as Staniloae writes. The inner authority of the entire Church encompasses all its members, i.e., clergy and the people alike, its history, interior life, synods, and their reception.[13] This common responsibility for the faith does not nullify the differences between various ministries in the Church. The priests and the bishops educate the faithful and verify their faith before the distribution of the Eucharist. The

12. Gregory of Nyssa, *On the Deity of the Son*, PG xlvii 557B, quoted in Ware, *The Orthodox Church*, 35.
13. Dumitru Staniloae, "Autoritatea Bisericii [The Authority of the Church]," *Studii Teologice* 16, no. 3–4 (1964): 198.

faithful, on their part, discern the faith of the clergy when that faith is reflected in sermons. The faithful can either accept the content of the sermon as reflective of the faith of the Church or raise their voice to express their rejection. In this sense, the 1848 encyclical of the Eastern patriarchs who responded to Pope Pius IX's claim of papal infallibility states, on the one hand, that the entire Church (clergy and laity) is infallible, and neither one bishop alone, nor all the bishops collectively. On the other hand, it affirms the distinction that the faithful are the "shields" of the truth, while bishops are the "judges."[14]

All these criteria for recognizing a council's ecumenical character, with their accompanying exceptions, show that Orthodoxy does not know an undisputed rule to establish the status of a council, and that the East has experienced a variety of expressions of conciliarity. As Schmemann writes, "in her history the Orthodox Church has had not one, but several patterns of councils, which in many respects differed rather substantially one from another.... The 'conciliar principle' firmly proclaimed by our whole Tradition cannot be simply identified with any of its multiple historical and empirical expressions."[15] Despite this lack of theological precision, throughout history and in varying degrees, the Church remained synodal at local, regional, and universal levels.

SYNODALITY IN THE CONTEMPORARY PARISH AND THE DIOCESE

The above historical considerations present synodality as an Orthodox charism. Unfortunately, this venerable tradition sometimes sounds hollow in contemporary discussions of history, the role of bishops, and canon law, which tend to backslide into abstract considerations about structures of power, giving insufficient attention to the faithful and to parish clergy. Such theologies are triumphalist—exulting a historical synodal tradition that worldwide Orthodoxy seems unable to match today—and exceedingly theoretical, remote from the concrete experience of the Church. And yet, *synodality remains an Orthodox charism* when considering the parish (where lay involvement is at its strongest) and national churches as they attend to their own internal matters.

Today, the most common experience of the Church is the parish community *gathered around the Eucharist*, involving the active participation of all the

14. Clément, *You Are Peter*, 13.
15. Schmemann, "Theology of Councils," 171–72.

faithful together with the priest. This image is intrinsically synodal when considering the multitude of ministries involved, e.g., chanters, choir, parish council, or priesthood. Moreover, in the Orthodox tradition of "Liturgy after the Liturgy," this eucharistic gathering represents the basis for other charitable and missionary ministries. In parish life, all ministries act together, in coordination with one another, and this common exercise of their responsibilities lies at the heart of synodality.

Even more potent is the liturgical image of the bishop celebrating the Liturgy in a local parish. Although a rare occurrence, it is a powerful image of the church gathered around its bishop, surrounded by a council of presbyters, deacons, and all the faithful in the celebration of the Eucharist. The presence of the bishop in a parish reminds the community of its synodal character; the parish is not an independent unit. It commemorates the local bishop and cannot celebrate a Liturgy without the *antimension*, which bears the signature of the local bishop. In turn, the bishop's ministry puts the parish in communion with other aspects of the Church: the bishop creates synodality within his diocese, nurturing each parish's communion with other parishes in his diocese, as for example when the bishop organizes clergy-laity conferences, diocesan retreats, or youth camps. Moreover, a diocesan bishop belongs to a synod in which bishops act synodally, thus placing each community from his jurisdiction in communion with parishes from all other jurisdictions represented at the synod. Lastly, the ministry of the bishop manifests the synodality of the Church to a different degree when the bishop represents his diocese in encounters with other Orthodox synods or with other Christians, contributing to the synodality of the entire Church—*Una Sancta*.

Synodality is also at the heart of *common decision-making*. As stated in chapter four, the community elects the parish council to oversee its day-to-day activity in collaboration with the priest. Past tensions between the council and the priest notwithstanding, many parishes today have a healthy pastoral life that regards all matters pertaining to the parish as the common task of the entire community. Parishes also hold general assemblies, in which all members come together to deliberate on the major aspects of parish life, including the mission of the community, the well-being of its ministries, the approval of the yearly budget, etc. This is a synodal practice that Orthodox Christians in North America—more than in other parts of the Orthodox world—experience on a regular basis. Such level of synodality is surprising for both Orthodox faithful in majority Orthodox countries and for Catholic faithful in the U.S., where the parish community has fewer decision-making abilities.

The diocese, too, has a council constituted from among both lay and ordained. It organizes regular clergy-laity assemblies that coordinate the ministries of the diocese, especially youth ministries, charity, and education. While
diocesan councils and clergy-laity assemblies are less involved in ministries than
their corresponding parish structures, the organization of the local diocese re-
tains an unmistakably synodal character.[16]

REGIONAL SYNODALITY TODAY

As our discussion of synodality transitioned from the parish to the diocese, the
role of the laity gradually decreased. This same trend is exhibited at regional
level, where synodality is manifested primarily through the ministries of the
bishops. This transition is somewhat justified since the bishop is responsible
for the interaction with other local churches. And yet, *regional synodality in
North America involves the laity, deacons, and priests*, as for example in International Orthodox Christian Charities (IOCC), Orthodox Christian Missions
Center (OCMC), the student organization Orthodox Christian Fellowship
(OCF), or Orthodox Theological Society in America (OTSA), all of which
transcend ethnic jurisdictional boundaries.

The communion between the clergy and the laity is also manifested synodally in clergy-laity conferences (or sobors) that Orthodox churches of various ethnicities organize in North America. Their authorities vary significantly,
some of them entrusting the delegates—laity and parish clergy—with the *election of bishops*, even though the ultimate decision rests with the synod of bishops.[17] Moreover, in North America, Western Europe, and elsewhere outside
majority Orthodox countries, there are *Episcopal Assemblies* that gather the
bishops of different ethnic jurisdictions in any given region. Even though it is

---

16. Today's practices of financial reports and audits involving the laity go back to the Church of the
Ecumenical Councils: "out of concern for financial accountability, the fourth ecumenical council (Chalcedon in 451) required each diocese to have an *oikonomos* (canon 25), to 'administer the Church's goods with
the advice of his own bishop' so that 'the administration of the Church will not be without checks and bal-
ances, the goods of the Church will not be dissipated, and the priesthood will be free from all suspicion.'...
The seventh ecumenical council (II Nicaea in 787, canon 11) developed elaborate enforcement mechanisms:
If a bishop fails to appoint an *oikonomos* for his Church, the metropolitan of the province may intervene
directly. So also, if a metropolitan fails to appoint an *oikonomos* for his Church, the patriarch may do
so." North American Orthodox-Catholic Theological Consultation, "A Common Response to the Joint
International Commission for the Theological Dialogue Between the Roman Catholic Church and the
Orthodox Church Regarding the Ravenna Document: 'Ecclesiological and Canonical Consequences of
the Sacramental Nature of the Church: Ecclesial Communion, Conciliarity and Authority'" (2009).

17. 2015 Statute of the OCA V.6.

not a synod in a technical sense, the Episcopal Assembly is a partial (and new) manifestation of synodality, practically dictated by the existence of parallel jurisdictions. The Assembly's main role is to find a solution to the uncanonical situation of parallel jurisdictions—a task that presently seems insurmountable. But various Assemblies succeeded in other areas of pastoral concern, such as providing a common translation of liturgical texts, as in the case of the German translation of St. John Chrysostom's Divine Liturgy, approved by the Episcopal Assembly of Germany in March 2017. In North America, the Episcopal Assembly blesses significant pan-Orthodox instances, such as IOCC, OCF, OCMC, and OTSA. The Assembly also delegates the members of ecumenical dialogues, as for example the North-American Orthodox-Catholic Theological Consultation. While these pan-Orthodox instances are not manifestations of synodality in the classical sense of the word, from an experiential perspective, they represent major pan-Orthodox synodal accomplishments, with an impact whose magnitude often surpasses contemporary episcopal synodality.

Episcopal synodality is *most efficient at the level of autocephalous churches because it is sustained by primacy*. At ecumenical encounters, the Orthodox have insisted on primacy as *primus inter pares* (first among equals), emphasizing the equality of all bishops and being hesitant to recognize more than a primacy of honor that is rather devoid of authority. Internally, however, the Orthodox are not hesitant about primacy. Primates of national churches have a significant degree of authority, as we shall see momentarily.

Autocephalous churches have developed various *models of synodality*. For example, the Patriarchate of Constantinople gathers the *synodos endemousa* (the permanent or the standing synod), which was initially composed of bishops living closer to the imperial capital. Today, bishops from Constantinople's territories around the world, by rotation, participate at monthly meetings of the *synodos endemousa* to discuss regular issues and to respond in a timely fashion to emergencies. This structure, in various forms, has been in place at least from the fourth century.[18] Other Orthodox churches, such as the Moscow Patriarchate, follow similar models. On the one hand, this practice of permanent synods represents a major sign of Orthodoxy's commitment to synodality, communal decision-making, and avoiding authoritarian temptations in the Church. On the other hand, when a permanent synod decides in matters that apply to the entire autocephalous church, not all bishops from that territory have decided in matters that affects their dioceses. In other words, the *synodos*

18. DeVille, *Everything Hidden*, 79.

endemousa is a structure that stands above the local diocese and the diocesan bishop does not always participate in the decision-making process that affects his diocese.

Ideally, all bishops would be equal, able to decide in their own jurisdictions in all local matters; for example, a local bishop should not need the approval of the archbishop for ordaining priests within his diocese. Moreover, each bishop should have a clearly delineated territory. Instead, in Western Orthodoxy there are overlapping jurisdictions, this also being the case in some traditionally Orthodox countries, such as Ukraine. Another instance where jurisdictions are not clearly delineated is that of auxiliary bishops. Theoretically, an auxiliary bishop has a title different than that of the archbishop of that region, but in fact their territories coincide and the auxiliary bishop serves under the archbishop. Equally problematic is the custom to ordain bishops for defunct sees, since in practice they become titular bishops, without a flock. Auxiliary and titular bishops, however, are more the exception than the rule, and so synods are mostly composed of bishops with real jurisdictions and flocks.

This synodal structure is particularly evident when several bishops *concelebrate the Divine Liturgy* in the order of processions and commemorations, based on their canonical order.[19] When the primate visits another diocese, he is the leader of the eucharistic service, even when the local bishop—who is the head of that specific local church—is present. In other words, the synodal order takes precedence over the principles of eucharistic ecclesiology. And yet, visiting bishops—including the primate—can visit a diocese only at the invitation of the local bishop, and thus the local bishop remains responsible for all aspects of ecclesial life in his diocese, in accordance with eucharistic ecclesiology. Synodality is also manifested in exchange of letters, mutual material assistance, collaboration on pastoral issues, and in the ancient tradition that ordinations of bishops must involve three (or in special circumstances two) neighboring bishops.[20]

19. Bishops throughout the Orthodox world are commemorated in diptychs. Various churches recognize different bishops, and so the diptychs differ from jurisdiction to jurisdiction. When bishops with different diptychs concelebrate, they follow the diptych of the hierarch in whose jurisdiction the Liturgy takes place. When, however, Orthodox representatives meet on neutral grounds (such as the WCC), delegates sometimes celebrate separate Liturgies.

20. Nicaea I, Canon 4

UNIVERSAL SYNODALITY TODAY

From an experiential perspective, synodality is at its strongest at parish, diocese, and regional levels, but not at the level of the universal Church. In the past, ecumenical councils, or even councils with world-wide representation that were not accepted as ecumenical, were part and parcel of the experience of the Church. If the ecumenical council gathers representatives of all local churches (more or less) and if its decisions are to be accepted by the entire Church, in the present context of schism, *it is practically impossible to convene an ecumenical council.*[21] The World Council of Churches does not claim to be such a council, although its Assemblies come the closest to an ecumenical council in a disunited Church. Hence, denominations can experience universal synodality only internally, in separation from other denominations. For example, the Catholic Church regularly convenes Synods of Bishops with worldwide representation—a practice established by Pope Paul VI in 1965, subsequently observed consistently, although with various degrees of success. These synods recommend to the Pope their findings, which become authoritative teaching only if the Pope ratifies them by virtue of his universal jurisdiction within the Catholic Church, an authority that the Synod of Bishops does not have.[22] For example, after the 2014–2015 Synods, the theology of the family that emerged from these councils became the basis of Pope Francis' 2016 apostolic exhortation, *Amoris Laetitia,* or *The Joy of Love.*

In the case of today's Orthodox Church, *a pan-Orthodox council* comes closest to universal synodality, but it is merely a remote possibility. *The 2016 Great and Holy Council of Crete* should have been an impetus for universal synodality, but the opposite happened when four of the fourteen national churches withdrew shortly before the Council. The Orthodox Church needs guidance on pastoral issues such as living a richer ecumenical life at the local level, interfaith marriages, rules of fasting, etc. But it seems that pan-Orthodox synodality is paralyzed by internal political conflicts and by fear of the segment of Orthodoxy that opposes ecumenism, openness to society, and progress. Concerning the latter, perhaps now is the time to postpone the attempts to appease them

---

21. Ravenna par. 39 states: "the break between East and West ... rendered impossible the holding of Ecumenical Councils in the strict sense of the term."

22. LG 25 lists three ways in which the magisterium can teach infallibly: 1. Bishops across the world agree unanimously; 2. Bishops convened in an ecumenical council; and 3. The Pope teaching *ex cathedra* with the intention of proclaiming an infallible dogma regarding matters of faith and morals. One should clarify that the latter is the rarest occurrence of the three.

and focus instead on Orthodoxy's immediate needs that have for too long remained unfulfilled.

This inability to gather in a pan-Orthodox council despite almost a century of preparations (though in full force since 1961), moderated Orthodox claims that synodality is its ecumenical charism, or even that it exists at all at the universal level. Despite a longstanding Eastern tradition of synodality and the caricaturist accusations that Catholics are authoritarians led by an infallible Pope that renders conciliarity unnecessary, the Second Vatican Council remains the highest standard of synodality within any given denomination.

Crete also radically challenged the Orthodox vision of Christian unity. Orthodox representatives to ecumenical dialogues claim that the ideal model of unity requires that bishops gather in the same synod and receive Communion together. This ideal of unity is often imposed as a condition for Orthodox-Catholic unity, when in fact it cannot be put into practice in world-wide Orthodoxy. Throughout history, intra-Orthodox unity endured even when local churches refused to participate in the same synod, including Crete. Moreover, eucharistic communion with a particular bishop does not represent the criterion for belonging to the Orthodox family. Occasionally, hierarchs of differing churches interrupt eucharistic communion with each other. Sometimes this interruption of communion goes even further, to apply to the faithful as well, as has happened in 2018 between the Patriarchates of Moscow and Constantinople over Ukrainian autocephaly, when the former interrupted commemorations and eucharistic communion with the latter, although Constantinople did not reciprocate the gesture. Shortly thereafter, three other autocephalous churches recognized Ukrainian autocephaly, so the Moscow Patriarchate ceased eucharistic communion with the bishops and faithful of the Church of Greece (with the exception of seven bishops and the faithful in their dioceses), as well as the Patriarchate of Alexandria and All-Africa, while the eucharistic schism with Cyprus extends only to the level of primates. And yet, in a deep sense, Orthodoxy remains one. Could this development help the cause of Christian unity? Will Orthodoxy continue to require eucharistic and synodal communion as conditions for unity with the Catholic Church? Or will it consider the similarities between the two schisms (East—West and Moscow—Constantinople) and reassess both the gravity of the issues separating the two churches and the motives for continuing in schism?

UNIVERSAL SYNODALITY REIMAGINED

Orthodoxy's current inability to manifest synodality at the pan-Orthodox level does not mean that universal synodality will forever remain imprisoned in a distant historical past. On the contrary, pan-Orthodox efforts need to continue with special attention to the involvement of the laity throughout the synodal process and to a full representation of all members of the Church in the council. Moreover, today Orthodoxy needs to creatively appropriate the tradition of the ecumenical councils; fundamentalism represents the greatest danger facing the proper reception of the Eastern conciliar tradition, not relativism or secularism. Finally, in order to restore universal synodality, the East needs to create a workable view of universal primacy based on precedents in the East (that is, avoiding the mistakes of the past) and in dialogue with the West, which has long experienced Papal primacy and universal jurisdiction (and here again, avoiding the mistakes of the past). To these themes we turn for the remainder of this chapter on synodality.

A re-imagined universal synodality needs to ascribe a *significant role to the laity, parish priests, and theologians*.[23] God works through his entire people, hence, a synodal church is participative and co-responsible. The contribution of the faithful is crucial both in their consultation before the council and in the process of reception. The faithful can be consulted today on a scale that earlier in history was simply un-imaginable, but now made possible by technological advances. For example, before the above-mentioned 2014–2015 Synods of Bishops on the Family, Catholic faithful were asked to submit online their answers to questions regarding family life, revealing in the process how diverse the Catholic faithful are in their opinions on family issues. To a lesser scale and limited to theologians, before the 2016 Council of Crete, numerous conferences throughout the world discussed the conciliar draft documents, scholars published articles, and North American theologians published commentaries on pre-conciliar drafts in a volume that some conciliar bishops read before Crete.[24]

---

23. In October 2021, the Catholic Church began its journey on the path entitled, "For a Synodal Church: Communion, Participation, and Mission," engaging its local and regional structures on a synodal path. An important stage will be the celebration of the XVI Ordinary General Assembly of the Synod of Bishops in October 2023, followed by the implementation phase. This synodal process ascribes a significant role to laity, parish priests, and theologians.

24. Nathanael Symeonides, ed., *Toward the Holy and Great Council: Theological Reflections* (New York: Greek Orthodox Archdiocese of America, 2016).

This process of consultation is traditional. Early councils included deacons (such as St. Athanasius the Great who served as a theological expert to bishop Alexander of Alexandria at Nicaea I and later on was instrumental in the reception of the Council) or emperors (Justinian at Constantinople II), even though only bishops voted on doctrinal matters.[25] The rule that only bishops are allowed to vote should not change, but it should be observed in the earnest, giving a vote only to bishops who represent a community of faithful and not to titular or honorific bishops ordained for defunct sees, since a bishop should vote only after consultation with the faithful and especially parish priests and theologians in his diocese. This consultation is especially important today, since it is no longer the case, as it was in the early church, that the most influential theologians were also bishops, and thus synodal decisions represented the consensus of the theological community.

Another important aspect of synodality has to do with the nature of synodal decisions. Although the synods of the early Church often addressed canonical issues, early synodality became known primarily for its doctrinal decisions. In that context it was understandable that bishops were attributed *charisma veritatis certum* — "the certain gift of truth,"[26] or the sure charism of truth. First of all, this charism did not function automatically. Richard McCormick argues that divine assistance is only effective to the extent to which it is accompanied by the proper human processes of gathering and assessing evidence.[27] A bishop has to inquire about the truth through earnest study and consultation with theologians and the faithful. Charisms do not work magically despite one's lack of effort. That is not to say that the Church arrives at the truth exclusively through human efforts. It is by the *sensus fidei*—understood as an instinct—that the faithful reject false teaching, as a music lover might react to false notes in a musical performance.[28] But this inspiration by the Spirit happens only as long as the bishop remains in the communion of the Church and inspiration is accompanied by human efforts, which are essential in this synergic quest for the truth.

---

25. The 1917–1918 Moscow Council experienced the highest level of lay participation in Orthodox history. It gathered more lay representatives (299) than clergy (265), ensuring lay participation from parish council, to diocesan and patriarchal structures. John Meyendorff and Nicholas Lossky, *The Orthodox Church: Its Past and Its Role in the World Today* (Crestwood, NY: St. Vladimir's Seminary Press, 1996), 112. While appreciating the extraordinary circumstances in which the Moscow Council took place, Afanasiev has a generally negative view of these changes, since the laity do not have the ministries of governance and witness. Afanassieff, *The Church of the Holy Spirit*, 65–69.

26. Irenaeus of Lyons, *Against Heresies*, IV:26:2, 124.

27. Richard A. McCormick, *Notes on Moral Theology: 1965 through 1980* (Lanham, MD: University Press of America, 1981), 261–66.

28. International Theological Commission, Sensus fidei *in the Life of the Church* (2014) par. 49, 62.

Second, today synodality addresses primarily issues of discipline, and thus theology needs to reimagine a new way of speaking of *charisma veritatis certum*, given that canonical decisions are not regarded as inspired teaching. A step in the right direction would be to acknowledge that the laity often have greater abilities in practical matters than the clergy, and so a greater participation of the laity in the process of synodality is necessary. Particularly important is the presence of women at councils, especially if the topic of marriage is on the agenda. Women have different experiences and perspectives compared to men. Their contribution can only improve the quality of a document addressing marriage, as in the case of the one approved at the Council of Crete, a document that was drafted and voted upon by a group of celibate male bishops.

The involvement of diverse categories of faithful in the synodal process is extremely important since the Orthodox hierarchy does not reflect the racial, socio-economical, and gender diversity of their constituents. Bishops speak primarily from their own personal perspective, which tends to be limited in scope: white, elderly, male, and economically privileged. Orthodoxy needs to ensure that the entire synodal process—from large-scale consultation to implementation—represents all the members of the Church, in all their diversity as the sure way of creating unity, as testified by the Tradition. St. Maximus the Confessor wrote in this sense that the Church reflects God's unifying work in all of us, since

> [the] holy church bears the imprint and [icon] of God since it has the same activity as he does by imitation and in figure ... It is in this way that the holy Church of God will be shown to be working for us the same effects as God, in the same way as the image reflects its archetype. For numerous and of almost infinite number are the men, women, and children who are distinct from one another and vastly different by birth and appearance, by nationality and language, by customs and age, by opinions and skills, by manners and habits, by pursuits and studies, and still again by reputation, fortune, characteristics, and connections: All are born into the Church and through it are reborn and recreated in the Spirit.... [The Church] gives to all a single, simple, whole, and indivisible condition which does not allow us to bring to mind the existence of the myriads of differences among them, even if they do exist, through the universal relationship and union of all things with it.[29]

The unifying activity of the Church and the process of consultation bring together on the same path (*syn-odos*) not only faithful from all walks of life

29. Maximus the Confessor, "*Mystagogia*," 186–87.

in a certain era, but also across the ages, in the process of reception. Today Orthodoxy needs to creatively receive the tradition of the ecumenical councils. Conciliar decisions and patristic writings need to be continuously made alive by understanding the context in which they were initially written, looking at the entire body of works in all its diversity, and applying them creatively to our new context. For example, as stated above, recent ecumenical dialogues revealed that the theological conflicts between the Oriental and Eastern Orthodox churches were primarily due to a terminological confusion. The two traditions share the same Christology and soteriology, so the anathemas of the third and fourth councils do not apply today. Nor do early centuries' interdictions of intercommunion with heretics refer to today's Catholics. In contrast, a fundamentalist repetition of conciliar decisions takes them out of their initial context, ignores the complexity of the arguments, intentionally overemphasizes some statements over others, and forcefully applies them in contemporary contexts in which the original authors would have never implemented them. That is fundamentalism, in short.[30] Today, the *greatest danger facing the proper reception of the Eastern conciliar tradition is not relativism or secularism, but fundamentalism.*

Jaroslav Pelikan said that

> *Tradition is the living faith of the dead; traditionalism is the dead faith of the living.* Tradition lives in conversation with the past, while remembering where we are and when we are and that it is we who have to decide. Traditionalism supposes that nothing should ever be done for the first time, so all that is needed to solve any problem is to arrive at the *supposedly unanimous testimony* of this homogenized tradition (emphases added).[31]

The contrast that Pelikan sets between Tradition and traditionalism is equivalent to the contrast set above between creative reception of conciliar decisions and fundamentalism. Historians of religion seem to deal with this methodological distinction consistently, in reaction to the misuse of synodal and patristic traditions. Florovsky contrasted the mechanical repetition of patristic formulae with a theology according to "the mind of the Fathers," or a *neo-Patristic synthesis.*[32] He recommends going beyond "archaic formulas,"

---

30. Hovorun considers fundamentalism among the most popular modern heresies in the Orthodox world, together with nationalism and anti-Semitism. Cyril Hovorun, *Political Orthodoxies: The Unorthodoxies of the Church Coerced* (Minneapolis: Fortress Press, 2018), 4, 89–116.

31. Jaroslav Pelikan, "Interview" in *U.S. News & World Report,* July 26, 1989.

32. Georges Florovsky, "Patristic Theology and the Ethos of the Orthodox Church," in *Aspects of Church History, Collected Works* 4 (Belmont, MA: Nordland, 1975), 17–18, 22, 29. "Address at 80 Years of

and simple "appeal to antiquity," providing Gregory Palamas as an example of "creative extension of ancient tradition" "in complete conformity with the mind of the Church," as opposed to a "theology of repetition," and the rediscovery of the "catholic mind," which is the language of the Scriptures, the worshipping Church, and the Fathers.[33]

The twentieth century witnessed an unprecedented resurgence of historical studies, with positive results that can hardly be overstated. Paradoxically, however, it also generated an overemphasis of history to the detriment of the present and of the future. After acknowledging the merits of neo-Patristic synthesis, Kalaitzidis asserts that it also resulted in introversion, trapping Orthodox theology in a "fundamentalism of tradition" or in a "fundamentalism of the Fathers." It created the idea that, in order to remain certain that we are within the limits of truth, we constantly need to take refuge in the past. In this sense, it is rather common to hear Orthodox theologians find solutions to all problems—past, present, and future—in the writings of the Fathers. Such an attitude does not account for the guiding work of the Spirit in the Church of our times. Neither does it correspond to Florovsky's desire to understand the "return to the Fathers" as thinking in this time and age "together with the Fathers." That is why Kalaitzidis advocates going "beyond the Fathers" as a proper Orthodox attitude much-needed today.[34]

It is important to pause for a moment on something that Kalaitzidis mentioned in passing, namely that those who embrace a "fundamentalism of tradition" remain certain that they are within the limits of truth. Mark Powell similarly explores the concept of *"epistemic certainty"* in Evangelical and Catholic traditions. Maximalist interpreters of authority within both these traditions look for a source of teaching where they can find the truth without room for interpretation, without further debate, a truth that remains applicable regardless of context. They find that place either in the literalist approach to the Bible or in papal infallible teachings, respectively. In the first case, biblical inerrancy is meant to counteract historical critical methods of scriptural interpretation and liberal Protestantism. In the second case, papal infallibility is hoped to guard against Protestant attitudes towards Scripture and Tradition, as well as then-modern challenges outlined in Pius IX's 1864 Syllabus of Errors:

Age" in Andrew Blane, "A Sketch of the Life of Georges Florovsky," in *Georges Florovsky: Russian Intellectual and Orthodox Churchman*, ed. Andrew Blane (Crestwood, NY: St. Vladimir's Seminary Press, 1993), 154.

33. Florovsky, "St. Gregory Palamas," 105–08, 44, 20. Florovsky, "The Church: Her Nature and Task," 58. Florovsky, "Western Influences in Russian Theology," 181–82.

34. Pantelis Kalaitzidis, "From the 'Return to the Fathers' to the Need for a Modern Orthodox Theology," *St. Vladimir's Theological Quarterly* 54, no. 1 (2010): 8–11.

"rationalism, indifferentism, socialism, communism, naturalism, free-masonry, separation of Church and State, liberty of the press, liberty of religion, progress, liberalism, and modern civilization."[35] Hence, Vatican I defined

> ... as divinely revealed dogma that when the Roman pontiff speaks *ex ca-*
> *thedra*, that is, when, in the exercise of this office as shepherd and teacher
> of all Christians, in virtue of his supreme apostolic authority, he defines
> a doctrine concerning faith or morals to be held by the whole church, he
> possesses, by the divine assistance promised to him in blessed Peter, that
> infallibility which the divine Redeemer willed his church to enjoy in de-
> fining doctrine concerning faith and morals. Therefore, such definitions of
> the Roman pontiff are of themselves, and not by the consent of the church,
> irreformable [*ex sese, non autem ex consensu ecclesiae irreformabiles esse*].[36]

The degree to which the First Vatican Council made infallible papal statements truly definitive and not subject to interpretation (or even correction) is debatable, but its hope to achieve epistemic certainty is not.[37] A maximalist reading of this text (among some Catholics and anti-ecumenical Orthodox) emphasizes that the Pope's doctrines are infallible in and of themselves, without the need for reception by the Church. A moderate reading (among most Catholics and pro-ecumenical Orthodox) accentuates the limitations that Vatican I placed on papal infallibility: the Pope has to speak *ex cathedra*, by virtue of his office (and not as an individual theologian, for example), his pronouncements have to refer to matters of faith and morals, with the intention to bind the whole Church, and his teachings participate in the infallibility of the entire Church without the possibility of speaking in isolation.

Maximalist Catholics share this claim to epistemic certainty not only with literalist evangelicals, but also with Orthodox fundamentalists. The latter are actually much closer to their Western counterparts than they would admit; it is only the source of authority that differs. Conciliar decisions, canonical norms, and patristic writings are, like papal statements or the literal meaning of Scripture, lifted up from their context to create an objective teaching that cannot be questioned and applied differently in various contexts. Orthodox

---

35. Mark E. Powell, *Papal Infallibility: A Protestant Evaluation of an Ecumenical Issue* (Grand Rapids, MI: Eerdmans, 2009), 2–28. For the context that gave rise to the Syllabus, especially its references to the relationship between Church and state in the events leading up to the French Revolution, see John Courtney Murray, "The Church and Totalitarian Democracy," *Theological Studies* 13, no. 4 (1952): 525–46.

36. *Pastor Aeternus* ch. 4, in Norman P. Tanner, ed., *Decrees of the Ecumenical Councils*, 2 vols., (Washington, DC: Georgetown University Press, 1990), II: 816.

37. Powell, *Papal Infallibility*, 2–19. Richard R. Gaillardetz, *Teaching with Authority: A Theology of the Magisterium in the Church* (Collegeville, MN: Liturgical Press, 1997), 193–254.

fundamentalism is a maximalist view that misrepresents ecumenical councils as an infallible episcopal authority shared in common, which is far from the Orthodoxy view of synodality outlined above. As with biblical inerrancy and papal infallibility, historical fundamentalism fails to deliver epistemic certainty.

It is important to acknowledge the temptation of epistemic certainty and not dismiss it lightly. First, epistemic certainty is a need with which all humans struggle. People are curious by nature and want to find *the* answer to their question. When one complex question has multiple conflicting responses, all valid in their own way, people tend to choose one answer to the detriment of the others. Paradox represents two different positions that apparently contradict each other but, taken separately, are each correct. We admire paradox but we are uncomfortable with it, and since we cannot solve it, we look for an external authority to offer us *the* unique answer that will satisfy our search. Fundamentalism is very tempting in this regard. But the Church is called to embrace paradox and live in the uncomfortable realm of personal and communal responsibility to listen to the Spirit and speak within the Tradition, with the voice with which Tradition would have spoken had it lived today. The Orthodox attitude is that of co-existence of diverse traditions.

The Scriptures, too, have preserved contradicting opinions and are comfortable with paradoxes. For example, in the first story of creation (Gn 1:1–2:4a), God creates the world in six days and humankind (male and female) is made after plants and animals. But in the second account of creation (Gn 2:4b–25), God creates the heavens and the earth in one day (Gn 2:4b), making Adam before plants and animals, and Eve only later. The New Testament is no different: in the synoptic Gospels Jesus eats the Last Supper on the first day of Passover (hence the Western practice of using unleavened bread for the Eucharist), while in the Gospel of John, the Last Supper takes place before Passover, as a regular meal, hence the Orthodox practice of using leavened bread for the Eucharist. And yet, the early Church resisted the temptation to recognize as canonical only one Gospel, instead canonizing diversity, paradox, and even contradiction. This mindset continued throughout the centuries.

Epistemic certainty should not be confused with faith certainty. Augustine, in the first chapter of his *Confessions*, writes, "our heart is restless until it rests in you."[38] This longing for putting an end to restlessness is also reflected in Ps 46:10, "be still and know that I am God," a favorite among hesychasts, the

---

38. Augustine, *Confessions*, trans. Henry Chadwick (New York: Oxford University Press, 1998), Book I.1, p. 3.

word *hesychia* meaning stillness. We certainly need to find our rest in truth, and it is there that we find the inspiration and power to face extreme challenges in the name of faith, including martyrdom. If one has arrived at the faith certainty that "Jesus is the Lord," one is willing to live and die by this faith. One does not live and die by uncertainty. However, believing with certainty that "Jesus is the Lord" (and being willing to die for it) does not mean that we cannot ask who Jesus was, and what we mean by his Lordship. Questioning does not weaken, but strengthens the faith.

Unlike biblical inerrancy, a spiritual reading of the bible that questions its literal meaning is certainly more beneficial than artificially trying to iron over the differences regarding Genesis and the Last Supper mentioned above. Unlike the maximalist view of Cardinal Manning, who at Vatican I argued that all papal statements are infallible, it is more fruitful to regard the Pope as having authority when he represents the consensus of the Church, thus avoiding the difficulty that John Henry Newman pointed out, namely that Pope Honorius embraced the monothelite heresy, for which reason the sixth ecumenical council condemned him and subsequent popes also condemned Honorius. Either Honorius was wrong, or the sixth ecumenical council and subsequent popes were wrong, thus challenging Manning's maximalist view of papal infallibility while still affirming papal infallibility as a gift to the Church in Newman's reading. Similarly, one could add another example against historical fundamentalism, namely that the creed of Nicaea was later revised at Constantinople, not simply by adding the articles about the Holy Spirit, but also deleting Nicaea's affirmation that the Son was born out of the essence of the Father and replacing it with the assertion that the Son was born of the Father before all ages.[39]

To put it simply, no Church reality speaks infallibly in and of itself: not the Pope, not the Ecumenical Council, not the literal meaning of the Scripture. But any person in the Church can speak infallibly if that person represents the consensus of the Church. And that person can be the Pope, an ecumenical council, or one's interpretation of the Bible, including the literal reading of some passages. The ultimate authority is the entire Church. This is the ultimate meaning of synodality.

---

39. Compare the two Creeds in Tanner, *Decrees of the Ecumenical Councils*, I:5–24.

PRIMACY: EAST AND WEST

This section does not attempt to offer a history of papal infallibility and primacy, although it will refer to several major studies on this theme. Rather, several experiential remarks will continue the discussion of the papacy in the same note as the previous section on epistemic certainty and will lead into an analysis of primacy in its various forms.

The first time I visited the Vatican, in 2012, I attended a Roman mass in St. Peter's Basilica. Prominent in front of us was *Cathedra Petri*, or the Chair of St. Peter, masterfully sculpted by Bernini. I was mesmerized by the beauty of the artwork, although, as a theologian, I chuckled when I saw above the chair a dove, representing the inspiration, or the Holy Spirit resting upon the Pope—the Vicar of Christ—as the dove rested upon Jesus at Baptism. I also noted the four doctors of the Church—Sts. Ambrose, Athanasius, John Chrysostom, and Augustine—two from the East and two from the West, all in accord with the teaching proclaimed by the one who sits on St. Peter's chair. The sight of the keys gave me another chuckle, thinking how Jesus' promise to give Peter the power of the keys to bind and loose (Mt 16:13–16) is in fact a post-resurrection appearance to Peter that was interposed back into the life of the historical Jesus,[40] and how binding and loosing was understood during Second Temple Judaism as the teacher's authority to say what is permissible and what is not among his disciples,[41] a far cry from the three-tiered papal tiara that Bernini placed between the keys to symbolize the Pope's authority.

But soon, this skeptical Eastern theologian noticed that the people who were gathering for the Mass spoke all the languages of the earth, and yet they all converged into one point. Then their diverse voices became one, as they sang the same melody, in the same language of the Mass. I am not in favor of living people worshiping in dead languages, but Latin was the only language that we all shared, and that is what united us at that moment. After the Mass, the multitudes gathered in St. Peter's square, outside the basilica. The square itself—conceived by the same Bernini—gathers pilgrims from all over the world in an embrace that brings them into one place. It was a Sunday when the Pope addressed the people that were gathered in the square, thousands or perhaps tens of thousands. Why did all these people listen to him and were so joyous to see him? Because he was their father—*papa*. This endearing term reflects the

40. Meier, *Companions and Competitors*, 228–35.
41. W. D. Davies and D. C. Allison, *The Gospel According to St. Matthew, vol. 2: Matthew 8–18* (London: T&T Clark, 1991), 639.

essence of Catholic identity: the Pope is their father. True, there are priests in parishes, bishops in dioceses, episcopal conferences, but transcending them all there is a father of 1.2 billion Catholics all over the world, namely the Pope— *il papa*—and he is their bishop.⁴²

Before this experience, I had, of course, studied the papacy in Orthodox institutions, I received a PhD from a Catholic institution, and had taught for six years at another Catholic university. Four years later I lived in Rome for three months, this time under a different Pope. I saw how he, too, gathered tens of thousands of faithful eager to hear him or to participate in the Paschal Liturgy that he celebrated in St. Peter's Square. These experiences solidified my experience of the papacy as one of the—if not *the*—most important elements of Catholic identity. This is a positive experience of the Pope. Faithful from around the world surround him in one place; he enables them to transcend their theological differences as secondary to their Catholic identity; he motivates them to surpass political divisions and embrace a common cause (as for example care for the environment—a divisive theme in the U.S.); and he has the authority to convene all bishops as a synod despite their centrifugal tendencies. All these elements of papal primacy are aspects of a ministry of unity that is much needed in Christianity today, including in Orthodoxy.

These experiential considerations about the Pope's ministry of unity are not without practical shortcomings. For example, the Pope's calling to become the mouthpiece of the Catholic Church cannot be overemphasized to the detriment of particularity of context and of diversity of opinions. A maximalist exercise of Petrine ministry results in uniformization of a Church that counts 1.2 billion faithful around the globe and countless more throughout history. Papal abuses abound throughout history, and so the skepticism of Orthodox, Protestant, and even many Catholics regarding papal authority is warranted.

---

42. The Pope has nineteen official titles. Pope in English, or *papa* in Italian, means father, a title that is also claimed by the Orthodox bishop of Alexandria and that was given to every bishop in the West until 1073, when it was restricted to the Bishop of Rome. Other papal titles include: the Vicar of Christ (although Vatican II affirmed that all bishops are vicars of Christ), Successor of the Chief of the Apostles, Successor or Vicar of Peter. These titles should be understood within Roman customs, where someone's successor or vicar had all the rights, prerogatives, and duties of the person they succeeded. Other titles harken back to Roman history; the Supreme Pontiff—Pontifex Maximus or Supreme Bridge Builder—was the title of the Roman emperor because he was chief among pagan priests. Richard P. McBrien, "The Papacy," in *The Gift of the Church: A Textbook on Ecclesiology in Honor of Patrick Granfield, O.S.B.*, ed. Peter C. Phan (Collegeville, MN: Liturgical Press, 2000), 316. In 2006, Benedict XIV dropped the title of Patriarch of the West, intending it as an ecumenical gesture towards Protestants who would rest assured that the papacy does not intend to have dominion over the entire West. But from an Orthodox perspective, that was one of the most appropriate titles for the Pope, whose authority in the West should be different from the exercise of his ministry in the rest of the world.

In the case of the first two, schism was the only option, so that the Pope would have no authority over them. That is why *ecumenical discussions are progressing so slowly on this subject*: we need to protect ourselves from the worst-case scenario. The Orthodox East still remembers the Fourth Crusade (1204) when Western armies sacked Constantinople and replaced Eastern bishops with Latin ones.[43] But this defensive attitude does not resonate with most faithful living in the West. Orthodox faithful emigrating to the Western world, when they first formed their communities, used Catholic churches as gathering places, often without paying any rent. Their neighbors and best friends are Catholic and their children go to Catholic schools. Such experiences are the polar opposite of the Fourth Crusade, since the West is the friendly neighbor, indeed, the sister or brother in Christ, and not a malevolent Pope. Even the recent popes have enjoyed much popularity around the world, and thus the ecumenical dialogue on the role of the papacy (still preparing for worst-case scenario based on negative historical memory) remains gravely incongruent with the experience of today's faithful who thirst for unity.

Not all historical memory is negative, of course.[44] The book of Acts, which documents the expansion of the Church from Jerusalem to the nations, ends with the hopeful image of Paul the Apostle in Rome, "proclaiming the kingdom of God and teaching about the Lord Jesus Christ with all boldness and without hindrance" (Acts 28:31). That is also where he entered the heavenly Kingdom, after being martyred, as was St. Peter. Being the place of martyrdom of Peter and Paul, Rome gained a prestige among Christians that far surpassed the fame that the imperial capital already enjoyed. The tradition of martyrdom continued and, to this day, pilgrims can visit catacombs that used to house large numbers of Roman bishops who gave their life for the faith. As early as Ignatius of Antioch's time, Rome was known as the one that "presides in love."[45]

43. In a tragic and ironic turn of events, the Crusaders were first excommunicated by pope Innocent III for attacking the city of Zara—another Catholic power. The pope lifted his sentence only when the crusaders vowed to refrain from attacking more fellow Christians. And yet, when exiled Byzantine prince Alexios IV (d. 1204) asked them to help his father Isaac II (d. 1204) regain his throne in exchange for sponsoring their crusade, they forgot their solemn vow not to attack fellow Christians and pope Innocent himself overcame his initial anguish when Alexios assured him that he would end the schism by submitting, together with the Patriarch, to the Pope. A. Edward Siecienski, *The Papacy and the Orthodox: Sources and History of a Debate* (New York: Oxford University Press, 2017), 283–86.

44. See George E. Demacopoulos, *The Invention of Peter: Apostolic Discourse and Papal Authority in Late Antiquity* (Philadelphia: University of Pennsylvania Press, 2013).

45. The greeting section of Ignatius' letter "To the Romans," from which this expression comes would make today's Orthodox and Protestants blush: Ignatius Theophorus to the Church on which the majesty of the most high Father and of Jesus Christ, His only Son, has had mercy; to the Church beloved and enlightened by the faith and charity of Jesus Christ, our God, through the will of Him who has willed all

Rome's ministry of presiding in love took many forms throughout the centuries and in different parts of the world. The saying attributed to Augustine, that when Rome has spoken the issue is concluded (*Roma locuta, causa finita*)[46] was an exaggeration throughout much of history. And yet, Rome had the privilege of receiving appeals from bishops who have been deposed by their provincial synods;[47] the Pope would initially order a new trial and, if necessary, only then would give a pronouncement. Besides disciplinary issues, the Bishop of Rome also heard appeals pertaining to dogmatic issues. Eastern saints such as John Chrysostom, Cyril of Alexandria, and Theodore the Studite have appealed to the Pope. Most notably, Maximus the Confessor found protection at the "most holy church of the Romans," "the sun of eternal light," which he considered as first among all the churches, having been entrusted with the power to bind and to loose.[48] Maximus' rhetoric regarding the papacy—and he is one among many—makes even today's ecumenically-minded Easterners blush. But it is an undisputable historical fact that most Roman bishops in the age of the councils were regarded as preeminent defenders of apostolic tradition. While all heresies condemned by the ecumenical councils arose in the East, being embraced by Patriarchs of Constantinople and emperors, all popes, with the exception of Honorius, remained firm in the true faith. At the Council of Chalcedon (451), the conciliar fathers proclaimed that "Peter has spoken through Leo." Of course, Leo's place as the successor of Peter was not enough in and of itself; Leo had to be in accord with the true faith confessed by Cyril of Alexandria: "Piously and truly did Leo teach, so taught Cyril."[49]

The Pope's venerable place among teaching authorities did not automatically translate into jurisdictional authority. By the time of Nicaea I (325), it did

things that exist—the Church in the place of the country of the Romans which holds the primacy. I salute you in the name of Jesus Christ, the Son of the Father. You are a Church worthy of God, worthy of honor, felicitation and praise, worthy of attaining to God, a Church without blemish, which holds the primacy of the community of love, obedient to Christ's law, bearing the Father's name." Ignatius, "To the Romans," in Saint Ignatius of Antioch (Theophorus), "The Letters," in *The Apostolic Fathers* (Washington, DC: The Catholic University of America Press, 1947), 106–7.

46. Although Augustine's text does not support such a strong interpretation, the basis of this saying is in a sermon where Augustine mentions that the decisions of two local councils have been sent to Rome—the Apostolic See—from where they received a response and now "The case is finished." See "Sermon 131 on John 6:53," in Augustine, *Sermons*, vol. III/4 – 131:10, 322.

47. Third canon of the Council of Sardica (343), reaffirmed at Trullo (691–692). The twelfth century Byzantine canonist Theodore Balsamon applied the right of appeal to the Patriarch of Constantinople. Joint Orthodox-Catholic Working Group, "Serving Communion," par. 7.3.

48. Maximus the Confessor, *Opuscula theologica et polemica* 11–12: PG 91, 137D–144C in Joint Orthodox-Catholic Working Group, "Serving Communion," par. 7.2.

49. Joint Orthodox-Catholic Working Group, "Serving Communion," par. 7.6.

not extend beyond the Roman province. It took almost a millennium for the papal authority to extend over the Western half of the empire. Throughout all these centuries, the Pope never had the authority to appoint bishops in the territories of the other ancient Patriarchates. His interventions in the East were of a different nature, usually as an arbiter in disputes. Thus, while the Church enjoyed relative unity in the first millennium, the Bishop of Rome exercised *two different types of authority*: a type of primacy that involved full authority in the West and a limited type of primacy that heard appeals and proclaimed the true doctrine in the East. One of the great tragedies of the schism between East and West is that, once separated from the East, the second type of papal primacy disappeared, and all that was left was a full patriarchal type authority that the Pope exercised wherever he could manifest his influence.[50] For example, as a result of the Fourth Crusade of 1204, he replaced Eastern bishops with Latin ones, thus manifesting a patriarchal type of authority in the East, an authority that was only beginning to expand. As John Quinn explains,

> With the discovery of the New World in the 15th century and the missionary expansion of the Latin Catholic Church in the 16th century and later, the patriarchal kind of papal government was gradually extended over the worldwide Catholic Church, bringing with it uniformity of liturgical language and practice, the choice and appointment of all bishops by the pope and the appointment of papal delegates in all countries where the Catholic Church had been planted.[51]

Quinn's last remark is quite important for a proper understanding of the development of the papacy, especially the *expansion of its religious and secular primacy*. Since Emperor Constantine moved the imperial capital and the Roman emperor resided in Constantinople beginning with 330, the Eastern Patriarchs had their secular authority limited by the Emperor and their religious authority by other Patriarchs. In the West, however, the situation was very different. There were no other apostolic sees besides Rome, so the Pope's religious authority was only nominally limited by other bishops. And since the

---

50. Papal authority varied greatly, depending on geography, historical era, or level of Church life. The authority of the Bishop of Rome was much more easily recognized in Italy than in Africa or Asia Minor. Similarly, the role of the Pope differed at four different levels: local-episcopal, metropolitan, patriarchal, and universal. Unfortunately, the lines separating these levels became less and less clear through the centuries. This confusion between Petrine responsibilities for the whole Church and for the West represents the very starting point of the schism between East and West, as Pope Benedict XVI suggests. Siecienski, *The Papacy and the Orthodox*, 140–41.

51. John R. Quinn, "Closer to Communion," in *America* November 24, 2014. http://americamagazine.org/

Emperor resided in the East, the Pope enjoyed an unusual amount of secular authority, exercised to the exasperation of Western princes. With the coronation of Charlemagne on Christmas day in 800 as "the Emperor of the Romans" at the hands of Pope Leo III in Rome, the papacy took full control over who holds the secular power in the Holy Roman Empire. Thus, the papacy gradually developed to have unchallenged power—secular and religious—in the West and throughout the world through Catholic missions. Such a view of primacy became unacceptable to the East.

While rejecting this type of Western primacy, the East continued to consider primacy as an essential condition of synodality. During the existence of the Byzantine Empire, that place was naturally assigned to *the bishop of Constantinople in the East*. After the move of the imperial capital from Rome to Constantinople in 330, the first major occasion to exalt the place of the New Rome in the ecclesiastical order (e.g., diptychs) was the second ecumenical council that took place, unsurprisingly, in Constantinople in 381. Its third canon justified the change on political grounds: "the bishop of Constantinople has the prerogatives of honor after the bishop of Rome, because this city is the New Rome."[52] The bishops of Alexandria and especially Rome did not accept this decision, even while receiving the doctrinal proclamations of the council. Decades later, canon 28 of the fourth ecumenical council in Chalcedon (451) elevated Constantinople to be equal to Rome—again justified by the presence of political authorities in the city—even though Constantinople remained second in rank to Rome.[53] The bishop of Constantinople was given the authority to ordain metropolitans and bishops for Pontus, Asia, Thrace, and the barbarian regions, an authority that Constantinople will later invoke to claim jurisdiction over the diaspora. The delegates of Pope Leo registered their protest in the acts of the council, and the Pope himself rejected this canon. The competition between the Old Rome and the New Rome was in full swing.

The tension intensified in the sixth century when Patriarch John the Faster of Constantinople adopted the *title "ecumenical,"* meaning that his authority extends over the entire civilized world. What exactly that meant remains

52. Emmanuel Lanne, "The Three Romes," in *The Holy Russian Church and Western Christianity*, ed. Giuseppe Alberigo and Oscar Beozzo (London, Maryknoll: SCM Press, Orbis, 1996), 12–13.

53. Canon 28 reads: "The Fathers [of 381] rightly granted its prerogatives to the see of Old Rome because this city is the imperial city. For the same reasons the 150 very pious bishops [of Chalcedon 451] have granted equal prerogatives to the most holy see of the New Rome, rightly judging that the city which is honored by the presence of the emperor and the senate, and which enjoys the same prerogatives as the old imperial city of Rome, is as great as that is in ecclesiastical matters, being the second after her." Lanne, "The Three Romes," 13.

debatable, since the Patriarch did not claim to have direct jurisdiction over the entire world. The Patriarch's action was probably more a sign of weakness than of strength, since he would not have had to claim the title "ecumenical" if his authority were undisputed. Also telling was Rome's reaction, which came from a position of strength. In response to the Patriarch of Constantinople's new title, Pope St. Gregory I the Great (590–604) adopted the title "the servant of the servants of God" (*servus servorum Dei*), a title that subsequent Popes have retained, as well. Despite these sixth century quarrels, the exact opposite happened in the ensuing centuries: Rome claimed universal jurisdiction, while Constantinople claimed a greater degree of primacy in the East.

As Edward Siecienski shows, in the years immediately preceding the schism, the *Pope's claim to an expanded authority and the Ecumenical Patriarch's strengthened position given the backing of the Byzantine emperor did not exclude one another.* There was even an Eastern proposal to recognize universal primacy as long as Constantinople was accorded first autonomy and second primacy in the East. Siecienski details the following proposal, which still has potential to bring East and West together:

> In 1024 Emperor Basil II and Patriarch Eustathius of Constantinople (1019–25) sent Pope John XIX (1024–32) a formula that they hoped would clarify the respective positions of Rome and Constantinople. They suggested that "the church of Constantinople might be called and regarded as universal in its own sphere (*in suo orbe*) just as Rome is throughout the world (*in universo*). On one level this formula was a gift to Rome, as it was prepared to "recognize the supreme power of the Roman See over the whole church and even Constantinople … reissuing the ordinances of Justinian II, of Phocas, and of Justinian I." True, there was also the suggestion that administratively Constantinople "should be admitted to be self-sufficient and autonomous," but given the relative impotence of the papacy at the time this was not an unreasonable request.[54]

Unfortunately, despite being initially inclined to accept this proposal, Pope John XIX's confidants persuaded him to reject it. But the proposal remains significant. It puts forth a possible solution to the schism between East and West, which clarifies that Rome's primacy in the East is not an absolute one, but guarantees Constantinople's autonomy and by extension the autonomy of all other Orthodox churches.

It is tempting to look only at *history for solutions to the current impasse;* this

---

54. Siecienski, *The Papacy and the Orthodox,* 242.

is the approach of the current ecumenical discussions about primacy. Extremely influential in this sense was the so-called "Ratzinger formula." In a lecture at Graz in 1976, long before being elected Pope Benedict XVI, Cardinal Ratzinger affirmed that, "as to the doctrine of primacy, Rome cannot claim more from the East than was formulated and practiced in the first millennium." In response, Siecienski cautions against attempting to extract a single model of papal authority in the first millennium. If anything, the first millennium suggests that the way forward is to accept that there are different ways in which papal authority can be exercised. Moreover, one should not take out of context the theological statements that some Eastern fathers have made either in favor or against papal authority. These patristic passages can be easily distorted when one does not consider whether the Pope was regarded as an ally or as an opponent in specific theological controversies. Eastern Fathers grant the Pope a special teaching authority, but never place him above the rest of the Church. At the same time, one should not overstate their case for an "anti-Roman affect," as if early Christianity refused to recognize Rome any special authority.[55]

One can draw from history the conclusion that Roman primacy is compatible with the Eastern tradition of synodality based on the autonomy of the local churches.[56] As a matter of fact, *in a future united Church, Orthodox theologians are ready to ascribe to Rome a position of primacy*, but not the kind of primacy that Rome now has in the Catholic Church.[57] The Orthodox should graciously acknowledge that Vatican I (1870) rushed to give the Pope more power than was necessary. The council's constitution, *Pastor Aeternus* states that the Pope does not merely have a primacy of honor; instead, he has episcopal, ordinary, and immediate universal jurisdiction, meaning that the authority of the Pope does not come from the Church or a council:

> [Ch. 1:] Therefore, if anyone says that Blessed Peter the apostle was not appointed by Christ the lord as prince of all the apostles and visible head of the whole church militant; or that it was a primacy of honor only and not one of true and proper jurisdiction that he directly and immediately received from our lord Jesus Christ himself: let him be anathema....

---

55. Siecienski, *The Papacy and the Orthodox*, 141–43.

56. Zizioulas points out that the apparent incompatibility between primacy and conciliarity is the result of the growing role of the papacy around the First Vatican Council, when some Catholic "conciliarist" theologians emphasized the idea that councils express the supreme authority of the Church in the hope to limit papal authority. Influenced by this conciliarist movement, numerous Orthodox theologians regarded synodality as an alternative to papal primacy. Zizioulas, *Lectures in Christian Dogmatics*, 120, 42.

57. Afanassieff, "Una Sancta," 27.

[Ch. 3:] if anyone says that the Roman pontiff has merely an office of supervision and guidance, and not the full and supreme power of jurisdiction over the whole church, and this not only in matters of faith and morals, but also in those which concern the discipline and government of the church dispersed throughout the whole world; or that he has only the principal part, but not the absolute fullness, of his supreme power; or that this power of his is not ordinary and immediate both over all and each of the churches and over all and each of the pastors and faithful: let him be anathema.[58]

The council's decision was motivated by Conciliarism (which advocated for the subordination of the Pope's authority to that of the council), Gallicanism (French secular powers usurping the Pope's authority over French bishops), and Ultra-Montane counterreactions (i.e., the exaggerated appeal to the Pope by bishops who sought approval for all matters "over the mountains" from Rome). Vatican I was also abruptly interrupted by the Franco-Prussian war, and so its work had to be continued decades later, at Vatican II (1962–1965), which attempted to place the papacy in the context of the entire episcopate and the entire Church.

But if Orthodox theologians adopt such an understanding attitude, Catholic theologians also have to admit that the teaching of their Church on the papacy remains controversial even after Vatican II. For example, *Lumen Gentium* 22 states that "the Roman pontiff, by reason of his office as Vicar of Christ, namely, and as pastor of the entire church, has full, supreme and universal power over the whole church, a power which he can always exercise unhindered." Vatican II conditions the synodality of the bishops upon the Pope, but papal authority does not depend on the bishops, even though it does not exclude the possibility that the Pope would collaborate with the other primates. Such a view of primacy is insufficient from an Orthodox perspective.

Again, papal primacy and Eastern ecclesiology are not incompatible. Zizioulas acknowledges repeatedly that in a unified Church, the bishop of Rome would enjoy a sort of universal primacy that would be neither a primacy of jurisdiction nor the prerogative of an individual, but the primacy of the local church of Rome, exercised in a synodal context. He continues:

Can there be unity of the Church without primacy on the local, the regional and the universal level in an ecclesiology of communion? We believe not. For it is through a "head," some kind of "primus," that the "many," be it

---

58. Tanner, *Decrees of the Ecumenical Councils*, II: 813–15.

individual Christians or local Churches, can speak with one voice. But a
"primus" must be part of a community; not a self-defined, but a truly relational ministry. Such a ministry can only act together with the heads of the
rest of the local Churches whose consensus it would express. A primacy of
this kind is both desirable and harmless in an ecclesiology of communion.[59]

Applying these conciliar principles and the provisions of the 34th Apostolic
Canon[60] to the vision of the papacy in a united Church, Zizioulas expects that
the Pope will act communally together with the other bishops, respecting the
fullness of the local Church. At the same time, the Pope would have a moral
and canonical authority that would enable him to convene councils and to express the common voice of the Church, as the mouthpiece of the entire Church
and of the consensus of the bishops with whom he is sacramentally equal. And
yet, in all these discussions on the authority of the Pope, it is important to remember that authority does not reside in his person as an individual, but as the
representative of his local Church that has primacy among other churches.[61]

Byzantine Catholic Churches provide another model of unity that accounts
for a different exercise of Papal primacy in the West and the East.[62] The 1995
Synod of the Greek Catholic Church in Lebanon approved nearly unanimously the following confession of faith: "Believe everything which the Orthodox
Church teaches and I am in communion with the bishop of Rome, in the role
that the Eastern Fathers accorded him before the separation." With the agreement of Patriarch Ignatius IV Hazim, Antiochian Orthodox Metropolitan
George Khodr responded: "I consider this profession of faith to set the necessary and sufficient conditions for re-establishing the unity of the Orthodox

---

59. John D. Zizioulas, "The Church as Communion," *Saint Vladimir's Theological Quarterly* 38, no. 1
(1994): 12.

60. The 34th Apostolic canon reads: "The bishops of every nation must acknowledge him who is first
among them and account him as their head, and do nothing of consequence without his consent; but each
may do those things only which concern his own parish, and the country places which belong to it. But
neither let him (who is the first) do anything without the consent of all; for so there will be unanimity,
and God will be glorified through the Lord in the Holy Spirit." "The Canons of the Holy and Altogether
August Apostles [Apostolic Canons]," trans. Henry R. Percival (Grand Rapids, MI: Eerdmans, 1899),
NPNF 14, 596.

61. John D. Zizioulas, "Primacy in the Church: An Orthodox Approach," in *Petrine Ministry and the
Unity of the Church: "Toward a Patient and Fraternal Dialogue": A Symposium Celebrating the 100th Anni-
versary of the Foundation of the Society of the Atonement, Rome, December 4–6, 1997*, ed. James F. Puglisi
(Collegeville, MN: Liturgical Press, 1999), 123–25. Bordeianu, "Primacies and Primacy according to John
Zizioulas," 14–19.

62. I have explored some themes in this sub-section in Radu Bordeianu, "'They Shall Beat Their
Swords into Plowshares': Orthodox – Eastern Catholic Conflicts and the Ecumenical Progress that They
Generated," in *Stolen Churches or Bridges to Orthodoxy*, ed. Vladimir Latinovic and Anastacia Wooden
(London: Palgrave Macmillan, 2021), 19–34.

Churches with Rome."[63] Similarly, Kallistos Ware acknowledges that the Orthodox are quick to point to the invalidity of Papal claims, but they find it rather difficult to speak positively about the role that the Pope should have in a united Church and, when they do, they come rather close to the model of Byzantine Catholic Churches.[64]

This is not to say that the model of Eastern Catholic Churches should be adopted wholesale. One the one hand, the genesis of these churches that were asked to recognize papal primacy but were promised that nothing else will change in their tradition, perhaps inadvertently, showed the recognition of papal primacy as a sufficient condition for unity. Rome did not regard the Filioque,[65] purgatory, azymes, and clerical celibacy as church-dividing issues that Easterners had to accept as pre-conditions for unity. Papal authority stood alone in this category, even while missionaries and apologists fervently defended the remaining issues against the Orthodox. In practice, however, the recognition of papal primacy was followed by a systematic process of Latinization. Examples of Latinization include the insertion of the Filioque in liturgical books, Roman missionaries trying to introduce the use of unleavened bread, and the obstruction of married priesthood in the West.[66] The efforts of some Popes to impede Latinization[67] did not put at ease the minds of Easterners who continue to distrust that Rome would use its authority without abusing it. And yet, Byzantine Catholic Churches have their own Code of Canon Law, their own practices, and a great degree of autonomy, which are elements that should inspire future discussions of Church unity.

63. Clément, *You Are Peter*, 88–89.

64. The Orthodox-Catholic International Commission's 1993 *Balamand Document*—whose reception, to put it politely, was rather cold on both sides—affirms the contrary: "'uniatism' can no longer be accepted either as a method to be followed nor as a model of the unity our Churches are seeking," in Borelli and Erickson, *The Quest for Unity*, 175–83.

65. Congar takes the lack of obligation for Oriental Catholic Churches to use the Filioque to imply that it is a theological opinion and not an obligatory dogma. Yves Congar, *I Believe in the Holy Spirit: The River of the Water of Life Flows in the East and in the West*, trans. David Smith, vol. 3 (New York: Seabury Press, 1983), 195–206.

66. The Congregation for the Oriental Churches issued in 1929 the decree, *Cum data fuerit*, which states that "priests of the Greek-Ruthenian Rite who wish to go to the United States ... and stay there, must be celibates." On June 14, 2014, Pope Francis authorized Cardinal Sandri to lift this ban.

67. For example, Benedict XIV's encyclical, *Allatatae Sunt* (*On the Observance of Oriental Rites*, 1755) is a response to missionaries who asked whether Armenians and Syrians united with Rome should adopt Latin practices. Citing a long list of popes who supported Greek practices, Benedict responded in the negative (#48, https://www.ewtn.com/library/ENCYC/B14ALLAT.HTM). Later on, Benedict the XVth established the Pontifical Oriental Institute (or the "Orientale") and created the Sacred Congregation for the Oriental Church, institutions meant to both protect the rights of the Eastern Catholic Churches and ensure the unity of the Catholic Church.

Among the many other proposals for unity,[68] it is perhaps best to end with *Afanasiev's suggestion that Orthodox and Catholics should share in the Eucharist even in the current state of theological divergence regarding the papacy.* While the West elevates Vatican I's teachings on papal primacy and infallibility to the level of dogma, Afanasiev proposes that the Orthodox should consider them as dogmas that are not received in the East. Indeed, dogmatic unity is the ideal, but rarely has that been the case throughout history. In the current state of animosity there are minimal chances of solving these differences, but they could be solved in a united church in the spirit of love. In the meantime, Afanasiev considers that the Orthodox and Catholic churches are already one, since each has a valid Eucharist.[69] He adds that, because of this unity manifested in the Eucharist, "the links between the Catholic Church and the Orthodox Church were never entirely broken and continue to exist until the present. The essential link between us is the Eucharist."[70] In other words, Afanasiev considers that the Catholic and Orthodox churches remain united despite their dogmatic differences, and thus they should commune eucharistically together.

To add to Afanasiev's proposal that Vatican I's teachings on papal primacy and infallibility should not impede intercommunion but be considered dogmas not received in the East, it is important to remember that these are the reasons why mixed Orthodox-Catholic marriages are required to stay divided eucharistically. The stakes could not be higher. And yet, the division continues even though it is difficult to support theologically, given that Vatican I took place in very unusual circumstances (Gallicanism, Ultra-Montanism, the Franco-Prussian war), and clearly Vatican II regarded it as not having had the last word. If that is the case, the Orthodox should simply adopt the following position: the Orthodox Church does not recognize Vatican I's teachings as dogmas received in the East; the Orthodox Church will not require that the Catholic Church renounce the teachings of Vatican I and II regarding the papacy, especially as they do not contradict any dogma proclaimed in an ecumenical council; the Orthodox Church allows its faithful to commune eucharistically with the Catholic Church.

It is true that this proposal does not establish episcopal communion, but

---

68. For example, DeVille proposes that a united Church should have a Permanent Ecumenical Synod, in which the role of the Pope would be to gather all the Eastern and Western patriarchs, preside over it (his presence representing the condition for the convening of the synod), promulgate and even veto the decisions of the synod, and in extreme circumstances have the prerogative to intervene in episcopal disputes. Adam A. J. DeVille, *Orthodoxy and the Roman Papacy: Ut Unum Sint and the Prospects of East-West Unity* (South Bend, IN: University of Notre Dame Press, 2011), 150–52.

69. Afanassieff, "Una Sancta," 24–28.

70. Afanassieff, "The Eucharist: Principal Link Between the Catholics and the Orthodox," 48–49.

that should not impede bishops to collaborate in matters pertaining to service to the world, for example. It is also true that this proposal appears rather imbalanced: the Orthodox Church does not change anything on its part, but it requires the Catholic Church to suspend its pretensions of papal universal primacy and obligation of infallible papal statements. And yet, as stated in a previous chapter, the Catholic Church did precisely that at the Second Vatican Council, when it agreed to extend eucharistic hospitality to Orthodox faithful, dependent on the consultation of the Orthodox bishops (*Orientalium Ecclesiarum* 29). All along, it has been up to the Orthodox Church to stop excluding its own faithful from Communion with the Catholic Church for a change that occurred in the Catholic Church, and which disproportionally affects the Orthodox faithful.

Since the discussion of the role of the Pope in a future united Church has slipped into the realms of theological speculation and idealistic musings, it is important to return to an *experiential approach to primacy in the East*. At a very superficial level, Orthodoxy has the solution to the tension between primacy and synodality: the Patriarch of Constantinople is *primus inter pares*—first among equals. Unfortunately, its practical application is far from providing an Eastern model of primacy that would have enough authority to make synodality possible, while also ensuring that no bishop stands above the others.

Constantinople certainly went *too far with its claim of primacy* in the past. For example, in what may sound both comical and aggravating today, in the fourteenth century, Patriarch Philotheos of Constantinople wrote to the princes of Russia: "Since God has appointed Our Humility as leader of all Christians found anywhere on the inhabited earth, as solicitor and guardian of their souls, all of them depend on me, the father and teacher of them all."[71] After the fall of Constantinople in 1453, other Orthodox leaders would make similar claims under the assumption that Christianity cannot endure without a "Rome," meaning a bishop who has primacy over all the rest.

Since the first Rome fell to the Goths and was now Catholic and the second Rome fell first under the West during the fourth crusade (1204) and then under the Ottomans (1453), who would take the role of *the third Rome?* In the early thirteenth century, an independent Bulgarian Patriarchate was established in the capital city of T'rnovo, which began being called the "Third Rome."[72] Later on in the same thirteenth century, after the Mongols sacked Kiev, the city

---

71. Quoted in MacCulloch, *Christianity*, 482.
72. MacCulloch, *Christianity*, 473.

of Novgorod replaced Kiev as the Orthodox capital of Rus' Orthodoxy and borrowed from T'rnovo the same title of "Third Rome."[73] The next center of Rus' Orthodoxy, namely Moscow, gradually made the same claim of being the "Third Rome." The tsars treated it with caution, as they feared that it gave the Church too much power. But the clergy and the people used it relentlessly, culminating with the letter of monk Filofei from the monastery of Pskov to Grand Prince Vasilii III of Moscow, in the mid-1520s. In it, Filofei reminds the prince that the first Rome fell away into heresy (by which he meant the *Filioque*, which he clumsily related to Apollinarianism), while the second Rome was overtaken by the unbelieving Ottomans. The tsar's destiny was to preside "in the new, third Rome, your mighty *tsarstvo* [empire], to shine like the sun throughout the whole universe, and to endure as long as the world endures: you are the only Tsar for Christians in the whole world.... Two Romes have fallen and the third stands. A fourth will not be."[74]

Despite such enthusiastic statements, the Third Rome theory did not enjoy wide influence in the Muscovite monarchy. It came back to prominence only with the rise of Slavophilism in the nineteenth century. The long suffering of the Russian Patriarchate under communism[75] certainly challenged any dreams of world-wide primacy. That is not to say that the communist authorities did not use the Patriarchate's standing in the Orthodox world to expand their own influence outside of the Soviet Union, but the secular authorities' intention was certainly not to bolster the position of the Patriarchate for religious reasons; it was primarily a means to counteract a Western-leaning Patriarchate of Constantinople. It is perhaps both surprising and sad to see that, after the fall of communism, the Moscow Patriarchate challenged Constantinople's standing with new vigor. Moscow regards itself as the gel that holds together the *Russky mir*—a presumed Russian world that includes many ex-Soviet territories that are no longer under Russian dominance politically, but are under the jurisdiction of the Moscow Patriarchate.[76] It also expands its territory by establishing

---

73. MacCulloch, *Christianity*, 513.

74. See MacCulloch, *Christianity*, 524–25. Lanne, "The Three Romes," 10–16.

75. See Meyendorff and Lossky, *The Orthodox Church*, 111–28.

76. The "Russian world" doctrine originated in the nineteenth-century Slavophile movement that advocated Panslavism (the doctrine of the unity of all Slavic nations under Russian leadership) and re-emerged under Patriarch Kirill of Moscow. Hovorun, *Political Orthodoxies*, 79. See also Cyril Hovorun, "Interpreting the 'Russian World,'" in *Churches in the Ukrainian Crisis*, ed. Andrii Krawchuk and Thomas Bremer (New York: Palgrave Macmillan, 2016), 163–71. For a condemnation of this ideology in the aftermath of Russia's invasion of Ukraine in 2022, see *A Declaration on the "Russian World"* (*Russkii Mir*) *Teaching*, https://publicorthodoxy.org/2022/03/13/a-declaration-on-the-russian-world-russkii-mir-teaching/

its own structures all over the world more than any other patriarchate, acting as if it has universal primacy of jurisdiction.

In contrast to these exaggerated claims of Eastern primacy stand the equal-ly *exaggerated claims of absolute equality among bishops*. It is true that all bishops are equal from a sacramental point of view, regardless of administrative rank. It is also true that one of the merits of Afanasiev's eucharistic ecclesiology was to emphasize the catholicity of the episcopal church, and not of the national autocephalous church—a unit that is "half political and half ecclesial.... To this latter, alone, modern Orthodox theology ascribes the ability to be free and autonomous. Orthodox theology indeed rejects the idea of primacy on the uni-versal scale, but it recognizes a partial primacy at the center of every autoceph-alous church, a primacy belonging to the head of that church."[77]

An experiential approach has the ability to embrace both the sacramental equality of all bishops and the reality that liturgical celebrations, administrative bodies, and synods require a primate with a real authority. In this realistic vein, none of the national Orthodox churches functions without a primate who has real authority. As Zizioulas writes,

> it would be a mistake to regard the authority of let us say a patriarch in relation to a synod in the Orthodox Church as simply a primacy of honor, as it is often stated by Orthodox theologians. There is certainly more to this primacy than simple "honor." The patriarch can convoke a synod and set its agenda. His presence is a *sine qua non* condition for all canonical delibera-tions, such as the election of bishops, etc. This means that the synod cannot function without its head.[78]

The authority of the primate within a national church thus includes call-ing the council, setting its agenda, ensuring the participation of the bishops in the council, and speaking on behalf of the council once a decision is made—a decision that the entire synod supports publicly. Moreover, the primate rep-resents the national church in its relations with secular authorities and other churches. This practical situation reveals primacy as an ecclesiological concept that extends the authority of the primate beyond his immediate jurisdiction, but only as commonly agreed within episcopal synodality, and not in a way

77. Nicolas Afanassieff, "The Church Which Presides in Love," in *The Primacy of Peter: Essays in Ecclesiology and the Early Church*, ed. John Meyendorff (Crestwood, NY: St. Vladimir's Seminary Press, 1992), 142–43.

78. John D. Zizioulas, "The Institution of Episcopal Conferences: An Orthodox Reflection," *The Jurist* 48 (1988): 381.

that supersedes the authority of the local bishop in his own diocese in pastoral matters.

One might wrongly assume that, if all Orthodox churches agree with the concept of a real primacy within their own borders, then automatically they all agree with this same concept of real primacy at pan-Orthodox and—in a united church—at universal level. Unfortunately, that is not the case. Many ills stem from Orthodoxy's refusal to have a pan-Orthodox primate with the same authority that primates have within their own national churches.

The most common way to refer to the authority of the Ecumenical Patriarch at pan-Orthodox level is that of *"primacy of honor"* (*presbeia tēs timēs*), as designated by the second ecumenical council. To clarify this terminology,

> The word *primacy* refers to the custom and use, already recognized by the first ecumenical councils as an ancient practice, whereby the bishops of Alexandria, Rome and Antioch, and later Jerusalem and Constantinople, exercised a personal ministry of oversight over an area much wider than that of their individual ecclesiastical provinces.... According to canon 34 of the Apostolic Canons, which is expressive of the Church's self-understanding in the early centuries and is still held in honor by many, though not all, Christians today, the first among the bishops in each nation would only make a decision in agreement with the other bishops and the latter would make no important decision without the agreement of the first.[79]

The understanding of primacy of honor varies greatly within Orthodoxy. The Russian Orthodox Church regards it as purely honorific, while the Patriarchate of Constantinople invokes it to convene councils, grant autocephaly, hear appeals, etc.[80] As Brian Daley conclusively shows, the Church of the councils did not know of a purely honorific type of primacy. When the 3rd canon of the Council of Constantinople (381) first introduced "primacy of honor" and when the 28th canon of the Council of Chalcedon (451) reaffirmed it, this type of primacy referred to a jurisdictional authority to make binding decisions, a first rank of leadership, pastoral responsibility, patronage (understood as reviewing and ratifying episcopal elections, ordaining bishops, mediating disputes, and being respected by the bishops who were expected to be loyal)—all these in an other-worldly sense and not in the sense in which imperial power was exercised. Later on, twelfth-century Byzantine writers such as Ioannis

---

79. WCC, *The Church*, par. 55.
80. Joint Orthodox-Catholic Working Group, "Serving Communion," par. II.4.

Zonaras and Theodore Balsamon presented a primacy that became devoid of real authority and largely ceremonial, referring to the order of liturgical commemorations, listings in synodal documents, the right to wear a Phrygian cap, a chain representing the office, a scepter, and the right to ride a horse.[81] The Russian interpretation of primacy of honor is rooted in this latter interpretation. Rejecting a ceremonial conception of primacy, however, Zizioulas applies the model of the primates of autocephalous churches discussed above to the Ecumenical Patriarch, whose authority would be real, well beyond a mere "primacy of honor,"[82] but it should not be confused with universal jurisdiction:

> The patriarch of Constantinople could not interfere in the affairs of the other patriarchates, but would be responsible for the canonical order within them and intervene only when asked to do so in cases of emergency or disturbance and anomaly of some kind. He would also be responsible for the convocation of councils dealing with matters pertaining to the entire Orthodox Churches, always with the consent of the other patriarchs.[83]

After the failure of the Ecumenical Patriarch to ensure the participation of all autocephalous churches at the Council of Crete in 2016, Zizioulas' contention that, as the *primus* in the East, the Patriarch of Constantinople convenes councils pertaining to issues that affect the entire Orthodox world strikes a tragic note. Without a doubt, a greater level of authority is necessary for an efficient exercise of the universal ministry of unity and of synodality—so dear to Orthodox hearts. It should be possible to exercise a pan-Orthodox form of primacy with real authority, similar to the primacy that national churches experience internally. An Eastern primate should be able to convene synods and set their agendas, speak for the entire Eastern Christianity, ensure that individual bishops follow the church's discipline within their own dioceses, hear appeals, and discipline bishops. Perhaps such a model of authority could make possible pan-Orthodox synodality and, if given to the Pope in a united Church, even universal synodality.

National interests, corroborated with the autocephaly of national churches that are administratively independent from one another and thus able to refuse

81. Brian E. Daley, "The Meaning and Exercise of 'Primacies of Honor' in the Early Church," in *Primacy in the Church: The Office of Primate and the Authority of Councils. Vol. 1: Historical and Theological Perspectives*, ed. John Chryssavgis (Yonkers, NY: St. Vladimir's Seminary Press, 2016), 37, 49–50. Brian E. Daley, "Position and Patronage in the Early Church: The Original Meaning of 'Primacy of Honour'," *Journal of Theological Studies* 44, no. 2 (1993): 529–53.

82. Zizioulas, "Primacy in the Church," 123.

83. Zizioulas, "Primacy in the Church," 122. Zizioulas, *Lectures in Christian Dogmatics*, 144–45.

to attend a pan-Orthodox council are the main reasons why pan-Orthodox synodality is so difficult today. It seems that one way out of this impasse is to ascribe a real primacy to a bishop who does not serve the interests of any state and to earnestly question Orthodoxy's understanding of the relationship between Church and nationality—the themes of the next chapter.

EIGHT

Nationality

Every foreign land is to them a fatherland,
and every fatherland a foreign land.

LETTER TO DIOGNETUS[1]

The epigraph of this chapter, written in the second century, illustrates quite well the bimillennial relationship between Church and nation. On the one hand, it affirms the love that Christians have for the lands in which they dwell; they do not need to renounce citizenship duties, respect for laws, and patriotism. On the other hand, it puts Christian identity above national identity since Christians are supposed to draw their distinctiveness from outside this world. Nationality is both an opportunity and a challenge for Orthodoxy. When the Church acts for living the Kingdom of God in its specific cultural, sociological, and national context, then the Church exists *for* the world. But Orthodoxy is also currently experiencing an unprecedented fragmentation due to the priority that national identity has over Orthodox unity. When serving the interests of the nation, the Church becomes *of* the world.

The *earliest Christians* lived with the expectation of Christ's imminent second coming and thus the end of this world, focusing almost exclusively on immediate problems and the Kingdom to come. They did not attempt to change social institutions (including problematic ones such as slavery) or to place much value on patriotism: "For here we have no lasting city, but we seek the city that is to come" (Heb 13:14). As Christianity became more and more persecuted,

---

1. "Letter to Diognetus," in *The Apostolic Fathers* (Washington, DC: The Catholic University of America Press, 1947), #5, 359.

Christians also anticipated the victory of Christ the King over the kingdoms of this world: "the Lamb ... is Lord of lords and King of kings" (Rv 17:14, cf. 19:16), or "the kingdom of the world has become the kingdom of our Lord and of his Messiah, and he will reign forever and ever" (Rv 11:15).

Unmistakable here is the confession of Jesus as Lord, a term that had significant political connotations. The first century Roman Emperor Domitian, who ruthlessly persecuted the Church, took for himself the title "our Lord and our God," or "*dominus et deus noster*."[2] In contrast, Christians were confessing together with Thomas that the risen Christ is "My Lord and my God" (Jn 20:28). To illustrate the courage of early Christians, Helmut Thielicke imagined a twentieth-century equivalent in which someone would have shouted "Jesus is Führer" in the midst of a Nazi rally.[3] Displaying the same courage, in mid-second century, Polycarp of Smyrna refused to say "Caesar is Lord," to "swear by the genius of Caesar," or to "curse Christ." As the acts of his martyrdom show, "As the Proconsul urged him and said: 'Take the oath and I release you; revile Christ,' Polycarp said: 'Eighty-six years have I served Him, and He has done me no wrong. How can I blaspheme my King who has saved me?'"[4]

Clearly, early Christians confessed Jesus, and not the Emperor, as their Lord. In the late second century, Tertullian went so far as to write that emperors—even good ones, who are necessary for the world—cannot be Christians since their ruling office is incompatible with Christianity: "Caesars, too, would have believed in Christ ... if Christians could have been Caesars."[5] Clearly Tertullian could not have envisaged the possibility of a Christian Caesar. On the contrary, Christians were intensely persecuted by an Emperor for whom, however, they prayed.

In 313, Christians were given freedom by emperor Constantine, whom they considered a saint equal to the Apostles. Soon thereafter, in 380, emperor Theodosius I decreed Christianity as the official religion of the Empire. That is not to say that Christians subsequently lived in peace; their own Church officials or nominally Christian emperors persecuted them. After the fall of Constantinople in 1453, much of the East lived under Ottoman occupation, followed by the emergence of nation states with their accompanying autocephalous national

2. Suetonius, *Domitian*, 13.

3. See Geoffrey Wainwright, "The Holy Spirit, Witness, and Martyrdom," in *It Is the Spirit Who Gives Life: New Directions in Pneumatology*, ed. Radu Bordeianu (Washington, DC: The Catholic University of America Press, 2022), 29.

4. "The Martyrdom of St. Polycarp," in *The Apostolic Fathers*, Fathers of the Church (Washington DC: The Catholic University of America Press, 1947), #9, 155–56.

5. Tertullian, "Apology," 21:24, 66.

churches, two world wars, militant atheist communism, and then a newfound freedom. Needless to say, throughout all these eras, the relationship between Church and the nation fluctuated greatly, but a common thread became the rise of ethnophyletism, which theoretically all Orthodox churches condemn, but in practice they all perpetuate through various levels of symphonia and through overlapping jurisdictions in the so-called "diaspora." Orthodoxy is in a dire need to transcend national and ethnic fragmentations, while acknowledging that it will exist differently in different contexts, whether it is the faith of the majority population or the minority. All these historical and theological elements can lead to a Kingdom-centered model for Church-state relations, and they all represent the focus of the present chapter.

ETHNOPHYLETISM

In 1870, Sultan Abdulaziz established a Bulgarian Exarchate in Constantinople, and two years later, he granted the Bulgarian Orthodox Church its autocephaly. Enraged, the Ecumenical Patriarch convened a council in Constantinople in the same year, 1872. With the support of the Patriarchs of Alexandria, Antioch, and the Archbishop of Cyprus, the council did not accept a parallel jurisdiction for Bulgarians in the Ottoman Empire and condemned ethnophyletism, which sets ethnicity over the principle of territoriality. In other words, the ecclesial autocephaly of a certain territory should not be granted on the basis of ethnic identity.[6]

The exact opposite happened both before and after the council of 1872, when new nation-states emerged, gaining their independence from the Ottoman Empire.[7] The newly independent state leaders then consolidated their independence by requesting the Patriarchate of Constantinople to grant autocephaly to the Orthodox churches within their new borders. The Ecumenical Patriarchate obliged. Thus emerged between 1850 and 1945 the Greek, Serbian, Romanian, Bulgarian, and Albanian autocephalous churches, established at the initiative of secular authorities, on grounds of ethnicity and nationality,[8] contrary to Constantinople's condemnation of ethnophyletism.

6. Accusing the Bulgarian Church of *phyletismos* (literally translated as "tribalism"), the council defined *phyletism* as bringing "national distinctions" into the Church and causing "controversies on ethnic grounds." Hovorun, *Political Orthodoxies*, 188.

7. Jean-Jacques Rousseau (1712–1778) first introduced the term nation in its modern understanding in his "Plan for the Constitution for Corsica" (1765). See Hovorun, *Political Orthodoxies*, 150.

8. The Serbian Orthodox Church first received its autocephaly in the thirteenth century but lost it

Despite its complexities, ethnophyletism represents, at its core, the favoring of ethnic character over Orthodox identity. It continues to have negative effects today, hence the 2016 Council of Crete's *Encyclical* recognized the authority of the 1872 Council of Constantinople that condemned "ethnophyletism as an ecclesiological heresy."[9] The most striking manifestation of this "ecclesiological heresy" is the existence of overlapping jurisdictions in the so-called "diaspora," where various national churches have established parallel structures based on ethnic and—sometimes within the same ethnicity—political grounds. Parallel jurisdictions exist even in traditionally Orthodox countries, as is the case of the Republic of Moldova—a territory that has ecclesial structures under the Patriarchates of Romania and Moscow. It is indeed an ecclesiological anomaly to assume that a bishop of a certain nationality cannot minister to Orthodox faithful of another nationality within his territory; this type of thinking is nothing more than a pretext for prioritizing national character over Orthodox identity.

Besides autocephaly and parallel jurisdictions, ethnophyletism is also perpetuated by the veiling of national pride in religious terms. In this sense, Kalaitzidis writes that

> [the] ideology of "National Orthodoxy"—as well as the analogous theories and mythologies of the Greeks as the "new chosen people of God", "Holy Russia" being the "Third Rome", the Slavophile movement, the medieval Christian kingdom of Serbia, the "Serbian people as the servant people of God", Antiochian uniqueness and Arabhood, the Latin character of Romanian Orthodoxy, etc.—do nothing but intensify the sense of geographical conditioning and isolation, our collective cultural narcissism and intellectual self-sufficiency, while also promoting a metaphysical essentialist view of an ethno-cultural identity that is unsusceptible to change within time and history, and which has come to be equated with the identity of the church.[10]

In this enthnophyletic vein, the nation is sacralized, to the expense of the faith that becomes insufficient to overcome national fragmentation. A return

during the Ottoman occupation; the granting of autocephaly in the nineteenth century is in fact its reinstatement. Moreover, the autocephaly of the Bulgarian Church was first unlawfully granted by the Sultan before the emergence of the independent Bulgarian state. Constantinople granted the autocephaly only in 1945, again at the insistence of secular authorities. Joint Orthodox-Catholic Working Group, "Serving Communion," 10.18–19.

9. *Encyclical* I.3 in Council of Crete, *Official Documents*.

10. Pantelis Kalaitzidis, "Church and State in the Orthodox World: From the Byzantine 'Symphonia' and Nationalized Orthodoxy, to the Need of Witnessing the Word of God in a Pluralistic Society," in *Religioni, Libertà, Potere*, ed. Emanuela Fogliadini (Milano: Vita e Pensiero, 2014), 73.

to first-century Christian consciousness is imperative—the time when Christianity was separating from the ethnic character of Judaism to include all nations and thus become the Israel of God, or "a chosen race, a royal priesthood, a holy nation, God's own people ... Once you were not a people, but now you are God's people" (1 Peter 2:9–10). Christianity is indeed a holy nation that gathers those who were previously separated in nations, but now are God's own people, above any national identity.

AUTOCEPHALY

The system of autocephaly is intrinsically related to national identity, and Orthodox churches are firmly allegiant to their nations. From an ecclesiastical point of view, it does not have to be so. Autocephaly simply means "having one's own head," in the sense that a church is free to elect its own head and to lead itself in all practical aspects of ecclesial life. Having a lesser degree of independence, an autonomous church receives the Holy Myron from its mother Church, which also approves its election of primates.[11] These ecclesiological structures do not have to align with nation-states, as it was not the case throughout most Christian history.

The ancient prerogative of all bishops in a province to consecrate new bishops and to gather in regional synods comes closest to today's understanding of autocephaly. That is the sense in which the third Ecumenical Council (431) recognized the autocephaly of the Church of Cyprus, and certainly not in the sense that Cyprus was a national church—an impossibility at that time in history.[12]

Having said this, the Church did not remain indifferent to the nation (understood not in its modern sense, but closer to ethnicity), especially in times of suffering. During the Ottoman occupation, the Orthodox Church was responsible not only for the care of the souls and bodies of its faithful, but also for saving the Orthodox "nation" (the *millet*) and the Greek culture from absorption into a Muslim, Turkish empire. In times of great peril, the Church

11. The Orthodox Church is a family of fourteen universally recognized autocephalous churches, nine of which are known as Patriarchates, and the autonomous churches of Sinai and Finland. Other churches are recognized are autocephalous or autonomous by some churches, but not by all.

12. Pantelis Kalaitzidis, "Ecclesiology and Globalization: In Search of an Ecclesiological Paradigm in the Era of Globalization (After the Previous Paradigms of the Local, Imperial, and National)," *St. Vladimir's Theological Quarterly* 57, no. 3–4 (2013): 498–99. Alexander Schmemann, *Church, World, Mission: Reflections on Orthodoxy and the West* (Crestwood, NY: St. Vladimir's Seminary Press, 1979), 92.

stood tall before the Sultan, for the survival and basic rights of the Christian nation. Those were times that Kalaitzidis rightly describes as "moments of exceptional historical urgency and need."[13] *The relationship between the nation and the Church was obviously positive in this case.* Elsewhere in the East, the Church took upon itself the duty to create a local culture by giving birth to a language in which people prayed and read the Scriptures, a local architecture, customs, literature, music, and so on. The Church's positive influence on culture cannot be underestimated.

The newfound *secular duties of the Orthodox Church* intensified exponentially with the gradual emergence of nation states, culminating with the liberation of most of the Orthodox East from the Ottoman Empire in the nineteenth century. As Schmemann explains,

> there emerged the idea of a *Christian nation*—with a national vocation, a kind of corporate "identity" before God. What is important for us here is that only at this stage in the history of the Eastern Church there appeared the notion of "autocephaly"—which, if not in its origin […], at least in its application, is a product not of ecclesiology, but of a *national* phenomenon…. "Autocephaly," i.e., ecclesiastical independence, becomes thus the very basis of national and political independence, the status-symbol of a new "Christian nation."[14]

Schmemann suggests here that the newly emerged independent nations have used religious structures to solidify their identity, as for example in the sixteenth century, when the Russian Church played almost no part in the process that led to its autocephaly; the process was led almost entirely by secular authorities.[15] That is not to say that churches were simply highjacked against their will. Both hierarchy and faithful already saw themselves as having a responsibility for their nation and saw the role of the state not as separate, but as intrinsically related to the role of the Church. Perhaps this inter-relation between the state and the Church reached its climax when Archbishop Makarios III, after having served ten years as the primate of Church of Cyprus, also became the first president of the nation, thus being the head of both

13. Kalaitzidis, "Church and State," 42.

14. Schmemann, *Church, World, Mission,* 98.

15. Schmemann, *Church, World, Mission,* 99. For the similarity between Orthodox experiences in Russia and Catholic experiences in France as they both shaped the later Orthodox view autocephaly as undermining intra-Orthodox unity and Orthodox-Catholic unity, see Adam A.J. DeVille, "Sovereignty, Politics, and the Church: Joseph de Maistre's Legacy for Catholic and Orthodox Ecclesiology," *Pro Ecclesia* 24, no. 3 (2015): 366–89.

Church and state from 1960 until 1977, being subjected to four assassination attempts and a coup d'état. In Cyprus as well as in the rest of the Orthodox world, to protect the nation was to protect the Church and, vice versa, to protect the Church was to protect the nation.

One might argue that the Church has the duty to follow secular structures, based on canon 17 of the fourth ecumenical council and canon 38 of the Quinisext council in Trullo, both of which prescribe that ecclesial and political structures should coincide. Kalaitzidis, however, argues that these norms do not automatically link ecclesial and political structures, but are rather "the seeds of what could be considered an early form of contextuality."[16] Without denying the merit of patriotism and love for country, one also has to question the uncritical association between national and ecclesiastical identities. After the fall of communism, the Orthodox East has experienced a new wave of emerging nations such as Montenegro and Ukraine. New Orthodox ecclesial structures that reinforce political independence have emerged in all these contexts. Their canonicity is intensely disputed for obvious political reasons and because worldwide Orthodoxy has not come an agreement regarding who grants autocephaly; Constantinople claims it is the only one who can do so, while Moscow has granted autocephaly to other churches, such as the OCA.

The practical result of the emergence of new Church structures along newly developed national lines is not so much a positive affirmation of patriotism and love for country, as a fragmentation of Orthodoxy that creates separation and even eucharistic schism. The level of intra-Orthodox disunity took a tragically different meaning in 2022, with the invasion of Ukraine by Russian armies that had the explicit support of the Moscow Patriarchate. Several autocephalous churches have condemned this fratricide, while others issued vague statements that called for the cessation of violence. Up until this writing, the Patriarch of Moscow continues to bless the invasion, despite the loss of life of his own spiritual children (numerous Ukrainians are under his jurisdiction) at the hands of his spiritual children, namely Russian soldiers. This fratricide has disastrous consequences regarding the loss of human life, property, ecclesial and cultural monuments, displacement of populations, and intra-Orthodox relations.

If autocephaly was intended to ensure each national church's ability to decide for itself in internal administrative matters, the above considerations about fragmentation prove that autocephaly soon devolved into what Nicolas Lossky calls, *"autocephalism,"* defined as the isolation and even competition of

16. Kalaitzidis, "Ecclesiology and Globalization," 495.

autocephalous churches based on national interests.[17] Nicolas Lossky criticizes
the resulting "autocephalist" ecclesiology, which regards the primate as "something of a 'super-bishop' who has more power than any of his brothers in the
episcopate," within the territory of the autocephalous church, which results at
the level of worldwide Orthodoxy into a "multiplied papism."[18]

Considering that the national church—and not the local diocese—is fully
Church and thus independent, autocephalist ecclesiology is a departure from
the eucharistic ecclesiology of the early Church. Theologically speaking, eucharistic ecclesiology remains the Orthodox ideal—an ideal that Orthodox observers at the Second Vatican Council enthusiastically advocated as an antidote
to Roman primacy. But they were also painfully aware of the practical reality
in the East, which remains fragmented on national grounds. As one of these
observes, Nikos Nissiotis, remarks,

> With no single governing head, each autocephalous Church being clothed
> with juridical authority, we tend to lose even the slightest, the most elemen-
> tary kind of coordination and initiative. Our eucharistic ecclesiology centred
> on the local Church and her sacraments saves us from replacing the catholic
> by a universalistic conception of the Church, but at the same time we risk be-
> coming the victims of our ambitions; these ambitions may spring from pride
> in the glorious past of one particular Church or in the power of a Church
> seeking to impose its will on the others, or may use the Orthodox tradition
> to maintain the national inheritance in the countries of the diaspora.[19]

Perhaps the nationalistic ills that Nissiotis writes about reached their peak
with the later emergence of the concept of *canonical territory*. Metropolitan Hilarion Alfeyev, the chairman of the Department of External Church Relations
of the Moscow Patriarchate, writes about the principle of "cultural canonical
territory" in "traditionally Orthodox countries": "This principle assumes that
the entire population of a state, which by its cultural roots belongs to the Orthodox tradition but which has lost its connection with the faith of its ancestors due to historical circumstances, is the potential flock of the local Orthodox
Church."[20]

17. Lossky, "Conciliarity-Primacy in a Russian Orthodox Perspective," 127–35. Similarly, Zizioulas
laments the "infiltration of the Church by nationalism and sometimes ethnophyletism. The idea of autocephaly has become autocephalism, that is, using the Church to serve national or phyletic interests." John
D. Zizioulas, "The Orthodox Church and the Third Millennium," *Sourozh* 81, no. August (2000): 22–23.
18. Lossky, "Conciliarity-Primacy in a Russian Orthodox Perspective," 129–30.
19. Nissiotis, "The Main Ecclesiological Problem," 60.
20. Bishop Hilarion Alfeyev, *Orthodox Christianity: The History and Canonical Structure of the Orthodox*

On the one hand, Alfeyev's remarks are justified; I remember vividly how, shortly after the 1989 Revolution in Romania, when the Orthodox Church was re-emerging after decades of communist persecution, evangelical missionaries were proselytizing Romanian Orthodox faithful, usually snatching the most pious believers instead of bringing to Christ those who did not believe. The Romanian Orthodox Church should have been allowed to first recover and claim the faithful on its territory, and then evangelical pastors could have done missions in the proper sense of the word.

On the other hand, the principle of canonical territory is a veiled tool of domination and a pretext for the repression of religious minorities. DeVille argues that the notions of canonical territory and ecclesial sovereignty have been surpassed by the "facts on the ground," as reflected in the Russian Orthodox Church's relationship with Ukraine, for example. While the Moscow Patriarchate considers that the boundaries of canonical territory should coincide with the boundaries of their corresponding sovereign state, the same Patriarchate expands its presence well beyond the boundaries of the Russian sovereign state, into Ukraine. The Moscow Patriarchate considers its presence in a different country as justified based on its view that Ukraine is part of the so-called *Russky mir* (the Russian world that is under the Moscow Patriarchate and used to be under the Soviet Union) and thus sees the Ukrainian Greek-Catholic presence in Ukraine as an intrusion in their canonical territory. That is not to say, however, that the principle of canonical territory is mutually binding. Moscow does not refrain from having a presence in Italy, for example, presumably the canonical territory of the Catholic Church.[21]

In concluding this section, far from arguing against the principle of autocephaly, I addressed the fragmented nature of world-wide Orthodoxy today due to the infusion of national identity in Church life via autocephalism, and I proposed the disassociation of autocephaly and nation-states. Such a proposal hearkens back to the earliest centuries of Christianity, before the Church's association with the empire in the fourth century, as well as the earliest instances of autocephaly afterward.

Church, vol. 1 (Yonkers, NY: St. Vladimir's Seminary Press, 2011), 341. For a contrasting view, see Kalaitzidis, "Church and State," 46–52.

21. DeVille, "Sovereignty, Politics, and the Church," 366–89.

SYMPHONIA

The Byzantine concept of *symphonia* or *synallelia* signifies the close relationship between Church and Empire. As Paul Ladouceur defines it,

> *symphonia* is characterized by the existence of two autonomous but inter-related sources of authority, the church and the empire. While each has its proper sphere and mode of activity, they overlap and collaborate for the furtherance of the Gospel and the Kingdom, yet without merging one with the other. Neither is subordinate to the other; the church does not absorb the state, nor the state the church. Historically this ideal situation was never fully achieved and was constantly put to the test, both in the Byzantium and later in the Russian Empire.[22]

FIG. 4

An illustrative symbol of *symphonia* is the double headed eagle: to the eagle that was the symbol of the Roman Empire headed by the emperor, it adds another head, namely the Patriarch of Constantinople. If one were to look cyn-ically (although quite realistically) at the multi-centennial history of the rela-tionship between the Byzantine emperor and the Church, one might point out that the two heads are looking in opposite directions, inflicting no small suf-fering about their common body—simultaneously citizens of the Empire and members of the Church. But at its best, *symphonia* was meant to protect the same body of citizens and faithful against dangers coming from all directions

---

22. Paul Ladouceur, *Modern Orthodox Theology: Behold, I Make All Things New* (New York: T&T Clark, 2019), 353.

both spiritual and material, and to have two heads working in harmony for the benefit of their common body. The presupposition was double: the emperor wants what is good for the Church and the Church supports the interests of the earthly empire (*basileia*), which are in conformity with the values of the heavenly Kingdom (*basileia*).

According to Eusebius of Caesarea, Constantine the Great was the ideal (or perhaps idealized) model of Byzantine symphonia, describing the emperor as an icon of the "heavenly sovereignty" who "frames his earthly government according to the pattern of the divine original" in "conformity to the monarchy of God."[23] Expressing the same socio-ecclesial ideal, Justinian writes in his famous Sixth *Novella*:

> There are two greatest gifts which God, in his love for man, has granted from on high: the priesthood and the imperial dignity. The first serves divine things, the second directs and administers human affairs; both, however, proceed from the same origin and adorn the life of mankind. Hence, nothing should be such a source of care to the emperors as the dignity of the priests, since it is for the [imperial] welfare that they constantly implore God. For if the priesthood is in every way free from blame and possesses access to God, and if the emperors administer equitably and judiciously the state entrusted to their care, general harmony (*symphonia*) will result, and whatever is beneficial will be bestowed upon the human race.[24]

John Meyendorff provides a threefold *critique of this symphonic ideal*. First, this dream of Byzantium as a universal Christian civilization, in which society is under the Christ-centered authority of both emperor and the Church, represents a combination of Roman and Christian universalisms. Second, it is based on the presupposition that all human activities are God-centered. As long as Christianity and Empire collided, this belief applied only to the eschaton and its anticipation in the sacraments. But with the "conversion" (scare quotes in Meyendorff's original) of Constantine the Great, this goal appeared reachable in history, without taking in consideration the fallen character of humanity.[25] And third, Meyendorff points out that Justinian embraced a "realized

23. Eusebius of Caesarea, "A Speech for the Thirtieth Anniversary of Constantine Accession," quoted in Nathaniel Wood and Aristotle Papanikolaou, "Orthodox Christianity and Political Theology: Thinking Beyond Empire," in *T&T Clark Handbook of Poltical Theology*, ed. Rubén Rosario Rodríguez (New York: T&T Clark, 2020), 339.

24. Quoted in John Meyendorff, *Byzantine Theology: Historical Trends and Doctrinal Themes* (New York: Fordham University Press, 1983), 213.

25. Aristotle Papanikolaou, *The Mystical as Political: Democracy and Non-Radical Orthodoxy* (Notre Dame, IN: University of Notre Dame Press, 2012), 55–86.

eschatology" that considered the Empire as the place where there is symphony between divine things and human affairs, based on the union between the divine and human natures in the Incarnation. The ideal humanity of Christ was manifested in the Byzantine Empire in which the unique person of Christ is the source of both imperial and ecclesial authority. Meyendorff does not mince words: he writes about "the fundamental mistake of this approach" being the belief that the Kingdom of God has come with power and is being manifested in the Byzantine Empire.[26] "There lies the tragedy of the Byzantine system: it assumed that the state, as such, could become intrinsically Christian."[27] In Byzantium, Eastern Christianity has come a long way from Tertullian, who laughed at the thought of Caesars being Christians and Christians being Caesars.[28]

To better understand the Byzantine ideal of *symphonia*, several *nuanced clarifications* are necessary. First, the Church's liturgical support for the emperor is not a fourth-century capitulation, but a much older custom. Rom 13:1–7 has often been used (and abused) to illustrate the duty to respect secular authorities: "Let every person be subject to the governing authorities; for there is no authority except from God, and those authorities that exist have been instituted by God" (Rom 13:1). Shortly thereafter, Tertullian argued that the Rome should not persecute Christians, since they earnestly pray for the emperor to the true God, as opposed to heathens who do not earnestly pray and who worship false gods: "Looking up to Him, we Christians ... constantly beseech Him on behalf of all emperors. We ask for them long life, undisturbed power, security at home, brave armies, a faithful Senate, an upright people, a peaceful world, and everything for which a man or a Caesar prays."[29] Moreover, Christians pray for the delay of the second coming of Christ, thus lending an aid to the longer duration of the Roman Empire.[30]

Second, the history of the Byzantine Empire does not represent a continuous submission of the Church to imperial power. On the contrary, during his trial, St. Maximus the Confessor made it clear that he blamed the emperor for

---

26. Kalaitzidis analyzes various liturgical hymns, Eusebius of Caesarea's works *Ecclesiastical History* and the *Life of Constantine*, and Justinian's *Novellae*. Kalaitzidis concludes that these lose the tension between the "already" and the "not yet" of the Kingdom, fully embracing a realized eschatology in their social order. Hence, "the Byzantines believed that their state and their society were the materialization of the kingdom of God on earth." Kalaitzidis, "Church and State," 68–70, here at 68.

27. Meyendorff, *Byzantine Theology*, 213–14.

28. Tertullian, "Apology," 21:24, 66.

29. Tertullian, "Apology," 30:4, 86.

30. Tertullian, "Apology," 32:1, 88. See also: "We pray, also, for the emperors, for their ministers and those in power, that their reign may continue, that the state may be at peace, and that the end of the world may be postponed." Tertullian, "Apology," 39:2, 98.

promulgating "The Typos," an act that legislated the heresies of monothelism and monoergism. Even when pressed about the Greek heritage that he shares with the emperor (as opposed to the faith of the Latins) and that the Church prays for the emperor, Maximus still gave priority to the purity of faith over the political order. His case is not simply an opposition between the Church and the Empire, since the emperor was in agreement with the Patriarch and the rest of the institutional church; it was rather an opposition between true faith and power, the latter having imperial, hierarchical, ethnic, and cultural overtones. *Symphonia* would again be challenged during the iconoclastic crisis, when the iconophile party represented by St. Theodore the Stoudite—then abbot of the monastery of Stoudios in the capital of the Empire—had no hesitation in telling Leo, "Your responsibility, Emperor, is with affairs of state and military matters. Give your mind to these and leave the Church to its pastors and teachers." That is why MacCulloch concludes, "the Church's reverence for the emperor remained conditional, even in Constantinople."[31] To give one more example from the Russian tradition, the sixteenth-century saints Philip Metropolitan of Moscow and Basil the Blessed "Fool in Christ" both protested Tsar Ivan the Terrible's bloodshed and injustices. As a result, St. Philip was martyred. St. Basil had already taken upon himself the "martyrdom" of being a "fool in Christ,"[32] and in a sense conquered the Tsar at his death, when the Tsar was one of his pallbearers.

Third, the idealized model of Byzantine *symphonia* continued to be invoked centuries after the fall of the Byzantine Empire in 1453, up until today. One such instance was communist Romania. Here I am not passing judgment on those who wrote in support of the persecuting atheist regimes that put an irresistible pressure upon them; this is simply an example of the survival of the *symphonia* model. As Ladouceur shows, in an attempt to ingratiate themselves to communist authorities and to ensure the survival of religion, the leaders of the Romanian Orthodox Church promoted the doctrine of "social apostolate." On the surface, this doctrine affirmed the Church's support for the Romanian state in its pursuit of peace, justice and other similar goals. Deep down, the social apostolate was closely tied with Romanian nationalism, clothed in a religious garment. Church leaders and theologians affirmed the Church's allegiance and obedience to both God and State, based on the New Testament and Church Fathers such as Origen, Tertullian, Gregory of Nazianzus, John

31. MacCulloch, *Christianity*, 451.
32. Ware, *The Orthodox Church*, 108.

Chrysostom, Augustine, Ambrose of Milan, Isidore of Pelusium and Maximus the Confessor. Leading Romanian hierarchs and theologians defended the doctrine of "social apostolate" as a continuation of the venerable tradition of *symphonia* as practiced both in the Byzantine Empire and in the Muscovy Kingdom.[33] Their example is by no means the exception, but rather the rule behind the Iron Curtain.

After the fall of communism, as Wood and Papanikolaou show, the principle of *symphonia* became the means "to provide a theological justification for autocracy against alternatives, including democracy. It has imbued Orthodox political thought with a predominantly 'royalist' orientation."[34] This royalist orientation of some Orthodox political theologies, as well as their negative reaction to democracy and human rights, represent pseudo-theological justifications to support autocratic leaders who are portrayed as defenders of so-called traditional moral values. They attempt to soothe the consciences of the faithful who are willing to overlook the sins of their secular leaders in exchange for the state's favoring of Orthodox structures and morals, although the latter are sometimes defined in questionable ways. Such an attitude is not only antithetical to the Church's calling to be prophetic and to conform itself to the Kingdom of God, it is also highly detrimental to the Church itself. In many majority-Orthodox countries, political regimes have extremely low approval ratings. The Church hurts itself by associating with these political regimes in exchange for ephemeral favors, attracting passionate criticisms and causing some to leave the Church. Secularization is not so much a "Western import," as it is the consequence of the East's allegiance with political powers.[35] It is most interesting to see how the nones in secular societies are not organized, but they create a common voice against Church structures. Who is organizing them? Sadly, the Church itself. As stated earlier, the second most important reason for which "nones" leave the Church is that they dislike organized religion. Under this umbrella fall "anti-institutional religion; religion focuses on power/politics, and religion causes conflict."[36]

33. Ladouceur, *Modern Orthodox Theology*, 162–65.
34. Wood and Papanikolaou, "Orthodox Christianity and Political Theology," 339. Ladouceur makes similar claims in regard to contemporary Russia in Ladouceur, *Modern Orthodox Theology*, 162–65.
35. Hovorun makes the following important distinctions: "*Secularism* is an ideology and a political agenda that ostracizes religion from the public square with the ultimate goal of exterminating religion altogether. This ideology is usually oppressive to religion. *Secular* describes the character of a political, social, or ecclesial space. It can be neutral or even beneficial for the church. Finally, *secularization* is an objective social or political process that leads to gradual abandonment of different social domains by religion." Hovorun, *Political Orthodoxies*, 14–15.
36. Pew Center, *Choosing New Church*, 29.

"Church" in this context does not mean parish life and ordinary faithful. The revival of the faith in Eastern Europe and the piety of the faithful remain central to what it means to be "Church" in that context. Rather, this term means here Church officials and ecclesial structures. In Romania, for example, the state is unable to provide decent wages and pensions, adequate hospitals and schools. At the same time, the government supports financially the majority of the cost of Orthodox priests' salaries and building projects of significant proportions, such as the cathedral dedicated to the Salvation of the Nation. In reaction, many Romanians protested with the chant, "hospitals, not cathedrals" (which rhymes in Romanian: *spitale, nu catedrale*). This choice is disingenuous since, first of all, the people do not trust the government to spend that money on hospitals and second, the Church helps many people in need with the money that it receives from the state. Still, the Church becomes a subject of criticism. Communist persecution was unable to detract the people from the faith. Decades after the 1989 Revolution, less than 0.01% of Romanians identified as atheists. As Tertullian wrote, the blood of the martyrs became the seed of Christianity. But the Church's credibility suffered greatly after the Revolution when it remained silent against the corruption and sinfulness of political powers in exchange for financial gain, privileges over other faiths, and political influence; in other words, power.

Herein lies *the crux of the problem: power*. The Church needs authority, not power. The more the Church uses the power of the state, the less moral authority it has. By using the means of this world, the Church becomes secular—of this world. And in this world, the lords use their power over the people. No matter who has the power, they will use it: persecuting Roman emperors, atheists like Stalin,[37] benevolent emperors like Constantine, or monothelite and iconoclast Patriarchs. Absolute power corrupts absolutely.

Has there ever been a time in history when Orthodoxy has turned a blind eye to the injustice of secular powers in exchange for worldly favors and the benefits have outweighed the costs? I do not think so. On the contrary, ecclesial structures that support autocratic states lose their moral authority, credibility, and do not fulfill their prophetic calling to stand up for justice and speak truth to power. *Symphonia* has done more damage to the Church from within than Roman, Ottoman, and communist persecutions have from without. The

---

37. Stalin created a ruthless structure of violence, especially directed against religion. Being responsible for the Holodomor (the massive famine in the early 1930s) and the Gulag (concentration camps), according to the estimation of Rudolf Rummel, Stalin murdered around 62 million of his own people. Hovorun, *Political Orthodoxies*, 74.

Church has moral authority when it does not have political power. For anything in between, moral authority and political power are indirectly proportional: one rises as the other falls.

"DIASPORAS": OVERLAPPING JURISDICTIONS

As Orthodoxy expanded beyond the borders of traditionally-Orthodox countries, its faithful emigrated primarily Westwards, accompanied by their national ideals. Besides constructive manifestations of ethnicity, they also amplified the negative effects of ethnophyletism, the fragmentation of autocephalism, and the symphonic understanding of national and ecclesial identities. It seems that the only way in which the Church will remain an icon of the Kingdom of God and not an icon of the kingdoms of this world is to decouple Orthodox identity from national identity. This de-coupling will be achieved when Orthodoxy achieves jurisdictional unity in the so-called "diaspora," replacing the current system of *overlapping jurisdictions*—a system that has a precedent in the seventh century.

In 688, the island of Cyprus became a territory under the shared administration of the Byzantine and Ottoman empires. The Orthodox population of the island relocated to Artake, near Cyzicus, together with their ecclesial administration under the leadership of Archbishop John I. There already existed an Eastern bishop of Cyzicus, so John's Cypriot Church became a parallel jurisdiction. This unusual situation was ratified at the Quinisext Council, whose 39th canon even allowed the Cypriot population to retain their autocephaly granted at the third ecumenical council. After less than a decade in Cyzicus, the Cypriot population returned to their island, and thus the existence of parallel jurisdictions came to an end. Clearly, such a short-lived exceptional situation forced by foreign invasions cannot be considered normative, even though the Quinisext Council acknowledged it.

Today, however, parallel jurisdictions are ingrained in the life of the Orthodox Church especially in the "diaspora," but also in majority Orthodox countries, such as the Republic of Moldova and Ukraine. In some Western European countries, Orthodox parishes exist for faithful who relocated temporarily for work and plan on returning to their homelands. Such parishes have a pronounced ethnic character, which poses a significant challenge to second-generation immigrants, who are less familiar with the language and culture of their country of origin than their parents. As more and more families decide not to return to their countries of origin, first- and especially second-generation immigrants long for a local, rather than an ethnic church.[38] That is especially the case in the United States, where immigration from the East has largely stopped decades ago.

Most of our discussion focuses on the North American context, where there already exists an Orthodox Church in America that received its autocephaly from the Moscow Patriarchate in 1970, and where the largest jurisdictions are made up of converts and second, third, and fourth generations Orthodox. On the one hand, U.S. Orthodoxy could be labeled, diaspora, without quotation marks. Various jurisdictions still identify by their nationality (Greek, Serbian, etc.), they have only recently developed church legislation specific to their American context, they all use different translations of liturgical texts with their specific variations regarding the *typikon*, and their bishops are not part of the same synod. Consequently, many resources are squandered by creating parallel structures: each jurisdiction has its own youth camp, liturgical texts, youth programs, online presence, etc., which could all be combined into one flexible pool of resources. Moreover, even though American Orthodoxy has the largest number of converts of all Orthodox churches, it remains highly Eurocentric; as a recent Pew Research study shows, 64% of American Orthodox Christians are either immigrants (49%) or children of immigrants (23%), making Orthodoxy the denomination with the highest such shares in the U.S.[39]

On the other hand, many—including this first-generation immigrant author whose children grew up in American parishes—find the title "diaspora" offensive. America is their homeland and the Orthodoxy that they experience in their parishes is not an import from a different culture, or an island of ethnicity; it is an icon of the Kingdom of God. American Orthodoxy has reached the level of a local church in many regards: it produced an Orthodox Study Bible, it coordinates college ministries with a very successful OCF, it has a tremendous

38. Marco Guglielmi points out important differences between the two main paradigms of the Orthodox diasporas (note the plural), namely North America and Western, Central, and Northern Europe, where the North American Orthodox communities tend to be more hybridized in their local environment. As Orthodox communities discover their new "glocal" identity, which blends global common traits and local features, Guglielmi hopes that diasporic churches would have an increasingly significant export of their pastoral approaches back to the mother churches, an export that is currently minimal, but could include a greater emphasis on social work and a reshaping of priestly ministry more focused on service. (Marco Guglielmi, *The Romanian Orthodox Diaspora in Italy: Eastern Orthodoxy in a Western European Country* (Cham, Switzerland: Palgrave Macmillan, 2022), 18, 112–25.) I would add to this list a greater lay involvement in the life (including leadership) of the parish, a greater sense of community among parishioners, and a more pronounced ecumenical openness, characteristic of Orthodox communities that are in the minority.

39. Pew Center, *Orthodox Christianity*, 25.

charitable impact in the U.S. and throughout the world through IOCC, and coordinates some of the most significant missionary efforts in world-wide Orthodoxy through OCMC. Especially the latter is a sure sign of ecclesial maturity: what started as a mission Church, now does its own missions. Hence, the title of the section, "diasporas," is between quotation marks.

A significant obstacle in the way of a united American Orthodox Church is the existence of parallel ethnic jurisdictions. Responding to the Chambésy mandate "to organize all the Orthodox faithful of every jurisdiction in the Region on a canonical basis,"[40] the Committee for Canonical Regional Planning of the U.S. Assembly of Canonical Bishops presented a proposal at its 2013 Assembly. The proposal was organized around two major principles: "one bishop in the same place and the concern to address the pastoral needs of Orthodox living in the region, including the diversity of national traditions."[41] It called for the establishment of ecclesiastical provinces and ethnic vicariates based on a thorough study of the membership, ethnicity, and financial resources of parishes, maintaining the number of canonical bishops to the current level. To the disappointment of the majority of participants, the representatives of the Bulgarian Orthodox Church and of ROCOR considered that the present situations of parallel jurisdictions is canonical as attested in their opinion by canon 39 of the Quinisext council, an argument already rejected above. Moreover, they argued that mother churches are justified in their desire to maintain a jurisdictional presence in the U.S., in order to provide pastoral care for their faithful. Severing ties with mother churches would be, in their estimation, "a matter of gravest spiritual peril to the souls of all our flocks in these lands."[42]

Because the Assembly of Bishops works on the principle of unanimity, it was unable—as were all other assemblies around the world—to fulfill their mandate to officially propose to the Council of Crete a viable model of Orthodox unity in the "diaspora." But the work already done should not be forgotten. It is viable to put each region under the jurisdiction of one bishop with several ethnic vicariates coordinated by priests, and assume that a bishop of a certain ethnic heritage can minister to faithful of other ethnicities, respecting their identity, customs, and traditions. If some jurisdictions (who have an infinitesimal number of faithful compared to the majority) refuse to join in the process

40. Article 5.e of the fourth Pre-Conciliar Pan-Orthodox Conference in Chambésy.

41. 2014 Report of the Committee for Canonical Regional Planning http://www.assemblyofbishops.org/committees/regionalplanning/committee-for-canonical-regional-planning-2014-annual-report

42. 2014 Report. See also the January 15, 2014 letter of Archbishop Kyrill (ROCOR) to Archbishop Demetrios (GOA and presiding bishop of the Assembly) at https://www.synod.com/synod/eng2014/20140115_ensynodletterarchbpdemetrios.html

of unification, they should not be allowed to derail the union of Orthodoxy, abusing the principle of unanimity as means of controlling the majority. These minority jurisdictions would remain in eucharistic communion with the rest of U.S. Orthodoxy, so that later on they might join the majority canonically. When realizing the importance of Orthodox unity and the realistic possibility of accomplishing it, places that no longer fit the description of "diaspora" such as the U.S. can no longer accept the current status quo of parallel jurisdictions, ethnophyletism, autocephalism, lack of synodality, and fragmentation.

TRANSCENDING ETHNIC BOUNDARIES
FOR EVANGELIZATION

National boundaries are not unsurpassable walls. Hopefully soon, Orthodox churches will find a balance between positive manifestations of national identity and the unifying power of their shared faith. The way to transcend national and ethnic boundaries is to regard Orthodox identity as of primary importance, surpassing all other differences. In this section I argue that a potential cure for nationalistic divisions is a stronger form of pan-Orthodox primacy, one that is devoid of allegiance to any specific ethnicity. Here, ethnicity is understood as belonging to a group classed according to common national and cultural identity.

It must be said from the outset that currently, Orthodoxy does not have a patriarchal see that is not tied to ethnicity. It is true that, while most Patriarchates are intrinsically allegiant to both a nation and a culture, some are not tied to the specific state in which they live: Constantinople to Turkey, Jerusalem to Israel, Alexandria to Egypt, and Antioch to Syria. And yet, each of them is greatly limited by the Greek (in the first three cases) or Arabic (in Antioch's case) cultures, even to the point of excluding other ethnicities from the upper echelons of leadership. Other times, some of these Patriarchates cave into the pressure exercised by other Patriarchates that are themselves aligned with the states in which they are located, thus becoming victims of the soft (or not so soft) power of other nations. These four Patriarchates are making efforts to surpass their ethnic limitations and there are encouraging signs in most of them, grounding Orthodox hopes of *a pan-Orthodox primate* who would not be suspected of having an ethnic, national, political, and dominating agenda. The Patriarchate of Constantinople is best positioned to exercise the role of Orthodox primacy, given its long history of Eastern primacy (especially after the schism with Rome) and its estranged relationship with the Turkish state, but only on the condition that Constantinople embraces other cultures besides Hellenism and its synod becomes reflective of world-wide Orthodoxy. Given the ecumenical character of the present book, it becomes natural to ask: how *could papal primacy serve as a model?*

Ecumenical dialogue is an opportunity to learn from one's partners and to enact beneficial changes. Having been involved in numerous ecumenical dialogues, at times I fear the contrary, namely that some participants agree to common statements only to the extent to which no change is required of their tradition and much change is required of the other. These low moments notwithstanding, dialogue is beneficial when one listens, understands, and changes. Orthodoxy has now an opportunity to learn from the lows and highs of papal primacy and, leaving aside the centuries of polemically defining Orthodoxy as the opposite of Catholicism, adapt to its own context some of the Catholic experiences.

Universal primacy is not automatically a cure for nationalistic fragmentation. As the greater part of two millennia of history show, the papacy was closely identified with a nation and with a culture; the overwhelming majority of popes were Italian and Catholics all around the world had to worship in Latin until mid-twentieth century. But since Vatican II, the Catholic Church has seen three popes of other nationalities and a proliferation of inculturation. These are positive manifestations of national and cultural neutrality of a papacy that resides in its own state, the Vatican. As mentioned repeatedly throughout this book, Rome still has long ways to go in the direction of inculturation and de-Latinization. But Catholic identity is now, unquestionably, the unifying factor among all Catholic churches, irrespective of their nationality. This priority of religious identity over ethnic differences is a model to follow in the East.

The East needs a primacy that is not determined by nation-states. This is the primacy of a local church, and not an individual. It cannot be a full and immediate jurisdiction, as when Constantinople claims authority over the "diaspora" based on canon 28 of the fourth ecumenical council, which granted Constantinople jurisdiction of the "barbarian lands," meaning territories outside the boundaries of the Roman Empire. Today Constantinople considers that "barbarian lands" include even territories of which the council was unaware, including North and South America, Australia, and East Asia.[43] Most other

---

43. https://www.patriarchate.org/-/territorial-jurisdiction-according-to-orthodox-canon-law-the-phenomenon-of-ethnophyletism-in-recent-yea-1

autocephalous churches do not recognize this claim and continue to establish parallel ethnic jurisdictions throughout the world.

The Roman-Catholic Church in the U.S. was in a similar situation up until the beginning of the twentieth century, when various waves of immigration brought to the new world Catholics of different ethnicities, often at odds with each other, both socially and ecclesiastically. Given Rome's authority, this situation of parallel ethnic jurisdictions ceased and now each diocese has one bishop, ministering to various ethnicities. While this is not the case of Byzantine Catholic Churches, which are still organized in parallel ethnic jurisdictions, Rome's successful intervention shows that a stronger primacy can unify of competing jurisdictions. As discussed in the previous sections, Orthodox autocephaly has a centrifugal effect and all attempts of canonical unity in the "diaspora" have thus far failed. A stronger pan-Orthodox primacy would ameliorate the situation, even without going as far as Constantinople's jurisdictional claims in the "diaspora."

As stated above, the Catholic Church can be a model here: universal primacy as defined by *Pastor Aeternus* at Vatican I was an exaggerated reaction to counteract the efforts of the new Western nations to limit the Pope's authority. There is much room in the middle for a primacy that is neither a direct, immediate, ordinary, and supreme power of jurisdiction (*Pastor Aeternus* 1–3), nor simply of honor, as understood by Moscow today. It would be naïve to hope that all autocephalous churches would simply accept this new primacy. Given most churches' attitudes toward the representatives of the Ecumenical Patriarchate who chair the Assemblies of Bishops around the world, it might even sound foolish to have such hopes. It does not help that many Eastern countries are circumspect of trans-national authorities and globalization, which they regard as detrimental to national identity. At the same time, however, all economies are global, and multi-national corporations are now a regular occurrence. Ordinary citizens (and thus the Orthodox faithful) in these countries live in a globalized world, with its own rules of behavior. In this context, it is impossible to postpone the question of global Orthodoxy and its concrete manifestations, including models of leadership.

The Orthodox primate could have the authority to oversee the ecclesial life of the "diaspora," including ensuring the establishment of a local synod that oversees the appointment of one bishop for each diocese, but his decisions could be overturned by a large percentage of votes of the primates of the other autocephalous churches. This presupposes that 1) the Orthodox primate convenes regular (ideally yearly) synaxes of the primates of autocephalous churches, 2) he can enforce the participation of all primates for example by having the right to use the vote of absent churches as he considers appropriate, 3) all primates identify the benefits of fully remaining part of this pan-Orthodox synodality that decides based on consensus, not unanimity, and 4) in the case in which a small group of churches refuses to work towards a common resolution—as in the case of the U.S. Assembly of Bishops discussed above—the majority moves on. Hopefully, no one will risk being left behind and no one would hesitate to follow a primate who is above national and ethnic interests.

Besides a stronger Eastern primacy, another way to transcend ethnic boundaries is through *a renewed focus on missions or evangelization*. Obviously, this space is insufficient to address properly the intrinsic connection between Orthodox liturgical life and the "Liturgy after the Liturgy," when the Church continues its worship in the form of service to the world, both near and far. Nor is it possible here to properly analyze the missionary efforts of saints Cyril and Methodius to the Slavs, Russian missionaries to China and Alaska, Archbishop Anastasios' apostolic ministry in post-communist Albania, or contemporary American missionaries who build homes, schools, hospitals, and preach the gospel all over the world. A proper discussion of missions or evangelization would also engage the dynamics between cradle Orthodox and converts; new opportunities for contextualized liturgical life; interreligious dialogue; multiple religious belongings; the Church's engagement with highly secularized societies; missions *ad intra* for those who suffer from oppression, economic injustice, and discrimination; and missions directed to the environment. But the following remarks should suffice to claim that the true nature of the Orthodox Church is missionary.

While traditionally Orthodoxy has taken the gospel to those who were unevangelized, the gradual association between Orthodoxy and Eastern nations resulted in a major missionary decline and an almost-exclusive inward focus. On the one hand, the world-wide Orthodox population has more than doubled in the last century; it now stands at nearly 260 million. On the other hand, the world's overall population has quadrupled, resulting in a significant percentage loss of Orthodox faithful compared to world population: from an estimated 7% in 1910, to 4% today.[44] Again, it is crucial to emphasize that Orthodoxy today represents merely 4% of the total world population—a humbling reality, difficult to fathom if one lives in a majority Orthodox country.

Why mention these statistics in the context of missions and nationality?

44. Pew Center, *Orthodox Christianity*, 6–7.

Because the main reason for Orthodoxy's diminishing numbers is *Eurocentrism*. In 1910, most Christians lived in Europe: 65% of world-wide Catholics, 52% of Protestants, and 91% of Orthodox. Now only 24% of Catholics and 12% of Protestants live in Europe but the Orthodox share is still 77%. During the twentieth century, Catholic and Protestant missionaries have (largely) abandoned the Eurocentric model of missions of the previous centuries. Hence, as the statistics above show, their missionary efforts have succeeded more than Orthodoxy's efforts. Orthodoxy remained centered in Europe—a continent with a declining population. Consequently, the percentage of Orthodox fell significantly over the last century not only compared to the world's population, but also among Christians, from 20% to 12%.[45] Without missions beyond European national borders and with an ethnically-focused presence in other parts of the world, Orthodoxy's numbers are bound to continue their free fall, mainly due to the unhealthy association between Orthodoxy and the nation—a European nation, specifically.

A century ago, Orthodoxy's Eurocentric character was not unique. Despite the fact that Jesus lived in the Near East, by the beginning of the twentieth century Christianity had become "a religion *from* Europe and, often, a religion *about* Europe [... to such degree that] the provocative aphorism was coined, apparently by Hilaire Belloc: 'The faith is Europe, and Europe is the faith.'"[46] The expansion of religious, political, and cultural European norms were part of a process of colonialization that resulted in a rather homogeneous world enabled by the British Empire on which the sun literally never set. This is not to say that all past missions were a form of colonialism or white imperialism. For example, saints Cyril and Methodius created the Slavonic alphabet (also called Cyrillic in honor of one of the brothers) and translated numerous biblical and liturgical texts for the newly converted Christians. Their opponents objected that there were "only three tongues worthy of praising God in the Scriptures, Hebrew, Greek and Latin," these being the languages in which Jesus' charge was written at the Crucifixion. But Cyril retorted: "Falls not God's rain upon all equally? And shines not the sun also upon all?"[47] Exporting an unaltered Greek culture by means of mission was not an option for the saint.

45. Pew Center, *Orthodox Christianity*, 6–7.
46. Pelikan, *Illustrated Jesus*, 236.
47. MacCulloch, *Christianity*, 462–63. African theologian Lamin Sanneh points out that Christianity adopted significant aspects of Greek culture from its beginning, instead of transmitting Jesus' words in Aramaic. This shows that Christianity is a "translated religion" and a "translating religion," rather than the possession of any culture, especially Western culture. Lamin Sanneh, *Whose Religion is Christianity? The Gospel beyond the West* (Grand Rapids, MI: Eerdmans, 2003), 97, 105.

For too long the East remained stuck in Cyril's opponents' mindset, that only some tongues are worthy of praising God. In a not-so-subtle form of cultural and political colonialism, national Orthodox churches remain focused on exporting their culture in new places where their immigration takes them, thus greatly limiting their mission. In this sense, Kalaitzidis considers that Orthodoxy's self-association with *national identity* is one of the main reasons for its *missionary inertia*. Autocephalous churches chose to export independently their own nationalism, which brought them in conflict with one another, rendering impossible a broad pan-Orthodox coordination of missionary efforts.[48]

Until the 1960s, most Orthodox theology either completely ignored missions or even showed animosity towards coordinated missionary efforts. Eucharistic ecclesiology was so prevalent, that the Liturgy became the exclusive constitutive element of the Church. In the context of this liturgical introversion, preaching the word of God to the world was considered a Protestant activity.[49] Communist persecution certainly exacerbated (though not caused singlehandedly) this situation by forbidding churches to act outside their temple walls in society at large and even less so in other countries. After the fall of communism, the proselytism of several evangelical churches that coerced faithful to convert away from Orthodoxy by offering them material advantages and denigrating Orthodox clergy, again contributed to the negative image of evangelization.

These anti-missionary attitudes persist today and are coupled with two other factors: first, missions are primarily directed *ad intra*, concerned with an increasingly secular society, and second, missions represent means of exporting a national culture to an ethnic population in the diaspora. And yet, miraculously, Orthodoxy has experienced an unprecedented missionary revival. Archbishop Anastasios' missionary work in Albania is comparable to that of the Apostles. The Orthodox presence in Southeast Asia takes such a local character and contributes so much to the well-being of the local populations, that it cannot be suspected of having primarily ethnic motivations. Last but not least, while the United States was still considered a missionary field just decades ago, it now houses some of (if not the) most significant missionary efforts in Orthodoxy, with the added bonus that these efforts are pan-Orthodox in character, as many

48. Pantelis Kalaitzidis, "New trends in Greek Orthodox theology: challenges in the movement towards a genuine renewal and Christian unity," *Scottish Journal of Theology* 67, no. 2 (2014): 144–45. Pantelis Kalaitzidis and Thomas FitzGerald, eds., *Orthodox Handbook on Ecumenism: Resources for Theological Education—"That They All May Be One"* (*John* 17, 21) (Oxford/Volos: Regnum Books International / Volos Academy Publications, 2013), 672–701.

49. Kalaitzidis, "New trends," 143–44.

national jurisdictions participate in missions together; what is impossible for world-wide Orthodoxy is possible in American pan-Orthodox missions. The missionary efforts of International Orthodox Christian Charities (IOCC), Orthodox Christian Mission Center (OCMC), and the Orthodox Mission Network stand out in this regard.

The shift away from missions entangled with cultures has been accompanied by another shift: now missions *to* the margins are concomitant with missions *from* the margins. What can the marginalized offer to those who are privileged? Those who have in abundance go through a conversion-like experience when they go to the lanes of the city and witness the frugality, the joy, and the solidarity of those who live there. Who is being evangelized? What are we learning and how are we transformed when we witness the presence of God in other cultures and religions? And finally, does mission always go one-way, from the evangelist to the evangelized,[50] from the rich to the poor, from the white to the black or brown? Moreover, missionaries, who were already the first ones to create dictionaries, grammars, and alphabets, are now paying even more attention to the contexts in which they go. Missionaries acknowledge that, in any place where they go to preach Christ for the first time, God was there before they arrived. Their first task is to understand what God told the people before the arrival of Christianity.

Truly listening to God in various contexts is a very difficult exercise, which challenges theological conclusions that have become normative long ago. But the Spirit speaks through these newly evangelized voices. Their differing approaches to Church life are not deviations from Orthodox truth, but adaptations to South American, African, or Asian realities. Not listening to these voices, no matter how different they may be from the Greco-Roman Orthodoxy that has become normative, means ignoring the Spirit who blows wherever it wills (Jn 3:8). An illustrative example in this regard is the place of the Eucharist in the life of the Church.

Until recently, I wholeheartedly agreed with the statement, "the Eucharist makes the Church," mostly because I found (and still find) convincing the eucharistic ecclesiologies of Afanasiev, Schmemann, and Zizioulas. But in my encounters with Christianity in India and in China, where missionaries are often forbidden to freely exercise their activities—including Baptisms and Liturgies—I recognized the unmistakable reality of a Church that was not eucharistic in a strict sense. Without invalidating eucharistic ecclesiology, but

50. Gaillardetz, *Ecclesiology Global Church*, 62.

providing it with important qualifications, an Orthodox theology of missions needs to ask whether there can be a Church without a regular eucharistic presence in some contexts; whether the Church is fully present in the healing and proclamation of the good news among the marginalized, but often without clerical structures; and whether diversity of faith can include non-eucharistic ecclesiologies. We cannot limit diversity to the (otherwise immensely inspiring) inculturation of Greek patristic traditions and liturgical practices in new missionary contexts, such as using rice wine in the Eucharist, reciting the "Our Father" with reference to "our daily rice" instead of bread, or iconographically depicting an Asian Jesus and the Twelve eating the Last Supper with chopsticks, as is sometimes the case in China. Perhaps at the end of this exercise, a more nuanced understanding of the eucharistic nature of the Church emerges: *the Eucharist makes the Church … but not always.* While the Eucharist remains central to Orthodox ecclesiology, it is not the only element that engenders the Church; rather, the Church emerges in a multitude of ways that do not involve the celebration of the Eucharist. Such a proposal would be more difficult to accept for those Orthodox Christians who regularly have access to the Eucharist and who enjoy religious liberty to assemble. And yet, Evdokimov's apophatic words resonate again: "We know where the Church is, but we cannot judge where the Church is not."[51] One has to rejoice that the Spirit is still at work, expanding the Body of Christ in new forms of teaching, discipline, worship, and mission that do not exist in traditionally Orthodox contexts, instead of absolutizing European inculturations of the gospel.

Unsurprisingly from a Kingdom-centered perspective, missions today represent primarily an opportunity to manifest the Kingdom of God through healing and proclamation. *Healing comes first.* Missionaries first go in places where they build hospitals, schools, water wells, homes, and do not require anything in exchange. That does not mean that they do not preach. On the contrary, according to the saying attributed to St. Francis of Assisi, "preach at all times; when absolutely necessary, use words." That is why, when missionaries manifest the healing power of the Kingdom of God, people often ask the missionaries, what is their motivation for showing love. The answer is a powerful proclamation of the good news to the poor as witness to the Lord. Thus, the purpose of evangelization is not primarily to expand churches and their institutions, but to be an icon of the Kingdom of God.

51. Evdokimov, *L'Orthodoxie*, 343.

DIFFERENT CONTEXTS

Orthodoxy could be caricaturized as a powerful, European faith. As with all caricatures, there is an element of truth. There are 13 Orthodox-majority countries in the world, all in or close to Europe. The three largest Orthodox populations are in Russia (101 mil.), Ukraine (34.8 mil.), and Romania (18.7 mil.),[52] but it should be noted that Ukrainian Orthodoxy is divided, and Romania has a sizeable emigrant population, making the Romanian Orthodox Church the second largest Patriarchate—an important detail for a Romanian author. Caricatures also exaggerate some elements. U.S. Orthodoxy is neither less Orthodox than European Orthodoxy, nor an aggregate of islands of European faith and culture. In fact, numerous Orthodox in the U.S. do not identify as having an Eastern European ethnic background, as for example in the Antiochian Archdiocese. Moreover, U.S. Orthodox members are more religious than their European counterparts. Statistics are illustrative in this regard: Russia has among the lowest levels of Orthodox religious observance—just 6% of Orthodox adults say attend church at least weekly and only 15% consider religion "very important" in their lives. Other ex-Soviet countries show similar percentages regarding the importance of religion, except for Armenia (53%) and Georgia (50%). All these ex-Soviet countries represent the majority of the world-wide Orthodox population. The percentages of Orthodox who consider religion "very important" are higher in other parts of Europe: 46 in Bosnia, 50 in Romania, and 59 in Greece. U.S. Orthodoxy stands in a reassuring third place in the world in this regard, at 52%, and 31% attend church at least weekly.[53] It seems that, at its best, Orthodoxy is not exclusively European.

Furthermore, Orthodoxy experiences today a wide variety of Church-state relationships. In some cases, the Orthodox Church is the national Church; in others, it wields an enormous influence on society because of its majority status; in other cases, it is only nominally in the majority, while most of its faithful are rather secularized; and in still other cases, Orthodoxy is a minute minority.

The Orthodox Church of Greece has the status of national church, which does not necessarily mean that it is the only faith recognized in Greece. Islam and Judaism, too, are recognized as public legal entities. Other Christian faiths, such as the Catholic Church, are registered as private legal associations.

---

52. Pew Center, *Orthodox Christianity*, 21–23.

53. Both U.S. and world-wide Orthodoxy rank lower compared to the 68% of U.S. overall Christians who consider religion "very important" in their lives and 47% attend church weekly. Pew Center, *Orthodox Christianity*, 10, 25.

Orthodox priests receive their salaries and pensions from the state, the Orthodox faith is taught in public schools, icons are present in public institutions,
public servants of the highest rank are sworn into service by the Archbishop or
his delegates, and until recently Orthodox bishops were consulted regarding
the building of places of worship for religious minorities.[54]

The situation in Russia is in many regards similar, with an added political
dimension. While Greece's political regimes have recently had varying degrees
of sympathy towards the Church, in Russia there seems to be complete support one for the other. The Russian Orthodox Church and the Russian State
assist each other in promoting public order; the Church does not protest the
regime's annexations of territories that are under the ecclesial jurisdiction of
the Moscow Patriarchate (and thus the fratricide that is taking place between
its own spiritual children); the state reinforces "spiritual security" and its related
legislation on non-governmental organizations which are obligated to register
as "Foreign Agents"—a category that has a negative impact on non-Orthodox
religious and theological institutions.[55]

As mentioned previously, the Moscow Patriarchate regards itself as having jurisdiction over the *Russky mir*—a presumed Russian world that includes
many ex-Soviet territories that are no longer under Russia's political dominance,
but remain under the jurisdiction of the Patriarchate. Moscow employs a rhetoric that includes expressions such as "Holy Russia" and "civilization," the latter
implying that Russian Orthodoxy represents its own world, which cannot be
judged according to the standards of other civilizations. Election by God and
Messianism are other rhetorical devices meant to justify its attempts to save other nations. This messianism is paradoxically coupled with isolationist attitudes
based on the assumption that the West is evil and, in order to preserve one's
purity, the East needs to isolate itself from the negative influence of the West.

As Papanikolaou shows, political and ecclesial authorities use the East-West
divide to define an Eastern type of democracy that includes "morality" as a result
of its Russian Orthodox past, in contrast with Western democracies that are
presumably godless, liberal, and support licentiousness. Papanikolaou continues: "some Russians have made common cause with such ultra-conservatives
in the West like Pat Buchanan and, ironically, American evangelical Christians,
even if evangelical Christians in Russia endure restrictions under the 1997 law
'On Freedom of Conscience and on Religious Association.'"[56]

54. Kalaitzidis, "Church and State," 43–44.
55. Kalaitzidis, "Church and State," 51.
56. Aristotle Papanikolaou, "Whose Public? Which Ecclesiology?," in *Political Theologies in Orthodox*

Too many members of the Church are freely joining in this kind of isola-tionist rhetoric and amplifying it. For more than a decade now—but especially after the Council of Crete, which brought to the forefront the divisiveness of anti-Western rhetoric—ecumenism is perceived as a threat. Simply being open to dialogue with the West is regarded as a renunciation of nation and Or-thodoxy. In fact, labeling a theologian as "Western" is so damaging that many ecumenically-minded theologians cannot function in their Eastern countries of origin. This kind of language plays into nationalistic rhetoric and causes fur-ther entrenching into divisive ideologies.[57] But it does not resonate with most of the faithful, especially the youth and the intellectuals. They look positively to the West and ecclesial rhetoric loses its credibility in their eyes. Anti-Western, isolationist attitudes have backfired not only in regard to Orthodoxy's place in the public sphere, but also in its relationship with the nationalist elements to which it panders. Despite the close relationship between the Moscow Patri-archate and the state, numerous Orthodox nationalists in Belarus, Moldova, and Russia have ceased their public commemorations of Patriarch Kirill after his very brief meeting with Pope Francis in 2016 in Havana. They refused to commemorate the Patriarch and considered him a traitor of the faith simply for having met the Pope.

Lavinia Stan and Lucian Turcescu describe the relationship between Church and state in Romania as different from other models: it is not a U.S.-type "wall of separation" between Church and state (with its own nuances), but it is not a national Church, either. Instead, it fits under the "dominant Church" model, in which the clergy and public-school teachers of Religion are remunerated by the state, legally the state is not allowed to interfere in Church matters, the Church has the exclusive rights to produce and sell liturgical items and Bibles, churches are tax exempt and do not pay for heating and electricity. In addition to the funds that the church collects tax-free, national and local authorities give significant amounts of public funds to the Church for construction projects and social programs. These include soup kitchens, daycare centers, after-school pro-grams, senior living centers, seminaries, publishing houses, radio and television stations. The authors argue that, from an economic perspective, at least, there is no full institutional differentiation between the state and the church. As a result

---

Christianity: Common Challenges—Divergent Positions, ed. Kristina Stoeckl, Gabriel Ingeborg, and Aristo-tle Papanikolaou (New York: T&T Clark, 2017), 229–42.

57. Hovorun writes in this regard: "For many Orthodox churches, nationalism has become a ticket to re-enter the secularized public and political space. Because nationalism is a card played by many political parties in the Orthodox nations, the churches also play this card to remain a part of the political process." Hovorun, *Political Orthodoxies*, 148.

of this special Church-state relationship, instead of the presence of religion being reduced out of the public sphere as one might expect in an increasingly secular society, the opposite is happening, namely a de-secularization, with religion being increasingly present in the public.[58]

The examples of Greece, Russia, and Romania suffice to show that the Byzantine model of *symphonia* is not a forgotten ideal of the past, but applies in different forms to contemporary democracies. Any form of *symphonia* comes with the words of caution that applied to the Byzantine context, as shown earlier. They are even amplified when realizing how poorly these Orthodox churches treat religious minorities with the help of the state. It is easy to be a moral people when being powerless. But how is a community going to be moral when it has power? How will a mighty national Church use its power in relationship to the weak? Will they heed the commandment "you shall also love the stranger, for you were strangers in the land of Egypt" (Dt 10:19), remembering their own experience of suffering under the Ottomans and the communists? Will they consequently refrain from causing the same suffering to the strangers who live among them (cf. Dt 16:11–14)? Will religion be a catalyst for inclusivity and respect, or, on the contrary, will the powerful oppress those of a different religion? In a true democracy, the majority has the duty to uphold the rights of the minority. Even more so, among people of faith, the powerful need to support the weak. Among the followers of Christ, those who are great should not lord it over the others as Gentiles do (Mt 20:24–26). That happens when Eastern European Orthodox immigrate to the West where they become weak, but are treated in a Christian way: they often receive Western churches as places of worship either with no rent or at a greatly reduced rate.

In the United States, there is a subtler type of *symphonia*. Here the Orthodox Church represents 0.3% of the population, so the state has no interest in favoring Orthodoxy and hierarchs do not have access to political power. Instead, the faithful freely align themselves with one of the two major political parties, merging not only religious and national identities, as in the East, but also political affiliation. Moreover, American society lives under an assumed separation of Church and state, but the reality is much more complex when considering the churches' tax-exempt status, for example. This situation brings to the forefront the Church's role in the democratic process of election.

Numerous countries around the world have free elections and some are

58. Lavinia Stan and Lucian Turcescu, *Church, State, and Democracy in Expanding Europe* (New York: Oxford University Press, 2011), 134–49.

ahead of U.S. democracy in voter representation and voting rights. But none of them mingles faith and elections to the level of the U.S. Here, pastors and faithful speak rather freely about elections, sometimes behind a very thin veil of subtilty as not to jeopardize their requirement to remain apolitical in order to maintain their church's tax-exempt status. Americans often motivate their electoral choices on religious grounds. Politicians routinely tout their support among religious groups. Sometimes it seems that both politicians and the (religious) public are taking the Lord's name in vain by religiously justifying unethical political choices.

Orthodox parishes are in an unprecedented situation: for the first time in the history of the Orthodox Church, they teach morality and the values of the Kingdom to voters. Previously, the faithful were either persecuted, or vassals of a benevolent empire, or under a monarchy. It was primarily after the fall of the Iron Curtain in the East and in the twentieth century in America, that Orthodox faithful became involved in truly democratic elections.[59]

In the U.S., political parties exert a significant influence on the "gospel" that is proclaimed based on a god created in our own political image and likeness. It is common in the U.S. to encounter Christians who rightly defend every species of animals and their habitats but agree with abortion as an acceptable means of family planning. And it is also common in the U.S. to encounter Christians who rightly call themselves pro-life in regard to life in the womb, but support the death penalty, invent "God-given" rights to proliferate guns, and oppose health-care reform and Christian treatment of immigrants or refugees. It is not the place here to discuss these major themes, nor the exceptional cases where some might find these positions morally defensible. But when such positions represent the norm, when morally problematic political positions are praised in religious language that takes the Lord's name in vain, surely the ravenous political wolf has come in sheep's clothing (cf. Mt 7:15).

Preachers must acknowledge their part in letting political views inform their preaching. At a meeting of our Priests-Rabbis dialogue in Pittsburgh, we all spoke frankly about our sincere intention to rise above politics, but also about the bias at work in our choice of topics for sermons. Those who regularly spoke against abortion rarely mentioned ecological concerns or the moral treatment of immigrants, and vice versa. This being the case, it is not surprising to see how political ideologies penetrate the attitudes of the faithful. While

---

59. Eastern Europe between the two World Wars and post-World War II Greece remain the exceptions that prove the rule.

comparable statistics for Orthodox parishes do not exist, a recent Pew Research study highlights these political differences among Catholics in the U.S.:

> Catholic Democrats and political independents are more likely than Catholic Republicans to say that working to help the poor is essential to their Catholic identity; two-thirds of Catholic Democrats and independents say this, compared with 56% of Catholic Republicans. And working to address climate change is seen as an essential part of Catholicism by far more Catholic Democrats (40%) and independents (32%) than Republicans (13%). By contrast, opposition to abortion factors more prominently in Catholic Republicans' sense of Catholic identity than it does for Catholic Democrats and independents. Four-in-ten Catholic Republicans (42%) say opposition to abortion is essential to what being Catholic means to them, compared with 30% of both Catholic Democrats and independents.[60]

Clearly, churches in the U.S. need to focus on their mission to inform and form their members to put the values of the Kingdom above political convictions. Moreover, by shaping voters (without alignment with a particular political party), churches in democratic societies go beyond the individual's responsibility to combat personal sin, and offer a communal answer to structures of sin. While emphasizing again that no political party—and thus no electoral vote—will coincide fully with the gospel, being fully involved in the life of the *polis* is an opportunity to enact the values of the Kingdom through governmental structures.

Given the risk of falsely sacralizing our own political views because we cannot think of ourselves voting against our moral values, the risk of aligning the institution of the Church with a certain political regime, and the risk of marginalizing some faithful because of their political views, it is better to avoid any alignment of Church and state, of preaching and electoral process.[61] Otherwise, the Kingdom of God conforms to the kingdoms of this world and not vice versa. Otherwise, we idolatrously worship a god created in our own political image and likeness. Otherwise, we call "good" "evil" because our political party tells us so. Otherwise, the "salt has lost its taste" (cf. Mt 5:13).

---

60. Pew Center, *U.S. Catholics Open to Non-Traditional Families*, 35.

61. Hovorun identifies the following advantages of separation of Church and state: the Church regains its self-awareness as different from the state; it learns how to act without coercing its positions and thus regains an apostolic ethos; and it receives protection from political influences. Hovorun, *Political Orthodoxies*, 198–99.

A KINGDOM-CENTERED MODEL OF
CHURCH-STATE RELATIONS

Nathaniel Wood and Aristotle Papanikolaou show that, while Orthodox theology came rather late to discussions of political theology, it is not inherently indifferent to politics. On the contrary, the reasons why some might see Orthodoxy as an unlikely dialogue partner in political Orthodoxy are in fact reasons for Orthodoxy's involvement in this field: divinization is not a Manichaean escape from this world, but rather a transformation of the social order in conformity to God's likeness. Moreover, the authors argue, numerous Orthodox answers to modern democracies, human rights theories, and secularization of the political sphere are rather reactionary, carrying over the centuries of reflection on the relationship between the Church and various imperial structures and attempting to simply rehash Byzantine models. And yet, Orthodoxy needs to earnestly engage the versatile Orthodox tradition with contemporaneity, resulting in a constructive Orthodox political theology.[62] Without attempting to offer a model of Orthodox political theology here, it is important to draw some general principles regarding Church-state relations based on the Kingdom-centered, experiential, and ecumenical perspectives offered in this book.

The Kingdom of God is already here … but not yet. On the one hand, the Kingdom of God is present in the Eucharist, in the community of the Church that offers glimpses of the eschaton, and in the world inasmuch as the world reflects the values of the Kingdom. On the other hand, the Kingdom of God is not yet present, so the Church has the mission to enact the values of the Kingdom and to proclaim that the Kingdom is of God, and not of "Caesar." The Kingdom of God is distinct from the kingdoms of this world, but the Church—as an icon of the Kingdom—is called to reflect the Kingdom, make the Kingdom present in the world, while not being of the world. In other words, Church and state should be different and separate in structures and mission. But the Church also needs to interact with the state as much as is needed for God to act in the world. This section attempts to unpack these principles.

The Kingdom of God is present in the Eucharist, gathering together people of all nationalities and political orientations, uniting Church members in ways in

---

62. Wood and Papanikolaou, "Orthodox Christianity and Political Theology," 337–51. Elsewhere, Papanikolaou presents an overview of various Orthodox models of Church-state relationships, which vary greatly and include, for example, Solov'ev's Christian liberalism, Bulgakov's version of liberation theology (my expression), Crainic's ethnocratic state, and Yannaras' and Guroian's critique of modern Western liberalism. Papanikolaou, *The Mystical as Political*, 34–53. See also Ladouceur, *Modern Orthodox Theology*, 333–60.

which no human institution can. Transcending all these differences and finding a new identity, the Eucharist becomes a manifestation of the Kingdom of God. At the same time, the experience of the community gathered in the Liturgy needs to irradiate beyond church walls: "Let us go forth in peace." For the majority of the twentieth century, Orthodox theology has emphasized eucharistic ecclesiology, and for good reasons. The works of Afanasiev, Zizioulas, Schmemann, and Staniloae have contributed to the revival of Orthodox theology and Church life to an unprecedented level. For Staniloae, for example, emphasizing the eucharistic nature of the Church was the only option, as he wrote under extreme limitations by communist censors who restricted the activity of the Church to its walls, forbidding any ecclesial manifestation outside its liturgy.

Today the Church permeates many aspects of society, being present in schools, hospitals, lay associations, and on the political scene. The Church cannot accept freely what communist censors have previously imposed on it, namely, an overemphasis on its eucharistic character and its retreat from these democratic, egalitarian, and moral principles that it now can transpose from within its walls into society. The opposite has already happened, where national ideals have permeated Church life, but ethnophyletism cannot have the last word. A Kingdom-centered ecclesiology thus affirms that the Kingdom of God is present in the community gathered in the Eucharist and that the Church is an icon of the transformation that God enacts in his Kingdom transcending national and political differences. This icon will only last for two hours a week, unless the Church expands it beyond the liturgical assembly. It is the mission of the community to offer the world glimpses of the eschaton by enacting the values of the Kingdom: healing and proclamation.

When going beyond church walls, one also discovers that the Kingdom of God is *already present in the world*, inasmuch as it reflects the values of the Kingdom. The remarks from the first chapter remain: the Church and the Kingdom are not coterminous, since the Kingdom is larger than the Church. Especially in preaching, but also in official documents, there is often an underlying assumption that society is hostile towards the Church. The Church feels permanently under attack. This is understandable given our long history of Roman, Ottoman, and communist persecutions, which taught us to take the defensive attitude of a persecuted Church. Visible symbols of this attitude are the numerous monasteries built as fortresses. Their walls have, in the past, protected both the faith and the nation. But today the Church needs to come out from behind its walls, into the nations that are generally peaceful and, at least nominally, Christian. Especially in majority Orthodox countries, "the world" is made up of baptized Christians, so an antagonizing attitude is not warranted. While protecting itself from the infection of nationalism and politicization, the Church needs to look towards the outside and manifest the values of the Kingdom: healing, peace, love, and proclamation. When these values are already manifested in just healthcare systems, governments that promote peace, and societies that value kindness, the Church can only rejoice at God's work in the world and sanctify it with grace.

The Kingdom is already present in the Eucharist and in the world … *but not yet*. Sometimes the antagonizing attitude of the Church towards the world—inasmuch as the latter is an instrument of sin—is not only justified, but also an imperative. No forces of evil will stand in the way of the Church, according to Jesus' promise that "the gates of Hades will not prevail against it" (Mt 16:18). It is unfortunate that the reference to the gates of Hades not prevailing against the Church is often interpreted according to a siege mentality: the Church is under siege, and we need to defend it by not being affected by the world, which is attacking us. But the image that Jesus is using, in actuality, is the reverse: the Church is on the offensive and Hades is under siege. The gates are a defense mechanism for Hades, not for the Church. The Church is not on the defensive; the Church is on the offensive against Hades, which keeps many imprisoned in a place of suffering and death. This realization forces us to abandon the siege mentality; the Church's task is not to defend itself from the impurities of the world, but to attack sin and injustice—Hades, in other words—knowing that the gates of Hades will not prevail. This insight is clearly connected with the resurrection of Jesus, who has conquered death and is now Lord. The icon of Jesus' descent into Hades shows the gates of Hades crumbled under his feet, and so Orthodox Christians sing, "The gates of Death have opened to You from fear, O Lord, and the gatekeepers of Hades were stricken when they saw You. For You have shattered the gates of brass, and the iron bars You have broken. You have led us out of darkness and the shadow of death, having broken our shackles."[63] Clearly, when looking at the icons of the descent into Hades, singing the above hymn, and understanding them in light of Matthew 16:18, one realizes that Christ has conquered Hades, has become Lord, and now his followers—the Church—have to share in his fight and victory over Hades, taking under siege sin, suffering, sickness, and death, whose gates will not prevail against the Church.

Sometimes the state represents Hades as structural sin, other times the state can be the Church's ally in its fight against sin. According to Jaroslav Pelikan, Western Christianity offers four distinct attitudes regarding the expectations that a Christian should have from the government. Martin Luther considered that the principles of the gospel do not apply to the act of governing because Jesus spoke about individual Christian life apart from a Christian's official duties when in position of authority. If, for example, Jesus forbade taking oaths, a person working in the government is required to do so. Consequently, a Christian should govern based on reason, not revelation. Distinguishing between the Kingdom of Christ and the kingdom of the world, Luther concluded that legislation is "the mirror of the Saxons," and not of the Eternal. In contrast to Luther, John Calvin advocated for Christian politics. Calvin considered that the duty of the government is to cherish and protect the worship of God, sound doctrine, the position of the Church in public life, and to adjust the life of society according to civil righteousness. Magistrates, therefore, are expected to channel the power of Christ through the power with which they are invested. In other words, the government has to be Christian and use its authority to build a Christian society. A third minority option is that of holy war in the name of Christ. Representatives range from crusaders, to Thomas Münzer—the radical reformer who took Christ's words that he did not come to bring peace but sword (Mt 10:34) to be a call for a Christian revolution that uproots corrupt governments to replace them with Christian governments—to liberation theology in the twentieth century. A fourth minority opinion is that of pacifism. Anabaptists and Quakers understood discipleship as separation from this world and thus did not take on the responsibilities of being magistrates and wielding the sword in military service. They did not intend to overturn governments, but refused to participate in governing, which made use of violence. Instead of waging war, they chose martyrdom,[64] as did, centuries later, Martin Luther King Jr.

Calvin's opinion regarding the role of government to create a Christian society seems to prevail among many Christians in the U.S. The participation of individual Christians in governing raises new possibilities. Sometimes the duty to change the kingdoms of this world according to the Kingdom of God falls on each individual member of the Church, as in elections. Other times, it falls on some members of the community who are filled with a prophetic spirit to speak for the rest; the most prophetic figures in history were not official

64. Pelikan, *Illustrated Jesus*, 178–80, 90–93.

representatives of their religions—prophet Jeremiah, Martin Luther King Jr., and, of course, Jesus of Nazareth. All Christians, according to their gifts, have the same duty to better their society. True, the Kingdom of God is not the Kingdom of "Caesar," but even Caesar can be persuaded to do the will of God.

In a certain sense, an ecclesiology oriented towards the Kingdom of God makes the discussions of the relationship between Church and state secondary, in the sense that the Church can be an icon of the Kingdom in any regime, ranging from militant atheist to benevolent rulers. As an icon of the Kingdom of God and not of Caesar, the Church can manifest the Kingdom of God regardless of its changing relationship with Caesar. When asked about whether it is lawful to pay taxes to Caesar, Jesus indirectly responded that regardless of what one has to give Caesar, even when paying the taxes to an occupier, one can still give oneself fully to God: "Give to Caesar the things that are Caesar's, and to God the things that are God's" (Mt 22:21). Just as the image of Caesar on the tax coin belongs to Caesar, so the image of God that is the entire person belongs to God, and the image (icon) of the Kingdom belongs to the King, regardless of who the Caesar is. Early Christians might have seemed delusional to their contemporaries, who witnessed the power of Caesar over their heavenly King, the Messiah. And yet the early Church confessed Jesus as Lord and reflected the values of God's Kingdom all around them in their preaching of the good news, in their care for the poor, in their love for one another, and in their service to one another. And in doing so, they fulfilled Jesus' mandate to continue his mission, without any help from—or even despite—their government. History often repeated itself, and the Church always found ways to stay true to its mission, even under governments with which it could not collaborate.

In times of persecution, the faithful and the hierarchy could not freely choose to have a relationship with the government. But in times of freedom, even when the majority of the Church thought that it could collaborate with secular governments or that the emperor was God's anointed, there were faithful who regarded such collaboration as a compromise. That is why monasticism developed in the fourth century, in response to the Church's close association with the empire—its leader and its citizens. Monastics embraced the ideal of detachment from the world so that the Church would not become worldly. They retreated from the world so they would not become of the world, and their charism remains essential in the Church. While this ideal weakened considerably throughout the centuries, it never disappeared: the Church is not *of* the world. Can the Church be *in* the world?

The fine line between being separate from the world and being involved in worldly affairs came to the forefront in early sixteenth-century Russia in the dispute between possessors and non-possessors. On the one hand, possessors led by Joseph, Abbot of Volokalamsk, considered that monastics had the duty to care for the sick and the poor, to show hospitality and to teach, for which they needed possessions; they considered that "the riches of the Church are the riches of the poor." On the other hand, non-possessors led by Nil Sorsky, criticized the monasteries that owned land (about a third of all land in Russia), acquired entire villages, and enslaved the peasants—their own brothers and sisters in Christ. Nil considered that monks should be detached from this world and its secular anxieties, leaving almsgiving as the duty of the laity. Wisely seeing merits in the teachings of both Joseph and Nil, the Russian Church canonized both saints.[65]

It is impossible to offer a clear-cut model of Church-state relations from all these examples. The Church is a stranger, a pilgrim along the path to a different world. But on its way to the heavenly Kingdom, it has the mission to transform the present world into the world to come. That is not to say that the Church is involved in societal aspects in the same manner as NGO's and political parties. The world, however, cannot become the Kingdom without the Church as leaven and icon. More than any worldly organizations, the Church's heart is beating for those who are oppressed, poor, sick, suffering, and in need. They are the Church, breathing the Spirit in, and sending the Spirit out, the Comforter who gives solace to the oppressed and who imparts blessings with its presence. As it looks towards the transformation of this world into the heavenly Kingdom and prays "Thy Kingdom come," the pilgrim Church is called to be an icon of the Kingdom in all the places through which it sojourns.

The Church must walk the fine line between complete withdrawal from the world and being of the world. Without taking to an extreme the separation of early monastics and non-possessors, or the identification of the Church with national ideals described in this chapter, the Church needs to resist the temptation of alignment with the state, and minister to the needs of this world. The Church is neither above this world as a master withdrawn into the ethereal, nor of this world as a servant of the kingdoms of this world. The Church is an icon, a presence of grace that makes it possible, as we say in the Liturgy, "for the Lord to act." Concretely, how can the Church walk this fine line? Perhaps Martin Luther King Jr. said it best:

65. Ware, *The Orthodox Church*, 104–8.

The church must be reminded that it is not the master or the servant of the state, but rather the conscience of the state. It must be the guide and the critic of the state, and never its tool. If the church does not recapture its prophetic zeal, it will become an irrelevant social club without moral or spiritual authority.[66]

66. Martin Luther King Jr. Sermon "A Knock at Midnight" (June 5, 1963) https://kinginstitute.stanford .edu/king-papers/documents/knock-midnight

Definitions of the Church

⟿

[In the Church, the community encounters a world
that is] purified, transfigured, filled again with divine beauty
and meaning—the very icon of the Kingdom of God.

ALEXANDER SCHMEMANN[1]

Having reached the end of his *Mystagogy*, St. Maximus meditated with trepidation on the impact of his work. Concerned that he lacked the authority of those who acquired the holy life, he wrote, "I do not want to have my written words to stand as an accuser in addition to my deeds."[2] If this beloved saint worried about the impact of his written words, what hope do I have? Dear reader, be kind, patient, and pray that these remarks about the Church will grow to bear good fruit. I wrote them as an individual theologian, scholar, teacher, priest, and faithful Orthodox Christian whose heart beats in the Church, with the Church, and for the Church. All that is left to do at this point is to offer a list of definitions of the Church that emerged throughout this book.

The Church is not precisely the same as the Kingdom of God. The Church is not separate from the Kingdom, either, as an icon is not the thing represented, but a visible sign, a presence, and an instrument of that thing represented. In this sense, the Church is an *icon of the Kingdom of God*. The Kingdom of God, fully manifested in the person of Jesus, expanded to include the community of disciples, which in turn became larger and larger, to include all the nations. And yet, the New Testament—at a time when most followers of Jesus were

---

1. Schmemann, *Of Water and the Spirit*, 118.
2. Maximus the Confessor, "*Mystagogia*," 214.

Jews—boldly affirms that the Church is "the Israel of God" (Gal 6:16) in the context of the Messiah's death, resurrection, and outpouring of the Spirit.

Jesus' followers began referring to their community as "the Body of Christ," and so the Church is the extended Jesus, or the extension of the Incarnation, having the same mission as the Messiah, namely to proclaim the good news and to heal the world of sin, suffering, and death. The early Church had the awareness of being the community of disciples that enact the values of the Kingdom of God, while praying for the Kingdom to come, as the Kingdom is already here, but not yet. The Church is both the experience and the expectation of the Kingdom. The eschaton thus becomes prescriptive of how the Church fulfills its mission here and now. In this sense, the Church already is what it will be. In the eschaton, when God will be "all in all," the entire world will be a Church, an icon of God, and we already experience that eschatological reality in the Church, as the above epigraph suggests.

The Church is *the community of the baptized*. As the rite of Christian initiation indicates, Baptism is much more than an abstract forgiveness of an individual's original sin; it is communitarian, marking one's entry into the Church. The rite also shows the Church as the renewed Israel, which partakes in the death and resurrection of Christ, becoming the Body of Christ. As the baptized unite themselves to Christ to such an extent that they "are properly called Christs," their being changes in two significant ways. First, Baptism moves them from "biological existence" to "ecclesial existence." In this sense, the Church is a mother who gives us birth in the waters of Baptism. Second, Baptism represents a consecration into universal priesthood, and thus the Church is the community of the baptized who are consecrated with the gift of the Holy Spirit into "a holy priesthood to offer spiritual sacrifices acceptable to God through Jesus Christ" (1 Pt 2:5).

The Church is the community of those who have been baptized not only with water, but also by blood or desire. These two alternative types of Baptism expand the boundaries of the Church considerably, to include for example children who died before being born. It is pastorally imperative to define the Church as the unity of heaven and earth, where parents pray for their unborn children and children pray for parents as one Body of Christ. The Church— *Una Sancta*—extends well beyond the canonical boundaries of the Orthodox Church, embracing all its children baptized validly. Consequently, when Catholics and Protestants convert to Orthodoxy, they are received by either Confession or Chrismation, since their baptism outside of Orthodoxy already made them members of the Church. Moreover, if a person consciously renounces their membership in the Church and later returns to Orthodoxy, they are not re-baptized, which implies the recognition of the permanent validity of baptism, despite one's personal choices in life: once baptized—always baptized.

The Church is *a family*—a community of love that includes persons who have a Christian identity from the moment of their conception or even before that, when the parents desire to have a child whom they will baptize into the Church; persons developing in the womb and up until their baptism, when they have a Christian identity by anticipation; baptized children for whom the community prays, who experience worship and learn about the faith in the family understood, in the words of John Chrysostom, as "a little Church"; Christians who are either single, monastics, married, or widowed; and cultural Orthodox who, although inactive as members of the church, are still a part of the family since they consider themselves Orthodox by culture, ethnicity, family traditions, beliefs, morality, and liturgical affinities.

The Orthodox Church offers the sacrament of Marriage to Protestants and Catholics who enter into a mixed marriage with an Orthodox. Moreover, some Orthodox consider that marriages contracted in Catholic and Protestant churches are valid, as intra-Church marriages. Mixed marriages are possible because the Church *Una Sancta* is one, extending beyond the canonical boundaries of Orthodoxy. At the same time, the Church remains divided, so non-Orthodox spouses generally do not commune eucharistically in the Orthodox Church, raising a significant theological question: if the two spouses become one "little church" in marriage and if "the Eucharist makes the Church," should the "little church" of mixed couples manifest the unified eucharistic being of the Church by engaging in eucharistic sharing in Orthodox parishes in the West as they already do in some Orthodox churches in the Middle East, for example?

The term "Church" has *a multitude of definitions*. In some casual conversations, the Church is the hierarchy or perhaps a body that interacts with governments mostly on secular terms. Other times, the Church is the clergy or an undefined teaching authority with clearly defined answers to every modern question imaginable. The Church—especially for theologians—is the Body of Christ, People of God, Bride of Christ, Temple of the Spirit, Pilgrim People, the diocese, the ethnic jurisdiction that is parallel to other ethnic jurisdictions, the national church, the entire Orthodoxy, Christian denominations, all of Christianity, or even the cosmos considering its sacramentality. The most immediate way in which a faithful person experiences the Church is through their own *parish*, understood as both community and building.

The prescriptions for painting the interior walls of a church illustrate that

the Church is the communion of the living worshipping in the pews and being censed as living icons, the saints depicted on the walls and symbolizing all
the departed, the angels, Virgin Mary, and Christ who has authority over all
(Pantocrator). Being depicted in the dome of the church, Christ is represented
as the head of the Church—a Church defined as the community that unites
heaven and earth. The Church on earth prays for those who are deceased and
to the saints, while the saints pray for the living and all worship God, so the
Church is a communion that surpasses the boundaries of time and space. In
fact, the community of the Church extends beyond human beings, since the
entire universe celebrates a cosmic Liturgy and is being transformed into a
Church through the priestly mediation of the human being.

The Church understood as the parish is a community of the faithful gathered together around the priest for the celebration of the Eucharist and other
services; for being an instrument of the Kingdom, bringing healing and proclamation of the good news to their locality and the world in general; and for
exercising the various charisms of its members for the building up of the Body
of Christ. This definition of the parish both challenges and agrees with the
eucharistic ecclesiology of Afanasiev, who considers that "the Church is where
the eucharistic assembly is." Most recent Orthodox theology converges around
Afanasiev's contention that the Church is eucharistic in nature, assuming that
the local church is the diocese and the bishop is the celebrant of the Liturgy. I
have proposed an experiential ecclesiology of the parish that earnestly considers the transition from the eucharistic assembly led by the bishop in the diocese
to the Liturgy presided over by the priest in the parish. In the parish, Christians experience concretely the Church that is one, holy, catholic, and apostolic.
In majority Orthodox countries the parish is the homogeneous community of
believers who share the same faith and the fullness of liturgical life. In American Orthodoxy, however, given the prevalence of mixed marriages, the parish
also includes Catholic and Protestant members.

The Church is the assembly of worshippers gathered in *the Liturgy* as
an icon of the Kingdom of God manifested visibly in the sacred space of the
church building. The communion that the faithful experience in the Liturgy
presupposes the act of gathering together in one place. And yet, an increasing
number of parishes stream their services online to respond to the needs of
those who are shut in, or are unable to come to church for reasons of health,
occupation, or travel. If these cases are usually in the minority, online worship
became the norm for the majority of Christians during the 2020 pandemic.
Extending the community of the faithful who gather in one place to the online

realm is a positive adaptation to the practical needs of our time, but exclusively virtual gatherings cannot supplant the community that shares the same physical space of the church building and the sacraments.

The Church defined as a building is God's dwelling place, built after the heavenly pattern, in which the community gets a glimpse of that eschatological Kingdom here and now. That is not to say that the Church is primarily a building. As the pilgrim Israel and as Jesus' body that was a temple walking in our midst, so the early Church regarded itself as a temple; the act of gathering was akin to constructing a spiritual building.

The Church gathered in the Liturgy is an icon of the work of Christ, and the offering of the Church is actually the offering of Christ through the entire Church, clergy and the people. Sometimes the priest acts as an icon of Christ, other times the priest is an icon of the worshipping congregation. The Liturgy shows that the entire community is priestly, not just the ordained, and the active participation of the faithful is an antidote to the clericalism that has drawn an edge between the clergy and the faithful through various practices such as the rare communion of the faithful.

The Eucharist also functions as a boundary marker, defining the limits of the Church. The Church is one and, at the same time, divided among "separated brethren." The concept of intercommunion struggles with this paradoxical, antinomical, and abnormal reality of schism: the Eucharist is both a sign of disunity and, because Orthodox and Catholics are united in a real sense, it can be a means towards unity.

Intercommunion existed throughout the entire history of the Church, so it is important to highlight the prophetic twentieth century Orthodox theologians who consider that intercommunion should be allowed on a limited basis, by *oikonomia*, based on the faith that we share in its most significant aspects and due to pastoral necessities. In the eschatological Kingdom there will be no Orthodox, Catholics, and Protestants, but all will be one in Christ. Refusing to allow others at the table does not reflect that Kingdom in the Liturgy. So, when we do not share the Eucharist with those who will be part of the eschatological Kingdom of God, we do not experience the eschaton in our Liturgy, but remain in its "not yet" dimension where the Church does not reflect the eschatological kingdom … yet. Opening up Orthodox-Catholic intercommunion on a limited basis would be a step in the right direction, without imposing papal primacy and infallibility as common dogmas. Even without episcopal communion (as with the non-Chalcedonians), Orthodox faithful should be allowed to receive Communion in the Catholic Church and Catholics in the Orthodox

Church, as Catholic discipline already allows it, despite the Orthodox rejection of papal dogmas.

Having affirmed the eucharistic nature of the Church, it would be reductive to regard the Eucharist as a substitute for all aspects of the Church, such as its work of healing and proclamation. Eucharistic ecclesiology cannot overshadow baptismal ecclesiology, charitable ecclesiology, or mission-centered ecclesiology—in other words, Kingdom-centered ecclesiology. On the contrary, the Church gathered in the Liturgy is later sent to celebrate "the Liturgy after the Liturgy" by healing the world of sin, sickness, racial and social injustice. The Church is God's healing presence in the world.

The entire Church is a priestly people, sharing in *the priesthood of Christ*. Today, a priest is the ordained leader of the parish, in line with a longstanding tradition to designate the ordained as priests. But the Church of the first three centuries referred to both clergy and laity as priests, in contrast with pagan religions and Judaism for which "priest" was a narrow cultic designation of those who offered sacrifices in a temple. Regardless of the contemporary usage of the term "priest," the distinction between the clergy and the people cannot take away the full participation of both the ordained and those who are not ordained in the priesthood of Christ.

Much has been said about the communion between clergy and laity, resulting in a much-needed redefinition of baptismal consecration and its priestly character. Ordained priesthood, however, still remains in need of redefinition in light of the communion between ordained and non-ordained priesthoods. Based on other proposals to understand ordination as ecclesial repositioning, I have suggested a reimagining of ordained priesthood in light of the ministries of various orders in Orthodox parishes. Although there is a single sacrament of Ordination, each of these orders have their own specific character, as opposed to being degrees of participation in the ministry of the bishop who would presumably have the fullness of Ordination, while the priest shares in that ordination to a lesser degree and the deacon to an even lesser degree.

In traditionally Orthodox countries, deacons are rather rare, almost exclusively surrounding the bishop. In the United States, however, more and more parishes have permanent deacons. When the deacon is a common presence in the parish, it becomes clear that the diaconate is not a stepping-stone towards the priesthood, but a ministry of eucharistic distribution and outreach. Women deacons have been a continuous presence in Orthodox history and their ministry has always been beneficial to the Church. Deaconesses are much needed in today's parishes and perhaps even more urgently in nuns' monasteries.

Theological treatises regard priesthood simply as a partial and delegated aspect of the ministry of the bishop; only the bishop has the fullness of ordination and is therefore considered the celebrant of the Eucharist and the father of the community. From an experiential perspective, however, the priest is the leader of the parish—a role that stems from the various roles that presbyters had in antiquity. The leadership role of the priest focuses on nurturing charisms, coordinating various aspects of parish life, including charity, administration, pastoral activities, teaching and presiding at the eucharistic assembly. In other words, the priest's calling is to be a servant leader and the spiritual father of the parish.

The bishop is a hierarch and the Church is a hierarchy not in the contemporary secular sense of inequality and dominance of the superiors over the subordinated, but, in Pseudo-Dionysian terms, as a communion of sanctification in which grace circulates both downward and upward. From this perspective, the Church is a communion between clergy and laity because their distinction involves a relationship of authority, not to be confused with power; power is imposed unwillingly upon one's subordinates, while authority is freely accepted by those who follow their leaders. Experientially speaking, the bishop appoints priests for the parishes under his jurisdiction, ordains the priests, and gives them the blessing to celebrate the Liturgy in his diocese. Moreover, the bishop is the leader of the diocese, the link between parishes within a diocese, and the connection with other dioceses around the world.

On the one hand, the Church is an institution, but not like other human organizations and ecclesiology cannot degenerate into a cynical account of power and worldly interests in the Church; the Church is not *of* the world, but an icon of the Kingdom of God. On the other hand, the Church is not only a divine—or divinely ordered—community; it is also a gathering of humans for a divine purpose and with human means, which implies that the Church's mission takes place *in* the world, *for* the world, while also remaining *above* the sinfulness of the world. At the intersection of these ecclesiological elements stands *synodality*: the Church is synodal.

In the first millennium, the Orthodox Church was synodal at all levels: parish, diocese, regional, and universal. Since then, Orthodoxy has become less synodal at the universal level, but increasingly conciliar in the parish, diocese, and autocephalous Church, with varying degrees of involvement of bishops, priests, and laity. In this latter sense, synodality remains an Orthodox charism.

The Church is synodal in the parish community gathered around the Eucharist, involving the active participation of all the faithful together with the priest, all ministries acting together, in coordination with one another. Synodality is also at the heart of common decision-making: the community elects the parish council to oversee its day-to-day activity in collaboration with the priest, and parishes hold general assemblies in which all members come together to deliberate on the major aspects of parish life, including the mission of the community, the well-being of its ministries, the approval of the yearly budget, etc.

The Church defined as the diocese or the national church is synodal primarily through the ministries of the bishops, who do not exercise their local ministries in isolation but synodally, and who are responsible for the interaction with other local dioceses. At these levels, synodality in North America also involves laics, deacons, and priests in the Church's charity (IOCC), missions (OCMC), college ministry (OCF), or theological research (OTSA), all of which transcend ethnic jurisdictional boundaries. Moreover, American Orthodox churches of various ethnicities convene clergy-laity conferences (or sobors), some of them entrusting the delegates—laity and parish clergy—with the election of bishops, even though the ultimate decision rests with the synod of bishops.

Episcopal synodality is most efficient at the level of autocephalous churches because it is sustained by primacy. Primates of national churches have a significant degree of authority, including calling the council, setting its agenda, ensuring the participation of the bishops in the council, and speaking on behalf of the council once a decision is made, and representing the national church in its relations with secular authorities and other churches.

The Church is synodal inclusive of all its members. The contribution of the laity, parish clergy, and theologians is crucial both in their consultation before the council and in the process of reception of councils. They can be consulted today on a scale that earlier in history was simply un-imaginable, but now made possible by technological advances, fully illustrating that a synodal church is participative and co-responsible. Moreover, today Orthodoxy needs to creatively appropriate the tradition of the ecumenical councils. Fundamentalism represents the greatest danger facing the proper reception of the Eastern conciliar tradition, not relativism or secularism. Finally, in order to restore universal synodality, the East needs to create a workable view of universal primacy based on precedents in the East and in dialogue with the West, while avoiding the mistakes of the past.

A future united Church should allow the Pope to confess the infallible teaching of the entire Church, but in a more synodal manner than current Catholic teaching allows. A future united Church should also ascribe primacy to Rome, but it will have to be more synodal than the current Catholic under-standing of papal primacy allows, and at least as synodal as national Orthodox churches led by primates with real authority.

Primacy is an essential condition of synodality. During the existence of the Byzantine Empire, that place was naturally assigned to the bishop of Con-stantinople in the East. Today, the Patriarch of Constantinople is *primus inter pares*—first among equals—a position that is impeded by both exaggerated claims of Eastern primacy and exaggerated claims of absolute equality among bishops. Perhaps an Eastern type of authority, modeled after the primacy and synodality that national churches experience, could again make possible pan-Orthodox synodality and, if given to the Pope in a united Church, even universal synodality.

The Church is *both national and supranational*. As the *Letter to Diognetus* states about Christians, "Every foreign land is to them a fatherland and every fatherland a foreign land." On the one hand, this quote illustrates the love that Christians have for the lands in which they dwell; Christians do not need to renounce citizenship duties, respect for laws, and patriotism. In this regard, the Church becomes the living icon of the Kingdom of God in a specific cultural, sociological, and national context. On the other hand, this quote sets Christian identity above national identity, otherwise the Church becomes a servant of the state and an agent of fragmentation.

Early Christians confessed Jesus, and not the Emperor, as their Lord. They prayed for the Emperor and were model-citizens of the Empire, but they ex-pected the Kingdom of God to be victorious over the kingdom of Caesar. The fourth century, however, inaugurated a significant shift: a realized eschatology which affirmed that the Kingdom of God has come with power and is being manifested in the Byzantine Empire. Ideally, Byzantine *symphonia* was meant to protect the same body of citizens and faithful against dangers both spiritual and material, and to have two heads working in harmony for the benefit of the body that they shared in common. The presupposition was double: the emper-or wants what is good for the Church and the Church supports the interests of the earthly empire (*basileia*), which are in conformity with the values of the heavenly Kingdom (*basileia*). Historically this ideal situation was never fully achieved.

The ideal of symphonic association between Church and state survived well past the fall of the Byzantine empire, although multiplied in the system of autocephaly that is based on national identity and on the Orthodox churches' firm allegiance to their nations. While autocephaly was intended to guarantee a

Church's freedom to elect its own head and to lead itself in all practical aspects of ecclesial life, it resulted in the fragmentation of world Orthodoxy due to the infusion of national interests in Church life via autocephalism.

In times of increasing nationalist fragmentation, the Church is called to be supranational. One way to transcend worldly boundaries is to recognize a pan-Orthodox primate who cannot be suspected of having an ethnic, political, and dominating agenda. The Ecumenical Patriarch is best positioned to exercise this role, on the condition that Constantinople embraces other cultures besides Hellenism and its synod becomes reflective of world-wide Orthodoxy. Another way to transcend ethnic boundaries is through a renewed focus on missions. While traditionally Orthodoxy has taken the gospel to those who were unevangelized, the later association between Orthodoxy and Eastern nations resulted in a major missionary decline and an almost-exclusive inward focus. Contrary to this trend, in many regards U.S. Orthodoxy can serve as a positive example of a Church that is no longer a "diaspora" mission territory, but a mature missionary Church: what started as a mission Church, now does its own missions.

It is impossible to offer a clear definition of the Church in its relationship with the state. The difficulty is both contextual and theological. Contextually, Church-state relations differ widely around the world. In some cases, the Orthodox Church is the national Church; in others, it wields an enormous influence on society because of its majority status; in other cases, it is only nominally in the majority, while most of its faithful are rather secularized; and in still other cases, Orthodoxy is a minute minority. Theologically, the Church is a stranger, a pilgrim along the path to a different world. But on its way to the heavenly Kingdom, it has the mission to transform the present world into the world to come. As it looks towards the transformation of this world into the heavenly Kingdom, as it prays "Thy Kingdom come," the pilgrim Church is meant to be an icon of the Kingdom in the places through which it sojourns. For this end, the Church must walk the fine line that avoids the extremes of complete withdrawal from the world and being *of* the world. The Church needs to resist the temptation of alignment with the state, and minister to the needs of this world. The Church is neither a master withdrawn into the ethereal, nor a servant of the kingdoms of this world, but rather the conscience, guide, and critic of the state. Above all, *the Church is an icon of the Kingdom of God in this world*, a presence of grace that makes it possible, as we say in the Liturgy, "for the Lord to act."

Having arrived at the end of this Kingdom-centered, experiential, and ecumenical ecclesiological study, it is impossible to provide a single, all-encompassing definition of the Church. It remains an apophatic experience of God, impossible to fully define in words, but felt intensely as the presence of God. When a person is baptized, the Church is there; when they grow up, the Church is there; when they get married and raise their own children, the Church is there; when they need spiritual nourishment and a community in which to live according to the values of the Kingdom, the Church is there; when they go into the heavenly Kingdom, the Church is there. In all circumstances, in a most profound sense, the Church is there, as icon of the Kingdom of God.

Selected Bibliography

Afanasiev, Nicholas. *The Church of the Holy Spirit.* Translated by Vitaly Permiakov. Notre Dame, IN: Notre Dame University Press, 2007.

———. "The Church Which Presides in Love." Translated by Katharine Farrer. In *The Primacy of Peter: Essays in Ecclesiology and the Early Church,* edited by John Meyendorff, 91–143. Crestwood, NY: St. Vladimir's Seminary Press, 1992.

———. "The Eucharist: Principal Link Between the Catholics and the Orthodox." Edited and translated by Michael Plekon. In *Tradition Alive: On the Church and the Christian Life in Our Time: Readings from the Eastern Church,* 47–49. Lanham, MD: Rowman & Littlefield, 2003.

———. "Una Sancta." Edited and translated by Michael Plekon. In *Tradition Alive: On the Church and the Christian Life in Our Time: Readings from the Eastern Church,* 3–30. Lanham, MD: Rowman & Littlefield, 2003.

Alberigo, Giuseppe, and Joseph A. Komonchak, eds. *History of Vatican II: Vol. V: The Council and the Transition: The Fourth Period and the End of the Council. September 1965– December 1965.* Maryknoll, NY: Orbis, 2006.

Alfeyev, Bishop Hilarion. *Orthodox Christianity: The History and Canonical Structure of the Orthodox Church.* Vol. 1, Yonkers, NY: St. Vladimir's Seminary Press, 2011.

Allison, Dale C. *Constructing Jesus: Memory, Imagination, and History.* Grand Rapids, MI: Baker Academic, 2010.

Aquinas, Thomas. *Summa Theologiae, Complete English Edition in Five Volumes.* Translated by Fathers of the English Dominican Province. Allen, TX: Christian Classics, 1981.

Augustine. *The City of God, Books XVII–XXII.* Translated by Gerald G. Walsh and Daniel J. Honan. The Fathers of the Church. Washington, DC: The Catholic University of America Press, 2008.

———. *Confessions.* Translated by Henry Chadwick. New York: Oxford University Press, 1998.

———. *Sermons.* Translated by Edmund Hill. Hyde Park, NY: New City Press, 1992–1994.

———. *St. Augustine: Sermons on the Liturgical Seasons.* Translated by Sister Mary Sarah Muldowney R. S. M. Washington, DC: The Catholic University of America Press, 1977.

———. *Tractates on the Gospel of John 28–54*. Translated by John W. Rettig. Fathers of the Church. Washington, DC: The Catholic University of America Press, 1993.

Baker, Matthew, and Seraphim Danckaert. "Georges Florovsky." In *Orthodox Handbook on Ecumenism: Resources for Theological Education—"That They All May Be One"* (*John 17, 21*), edited by Pantelis Kalaitzidis and Thomas FitzGerald, 211–15. Oxford/ Volos: Regnum Books International / Volos Academy Publications, 2013.

Balthasar, Hans Urs von. *Cosmic Liturgy: The Universe According to Maximus the Confessor.* Translated by Brian Daley. Communio Books. Ft. Collins, CO: Ignatius Press, 2003.

Basil the Great. "Letter 114. To Cyriacus and His Followers at Tarsus." Translated by Sister Agnes Clare Way. In *Saint Basil. Letters. Volume I (1–185)*. Fathers of the Church, 241–42. Washington DC: The Catholic University of America Press, 1951.

Bede, *Ecclesiastical History of the English People*, ed. Bertram Colgrave and R. A. B. Mynors. Oxford: Clarendon Press, 1969.

Behr, John. "The Trinitarian Being of the Church." *Saint Vladimir's Theological Quarterly* 48, no. 1 (2003): 67–88.

Behr-Sigel, Elisabeth. "The Ordination of Women: Also a Question for the Orthodox Churches." In *The Ordination of Women in the Orthodox Church*, edited by Elisabeth Behr-Sigel and Kallistos Ware, 11–48. Geneva: WCC Publications, 2000.

Bernier, Paul. *Ministry in the Church: A Historical and Pastoral Approach*. Second ed. Maryknoll, NY: Orbis, 2015.

Blane, Andrew. "A Sketch of the Life of Georges Florovsky." In *Georges Florovsky: Russian Intellectual and Orthodox Churchman*, edited by Andrew Blane, 11–217. Crestwood, NY: St. Vladimir's Seminary Press, 1993.

Bobrinskoy, Boris. *The Mystery of the Church: A Course in Orthodox Dogmatic Theology.* Translated by Michael Breck. Yonkers, NY: St. Vladimir's Seminary Press, 2012.

Bordeianu, Radu. "Baptism as Entry into the Church, The Boundaries of the Church, and Mutual Recognition among Churches." In *Tendances et directions dans les recherches actuelles des théologiens orthodoxes roumains de la diaspora*, edited by Ciprian C. Apintiliesei and Constantin Pogor, 101–20. Paris: Editions du Cerf, 2022.

———. "*The Church: Towards A Common Vision*: A Commentary in Light of the Inter-Orthodox Consultation at Agia Napa in Cyprus." *Exchange: Journal of Missiological and Ecumenical Research (Brill)* 44, no. 3 (2015): 231–49.

———. *Dumitru Staniloae: An Ecumenical Ecclesiology*. Ecclesiological Investigations. New York, London: T&T Clark/Continuum, 2011.

———. "Eucharistic Hospitality: An Experiential Approach to Recent Orthodox Theology." *Journal of Ecumenical Studies* 54, no. 1 (2019): 5–24.

———. "Getting from Conflict to Communion: Ecclesiology at the Center of Recent Lutheran-Orthodox Dialogues and the 2016 Orthodox Council of Crete." *Worship* 91, no. Nov. (2017): 518–39.

———. "Local Synodality: An Unnoticed Change." In *Changing the Church: Transformations of Christian Belief, Practice, and Life*, edited by Mark Chapman and Vladimir Latinovic, 341–49. London: Palgrave Macmillan, 2021.

———. "Maximus and Ecology: The Relevance of Maximus the Confessor's Theology of Creation for the Present Ecological Crisis." *The Downside Review* 127, no. 447 (2009): 103–26.

———. "Orthodox Observers at the Second Vatican Council and Intra-Orthodox Dynamics." *Theological Studies* 79, no. 1 (2018): 86–106.

———. "Primacies and Primacy according to John Zizioulas." St. *Vladimir's Theological Quarterly* 58, no. 1 (2014): 5–24.

———. "'They Shall Beat Their Swords into Plowshares': Orthodox–Eastern Catholic Conflicts and the Ecumenical Progress that They Generated." In *Stolen Churches or Bridges to Orthodoxy*, edited by Vladimir Latinovic and Anastacia Wooden, 19–34. London: Palgrave Macmillan, 2021.

———. "The Unity We Seek: Orthodox Perspectives." In *The Oxford Handbook of Ecumenical Studies*, edited by Geoffrey Wainwright and Paul McPartlan, 577–93. New York: Oxford University Press, 2021.

Borelli, John, and John H. Erickson, eds. *The Quest for Unity: Orthodox and Catholics in Dialogue*. Crestwood, NY: St. Vladimir's Seminary Press, 1996.

Bradshaw, Paul. *Rites of Ordination: Their History and Theology*. Collegeville, MN: Liturgical Press, 2013.

Bria, Ion. *The Liturgy after the Liturgy: Mission and Witness from an Orthodox Perspective*. Geneva: WCC Publications, 1996.

Bucur, Bogdan G. "Anti-Jewish Rhetoric in Byzantine Hymnography: Exegetical and Theological Contextualization." St. *Vladimir's Theological Quarterly* 61, no. 1 (2017): 39–60.

Bulgakov, Sergius. "By Jacob's Well." In *Tradition Alive: On the Church and the Christian Life in our Time: Readings from the Eastern Church*, edited by Michael Plekon, 55–65. Lanham, MD: Rowman & Littlefield, 2003 (orig. 1933).

Calivas, Alkiviadis C. "Reflections on the 'Johnstown' Pastoral Statement on Orthodox-Roman Catholic Marriages." In *InterMarriage: Orthodox Perspectives*, edited by Anton C. Vrame, 166–87. Brookline, MA: Holy Cross Orthodox Press, 1997.

Calvin, John. *A Harmony of the Gospels Matthew, Mark and Luke*. Translated by T. H. L. Parker. Vol. 2, Grand Rapids, MI: Eerdmans, 1995.

Center, Pew Research. *America's Changing Religious Landscape: Christians Decline Sharply as Share of Population; Unaffiliated and Other Faiths Continue to Grow*. 2015. www.pewresearch.org.

———. *Choosing a New Church or House of Worship*. 2016. www.pewresearch.org.

———. *Many Americans Hear Politics from the Pulpit*. 2016. www.pewresearch.org.

———. *One-in-Five U.S. Adults Were Raised in Interfaith Homes: A Closer Look at Religious Mixing in American Families*. 2016. www.pewresearch.org.

———. *Orthodox Christiniaty in the 21st Century*. 2017. www.pewresearch.org.

———. *U.S. Catholics Open to Non-Traditional Families: 45% of Americans Are Catholic or Connected to Catholicism*. 2015. www.pewresearch.org.

Christian, Robert. "Bonds of Communion among Parishes and among Priests." In *What Is a*

Parish? Canonical, Pastoral, and Theological Perspectives, edited by Thomas A. Baima and Lawrence Hennessey, 130–44. Chicago: Hillenbrand Books, 2011.

Chryssavgis, John. *Remembering and Reclaiming Diakonia: The Diaconate Yesterday and Today*. Brookline, MA: Holy Cross Orthodox Press, 2011.

Clement of Alexandria. "Stromateis, Book Three." Translated by John Ferguson. In *Stromateis, Books 1–3*. Fathers of the Church, 256–326. Washington, DC: The Catholic University of America Press, 1992.

Clement of Rome. "The Letter of St. Clement of Rome to the Corinthians." Translated by Francis X. Glimm. In *The Apostolic Fathers*. Fathers of the Church, 1–58. Washington, DC: The Catholic University of America Press, 1947.

———. "The So-Called Second Letter of St. Clement." Translated by Francis X. Glimm. In *The Apostolic Fathers*. Fathers of the Church, 59–79. Washington, DC: The Catholic University of America Press, 1947.

Clément, Olivier. *Orient-Occident: deux passeurs, Vladimir Lossky et Paul Evdokimov*. Perspective orthodoxe; no 6. Genève: Labor et Fides, 1985.

———. *You Are Peter: An Orthodox Theologian's Reflection on the Exercise of Papal Primacy*. New York: New City Press, 2003.

Coakley, Sarah. *God, Sexuality, and the Self: An Essay 'On the Trinity'.* Cambridge: Cambridge University Press, 2013.

Cohen, Will. "Does the Long-Contested Question of Orthodox Ecumenism Remain Open after Crete?". *International Journal of Systematic Theology* 23, no. 1 (2021): 11–25.

———. "Why Ecclesial Structures at the Regional Level Matter: Communion as Mutual Inclusion." *Theological Studies* 75, no. 2 (2014): 308–30.

Coman, Viorel. *Dumitru Staniloae's Trinitarian Ecclesiology: Orthodoxy and the Filioque*. New York: Fortress / Lexington, 2019.

Commission, International Theological. *The Hope of Salvation for Infants Who Die Without Being Baptized*. 2007. http://www.vatican.va/roman_curia/congregations/cfaith/cti_documents/rc_con_cfaith_doc_20070419_un-baptised-infants_en.html.

Congar, Yves. *I Believe in the Holy Spirit: The River of the Water of Life Flows in the East and in the West*. Translated by David Smith. Vol. 3, New York: Seabury Press, 1983.

———. "My Path-Findings in the Theology of Laity and Ministries." *The Jurist* 32, no. 2 (1972): 169–88.

Constantelos, Demetrios, J. "Mixed Marriage in Historical Perspective." In *InterMarriage: Orthodox Perspectives*, edited by Anton C. Vrame, 62–70. Brookline, MA: Holy Cross Orthodox Press, 1997.

Consultation, Inter-Orthodox. *A Response to the Faith and Order Study: The Nature and Mission of the Church: A Stage on the Way to a Common Statement (Faith and Order Paper 198, 2005 WCC), Agia Napa / Paralimni, Cyprus, 2–9 March 2011*. 2011. http://www.ec-patr.org/docdisplay.php?lang=en& id=1310&tla=gr.

Consultation, North American Orthodox-Catholic Theological. "Baptism and 'Sacramental Economy' (1999)." In *The Journey Toward Unity: The Orthodox-Catholic Dialogue*

Statements, edited by Ronald Roberson, Thomas FitzGerald and J. Figel. Fairfax, VA: Eastern Christian Publications, 2016.

———. "The Filioque: A Church-Dividing Issue? An Agreed Statement of the North American Orthodox-Catholic Theological Consultation. Saint Paul's College, Washington, D.C. October 25, 2003." In *The Journey Toward Unity: The Orthodox-Catholic Dialogue Statements*, edited by Ronald Roberson, Thomas FitzGerald and J. Figel, 153–83. Fairfax, VA: Eastern Christian Publications, 2016.

Cooper, Adam G. *The Body in St. Maximus the Confessor: Holy Flesh, Wholly Deified.* The Oxford Early Christian Studies. Oxford, NY: Oxford University Press, 2005.

Cooper, Kate. *Band of Angels: The Forgotten World of Early Christian Women.* New York: Overlook Press, 2013.

Crete, Council of. *Official Documents.* 2016. https://www.holycouncil.org/official-documents.

Cyprian of Carthage. *Letters (1–81).* Translated by Sister Rose B. Donna. Fathers of the Church. Washington, DC: The Catholic University of America Press, 1964.

———. "The Unity of the Church." Translated by Roy J. Deferrari. In *Treatises*, 89–124. Washington, DC: The Catholic University of America Press, 1958.

Cyril of Jerusalem. "Lenten Lectures (Catecheses) I–XII." Translated by Leo P. McCauley. In *The Works of Saint Cyril of Jerusalem Volume 1*. Fathers of the Church, 91–252. Washington DC: The Catholic University of America Press, 1969.

———. "Mystagogical Lectures." Translated by Anthony A. Stephenson. In *The Works of Saint Cyril of Jerusalem Volume 2*. Fathers of the Church, 141–206. Washington DC: The Catholic University of America Press, 2000.

Daley, Brian E. "The Meaning and Exercise of 'Primacies of Honor' in the Early Church." In *Primacy in the Church: The Office of Primate and the Authority of Councils. Vol. 1: Historical and Theological Perspectives*, edited by John Chryssavgis, 35–50. Yonkers, NY: St. Vladimir's Seminary Press, 2016.

———. "Position and Patronage in the Early Church: The Original Meaning of 'Primacy of Honour.'" *Journal of Theological Studies* 44, no. 2 (1993): 529–53.

Davies, W.D., and D.C. Allison. *The Gospel According to St. Matthew, vol. 2: Matthew 8–18* London: T&T Clark, 1991.

de Lubac, Henri. *Corpus Mysticum: The Eucharist and the Church in the Middle Ages.* Translated by Gemma Simmonds and Richard Price. Notre Dame, IN: Notre Dame Press, 2007.

Demacopoulos, George E. "Crociate, Memoria e Perdono Nella Construzione dell'Identità Cristiana." In *Misericordia e Perdono*, 337–54. Bose, Italy: Qiqajon Comunità Bose, 2016.

———. *The Invention of Peter: Apostolic Discourse and Papal Authority in Late Antiquity.* Philadelphia: University of Pennsylvania Press, 2013.

Denysenko, Nicholas E. *Chrismation: A Primer for Catholics.* Collegeville, MN: Liturgical Press, 2014.

———. *Liturgical Reform After Vatican II: The Impact on Eastern Orthodoxy.* Minneapolis: Fortress Press, 2015.

DeVille, Adam A. J. *Orthodoxy and the Roman Papacy: Ut Unum Sint and the Prospects of East-West Unity*. Notre Dame, IN: University of Notre Dame Press, 2011.

———. "The Sacrament of Orders Dogmatically Understood." In *The Oxford Handbook of Sacramental Theology*, edited by Hans Boersma and Matthew Levering, 531–44. New York: Oxford University Press, 2015.

———. *Everything Hidden Shall Be Revealed: Ridding the Church of Abuses of Sex and Power*. Brooklyn, NY: Angelico Press, 2019.

———. "Sovereignty, Politics, and the Church: Joseph de Maistre's Legacy for Catholic and Orthodox Ecclesiology." *Pro Ecclesia* 24, no. 3 (2015): 366–89.

"The Didache or Teaching of the Twelve Apostles." Translated by Francis X. Glimm. In *The Apostolic Fathers*, 165–86. Washington, DC: The Catholic University of America Press, 1947.

Dionysius the Areopagite, Pseudo. *Pseudo-Dionysius: The Complete Works*. Translated by Colm Luibheid and Paul Rorem. The Classics of Western Spirituality. New York: Paulist Press, 1987.

Dragas, George D. "The Manner of Reception of Roman Catholic Converts into the Orthodox Church with Special Reference to the Decisions of the Synods of 1484 (Constantinople), 1755 (Constantinople) and 1667 (Moscow)." *Greek Orthodox Theological Review* 44, no. 1–4 (1999): 235–71.

Erickson, John H. "On the Cusp of Modernity: The Canonical Hermeneutic of St. Nikodemos the Haghiorite" (1748–1809)." *St. Vladimir's Seminary Quarterly* 42, no. 1 (1988): 45–66.

———. "Organization, Community, Church: Reflections on Orthodox Parish Polity in America." In *The Orthodox Parish in America: Faithfulness to the Past and Responsibility for the Future*, edited by Anton C. Vrame, 67–82. Brookline, MA: Holy Cross Orthodox Press, 2003.

———. "Reception into the Orthodox Church: Contemporary Practice." *The Ecumenical Review* 54, no. 1 (2002): 66–75.

Evdokimov, Paul. *L'Orthodoxie*. Paris: Desclée de Brouwer, 1979.

———. *The Sacrament of Love: The Nuptial Mystery in the Light of the Orthodox Tradition*. Translated by Anthony P. Gythiel and Victoria Steadman. Crestwood, NY: St. Vladimir's Seminary Press, 1985.

Fagenblat, Michael. "The Concept of Neighbor in Jewish and Christian Ethics." In *The Jewish Annotated New Testament*, edited by Amy-Jill Levine and Marc Zvi Brettler, 540–43. New York: Oxford University Press, 2011.

FitzGerald, Thomas, and Peter Bouteneff, eds. *Turn to God, Rejoice in Hope: Orthodox Reflections on the Way to Harare: The Report of the WCC Orthodox Pre-Assembly Meeting and Selected Resource Materials*. Geneva: Orthodox Task Force, WCC, 1998.

Flannery, Austin, ed. *Vatican Council II: The Conciliar and Postconciliar Documents*. New Revised ed Vol. 1. Northport, NY: Costello Publishing Company, 1998.

Florovsky, Georges. "The Boundaries of the Church." In *Ecumenism I: A Doctrinal Approach*,

Collected Works of Georges Florovsky, Emeritus Professor of Eastern Church History, Harvard University; vol. 13, 36–45. Belmont, MA: Nordland, 1989.

———. "The Catholicity of the Church." In *Bible, Church, Tradition*. Collected Works of Georges Florovsky, Emeritus Professor of Eastern Church History, Harvard University; vol.1, 37–55. Belmont, MA: Nordland, 1972.

———. "The Church: Her Nature and Task." In *Bible, Church, Tradition; Collected Works vol. 1*, 57–72. Belmont, MA: Nordland, 1972.

———. "Confessional Loyalty in the Ecumenical Movement." In *The Patristic Witness of Georges Florovsky: Essential Theological Writings*, edited by Brandon Gallaher and Paul Ladouceur, 279–88. London: T&T Clark, 2019.

———. "The Historical Problem of a Definition of the Church." In *Ecumenism II: A Historical Approach*. Collected Works of Georges Florovsky, Emeritus Professor of Eastern Church History, Harvard University; vol. 14. Belmont, MA: Nordland, 1989.

———. "Patristic Theology and the Ethos of the Orthodox Church." In *Aspects of Church History, Collected Works 4*, 11–30. Belmont, MA: Nordland, 1975.

———. "The Predicament of the Christian Historian." In *Christianity and Culture; Collected Works, vol. 2*, 31–65. Belmont, MA: Nordland, 1974.

———. "St. Cyprian and St. Augustine on Schism." In *Ecumenism II: Collected Works vol. 14*, 48–51. Belmont, MA: Nordland, 1989.

———. "St. Gregory Palamas and the Tradition of the Fathers." In *Bible, Church, Tradition; Collected Works vol. 1*, 105–20. Belmont, MA: Nordland, 1972.

———. "Western Influences in Russian Theology." In *Aspects of Church History, Collected Works 4*, 157–82. Belmont, MA: Nordland, 1975.

Ford, David C., and Mary Ford. *Marriage as a Path to Holiness: Lives of Married Saints.* South Cannan, PA: St. Tikhon's Seminary Press, 1999.

Frederick Frost, Carrie. *Maternal Body: A Theology of Incarnation from the Christian East.* Mahwah, NJ: Paulist Press, 2019.

Fries, Heinrich, and Karl Rahner. *Unity of Churches: An Actual Possibility.* New York: Fortress, 1985.

Gaillardetz, Richard R. "The Ecclesiological Foundations of Ministry within an Ordered Communion." In *Ordering of the Baptismal Priesthood*, edited by Susan Wood, 26–51. Collegeville, MN: Liturgical Press, 2003.

———. *Ecclesiology for a Global Church: A People Called and Sent.* Maryknoll, NY: Orbis, 2008.

———. *Teaching with Authority: A Theology of the Magisterium in the Church.* Collegeville, MN: Liturgical Press, 1997.

Gallaher, Brandon (Anastassy). "Bulgakov and Intercommunion." *Sobornost* 24, no. 2 (2002): 9–28.

George, Francis Cardinal. "The Parish in the Mission of the Church." In *What is a Parish? Canonical, Pastoral, and Theological Perspectives*, edited by Thomas A. Baima and Lawrence Hennessey, 18–38. Chicago: Hillenbrand Books, 2011.

Golitzin, Alexander. "Scriptural Images of the Church: An Eastern Orthodox Reflection."

In *One, Holy, Catholic and Apostolic: Ecumenical Reflections on the Church*, edited by Tamara Grdzelidze, 255–66. Geneva: WCC Publications, 2005.

Golitzin, Alexander, and Bogdan G. Bucur (ed.). *Mystagogy: A Monastic Reading of Dionysius the Areopagita*. Edited by Bogdan G. Bucur. Collegeville, MN: Cistercian Publications, 2013.

Gratsias, Emmanuel. "The Effect of Mixed Marriage on the Parish." In *InterMarriage: Orthodox Perspectives*, edited by Anton C. Vrame, 146–51. Brookline, MA: Holy Cross Orthodox Press, 1997.

Greek Orthodox Holy Week & Easter Services. Translated by Fr. George Papadeas. Daytona Beach, FL: Patmos Press, 2016.

Gregory of Nyssa. *The Life of Moses*. Translated by Abraham J. Malherbe and Everett Ferguson. The Classics of Western Spirituality. New York: Paulist Press, 1978.

Gregory Palamas. *The Homilies*. Translated by Christopher Veniamin. Waymart, PA: Mt. Tabor Publishing, 2009.

———. *The Triads*. Translated by Nicolas Gendle. Edited by John Meyendorff. Mahwah, NJ: Paulist Press, 1983.

Groppe, Elizabeth T. "The Contribution of Yves Congar's Theology of the Holy Spirit." *Theological Studies* 62, no. 3 (2001): 451–78.

Guglielmi, Marco. *The Romanian Orthodox Diaspora in Italy: Eastern Orthodoxy in a Western European Country*. Cham: Palgrave Macmillan, 2022.

Hahnenberg, Edward P. "Learning from Experience: Attention to Anomalies in a Theology of Ministry." In *A Church with Open Doors: Catholic Ecclesiology for the Third Millenium*, edited by Richard R. Gaillardetz and Edward P. Hahnenberg, 159–80. Collegeville, MN: Liturgical Press, 2015.

Harrington, Daniel J. *The Church According to the New Testament: What the Wisdom and Witness of Early Christinity Teach Us Today*. Franklin, WI: Sheed&Ward, 2001.

Hart, David Bentley. *That All Shall Be Saved: Heaven, Hell, and Universal Salvation*. New Haven, CT: Yale University Press, 2019.

Hart, David Bentley, and John Chryssavgis, eds. *For the Life of the World: Toward a Social Ethos of the Orthodox Church*. Brookline, MA: Holy Cross Orthodox Press, 2020.

Herbel, D. Oliver. *Turning to Tradition: Converts and the Making of an American Orthodox Church*. New York: Oxford University Press, 2014.

Heschel, Abraham. *Man's Quest for God: Studies in Prayer and Symbolism*. New York: Scribner, 1954.

Hinze, Bradford E. "Ecclesial Repentance and the Demands of Dialogue." *Theological Studies* 61, no. 2, June (2000): 207–38.

Hoge, Dean R. "Sociological Research on Interfaith Marriage in America." In *InterMarriage: Orthodox Perspectives*, edited by Anton C. Vrame, 83–96. Brookline, MA: Holy Cross Orthodox Press, 1997.

Hoover, Brett C. "A Place for Communion: Reflections on an Ecclesiology of Parish Life." *Theological Studies* 78, no. 4 (2017): 825–49.

Hopko, Thomas. *Christian Faith and Same-Sex Attraction: Eastern Orthodox Reflections.* Ben Lornond, CA: Conciliar Press, 2006.

———. "The Orthodox Parish in America." In *The Orthodox Parish in America: Faithfulness to the Past and Responsibility for the Future*, edited by Anton C. Vrame, 1–10. Brookline, MA: Holy Cross Orthodox Press, 2003.

Hovorun, Cyril. "Interpreting the 'Russian World.'" In *Churches in the Ukrainian Crisis*, edited by Andrii Krawchuk and Thomas Bremer, 163–71. New York: Palgrave Macmillan, 2016.

———. *Political Orthodoxies: The Unorthodoxies of the Church Coerced.* Minneapolis: Fortress Press, 2018.

———. *Scaffolds of the Church: Towards Poststructural Ecclesiology.* Cambridge: James Clarke & Co, 2017.

Hughes, Edward. "Reflections on Mixed Marriage in the Context of Parish Ministry." In *InterMarriage: Orthodox Perspectives*, edited by Anton C. Vrame, 152–57. Brookline, MA: Holy Cross Orthodox Press, 1997.

Hyppolitus. *On the Apostolic Tradition.* second ed. Edited by Alistair C. Stewart. Crestwood, NY: Saint Vladimir's Seminary Press, 2015.

Ignatius of Antioch (Theophorus). "The Letters." Translated by Gerald G. Walsh. In *The Apostolic Fathers*, 81–130. Washington, DC: The Catholic University of America Press, 1947.

Irenaeus of Lyons. *Irenaeus on the Christian Faith: A Condensation of Against Heresies.* Translated by James R. Payton. Cambridge: James Clarke, 2012.

Jensen, Robin M. "Icons and Iconography." In *The Cambridge Dictionary of Christian Theology*, edited by I. A. et al. McFarland, 232–34. New York: Cambridge University Press, 2011.

Jillions, John A. "Ecumenism and the Paris School of Orthodox Theology." *Theoforum* 39 (2008): 141–74.

———. "Three Orthodox Models of Christian Unity: Traditionalist, Mainstream, Prophetic." *The International Journal for the Study of the Christian Church* 9, no. 4 (2009): 295–311.

John Chrysostom. "Homily 4 on 2 Thessalonians 2:6–9." Translated by Gross Alexander. In *Saint Chrysostom: Homilies on Galatians, Ephesians, Philippians, Colossians, Thessalonians, Timothy, Titus, and Philemon*. NPNF I:XIII. Grand Rapids: MI: Eerdmans, 1988.

———. "Homily 20 on Ephesians 5:22–24." Translated by Gross Alexander. In *Saint Chrysostom: Homilies on Galatians, Ephesians, Philippians, Colossians, Thessalonians, Timothy, Titus, and Philemon*. NPNF I:XIII, 143–52. Grand Rapids, MI: Eerdmans, 1988.

———. "Homily 50 on Mt 14:23–24." Translated by George Prevost. In *St. John Chrysostom, on the Gospel of St. Matthew*. NPNF I:X, 300–04. Grand Rapids, MI: Eerdmans, 1888.

———. "Homily 86 (John 20.10–23)." Translated by Sr. Thomas Aquinas Goggin. In *Commentary on Saint John the Apostle and Evangelist, Homilies 48–88*. Fathers of the Church, 446–57. Washington, DC: The Catholic University of America Press, 1959.

———. *On Wealth and Poverty.* Translated by Catharine P. Roth. Crestwood, NY. St. Vladimir's Seminary Press, 1984.

John of Damascus. *Three Treatises on the Divine Images*. Crestwood, NY: St. Vladimir's Seminary Press, 2003.

Joint Orthodox-Catholic Working Group, St. Irenaeus "Serving Communion: Re-thinking the Relationship between Primacy and Synodality." (2018).

Justin Martyr. "First Apology." Translated by Thomas B. Falls. In *Saint Justin Martyr: The First Apology, the Second Apology, Dialogue with Trypho, Exhortation to the Greeks, Discourse to the Greeks, the Monarchy or the Rule of God*. Fathers of the Church. Washington, DC: The Catholic University of America Press, 1965.

Kalaitzidis, Pantelis. "Church and State in the Orthodox World: From the Byzantine 'Symphonia' and Nationalized Orthodoxy, to the Need of Witnessing the Word of God in a Pluralistic Society." In *Religioni, Libertà, Potere*, edited by Emanuela Fogliadini, 39–74. Milano: Vita e Pensiero, 2014.

———. "Ecclesiology and Globalization: In Search of an Ecclesiological Paradigm in the Era of Globalization (After the Previous Paradigms of the Local, Imperial, and National)." St. *Vladimir's Theological Quarterly* 57, no. 3–4 (2013): 479–501.

———. "From the 'Return to the Fathers' to the Need for a Modern Orthodox Theology." St. *Vladimir's Theological Quarterly* 54, no. 1 (2010): 5–36.

———. "New trends in Greek Orthodox theology: challenges in the movement towards a genuine renewal and Christian unity." *Scottish Journal of Theology* 67, no. 2 (2014): 127–64.

———. "Quelques réflexions conclusives au term du colloque." *Contacts* 243 (2013): 607–27.

Kalaitzidis, Pantelis, and Thomas FitzGerald, eds. *Orthodox Handbook on Ecumenism: Resources for Theological Education—"That They All May Be One" (John 17, 21)*. Oxford/ Volos: Regnum Books International / Volos Academy Publications, 2013.

Kappes, Christiaan. "A New Narrative for the Reception of Seven Sacraments into Orthodoxy: Peter Lombard's *Sentences* in Nicholas Cabasilas and Symeon of Thessalonica and the Utilization of John Duns Scotus by the Holy *Synaxis*." *Nova et Vetera* 15, no. 2 (2017): 465–501.

Karmiris, John N. *The Status and Ministry of the Laity in the Orthodox Church*. Brookline, MA: Holy Cross Seminary Press, 1994.

Kinnamon, Michael, and Brian E. Cope. *The Ecumenical Movement: An Anthology of Key Texts and Voices*. Grand Rapids, MI: Eerdmans, 1997.

Krindatch, Alexei, ed. *Atlas of American Orthodox Christian Monasteries*. Brookline, MA: Holy Cross Orthodox Press, 2016.

———. *Eight Facts about Church Atttedance in US Orthodox Christian Churches*. http://assemblyofbishops.org/news/research 2010.

———. *Exploring Orthodox Generosity: Giving in US Orthodox Parishes*. http://assembly ofbishops.org/news/research 2015.

———. *Fast Questions and Fast Answers about the Geography of Orthodoxy in America*. 2018. http://assemblyofbishops.org/news/research.

———. *Orthodox Christian Churches in 21st Century America: A Parish Life Study*. http://assemblyofbishops.org/news/research 2018.

———. *Orthodox Church Today.* Berkeley, CA: Patriarch Athenagoras Orthodox Institute, 2008.

———. *Young Adults and Young Adult Ministries in American Orthodox Christian Parishes.* http://assemblyofbishops.org/news/research 2017.

Küng, Hans. *The Church.* Garden City, NY: Image Books, 1976.

L'Huillier, Peter. "Episcopal Celibacy in the Orthodox Tradition." *St. Vladimir's Theological Quarterly* 35, no. 2–3 (1991): 271–300.

Ladouceur, Paul. *Modern Orthodox Theology: Behold, I Make All Things New.* New York: T&T Clark, 2019.

Lanne, Emmanuel. "La Perception en Occident de la participation du Patriarcat de Moscou à Vatican II." In *Vatican II in Moscow (1959–1965): Acts of the Colloquium on the History of Vatican II. Moscow, March 30–April 2, 1995,* edited by Alberto Melloni, 111–28. Leuven: Library of the Faculty of Theology K. U. Leuven, 1997.

———. "Quelques questions posées à l'Église orthodoxe concernant la 'communicatio in sacris' dans l'eucharistie." *Irénikon* 72, no. 3–4 (1999): 435–52.

———. "The Three Romes." In *The Holy Russian Church and Western Christianity,* edited by Giuseppe Alberigo and Oscar Beozzo, 10–18. London, Maryknoll, NY: SCM Press, Orbis, 1996.

Larin, Vassa. "'Active Participation' of the Fatihful in Byzantine Liturgy." *Saint Vladimir's Theological Quarterly* 57, no. 1 (2013): 67–88.

———. "What is 'Ritual Im/Purity' and Why?". *St. Vladimir's Theological Quarterly* 52, no. 3–4 (2008): 275–92.

Latinovic, Vladimir. "Konservativer als zuvor? Die orthodoxe Beteiligung am ökumenischen Dialog." In *Damit alle eins seien: Programmatik und Zukunft der Ökumene,* edited by Bernd Jochen Hilberath, Hans Küng and Johanna Rahner, 111–33. Ostfildern: Grünewald Verlag, 2015.

"Letter to Diognetus." Translated by Gerald G. Walsh. In *The Apostolic Fathers,* 351–70. Washington, DC: The Catholic University of America Press, 1947.

Lewis, C. S. *Mere Christianity.* New York: HarperCollins, 2001.

Limouris, Gennadios, ed. *Orthodox Visions of Ecumenism: Statements, Messages and Reports of the Ecumenical Movement 1902–1992.* Geneva: WCC Publications, 1994.

———, ed. *The Place of the Woman in the Orthodox Church and the Question of the Ordination of Women: Inter-orthodox Symposium, Rhodos, Greece 30 October–7 November 1988.* Katerini: Tertios, 1992.

Lockwood, Christopher. "Hagismos: Water Symbolism in Orthodox Christianity." *St. Vladimir's Theological Quarterly* 61, no. 1 (2017): 5–38.

Loisy, Alfred. *L'Évangile et l'Église.* Second ed. Bellevue: Picard, 1903.

Lossky, Nicholas. "Conciliarity-Primacy in a Russian Orthodox Perspective." In *Petrine Ministry and the Unity of the Church: "Toward a Patient and Fraternal Dialogue": A Symposium Celebrating the 100th Anniversary of the Foundation of the Society of the Atonement, Rome, December 4–6, 1997,* edited by James F. Puglisi, 127–35. Collegeville, MN: Liturgical Press, 1999.

MacCulloch, Diarmaid. *Christianity: The First Three Thousand Years*. New York: Penguin Books, 2009.

Mamalakis, Philip. *Parenting Toward the Kingdom: Orthodox Principles of Child-Rearing*. Chesterton, IN: Ancient Faith Publishing, 2016.

Mannion, Gerard. *Ecclesiology and Postmodernity: Questions for the Church in Our Time*. Collegeville, MN: Liturgical Press, 2007.

"The Martyrdom of St. Polycarp." Translated by Francis X. Glimm. In *The Apostolic Fathers*. Fathers of the Church, 146–66. Washington DC: The Catholic University of America Press, 1947.

Matera, Frank J. "Theologies of the Church in the New Testament." In *The Gift of the Church: A Textbook on Ecclesiology in Honor of Patrick Granfield, O.S.B.*, edited by Peter C. Phan, 3–22. Collegeville, MN: Liturgical Press, 2000.

Maximos the Confessor. *On Difficulties in the Church Fathers: The Ambigua*. Translated by Nicholas Constas. 2 vols. Cambridge, MA: Harvard University Press, 2014.

———. "The Church's Mystagogy in Which Are Explained the Symbolism of Certain Rites Performed in the Divine Synaxis." Edited and Translated by George C. Berthold. In *Maximus Confessor: Selected Writings*. Classics of Western Spirituality, 183–225. New York: Paulist Press, 1985.

———. *Questions and Doubts*. Translated by Despina D. Prassas. DeKalb, IL: Northern Illinois University Press, 2010.

McBrien, Richard P. "The Papacy." In *The Gift of the Church: A Textbook on Ecclesiology in Honor of Patrick Granfield, O.S.B.*, edited by Peter C. Phan, 315–36. Collegeville, MN: Liturgical Press, 2000.

McCormick, Richard A. *Notes on Moral Theology: 1965 through 1980* Lanham, MD: University Press of America, 1981.

McPartlan, Paul. "The Body of Christ and the Ecumenical Potential of Eucharistic Ecclesiology." *Ecclesiology* 6, no. 2 (2010): 148–65.

Meier, John. *Companions and Competitors, vol. 3 of A Marginal Jew: Rethinking the Historical Jesus*. New York: Doubleday, 2001.

Melloni, Alberto, Federico Ruozzi, and Enrico Galavotti, eds. *Vatican II: The Complete History*. Mahwah, NJ: Paulist Press, 2015.

Meyendorff, John. *Byzantine Theology: Historical Trends and Doctrinal Themes*. New York: Fordham University Press, 1983.

———. *Marriage: An Orthodox Perspective*. Crestwood, NY: St. Vladimir's Seminary Press, 1984.

Meyendorff, John, and Nicholas Lossky. *The Orthodox Church: Its Past and Its Role in the World Today*. Crestwood, NY: St. Vladimir's Seminary Press, 1996.

Meyendorff, Paul. "Liturgical Life in the Parish: Present and Future Realities." In *The Orthodox Parish in America: Faithfulness to the Past and Responsibility for the Future*, edited by Anton C. Vrame, 143–53. Brookline, MA: Holy Cross Orthodox Press, 2003.

Mihai, Vasile. *Orthodox Canon Law: Reference Book*. Brookline, MA: Holy Cross Orthodox Press, 2014.

Murray, John Courtney. "The Church and Totalitarian Democracy." *Theological Studies* 13, no. 4 (1952): 525–63.

Nissiotis, Nikos. "Is the Vatican Council Really Ecumenical?". *The Ecumenical Review* 16, no. 4 (1964): 357–77.

———. "The Main Ecclesiological Problem of the Second Vatican Council and the Position of the Non-Roman Churches Facing It." *Journal of Ecumenical Studies* 2, no. 1 (1965): 31–62.

Oepke, Albrecht. "Bapto, Baptizo, Baptismos." Translated by G. W. Bromiley. In *Theological Dictionary of the New Testament*, edited by Gerhard Kittel, 529–46. Grand Rapids, MI: Eerdmans, 1964/1993.

Origen. *The Commentary of Origen on the Gospel of St Matthew, Volume II*. Translated by Ronald E. Heine. Oxford Early Christian Texts. New York: Oxford University Press, 2018.

Osborne, Kenan B. "Envisioning a Theology of Ordained and Lay Ministry: Lay/Ordained Ministry—Current Issues of Ambiguity." In *Ordering of the Baptismal Priesthood*, edited by Susan Wood, 195–227. Collegeville, MN: Liturgical Press, 2003.

———. *Reconciliation and Justification: The Sacrament and Its Theology*. Eugene, Ore.: Wipf and Stock, 2001.

Papanikolaou, Aristotle. *The Mystical as Political: Democracy and Non-Radical Orthodoxy*. Notre Dame, IN: University of Notre Dame Press, 2012.

———. "Whose Public? Which Ecclesiology?". In *Political Theologies in Orthodox Christianity: Common Challenges—Divergent Positions*, edited by Kristina Stoeckl, Gabriel Ingeborg and Aristotle Papanikolaou, 229–42. New York: T&T Clark, 2017.

Patsavos, Lewis J. "The Canonical Response to Intra-Christian and Intra-religious Marriages." In *InterMarriage: Orthodox Perspectives*, edited by Anton C. Vrame, 71–82. Brookline, MA: Holy Cross Orthodox Press, 1997.

Pelikan, Jaroslav. *The Christian Tradition: A History of the Development of Doctrine*. Vol 1: *The Emergence of the Catholic Tradition (100–600)*. Chicago: The University of Chicago Press, 1971.

———. *The Illustrated Jesus Through the Centuries*. New Haven, CT: Yale University Press, 1997.

Petersen, Elizabeth, and Jannie Swart. "Via the Broken Ones: Towards a Phenomenological Theology of Ecclesial Leadership in Post-Apartheid South Africa." *Journal of Religious Leadership* 8, no. 2 (2009): 7–34.

Pius XI, Pope. *Mortalium Animos*. 1928.

Plekon, Michael. *Saints as They Really Are: Voices of Holiness in our Time*. Notre Dame, IN: University of Notre Dame Press, 2012.

Powell, Mark E. *Papal Infallibility: A Protestant Evaluation of an Ecumenical Issue*. Grand Rapids, MI: Eerdmans, 2009.

Proeschold-Bell, Rae Jean, and Patrick J. McDevitt. "An Overview of the History and Current Status of Clergy Health." *Journal of Prevention and Intervention in the Community* 40, no. 3 (2012): 177–79.

Purpura, Ashley M. *God, Hierarchy, and Power: Orthodox Theologies of Authority from Byzantium*. New York: Fordham University Press, 2018.

Rahner, Karl. "Of the Structure of the People in the Church Today." In *Theological Investigations 12: Confrontations 2*, 218–28. New York: Seabury, 1974.

Rapp, Claudia. *Brother-Making in Late Antiquity and Byzantium: Monks, Laymen, and Christian Ritual*. New York: Oxford University Press, 2016.

Rich, Bryce E., Robert M. Arida, Susan Ashbrook Harvey, David Dunn, Maria McDowell, and Teva Regule. "Marriage, Family, and Scripture." In *Toward the Holy and Great Council: Theological Reflections*, edited by Nathanael Symeonides, 85–89. New York: Greek Orthodox Archdiocese of America, 2016.

Riou, Alain. *Le Monde et l'Église selon Maxime le Confesseur*. Théologie Historique 22. Paris: Beauchesne, 1973.

Roccucci, Adriano. "Russian Observers at Vatican II: The 'Council for Russian Orthodox Church Affairs' and the Moscow Patriarchate Between Anti-Religious Policy and International Strategies." In *Vatican II in Moscow (1959–1965): Acts of the Colloquium on the History of Vatican II. Moscow, March 30–April 2, 1995*, edited by Alberto Melloni, 45–69. Leuven: Library of the Faculty of Theology K. U. Leuven, 1997.

Roeber, A.G. *Mixed Marriages: An Orthodox History*. Yonkers, NY: St. Vladimir's Seminary Press, 2018.

Rosu, Alexandru. "Fr. Dumitru Staniloae's View on Laymen's Participation in the Infallibility of the Church." *Ecumenical Review Sibiu / Revista Ecumenica Sibiu* 6, no. 1 (Apr. 2014): 28–46.

Russell, Norman. "Deification." In *The Cambridge Dictionary of Orthodox Theology*, edited by Ian A. McFarland, David Fergusson, Karen Kilby and Iain R. Torrance. Cambridge: Cambridge University Press, 2011.

———. "Theosis and Gregory Palamas: Continuity or Doctrinal Change?". *Saint Vladimir's Theological Quarterly* 50, no. 4 (2006): 357–79.

Sanneh, Lamin. *Whose Religion is Christianity? The Gospel beyond the West*. Grand Rapids, MI: Eerdmans, 2003.

The Sayings of the Desert Fathers: The Alphabetical Collection (Rev. Ed.). Translated by Benedicta Ward. Collegeville, MN: Liturgical Press, 1984.

Schmemann, Alexander. *Church, World, Mission: Reflections on Orthodoxy and the West*. Crestwood, NY: St. Vladimir's Seminary Press, 1979.

———. *The Eucharist: Sacrament of the Kingdom*. Crestwood, NY: St. Vladimir's Seminary Press, 1988.

———. *For the Life of the World: Sacraments and Orthodoxy*. Second ed. Crestwood, NY: St. Vladimir's Seminary Press, 1973.

———. *Of Water and the Spirit: A Liturgical Study of Baptism*. Crestwood, NY: St. Vladimir's Seminary Press, 1974.

———. "Towards a Theology of Councils." *St. Vladimir's Seminary Quarterly* 6, no. 4 (1962): 170–84.

Schmemann, Juliana, ed. *The Journals of Father Alexander Schmemann 1973–1983*. Crestwood, NY: St. Vladimir's Seminary Press, 2000.

Schmidt, Karl Ludwig. "Basileus, Basileia." Translated by G. W. Bromiley. In *Theological Dictionary of the New Testament*, edited by Gerhard Kittel, 564–93. Grand Rapids, MI: Eerdmans, 1964/1993.

Schneiders, Sandra M. "Whose Sins You Shall Forgive… The Holy Spirit and the Forgiveness of Sin(s) in the Fourth Gospel." In *It Is the Spirit Who Gives Life: New Directions in Pneumatology*, edited by Radu Bordeianu, 53–85. Washington, DC: The Catholic University of America Press, 2022.

Siecienski, A. Edward. "Holy Hair: Beards in the Patristic Tradition." *St. Vladimir's Seminary Quarterly* 58, no. 1 (2014): 41–68.

———. *The Papacy and the Orthodox: Sources and History of a Debate*. New York: Oxford University Press, 2017.

Slagle, Amy. *The Eastern Church in the Spiritual Marketplace: American Conversions to Orthodox Christianity*. DeKalb, IL: Northern Illinois University Press, 2011.

Sobrino, Jon. *Witnesses to the Kingdom: The Martyrs of El Salvador and the Crucified Peoples*. Maryknoll, NY: Orbis, 2003.

Spence, Michael. *Priest Acting in Persona Christi" The Mystery of Faith: Reflections on the Encyclical Ecclesia de Eucharistia*. Blackrock, Ireland: Columba Press, 2005.

Spinks, Bryan D. *Do This in Remembrance of Me: The Eucharist from the Early Church to the Present Day*. London: SCM Press, 2013.

Stan, Lavinia, and Lucian Turcescu. *Church, State, and Democracy in Expanding Europe*. New York: Oxford University Press, 2011.

Staniloae, Dumitru. "Autoritatea Bisericii [The Authority of the Church]." *Studii Teologice* 16, no. 3–4 (1964): 183–215.

———. "Creatia ca dar si Tainele Bisericii [Creation as Gift and the Sacraments of the Church]." *Ortodoxia* 28, no. 1 (1976): 10–29.

———. "Elemente de antropologie ortodoxa [Elements of Orthodox Anthropology]." In *Volumul omagial dedicat Patriarhului Nicodim [Celebratory Volume Dedicated to Patriarch Nicodim]*, 236–43. Bucuresti, 1946.

———. *The Experience of God: Orthodox Dogmatic Theology—The Sanctifying Mysteries*. Translated by Ioan Ionita and Robert Barringer. Vol. 5, Brookline, Mass.: Holy Cross Orthodox Press, 2013. Teologia Dogmatica Ortodoxa.

———. *The Experience of God: Revelation and Knowledge of the Triune God*. Translated by Ioan Ionita and Robert Barringer. Second ed. Vol. 1, Brookline, Mass.: Holy Cross Orthodox Press, 1998. 1994. Teologia Dogmatica Ortodoxa.

———. *Iisus Hristos sau restaurarea omului [Jesus Christ or the Restoration of Humankind]*. Second ed. Craiova: Editura Omniscop, 1993. 1943.

———. "Sinteza ecclesiologica [Ecclesiological Synthesis]." *Studii Teologice* 7, no. 5–6 (1955): 262–84.

———. "Slujirile bisericesti si atributiile lor [Ecclesial Ministries and their Attributions]." *Ortodoxia* 22, no. 3 (1970 1970): 462–69.

———. *Spiritualitate si comuniune in Liturghia Ortodoxa* [*Spirituality and Communion in the Orthodox Liturgy*]. Craiova: Editura Mitropoliei Olteniei, 1986.

———. "Temeiurile teologice ale ierarhiei si ale sinodalitatii [The Theological Foundations of Hierarchy and Synodality]." *Studii Teologice* 22, no. 3–4 (1970): 165–78.

———. *Teologia Dogmatica Ortodoxa* [*Orthodox Dogmatic Theology*]. Second ed. Vol. 3, Bucharest: EIBMBOR, 1997. Teologia Dogmatica Orthodoxa 1978.

Staniloae, Dumitru, and M. A. Costa de Beauregard. *Mica dogmatica vorbita: dialoguri la Cernica* [*Brief Spoken Dogmatics: Dialogues at Cernica*]. Translated by Maria-Cornelia Oros. Sibiu: Deisis, 1995. Ose comprendre que je t'aime (Paris: Le Cerf, 1983).

Stylianopoulos, Theodore G. "Toward a Theology of Marriage in the Orthodox Church." In *InterMarriage: Orthodox Perspectives*, edited by Anton C. Vrame, 1–33. Brookline, MA: Holy Cross Orthodox Press, 1997.

Sullivan, Francis A. *The Church We Believe In: One, Holy, Catholic and Apostolic*. New York: Paulist Press, 1988.

Symeonides, Nathanael, ed. *Toward the Holy and Great Council: Theological Reflections*. New York: Greek Orthodox Archdiocese of America, 2016.

Taft, Robert F. "The Byzantine Office in the Prayerbook of New Skete: A Critique." *Orientalia Christiana Periodica* 48 (1982): 336–70.

Tanner, Norman P., ed. *Decrees of the Ecumenical Councils*. 2 vols. Washington, DC: Georgetown University Press, 1990.

Tavard, George H. "The Ecclesial Dimension of Spirituality." In *The Gift of the Church: A Textbook on Ecclesiology in Honor of Patrick Granfield, O.S.B.*, edited by Peter C. Phan, 215–30. Collegeville, MN: Liturgical Press, 2000.

Tertullian. "Apology." Translated by Rudolph Arbesmann, Sr. Emily J. Daly and et al. In *Tertullian, Apologetical Works and Minucius Felix, Octavius*. The Fathers of the Church. Washington, D.C.: Catholic University of America Press, 1950.

———. *Homily on Baptism*. Translated by Ernest Evans. London: SPCK, 1964.

———. "To His Wife (Ad Uxorem)," in *Tertullian, Part Fourth; Minucius Felix; Commodian; Origen, Parts First and Second*, transl. S. Thelwall, ANF IV, 39–49. Grand Rapids, MI: Eerdmans, 1885.

Theokritoff, Elizabeth. *Living in God's Creation: Orthodox Perspectives on Ecology*. Crestwood, NY: St. Vladimir's Seminary Press, 2009.

Thompson-Uberuaga, William. *Your Kin-dom Come: The Lord's Prayer in a Global Age*. Eugene, OR: Cascade Books, 2018.

Thumberg, Lars. *Man and the Cosmos: The Vision of St. Maximus the Confessor*. Crestwood, NY: St. Vladimir's Seminary Press, 1985.

Tillard, J.-M.-R. *Church of Churches: The Ecclesiology of Communion*. Translated by R. C. De Peaux. Collegeville, MN: Liturgical Press, 1992.

Tillich, Paul. *A History of Christian Thought: From Its Judaic and Hellenistic Origins to Existentialism*. New York: Simon and Schuster, 1968.

Turcescu, Lucian. "Eucharistic Ecclesiology or Open Sobornicity?". In *Dumitru Staniloae:*

Tradition and Modernity in Theology, edited by Lucian Turcescu, 83–103. Iasi, Romania; Palm Beach, FL: Center for Romanian Studies, 2002.

Uzukwu, Elochukwu E. "Ministry with 'Large Ears'—Approaches to Dynamic African Patterns of Reform and Renewal in the Church Today." In *'Ecclesia semper reformanda': Renewal and Reform beyond Polemics*, edited by Peter De Mey and Wim François. Bibliotheca Ephemeridum Theologicarum Lovaniensium, 337–59. Leuven: Peeters, 2020.

Velati, Mauro. *Separati ma fratelli: Gli osservatori non-cattolici al Vaticano II (1962–1965)*. Bologna: Il Mulino, 2014.

Wainwright, Geoffrey. "The Holy Spirit, Witness, and Martyrdom." In *It Is the Spirit Who Gives Life: New Directions in Pneumatology*, edited by Radu Bordeianu, 22–52. Washington, DC: The Catholic University of America Press, 2022.

———. *Methodists in Dialogue*. Nashville: Kingswood, 1995.

Ware, Kallistos. "The Holy Spirit in the Liturgy of St. John Chrysostom." In *It Is the Spirit Who Gives Life: New Directions in Pneumatology*, edited by Radu Bordeianu, 89–121. Washington, DC: The Catholic University of America Press, 2022.

———. "Intercommunion: The Decisions of Vatican II and the Orthodox Standpoint." *Sobornost* 4, no. Winter (1966): 258–72.

———. *The Orthodox Way*. Rev. ed. Crestwood, NY: St. Vladimir's Seminary Press, 1995.

———. "Church and Eucharist, Communion and Intercommunion." *Sobornost* 7, no. 7 (1978): 550–67.

———. *The Orthodox Church*. New ed. London, New York: Penguin Books, 1997.

WCC. *The Church: Towards a Common Vision*. Geneva: WCC Publications, 2013.

———. *The Nature and Mission of the Church: A Stage on the Way to a Common Statement*. Geneva: WCC Publications, 2005.

Williams, Rowan. *Why Study the Past? The Quest for the Historical Church* Grand Rapids, MI: Eerdmans, 2015.

Wood, Nathaniel, and Aristotle Papanikolaou. "Orthodox Christianity and Political Theology: Thinking Beyond Empire." In *T&T Clark Handbook of Poltical Theology*, edited by Rubén Rosario Rodríguez, 337–51. New York: T&T Clark, 2020.

Wright, N. T. *The Challenge of Jesus: Rediscovering Who Jesus Was and Is*. Downers Grove, IL: InterVarsity Press, 1999.

Wybrew, Hugh. *The Orthodox Liturgy: The Development of the Eucharistic Liturgy in the Byzantine Rite*. Crestwood, NY: St. Vladimir's Seminary Press, 2001.

Zizioulas, John D. *Being as Communion: Studies in Personhood and the Church*. Contemporary Greek Theologians; no. 4. Crestwood, NY: St. Vladimir's Seminary Press, 1985.

———. "The Church as Communion." *Saint Vladimir's Theological Quarterly* 38, no. 1 (1994): 3–16.

———. *Communion and Otherness: Further Studies in Personhood and the Church*. Edited by Paul McPartlan. New York: T&T Clark—Continuum, 2006.

———. *Eucharist, Bishop, Church: The Unity of the Church in the Divine Eucharist and the Bishop During the First Three Centuries*. Translated by Elizabeth Theokritoff. Brookline, MA: Holy Cross Orthodox Press, 2001.

————. "The Institution of Episcopal Conferences: An Orthodox Reflection." *The Jurist* 48 (1988): 376–83.

————. *Lectures in Christian Dogmatics.* Edited by Douglas H. Knight. New York: T&T Clark, 2008.

————. "The Mystery of the Church in Orthodox Tradition." *One in Christ* 24, no. 4 (1988): 294–303.

————. "The Orthodox Church and the Third Millennium." *Sourozh* 81, no. August (2000): 20–31.

————. "Primacy in the Church: An Orthodox Approach." In *Petrine Ministry and the Unity of the Church: "Toward a Patient and Fraternal Dialogue": A Symposium Celebrating the 100th Anniversary of the Foundation of the Society of the Atonement, Rome, December 4–6, 1997,* edited by James F. Puglisi, 115–25. Collegeville, MN: Liturgical Press, 1999.

————. "The Theological Problem of 'Reception.'" *One in Christ* 21, no. 3 (1985): 187–93.

Zusak, Markus. *The Book Thief.* New York: Knopf, 2005.

Index